A HISTORY OF
Rich County

A HISTORY OF ═══════

Rich County

Robert E. Parson

1996
Utah State Historical Society
Rich County Commission

ISBN 0-913738-02-6
Library of Congress Catalog Card Number 96-60061
Map by Automated Geographic Reference Center—State of Utah
Printed in the United States of America

Utah State Historical Society
300 Rio Grande
Salt Lake City, Utah 84101-1182

Dedicated to
A. J. Simmonds
Without whose encouragement and knowledge of
Utah history sources this work would not have been possible.

And to the people of Rich County.

Contents

General Introduction

When Utah was granted statehood on 4 January 1896, twenty-seven counties comprised the nation's new forty-fifth state. Subsequently two counties, Duchesne in 1914 and Daggett in 1917, were created. These twenty-nine counties have been the stage on which much of the history of Utah has been played.

Recognizing the importance of Utah's counties, the Utah State Legislature established in 1991 a Centennial History Project to write and publish county histories as part of Utah's statehood centennial commemoration. The Division of State History was given the assignment to administer the project. The county commissioners, or their designees, were responsible for selecting the author or authors for their individual histories, and funds were provided by the state legislature to cover most research and writing costs as well as to provide each public school and library with a copy of each history. Writers worked under general guidelines provided by the Division of State History and in cooperation with county history committees. The counties also established a Utah Centennial County History Council to help develop policies for distribution of state-appropriated funds and plans for publication.

Each volume in the series reflects the scholarship and interpretation of the individual author. The general guidelines provided by the Utah State Legislature included coverage of five broad themes encompassing the economic, religious, educational, social, and political history of the county. Authors were encouraged to cover a vast period of time stretching from geologic and prehistoric times to the present. Since Utah's statehood centennial celebration falls just four years before the arrival of the twenty-first century, authors were encouraged to give particular attention to the history of their respective counties during the twentieth century.

Still, each history is at best a brief synopsis of what has transpired within the political boundaries of each county. No history can do justice to every theme or event or individual that is part of an area's past. Readers are asked to consider these volumes as an introduction to the history of the county, for it is expected that other researchers and writers will extend beyond the limits of time, space, and detail imposed on this volume to add to the wealth of knowledge about the county and its people. In understanding the history of our counties, we come to understand better the history of our state, our nation, our world, and ourselves.

In addition to the authors, local history committee members, and county commissioners, who deserve praise for their outstanding efforts and important contributions, special recognition is given to Joseph Francis of Morgan County for his role in conceiving the idea of the centennial county history project and for his energetic efforts in working with the Utah State Legislature and State of Utah officials to make the project a reality. Mr. Francis is proof that one person does make a difference.

ALLAN KENT POWELL
CRAIG FULLER
GENERAL EDITORS

Introduction

Early Bear Lake settler Joseph C. Rich remarked to his future wife Ann Eliza Hunter in 1863 that "only men with plenty of hair on 'em are tough enough to stand the climate of Bear Lake." To those who endured, raised families, and whose names became linked with the area, the rigorous climate of Rich County became something to be celebrated. Not just anyone could make a go of it in Rich County. And not just anyone did. The early history of Rich County is peppered with examples of settlers who came, spent one winter in the area, and then left the next spring. The paths of outgoing settlers crossed the paths of other incoming settlers as the population of Rich County has either declined or remained static during much of its history.

Although its climate is extreme, the area is a land of extreme beauty. Hardly anyone who ever traversed the area has failed to note that fact. "What a country!" Rich exclaimed to Ann Eliza. The country Rich described was one full of wild game, fish, water, timber, and grass. It had been an important point of operations for early fur trapping activities in the late 1820s. Prior to the fur trade era, Rich

County was claimed by both Shoshoni and Blackfoot Indians, who fought one another for preeminence in the area. Diarists who traveled the Oregon Trail during the 1840s, following the meanderings of the Bear River northwest to present-day Montpelier, Idaho, and on to Oregon, often commented on the region's abundant resources. Bear Lake Valley and the upper Bear River Valley were among the areas of consideration for Mormon settlement in 1847. But the prospects of establishing successful agricultural communities that far north were problematic. Therefore, during their first decade in the Great Basin, Mormons concentrated their colonizing efforts in the Salt Lake Valley, the lower Bear River Valley, and points south. Not until 1863 did Mormon colonists under Charles C. Rich found settlements at Paris and St. Charles.

Rich County lies in the northeast notched corner of Utah and borders on Cache, Morgan, Summit, and Weber counties and the states of Idaho and Wyoming. The county contains approximately 1,023 square miles and ranges in elevation from 5,924 feet at the shore of Bear Lake to 9,148 feet at Monte Cristo Peak. Its elevation and location made the settlement of Rich County difficult, as it was isolated from other areas of settlement. Brigham Young remarked to Charles C. Rich in 1866 that he would be happy to visit the Bear Lake communities as soon as a passable road was constructed. There was no easy route into the valley, and the county's geographic isolation has continued to play an important part in its development. Today, connections to areas outside the county are possible only by two-lane highways, and until the 1950s some of these connections were gravel roads.

The communities of Rich County are isolated geographically from the rest of the state, and they are isolated from each other. The Bear Lake and Bear River valleys comprise the two main geographic regions of the county. The communities of Laketown and Garden City in Bear Lake Valley have more in common with the communities of Paris, Fish Haven, and St. Charles, Bear Lake County, Idaho, than with Woodruff and Randolph in the Bear River Valley. Similarly, Woodruff and Randolph have more in common with communities in southwestern Wyoming than they have with Laketown and Garden City. When Mormon settlers first established themselves at Paris and

St. Charles, they assumed that the entire Bear Lake Valley was part of Utah Territory. The Utah Territorial Assembly agreed and created Rich County (then called Richland County) in 1866, placing the county seat at St. Charles. The 1872 federal survey of the region, however, showed that about half of Bear Lake Valley, including the county seat, belonged to Idaho. The territorial assembly then moved the county seat to Randolph. The two parts of the county were connected by little more than a horse trail leading southeast from Laketown, over the mountain divide to Otter Creek, and down into Randolph. As a result, the two settled areas of Rich County developed somewhat independently from each other.

That separation can be seen in the educational development of the county. Although the trend in education throughout the history of Rich County has been towards consolidation, that goal has not been accomplished without significant turmoil. Prior to 1915 the county was divided into eight separate school districts, each with its own school board. Even after state legislation mandated that counties consolidate school districts under one board, the county continued to recognize four distinct areas and continued to operate separate schools at Woodruff, Randolph, Laketown, and Garden City. In 1928 the closing of the high school in Garden City resulted in a rift between Garden City and Laketown residents. The rift widened over the years, especially after 1948 when further consolidation threatened to relocate seventh and eighth grade students from Garden City to Laketown schools. Garden City residents responded by sending their intermediate students to a school in Paris, Idaho. Differences eventually were worked out, and the Garden City students returned to attend school in Laketown. Still, the county's educational history helps illustrate the geographic peculiarities of Rich County. The general trend toward consolidation was necessary in order to provide the best possible facilities for the county's students; however, older county residents continued to regret the loss of the autonomy that individual community schools have provided them, and reconciliation was a slow process.

The administration of local churches within the county also illustrates the county's geographic split. The residents of the county predominantly have been members of the Church of Jesus Christ of

Latter-day Saints. Initially members of the LDS church living in Woodruff, Randolph, Laketown, and Garden City, Utah, were part of the Bear Lake Stake which also included members of the church living in Bear Lake County. The stake also included communities in southwestern Wyoming, from Star Valley to Evanston. Admittedly, the stake was too large to administrate efficiently; nevertheless, when a new stake was created in 1898, LDS church leaders chose to disregard county boundaries and relied instead on natural geographic boundaries. As a result, the communities of Laketown and Garden City remained part of Bear Lake Stake while Woodruff and Randolph joined the communities in southwestern Wyoming to become the Woodruff Stake.

Church fellowship in Rich County, particularly during the early period, had influenced political affairs as well. The eventual affiliation of LDS church members from Randolph, Woodruff, Laketown, and Garden City in one stake helped remove the geographical gap. More recently with the reorganization of church members in the county into different stakes, the county has been able to maintain the bridge over the geographical gap with improved roads, a unified school system, and common development of water resources.

Geography has influenced the economic developments of the Bear Lake Valley and the Bear River Valley segments of the county. Although agriculture remains the primary economic base for the entire county, Laketown and Garden City also derive significant revenue from tourism. More than a century ago, residents of Garden City foresaw a time when that area would be transformed into a recreational mecca. They looked forward to the day when pleasure seekers from throughout the world would travel to Garden City to enjoy the azure waters of Bear Lake. However, that time was not as rapidly forthcoming as many of the early settlers assumed it would be. No one could deny that the Bear Lake area held strong potential for recreation, but the sudden influx of visitors never materialized. Early lakeshore resorts, such as Fish Haven and Ideal Beach, enjoyed significant early success, but Utah Power and Light's operation of the Lifton Pumping Plant on the lake's north shore in 1919 eventually lowered the level of the lake, leaving the resorts high and dry. By

1929, pumping for both irrigation water and hydroelectric power had lowered the level of Bear Lake fourteen feet.

The national economic depression which followed 1929 further affected the resorts around Bear Lake as well as other Rich County communities. Livestock prices fell dramatically, and this, coupled with the onset of a drought, crippled the agricultural economy of Rich County. Despite the financial hardships endured by county residents during the Great Depression, Rich County communities did experience some benefit from programs offered by the federal government. Under Public Works Administration projects, culinary water systems were constructed at Woodruff, Garden City, and Pickleville. The county also received funding for the construction of a new courthouse.

The privations of the Great Depression continued with the outbreak of World War II. That war, however, brought increased demand for food and fibre, and once the war abated Rich County residents began enjoying a period of relative affluence. However, fewer agricultural jobs, brought about by an increase in farm mechanization coupled with out-migration for non-farm employment, decreased the population of the county. Agriculture has remained the backbone of Rich County's economy; but beyond supporting individuals already operating farms and ranches, agriculture has been unable to provide employment for additional population increases.

During the years from 1900 to 1980 the population of Rich County fluctuated between approximately 1,650 and 1,800 people. In the 1980s, however, the county experienced a population boom brought about by an increase in recreational development and by oil and gas exploration. By 1983 the county's population had increased to 2,400 up from 1,600 in 1970. It appeared at the time that the population boom would continue, and it became common for developers to compare the Bear Lake area of Rich County to the area of Lake Tahoe, Nevada. Estimates of a population approaching two hundred thousand were frequently cited by developers and promoters.

At the same time that developers were scrambling to capitalize on the recreational boom, seismic crews were combing the overthrust belt in the vicinity of Woodruff and Randolph for potential sites for oil and gas wells. The increase in county population brought about by oil exploration and recreational development strained the county's ability to provide adequate housing, services, and education; but the sudden increase also awakened in residents the need for community planning. During the 1980s the county undertook to increase culinary water supplies, provide sewage treatment plants, re-zone property districts, and in general prepare for what was expected to be inevitable and continual growth. By 1990, however, the county's population had again subsided to below two thousand inhabitants. The boom had busted. Nevertheless, the improvements and planning initiated during the 1980s placed the county in an enviable position to deal with whatever the future might bring.

Dealing successfully with the future, however, will hinge on the ability of county leaders and residents to juggle traditional values with an ever-increasing influx of new ideas. Rich County has maintained its rural, Mormon, agricultural lifestyle for more than 120 years. Although new technologies have been readily accepted and deployed in the agricultural sector, making Rich County a state leader in livestock production, these new inventions have not altered the county's traditional, rural lifestyle. Rather, they often have served to reinforce it. Nevertheless, just as development and change have affected other rural areas of the state, Rich County eventually will also come to a crossroads. At that time, county residents will have to decide what changes they can accept as well as what changes they will not. A familiarity with the county's history can only help in the decision-making process, and it is hoped that these decisions will be aided through this examination of the historical past.

Special thanks is extended to the Rich County Commission, particularly Commissioner Blair Francis, who spearheaded this project in the county. Thanks are also extended to the staff and officials at the Rich County Courthouse, particularly Rich County Recorder Debra Ames and County Clerk Pamela Shaul. This project was aided by the help and encouragement of numerous individuals in the county, most importantly, Willa Kennedy, Helen Cornia, Lori Cornia, Annie Wamsley, Clayton Robinson, Mar Jean Thomson, and Ralph Johnson. Previous written histories served as a blueprint for the writing of this volume, and the author is indebted to the authors and contributors to *The First Hundred Years In Woodruff* and to Mar Jean

S. Thomson, Steven L. Thomson, and Jane D. Digerness, for *Randolph: A Look Back.* Compiled by the late Mildred Hatch Thomson, the book *Rich Memories* was also an indispensable volume in writing this history.

Writing about the settlement of Rich County required an understanding of Mormon pioneers. In part, this book is dedicated to the memory of the rugged pioneering Mormon families who settled and established homes in Rich County. The author appreciates the courtesy and professionalism of the staff at the LDS Church Archives, particularly Scott Christiansen and Ronald Watt, for their help in accessing the various manuscript histories of the branches, wards, and stakes which have at one time or another been a part of the county.

Much of the research for this book was undertaken in the Division of Special Collections and Archives at Utah State University, using resources collected and made available through the efforts of the division's staff. Special thanks is extended to Peter F. Schmid, Bradford Cole, Noel Carmack, Ann Buttars, and especially to the late A. J. Simmonds, to whom this book is also dedicated.

The author also acknowledges the tireless efforts of the staff at the Utah State Historical Society, particularly Craig Fuller, Kent Powell, and Jay Haymond, for their encouragement and criticism on each step of this project. The Utah State Legislature should be commended for funding the county history program, and the author wishes to particularly acknowledge the untiring efforts of Joseph Francis of Morgan County for his gentle proddings of that honorable body.

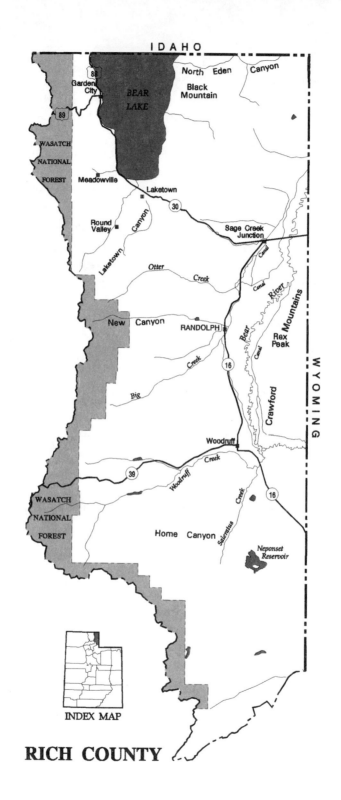

IDAHO

88
Garden
City

BEAR
LAKE

North Eden Canyon

Black
Mountain

89

WASATCH

NATIONAL

FOREST

Meadowville

Laketown

30

Sage Creek
Junction

Round
Valley

Canyon

Laketown

Otter

Creek

Canal

Canal

Bear

River

Rex
Peak

Mountains

WYOMING

New Canyon

RANDOLPH

16

Canal

Creek

Big

Crawford

Woodruff

Creek

39

Woodruff

Creek

16

WASATCH

NATIONAL

FOREST

Home Canyon

Solomibus

Creek

Neponset
Reservoir

INDEX MAP

RICH COUNTY

"The Very Land Itself . . ."

PREHISTORY AND PRESETTLEMENT IN RICH COUNTY

The history of Rich County, Utah, is two-fold. It is obviously the history of people—both Native American and later immigrants—their communities, social life, and customs, but tied closely to the people is the land itself. And the inhabitants of Rich County, in any given historic period, have come to identify strongly with their environment. The Shoshoni viewed Bear Lake Valley with the same sort of spiritual reverence that Randolph resident Mildred Hatch Thomson expressed nearly one-hundred years later. We greet "the morning sun," Thomson wrote, "over the tall peaks of the Crawford Mountain, its face . . . jagged and almost perpendicular . . . sparsely timbered with cedar and pine wears a purplish, blue hue."[1]

The history of human habitation is not much more than a blink of the eye when compared to the entirety of geologic history. For close to 500 million years, throughout the greater portion of Paleozoic and Mesozoic periods, Rich County was covered by an inland sea. Rich County occupied part of what geologists refer to as the "cordilleran geosyncline." This down-sloping area of North America allowed a great sea to encroach inland, leaving behind

deposits of sandstone, shale, and limestone. The period was characterized by gradual, "gentle" uplifting and down-warping, and the sea
advanced and retreated accordingly.

Towards the close of the Mesozoic period, perhaps 70 million
years ago, gentleness gave way to violence. This is called by geologists
the Laramide Revolution, one of the most catastrophic episodes in
geologic history. The land heaved and buckled from the earth's internal forces. Huge fractures in the land's surface appeared as tremendous pressures forced fault blocks over each other, pushing the mass
of rock and sediment northward for more than a hundred miles.
Monstrous chunks of quartzite, limestone, and sandstone, deposited
eons before by shallow inland seas and waterways, rose from the sea
floor and were pushed some 20,000 feet upwards. The sea, which had
sat undisturbed for millions of years, now receded to the west, washing and eroding the desolated landscape.

If, as one group of historians writes, we had the benefit of time-
lapse photography, "we could watch as the area now known as Utah
folded, heaved, buckled, cracked and bent, while rain, snow, flowing
water and in some areas, ice constantly wore away at every elevation."
We could watch with fascination the alternating wet and dry cycles,
the creation of great rivers and swamps, their succession by deserts,
the advance and retreat of the oceans, until finally, as the time-lapse
pictures moved closer to the present, we would witness the creation
of the present landscape.[2]

The Laramide Revolution disturbed the sediments laid down
during the preceding periods, twisting, folding, bending, and perma-
nently lifting them above sea level The extensive faulting activity
resulted in the creation of the Bannock Overthrust, according to G.
B. Richardson, "one of the major structural features of the Rocky
Mountains."[3] Evidence of the Bannock Overthrust in Rich County is
visible on the mountains west and northwest of Garden City, where
rocks—in this case quartzite and limestone—from different ages
come into contact with one another. The deposition of the two materials was separated by several hundred million years, indicating the
magnitude of the force necessary to thrust one fault block over the
top of the other. Further evidence of overthrusting is seen, among

other places, northwest of Meadowville and along the cliffs border-
ing Cheney Creek.[4]

Rich County's geologic history has created a great diversity, from
miles of lake shore to steep mountain slopes. The mountains which
arose during the Laramide period have since been eroded into mere
shadows of their former selves. George R. Mansfield postulated:

> The height of the mountains produced by this great orogenic dis-
> turbance can only be conjectured. The stratigraphic throw pro-
> duced by the fault was between 15,000 and 20,000 feet. If all this
> amount was added to the present elevation of the fault trace a
> maximum height of about 25,000 feet might be produced.[5]

The Laramide period, in large measure, created the present-day
landscape. Our inheritance from geologic time—the present lay of
the land—and the climate have themselves played crucial roles in
influencing regional and local history and prehistory. For native cultures, changes in climate from cool and wet to warm and dry, and
back again, helped define areas suitable for seasonal hunting and
gathering and influenced patterns of migration. Climate, altitude,
and topography also helped determine activities of white Americans.
When compared to Cache Valley and the Salt Lake Valley, the extreme
climate of Rich County retarded settlement. One western historian
characterized this area of northern Utah and southeastern Idaho as
an area crossed over by people in order to get elsewhere.[6] The region's
high altitude and aridity were strong factors persuading settlers to
continue on to milder, wetter climates in California and Oregon.

Rich County, like the rest of Utah, is semi-arid although precipitation ranges from less than seven inches annually in the west deserts
of the state to more than forty inches annually along the peaks of the
Wasatch Range.[7] Geographically, Utah is divided into three major
provinces: the Basin and Range, encompassing most of the western
portion of the state; the Colorado Plateau, encompassing the eastern
portion of the state; and the Rocky Mountain Province, which
includes the Wasatch Front north to the Idaho border and east to
include Summit and Rich Counties.[8]

Rich County has an area of 1,023 square miles and is made up of
five distinct geographic areas: the Bear River Plateau, Bear Lake Basin,

Bear River Valley, Bear River Range, and the Crawford Mountains. The largest of these areas, the Bear River Plateau, is bordered on the west by the Bear Lake Basin, which occupies the northwestern corner of the county, and on the east by the Bear River Valley, which sits along the county's eastern border. The Bear River Mountains, the northernmost extension of the Wasatch Range, separates Rich County from Cache County, Weber County, and Morgan County to the west. Similarly, the Crawford Mountains separate a portion of Rich County and Utah from Wyoming to the east.

The county's elevation ranges from 5,924 feet at the shore of Bear Lake to 9,148 feet at Monte Cristo Peak. High elevation contributes to a cold mean temperature for the county of only 41 degrees Fahrenheit, with tremendous shifts in day and nighttime temperatures. Seasonal extremes are also common. The warmest temperatures at Woodruff can approach 100 degrees in July and drop to as low as 50 degrees below zero during winter.

The county is traversed in part by the Bear River, which enters the county east of Woodruff. The river begins high in the Uinta Mountains and flows north through Utah to Wyoming and back again, entering Idaho in the vicinity of Dingle. The Bear is the major river in Rich County. Other streams in the county which are tributary to the Bear River include Saleratus, Crane, Woodruff, Birch, Big, Little, and Otter creeks, which all flow eastward. Streams in the county which are tributary to Bear Lake include Swan, Cheney, Tufts, and Big creeks (in the vicinity of Laketown) which all flow from the west to the east; and North and South Eden creeks, which flow westward from the east.[9]

At times during the course of recent geologic history, these streams became raging torrents; at other times they virtually dried up. As wet cycles greatly increased the volume of streams and rivers flowing from the higher elevations, those waterways cut deeply into the sedimentary deposits of previous periods. Bear Lake at one time rose about thirty-nine feet above its current level. Its southern boundary extended to the north-central portion of Round Valley. There is now little indication of the shallow bay which occupied Round Valley, but evidence of the lake's high level is prominent in the terraces between North and South Eden canyons on the east side of the lake.[10] At least two other major lake levels at approximately 10–foot intervals are also visible. Warm and dry climatic periods were times of deposition, during which streams deposited material on the valley floors. Prior to about 18,000 years ago, the Bear River is thought to have flowed through the lake. However, periods of deposition eventually created a natural dam across the north end of Bear Lake Valley, pushing the channel of the Bear River farther to the east and allowing Bear Lake to expand.[11]

The waters of Bear River and Bear Lake commingled by means of the natural channel between Bear Lake, Mud Lake, and Bear River. As late as 1899, prior to the regulation of Bear Lake by Utah Power and Light Company, Clarence T. Johnston and Joseph A. Breckons mentioned flood waters from Bear River commingling with waters from Bear Lake through Mud Lake to the north.[12] During the early settlement period, water from Bear Lake also mingled with that of area sloughs, rivers, and streams. On a trip from Paris, Idaho, to Montpelier, one traveler remarked:

> I noticed my driver was making for what seemed to me to be a lake six or eight miles wide; on asking for the name of the lake imagine my surprise and horror to find that this was the overflow from the sloughs and rivers . . . Pointing to a black spec [sic] far out in the water, my driver informed me that it was the bridge over Ovid Creek.[13]

The water supply of Bear Lake Basin has historically played an important role downstream. Although prehistoric Lake Bonneville, which covered much of Utah during the late Pleistocene period (12,000 to 14,000 years ago), was never actually connected to Bear Lake, the high stages of Bear Lake correspond in time to the existence of Lake Bonneville. Furthermore, the Bear River and its tributaries and Bear Lake and its tributaries were the major contributors to the Cache Bay portion of Lake Bonneville, west of the Bear River Range.

In writing about the Pleistocene period, Richard C. Bright noted the interrelatedness between Lake Bonneville and Lake Thatcher to the north. Lake Thatcher occupied that area of southern Idaho consisting of Gem and Gentile valleys. The northern part of the Thatcher Basin drains to the Portneuf River, while the southern part drains to the Bear River. Fossilized remains found at the site of Lake Thatcher and at Utah Lake also suggested to Bright that the two were at one time connected, "probably via Lake Bonneville." He also surmised that the Snake River was at one time connected to points south, including the Portneuf Valley in southeastern Idaho.[14]

Events in the geologic past were almost always regional in nature. The geologic events which shaped Rich County also shaped Cache Valley, the remainder of Utah, and most of the Intermountain West. The most recent geologic history, which has left the topography of the region in its present form, has helped determine the activities of humans on the land.

Prehistoric Inhabitants

The importance of climate and other "features of the natural landscape are so interrelated with one another," noted Julian S. Steward, "that great altitude, heavy rainfall, relative abundance of edible foods, sources of water, and consequently population concentration largely coincide."[15] Furthermore, according to Merle W. Wells, "major changes in climate" have completely altered the Great Basin region. Wells explains how climate has impacted both human and animal populations; he writes that as desert conditions succeeded wet glacial periods, "elephants [mammoths] could no longer be found ... [and] early hunters followed the game, moving north and east to stay with the cooler, wetter climate."[16] As one group of people moved out of the area, others moved in. The movement of human and animal life in and out of areas of the Intermountain West brought about major cultural changes eight thousand years ago, Wells concludes.[17]

Native cultures have occupied areas of the Great Basin and Intermountain West for approximately the last fourteen thousand years.[18] Early Indian cultures were highly migratory, moving with the seasons in order to successfully practice their subsistence hunting-gathering lifestyle. Permanent dwellings and campsites, with the exception of more extended winter camps, were generally not a part of prehistoric Indian culture; and extended family groups constituted developed social organization among prehistoric Indians.

Distinct Indian cultures, such as that of the Shoshoni which eventually came to dominate the Rich County area, developed gradually. Tribal organization, as presently understood, did not exist at the time the first Native Americans migrated over the Bering Straits during the last ice age (possibly as early as twenty thousand years ago.) The Shoshoni may actually have arrived in southeastern Idaho, northeastern Utah, and southwestern Wyoming as recently as only five hundred to six hundred years ago. The archaeological record, for the most part, is insufficient to allow modern researchers to fully date and document the transition of different Indian cultural groups from one area to another.[19]

Little archaeological work has been done in Rich County itself; but it is reasonable to assume that Indian groups to the west, east, and north of Rich County also included the lands of Rich County, Utah, and Bear Lake County, Idaho, in their traditional hunting and gathering area.[20] The south shore of Bear Lake was the site of two fur trappers' rendezvous in 1827 and 1828, and the site had quite likely been used for Indian gatherings prior to the trappers' era. As late as 1872, the Shoshoni and Bannock Indians continued to use the Bear Lake Valley as a meeting place.[21] There is reason to believe that this activity preceded the fur trade, possibly by millennia.

Early ancestors of present-day Indian groups were hunters and gatherers who tended to travel in small, extended family groups, sometimes moving camp as much as fifty to one hundred times a year.[22] Their diet seemed to be based mostly upon plant foods. George C. Frison explains that "the availability of plant food for human groups changed throughout the year, as it did for animals." From early spring to late fall, inhabitants altered their diets to correspond with seasonal changes and plant growth. The nomadic lifestyle was necessary in order to subsist because "fruits and berries appear and disappear rapidly, but since the same plants often grow at different elevations, they may be mature at one elevation and immature higher up."[23]

Many of the plants relied upon by humans were also consumed by animals, and this could facilitate the capture of certain small animals that then became part of the Indians' subsistence diet. Hunting was an absolute necessity to prehistoric cultures; it provided alternative foods as well as skins for clothing and shelter.[24] Frison notes that prehistoric peoples seldom limited themselves to only one type of

food and that "specializations were often the road to disaster."[25]
Prehistoric Americans utilized whatever food was available, including small rodents and insects.

Although most hunting was done by individuals or small family
groups, scholars believe that the hunting of large animals was often
done in concert with others: "When taking buffalo, antelope, rabbits,
deer, mountain sheep, and, under certain conditions, water fowl, fish,
and even insects," noted Julian H. Steward, "collective effort increased
manyfold what an individual hunter could have procured." [26] Perhaps
the most important example of collective hunting involved the buffalo, or bison.

Bison became the large animal of choice for hunters after the
extinction of the mammoth, perhaps twelve to thirteen thousand
years ago,[27] and bison herds ranged both east and west of the Rocky
Mountains in northern Utah and southeastern Idaho. Huge herds
roamed the Green and Bear river valleys until the 1830s and 1840s.[28]
Even after the Cache Valley and Bear River Valley herds disappeared,
many Shoshoni, particularly the northern bands, continued to hunt
buffalo communally. The acquisition of the horse made it possible
for Indian groups to travel eastward to participate in annual buffalo
hunts on the Great Plains.

For the area Indians, the acquisition of the horse was a most
important event, helping alter their lifeways and culture. The horse
may have entered into Shoshoni culture as early as the mid-1700s via
the contact with mounted Ute tribes to the south who were in closer
contact with the Spanish, who introduced horses to the American
continents in historic times. The acquisition of the horse, coupled
with the arrival of fur traders and subsequent introduction of
firearms, helped bring about the rapid extermination of bison herds
in northern Utah and southeastern Idaho.

Acquisition of the horse also changed Native American social
patterns. By improving hunting methods, individual families were
better able to combine together into bands. With the increased use of
buffalo hides and contact with Plains Indians, temporary grass shel-
ters were gradually replaced by lodges and tepees as Shoshoni and
Bannocks banded together in more permanent villages.[29]

Indians had hunted buffalo, however, for perhaps eleven thousand years before they acquired the horse, and they had devised many ingenious ways of doing so, including the construction of elaborate corrals, traps, and jumps in order to capture and kill their prey. Their success in these ventures depended upon their knowledge of the land and their knowledge of animal behavior. Communal hunts for large animals such as buffalo, antelope, and deer were of necessity well-planned events. In his evaluation of the Ruby Bison Corral used by Native Americans to trap bison in the Powder River Basin, Wyoming, George C. Frison explains:

> The Ruby bison pound reflects a high level of knowledge, resourcefulness, and dedication in prehistoric bison procurement. If they were present today in their original form, the structures involved in the procurement operation would be adequate for corralling buffalo or cattle, and were probably equal or even superior to many present-day cattle corrals and might even be considered as their prototype.[30]

No archaeological evidence has been found in the Bear River or Bear Lake valleys to confirm or suggest the use of bison corrals. Bison were present in the area in large numbers, however, and were procured by prehistoric hunters as is evidenced by remains of a bison kill unearthed in the vicinity of Woodruff.[31]

Lush meadow lands along the Bear River and in southern Bear Lake Valley were excellent habitat for bison herds. This same habitat also made the area attractive for more recent cattle operations. Prehistoric hunters, in some ways, faced similar problems to modern day cattle ranchers, but the amount of work required under prehistoric conditions was much greater. Even so, a contemporary cattle operation is difficult and labor intensive; today, however, a corral would most likely be constructed with a post-hole digger and chain saw, or the lumber bought ready-cut and transported to the area with a four-wheel drive pickup truck. One or two men could build a "bison-proof" corral in less than three days. George Frison estimates that in the prehistoric West the construction of a corral such as the Ruby site may have taken upwards of two weeks to complete and required the labor of at least twenty adult males.[32]

In addition to corralling their prey, prehistoric Indians also devised other hunting methods, including the bison jump. The jump required that the hunters drive their prey over a cliff or into a deep sinkhole in order to kill or cripple a number of the animals. In contrast to the corral where small numbers of animals were best handled, a successful jump required large herds. According to Frison, it would be virtually impossible, even for experienced cowhands on horseback, to cause a small herd of bison to jump over a cliff. Large numbers of animals were needed so that by the time the lead animals realized the danger, the momentum of the stampede would be enough to force them over the cliff or into the sink hole.[33]

A great deal of waste inevitably occurred with bison jumps; however, it is clear that prehistoric Indians, like their historic counterparts, dried or "jerked" meat for winter use. They also cached bulbs, seeds, and nuts for later use. Yet the subsistence lifestyle of prehistoric Americans made for a tenuous existence at best, with starvation a constant possibility. Some prehistoric Indians, such as the Anasazi in southeastern Utah and some Fremont Indian groups in the Great Basin, simply disappeared; whether they migrated out of the area or succumbed to starvation or to abrupt climatic change is not known. Yet as one cultural group abandoned or disappeared from an area, other cultural groups generally moved in.[34] Some areas did remain uninhabited for long periods of time. At the time of white and Indian contact, during the earliest historic period, the dominant Indian culture in the Rich County area was Shoshoni. It is not known, however, if their ancestors were the prehistoric inhabitants of the region.[35]

The Shoshoni Indians proved extremely adaptive after moving into the area. Their approach to the land and its resources was in many ways not unlike that of the white settlers who followed. Their main concern was for the perpetuation of their families and traditions, and they, like the white settlers who followed, sought to shape their environment to suit their needs. Indians were limited in their abilities to shape their environment by a lack of technological means, yet Shoshoni Indians freely adopted and adapted to new ideas and technologies which came via their contact with whites and which did not conflict with their view of the world. Shoshonis rejected the notion of a permanent agricultural-based society, which conflicted with their traditional viewpoint; however, the acquisition of the horse and the use of firearms, both of which helped perpetuate their traditional hunting culture, were accepted without question, and, in the case of the horse, eventually became a symbol of wealth and prestige, defining an individual's social standing.

Indians did not simply coexist with their environment. While it is true that in their traditional culture Indians were not equipped to greatly impact their surroundings, and also true that their hunting and gathering society was environmentally more benign than was the white culture which followed, Indians did seek to modify their surroundings to suit their needs.

Competition for the land and its resources in the West was important long before the arrival of white immigrants who eventually dispossessed all Indians regardless of tribal affiliation. After the demise of Indian power, competition for the land's resources continued among whites. The Shoshoni and Blackfoot tribes had battled one another for preeminence throughout the Northwest, and the Ute and Shoshoni did likewise throughout the Great Basin. Even after the arrival of white fur traders and trappers, Indian tribes often divided their allegiances between competitive fur companies carrying on their warring tradition.

The Fur Trade

The first contact between white Americans and Shoshoni Indians probably occurred at the time of the Lewis and Clark expedition in 1803, although it is conceivable that the Shoshoni were in contact with British fur traders in the Pacific Northwest prior to that time. It is also possible that contact between the Spanish and Shoshoni had taken place in the Great Basin prior to 1800. The first contact between white Americans and Indians in the Rich County area appears to have occurred when the first fur trapping expedition to the region entered Bear River Valley in 1811 under the command of Joseph Miller. They were employed by John Jacob Astor's fur company and were part of the Wilson Price Hunt expedition. They separated from the main group at Fort Henry in eastern Idaho and traveled south to the Portneuf River and then to the Bear River near Preston, Idaho. The river, named for a time for Miller, was assumed to flow west to the Pacific Ocean. That assumption would linger for

Trappers, such as those depicted in this painting by J. Macdonald, used the Bear Lake Valley extensively from 1824 through 1836. (Special Collections, Utah State University, Logan.)

some time. That fall the party traveled east along the Bear to the area of present-day Soda Springs.[36] Robert Stuart wrote on 20 August 1812 that the Miller expedition had made contact with local Indians, albeit not under the friendliest of circumstances:

> ... we found John Hobough fishing and in an instant Mr. Miller[,] Edward Robinson and Jacob Reznor who had been similarly employed. . . . They had on leaving the Party at Henry's Fort last Fall, gone 200 Miles South, where they made that season's Hunt on a River which must discharge itself into the Ocean to the Southard of the Columbia—From thence they steered 200 more due East where they found about Sixty lodges of Arapahays, who robbed them—they then left them and continued their journey 50 miles, where they wintered, and early in the Spring were overtaken by the same Rascals [who] robbed [them] of all their horses and almost everything else.[37]

The detached Astorians (as they have come to be called) likely had entered the Bear Lake Valley as well and had trapped in the vicinity of Georgetown and Bennington before returning to the Bear River and following its course to the east. Even though Miller and his associates entered the Bear Lake Valley, they never in fact saw the lake. It is possible to be in the vicinity of present-day Georgetown or Bennington and not have Bear Lake visible, which is probably as far into the valley as Miller's party ventured. Robert Stuart's map, part of which is based upon Miller's description of the area, accurately represents the meanderings of the Bear River (especially the big bend at Soda Springs), but Bear Lake is conspicuously absent.[38] The group then followed the Bear River south to the headwaters of the Green River where they spent the winter.

The party's main purpose was to trap beaver, not to explore the country. If they encountered beaver in sufficient numbers, there was little reason to explore elsewhere. Indians also kept them occupied. Robert Stuart's party found the Miller group on the Snake River in August 1812, as mentioned above, tired, hungry, and utterly destitute. Stuart outfitted Robinson, Hobough, and Reznor, who decided to remain in the mountains for another year, hoping to improve their financial situation before returning east. Joseph Miller joined up with Stuart's party to return immediately to St. Louis. It was largely from the information which Stuart gleaned from Miller that the group was able to travel south and east and eventually negotiate South Pass at the foot of the Wind River Range in November 1812, the first whites to do so.[39] The celebrated South Pass would, for future generations of overland emigrants, mark the route of the Oregon Trail.

Miller's geographical savvy was indeed impressive. Yet his journey missed one important landmark—Bear Lake. The first reference to Bear Lake comes from Scottish fur trapper Donald McKenzie, who worked for the British-owned Northwest Fur Company. McKenzie referred to "Black Bears" Lake in a 10 September 1819 letter to his superior, Alexander Ross. McKenzie's casual reference suggests that he attached no particular importance to being at Black Bears' Lake, nor did he lay claim to discovering the lake. His letter to Ross was terse:

> We have passed a very anxious and troublesome summer. War parties frequent. In danger often; but still we do not despair. Time

and perseverance will do much. You will make no arrangements
for forwarding our supplies, we have had enough of that already,
I will accompany the spring returns and try to be at Fort Nez
Perces by the 20th of next June.[40]

Black Bears' Lake was a name attached to Bear Lake by the British
fur trappers. Americans referred to the lake variously as Sweetwater,
Little Lake, or Weaver's (Weber) Lake, the latter named for John H.
Weber of the Ashley-Henry Fur Company. The Weber River and
Weber County in Utah are also named for him.[41]

The Bear Lake region and Bear River Valley portions of Rich
County, along with Cache Valley to the west, were at the very heart of
the American fur trade experience. In 1822 two St. Louis entrepreneurs, William Ashley and Andrew Henry, combined their resources
to form the Ashley-Henry Fur Company. With Ashley's business
sense and Henry's geographic knowledge, the company largely rede-
fined the fur trade through the concepts of the "free trapper" and the
mountain rendezvous. Until that time, American companies such as
the Missouri Fur Company (operated in 1822 by Joshua Pilcher) had
largely adopted the British method of employer/employee relations.
The trappers, or *engages* in the language of the fur trade, worked for
the company for a set wage. Ashley gradually introduced the idea of
"initiative" by paying the trappers a portion of their catch.[42]
Advertising in February 1822, Ashley sought

> to engage ONE HUNDRED MEN, to ascend the river Missouri to
> its source, there to be employed for one, two, or three years. For
> particulars enquire of Major Andrew Henry, near the Lead Mines,
> in the County of Washington, (who will ascend with, and com-
> mand the party) or to the subscriber at St. Louis. *Wm. H. Ashley.*[43]

Some of the most well-known names in fur trade history would
begin with the Ashley-Henry Company, and a good many of these
would spend time trapping, trading, and plying their profession
within northern Utah, and in southern Bear Lake Valley, in particular.
Among those responding to Ashley's advertisement were Jim Bridger,
Tom Fitzpatrick, Jedediah Smith, and David Jackson.[44] During the
years of Ashley's active participation, other notables also followed

him westward. Among them were William Sublette, James Clyman, Hugh Glass, Thomas Smith, and John H. Weber.[45]

Weber, a captain in Ashley's first expedition, began trapping the region of present-day Cache and Rich counties in 1822. Daniel Potts, who accompanied Weber, provides the first written description of Bear Lake and the surrounding area. It is interesting to note that Potts describes Bear Lake Valley from south to north and that his group's entrance into the region followed the Bear River from its head. Weber's party, therefore, traversed portions of present-day Rich County.

> The first valley as you approach from the head of the river, is a small sweet lake, about 120 miles in circumference, with beautiful clear water, and when the wind blows has a splendid appearance. . . . The valley is scantily supplied with timber, as is the case with most of the low grounds of this country.[46]

The scenic setting of Bear Lake made it a favorite meeting place for trappers and Indians. Prior to the trappers' arrival, Shoshoni, Bannock, and Ute Indians had used the area for generations as an annual gathering place. The southern shore of Bear Lake became the American fur trappers' center of operations from 1827 to 1830. The first of two mountain rendezvous was held at the south shore near present-day Laketown in 1827; the second was held a year later. These were the third and fourth such events; the first having been held at the confluence of Henry's Fork on the Green River in southwestern Wyoming, and the second occurring in Cache Valley on the Blacksmith Fork River.[47] The rendezvous, in conjunction with the "free trapper" concept, was unique to American fur trade activities. By holding a rendezvous, Ashley could supply his trappers with provisions for the upcoming season, which in turn allowed the trappers to remain in the mountains throughout the year. The rendezvous also allowed the trappers and their Indian partners an opportunity to socialize and play. The rendezvous became a much-anticipated event. James Beckwourth recalled the 1826 event in Cache Valley. He mentions that there were brought that year

> three hundred pack mules, well laden with goods and all things necessary for the mountaineers and the Indian trade It may well be

Trapper rendezvous, such as the one on the Green River in 1837 depicted in this painting by Alfred Jacob Miller, were held at Bear Lake in 1827 and 1828. (Special Collections, Utah State University, Logan.)

supposed that the arrival of such a vast amount of luxuries from the East did not pass off without a general celebration. Mirth, songs, dancing, shouting, trading, running, jumping, singing, racing, target-shooting, yarns, frolics, with all sorts of extravagances that white men or Indians could invent, were freely indulged in. The unpacking of the *medicine water* contributed not a little to the heightening of our festivities.[48]

The rendezvous in Cache Valley appears to have passed without incident. Not so the subsequent "jubilee" on the shores of Bear Lake. Daniel Potts recorded that event's rather inauspicious beginnings.

A few days previous to my arrival at this place [Bear Lake] a party of about 120 Black feet approached the camp and killed a Snake and his squaw the alarm was immediately given and the Snakes Utaws and Whites sallied forth for the Battle the enemy fled to the Mountain to a small concavity thickly grown with small timber surrounded by open ground In this engagement the squaws whe[were] busily engaged in throwing up batterys and dragging off the dead there was only six whites engaged in this battle who immediately advanced within Pistol shot and you may be assured that almost every shot counted one the loss of the Snakes was three killed and the same wounded that of the Whites one wounded and two narrowly made their escape that of the Utaws was none though who gained great applause for their bravery the loss of the enemy is not known six where found dead on the ground besides a great number where carried off on Horses . . . [49]

After that attack, the gathering proceeded in much the same manner as had the previous year's rendezvous in Cache Valley. William Sublette, David Jackson, and their trapping partners brought more than 7,400 pounds of beaver pelts, turning them over to the company representative at three dollars per pound.[50] After business matters were cleared, the rendezvous got down to its secondary but equally important purpose—celebrating.

The exact number of participants in the Bear Lake rendezvous is unknown. It is known, however, that Ashley had about fifty men in the field in 1826; and it is assumed that the Missouri Fur Company had an equal or greater number. Those "freemen" trapping with Peter Skene Ogden for the British-owned Hudson's Bay Company may also have participated. The possibility exists that between 150 and 200 trappers met at the south shore of Bear Lake. The trappers were probably outnumbered five to one by Indians—mostly Shoshonis, Bannocks, and Utes. Thus, between 1,000 and 1,500 individuals indulged in what author Don Berry records as "general rampaging, fighting, fornicating, drinking, singing, lying, dancing, eating, shouting, [and] shooting."[51]

In other words, it was an outright celebration. The arrival of Jedediah Smith at the 1827 Bear Lake rendezvous was announced by one volley of cannon fire, the first heard in the valley and the only reference to that cannon ever having been used. The cannon, a four-pounder mounted on a carriage and pulled by two mules, had been brought overland from St. Louis by William Ashley's men under the direction of General A. Malcomb. The cannon holds the distinction of being the first wheeled vehicle to cross South Pass. Smith's arrival was a welcome sight to the trappers, for he had not been heard from since leaving the 1826 rendezvous in Cache Valley. Smith had traveled southwest, explored the Great Salt Lake, moved south to the Sevier River, and then navigated the Virgin and Colorado rivers, before crossing the Mohave Desert and ultimately ending up in San

Bernardino Valley, California. His party was the first to successfully travel a southern route to California.[52]

Perhaps more important to those assembled on the south shore of Bear Lake, although Smith's accomplishment was certainly not lost on his fellow fur trappers, was his status within the fur company. Smith had been Ashley's second-in-command, and, in July 1826, Ashley sold his share of the company along with certain goods to Smith, David Jackson, and William Sublette. Their understanding was that Ashley, or his agent, would deliver goods to them the following year "at or near the west end of the little lake of the Bear River."[53]

Ashley was not at the rendezvous in 1827, instead sending his "agent." The normal and most accessible route into Bear Lake Valley was via the Bear River from the north. It followed that the most logical choice for a rendezvous site was at the north end of the lake. Yet the rendezvous actually took place at the opposite end of the lake, a fact which Dale Morgan conjectures may mean that the trappers met near the point where the Bear Lake Outlet flows into the Bear west of present Montpelier, Idaho. It is possibly material, Morgan concludes, that travel guides in the 1850s applied the name "Ashley Creek to the present Georgetown Creek in this area."[54] With their preference for the southern shore, it is possible that the fur trappers' Indian partners may have influenced the choice of the site.

One of the most far-reaching outcomes of the 1827 Bear Lake rendezvous was the lessening of Indian tensions. Possibly as an outgrowth of the battle which preceded the arrival of Daniel Potts, in which several of the trappers emerged heroic, the Americans were able to arrange a truce among themselves, the Utes, and the Shoshonis. The Americans already enjoyed amicable relations with the Shoshoni; more important in this matter was the truce between the two Indian tribes.[55]

Enmity existed between the Utes and Shoshonis similar to that which existed between the Shoshonis and the Blackfeet: they had been competitors for the region's resources long before the arrival of white men. The arrival of white trappers and traders increased the demand for the region's resources; it thereby increased the competitive tensions between Indian tribes. Moreover, tribes tended to ally themselves with different groups of trappers and traders. The

Jim Bridger, mountain man who spent considerable time trapping and trading in northern Utah and southwestern Wyoming. (From painting by Waldo Love. Original at the Colorado State Historical Society, Denver, Colorado. Photograph in Special Collections, Utah State University, Logan.)

Blackfeet remained relatively loyal to the British trappers and traders working south from the Oregon Territory under the banner of the Hudson's Bay Company. The Shoshonis, and after 1827, the Utes were traditional enemies of the Blackfeet and remained loyal to the Americans, "with lasting benefits," according to Dale Morgan, for "from this time both tribes were consistently friendly to the mountain men, the Snakes [Shoshoni] in particular acquiring an enduring reputation for friendliness."[56]

Still, competition remained keen. Bear Lake Valley was in actuality in neither American nor British territory. The Americans had acquired a large portion of the trans-Mississippi West in 1803 with the Louisiana Purchase and had come to an agreement with England in 1818 to jointly share and occupy the Oregon country south of the fifty-fourth parallel. That agreement was continued in 1827. Western land below the forty-second parallel, however, remained in Mexican hands, the Mexicans having acquired the land after gaining their independence from Spain in 1821. The Mexicans protested vigorously the treaty arranged by the Americans at Bear Lake between the Snakes and Utes. One of their reports read in part:

> at four days journey beyond the lake of Timpanagos [Utah Lake], there is a fort situated in another lake, with a hundred men under the command of a general of the United States of North America, having with them five wagons and three pieces of artillery; that they arrived at the said fort in May, and left it on the 1st of August of the year last past, with a hundred horses loaded with otter skins; that said general caused a peace to be made between the barbarous nations of the Yutas Timpanagos and the Comanches Sozones, and made presents of guns, balls, knives, &c. to both nations; that the Yuta Timpanago Indian, called *Quimanuapa*, was appointed general by the North Americans . . . [57]

The Mexican government, however, was working at a distinct disadvantage in this matter—they were not there. In the remote western reaches of North America, the only way to effectively lay claim to an area was to physically hold on to it. Morgan summarizes: "The gathering at Bear Lake was indeed a trespass on the soil of Mexico . . . , but none of the mountain men knew where that vague abstraction, the boundary line, really ran. Nor did they care. Effective sovereignty was exercised here by no nation; law was what could be agreed on with friendly Indians and enforced on others."[58]

Clashes occurred often on the frontier which involved every configuration possible: Indian versus Indian, trapper versus Indian, and trapper versus trapper. It was not unusual for trappers from the Hudson's Bay Company to desert to the Americans, or vice-versa. The British fur trapper Peter Skene Ogden, in 1826, recorded making contact with a "Party of Americans and some of our deserters of last year."[59] The long arm of the Hudson's Bay Company,[60] whose initials HBC Americans referred to as "Here Before Christ," seemed to reach everywhere.

The Americans, operating under Smith, Jackson, and Sublette, and the HBC, under the command of Ogden, spent a rather tense winter in the region in 1828. An expedition under William Sublette left Bear Lake headquarters in August, pushing northward into the Snake River Basin, the domain of the HBC. By October, destitute of supplies, they were forced to purchase provisions at an inflated price from Ogden. By late November, winter had arrived with a vengeance and Sublette was forced to retreat again to the Bear River. According to Don Berry, "Americans all over the mountains were in trouble." The severe winter caused a shortage of game, and even at the trappers' headquarters at Bear Lake, Americans were reduced to eating horses and dogs.[61]

At the rendezvous of 1830, at Green River, William Sublette had had enough and proposed dissolving his partnership with Jackson and Smith. Like Ashley three years earlier, Sublette retired to St. Louis to become the supplier of the successor organization, the Rocky Mountain Fur Company (RMFC). The new company was formed by five partners: Tom Fitzpatrick, James Bridger, Milton Sublette (William's brother), Henry Fraeb, and Jean Baptiste Gervais. They were arguably the most experienced trappers operating in the mountains. They also were arguably the poorest. The RMFC continued its base of operations in the Bear Lake and Bear River valleys. The company's success, however, depended on its ability to compete with the American Fur Company, which had decided to expand its area of operations from the upper Missouri into the Rocky Mountains. What the American Fur Company (or simply "the company," as the RMFC referred to it) lacked in expertise, it more than made up for in brains and capital. Headed by Kenneth McKenzie, who had great business skills, the AFC was bankrolled by none other than John Jacob Astor. Its access to capital was enormous, and in order to eventually outcompete the RMFC, all that was necessary was to gain some experience—experience gained largely at the expense of RMFC. It became the AFC's *modus operandi* to shadow the RMFC trappers, essentially going to school in order to learn the trade. By the mid-1830s their men had learned their lessons well and had managed to compete with the best trappers in the mountains.

Both companies competed for the same resources. Both frequented the Bear Lake and Bear River valleys. Perhaps the most precise (and most flowery) description of the Bear Lake region comes from the pen of Warren Angus Ferris, who spent six years (1830 to 1835) in the central Rockies as an employee of the AFC. Ferris's description is also the first reference to fur traders entering the Bear Lake Valley from the west. Ferris most likely entered Bear Lake Valley from Cache Valley through Logan Canyon.

> From the precipitous western sides of the height on which we stood, one of the most agreeable prospects imaginable, saluted and blessed our vision. It was the Little Lake, which from the foot of the mountain beneath us, stretches away to the northward washing the base of the cordillera that invests it. It is fifteen miles long and about eight in breadth and like Nemi, "Navelled in the hills," for it is entirely surrounded by lofty mountains, of which those on the western side are crowned with eternal snow. It gathers its waters from hundreds of rivulets that come dancing and flashing down the mountains, and streams that issue not infrequently from subterranean fountains beneath them. At the head of the lake opposite, and below us, lay a delightful valley of several miles extant, spotted with groves of aspen and cottonwood, and beds of willows of ample extent.
>
> When first seen the lake appeared smooth and polished like a vast field of glass, and took its colour from the sky which was clear unclouded blue. It was dotted over by hundreds of pelicans white in their plumage as the fresh-fallen snow. While we yet paused, gazing rapturously upon the charmed prospect, and feasting our eyes upon its unhidden beauties, we were over-taken by a tremendous gale of wind accompanied with rain, which dissipated in a moment a lovely cottage Fancy had half constructed upon the quiet margin of the sleeping lake. Beautiful to behold is a fair young female in the soft slumber of health and innocence, but far more beautiful when startled to consciousness from her gentle rest, and bright colors chase one another across her cheeks and bosom. So with the lake, which far from losing a single attraction when

roused by the wind from its repose, became even more enchanting than before; for the milk-white billows rolling like clouds over its deep blue surface seemed to add a bewitching something to the scene that did not appear to be wanting until the attention of the observer was directed to it, when it became too essential to be spared.[62]

The AFC's keen sense of competition was augmented when the RMFC's supplier, William Sublette, had a change of heart. Sensing the precarious economic situation of his brother Milton's company, William approached the AFC with an offer: if the AFC trappers would confine themselves to the Missouri River, the RMFC would agree to confine itself to Bear Lake and the Great Basin. William Sublette knew that he had a good deal of leverage in the negotiations. Competition with the RMFC had proven to be expensive, and in 1834 John Jacob Astor, a man whose business sense paralleled his bank account, foresaw the ultimate demise of the fur trade and withdrew from the AFC. The agreement was struck; although the RMFC survived another year, William Sublette's finaglings and Astor's withdrawal ultimately spelled doom for the company.[63]

The fur trade in the Rocky Mountains came and went with meteoric speed. The beaver population in the West became severely depleted during the 1830s. Furthermore, by 1837 the national economy had collapsed in a financial panic brought on in part by President Andrew Jackson's war with the Bank of the United States (BUS). As Jackson removed BUS deposits and placed them in his own favored banks, he inadvertently fueled a land-speculation boom. "The greater fool theory" was popular in the West; it operated upon the calm assumption that once land had been purchased by a speculator, a "greater fool" would inevitably come along and purchase the land for more. The problem with the theory, however, was the finite number of "fools." In his attempt to slow the pace of land speculation, Jackson exacerbated the situation by issuing a "Species Circular" which demanded that all land transactions be made with hard currency. As a result, fortunes rapidly disappeared as banks and businesses failed on a mammoth scale.

In addition to the financial crunch caused by bank failures, the fur trade suffered further by the decreased demand for beaver pelts brought on by the fickle tastes of fashion. This change in taste, though bad for the trappers, was good for the beaver, which otherwise may have experienced a fate similar to that of the bison. The fur trade provided a most important link between the settled and unsettled portions of the United States. The early successes of the great western migration which followed the years of the fur trade hinged on the geographical knowledge gained by the trappers. Trappers such as Kit Carson, Tom Fitzpatrick, and Moses Black Harris, among others, used their special knowledge to guide immigrant trains to Oregon and California and also to guide government surveys in their reconnaissance of the West. By 1840 most of the name players in the American fur trade had either retired, gone broke, or perished. Jedediah Smith, for instance, died near Santa Fe in May 1831, presumably from hostile Indians.[64] William Sublette, though he holds the distinction of guiding the first wagon train successfully through South Pass in 1830, eventually settled in St. Louis and lost most of his wealth in the years following the Panic of 1837.[65] The mountain men who prospered after 1840 were those who became guides for overland wagon trains or government surveys or those who made the transition from trapping to trading. James Bridger established an outpost on Black's Fork of the Green River in southwestern Wyoming in 1843; Thomas "Pegleg" Smith established a similar outpost in the Bear Lake Valley.

Pegleg Smith is Bear Lake's most famous mountain man. Like James Bridger, who incidentally was Pegleg's major competitor, Smith was one of a small handful of trappers who remained in the West after the decline of the fur trade. He first came west with the Ashley-Henry group in 1823 and remained in the mountains until 1850.[66] Smith may have first seen the Bear Lake Valley at the 1827 rendezvous. It was during the following fall's hunt on the Green River that an Indian bullet shattered (or an arrow poisoned, depending upon which version of the story one reads) his left foot and lower leg. According to some accounts, Smith amputated the damaged appendage himself. Other accounts suggest that he was aided by his partner James Cockrell.

Aided by the many retellings of the Pegleg Smith story, the Pegleg Smith legend prospered. Smith himself was certainly not above

Bear Lake Valley's most celebrated mountaineer, Thomas Peg-leg Smith. (Engraving in *Hutchings' California Magazine, reproduced in Sardis W. Templeton, The Lame Captain: The Life and Adventures of Pegleg Smith.*)

embellishment and, in fact, retold his story many times over the years while operating his trading post at the north end of Bear Lake Valley. Not only did the legend prosper, but as a trader, so did Smith. By the 1840s the south end of the Bear Lake Valley lay directly in the path of overland travelers. Smith took advantage of his fortuitous location, the success of which was augmented by his expertise as a horse thief. In company with outlaw Indian bands, Smith led many trips to plunder Mexican haciendas in California, sometimes returning with upwards of five thousand animals.[67]

Although a one-legged man operated under a disadvantage as a trapper, Smith compensated for his handicap by keeping four legs of horseflesh under him most of the time. And it was his switch to trafficking in horseflesh that enabled him to remain in the mountains after the decline of the fur trade.

Overland Trail

Edward Henry Lenox, a traveler on the Oregon Trail, encountered Pegleg Smith in 1843 in the Bear River Valley and provided the first mention of Smith's outpost.[68] The outpost grew considerably over the next year. It is not clear from Lenox's mention whether Smith had any actual buildings in 1843 or was simply living with his Indian partners, conducting business out of a tepee. In 1844, however, John Minto encountered Smith at Fort Hall, the next stop on the Oregon Trail, a hundred miles north and west of Pegleg's permanent base. Judging from Minto's description of Smith, it is clear that business had been good. "He was now dressed in navy blue and would have been adjudged a steamboat captain at St. Louis."[69]

Throughout the 1840s Smith prospered. Sardis W. Templeton, Smith's biographer, notes that his outpost became progressively more elaborate with one or two log cabins in addition to Indian Lodges. One of these was furnished eventually with a stove, table, and chairs, and here Smith's invited guests enjoyed mountain meals that were almost elaborate. Brandy and whiskey were served, and the dinners often became jovial affairs and prolonged into the evening. There are indeed few sour notes in the many journals that tell of the Bear River Valley in these days.[70]

In 1847 Smith also made an effort to grow vegetables and grains for the overland market. Frustrated by frosts and insects, however, he eventually gave up on the idea and purchased these items from Mormon settlements in the Salt Lake Valley. It was not unusual for there to be one or two Mormon families at Smith's outpost during this time.[71] He retained cordial relations with Mormon church president Brigham Young over the next three years. His frustrating experiences with farming in the Bear Lake Valley may have dampened Young's enthusiasm for encouraging Mormon settlement there. The Mormon leader postponed settlement of the Bear Lake Valley until passage of the Homestead Act in 1862 which forced him to make that decision.

With a large part of the western migration passing through

Covered wagons, such as the one in this photograph, carried immigrants along the Oregon Trail. Although immigrants often remarked about the lushness of the Bear River Valley, most stayed only long enough to refresh their stock. (Special Collections, Utah State University, Logan.)

Smith's front yard in Bear Lake Valley, it would seem bad timing on his part to have abandoned the post in 1850. The 1849 season had been a watershed year for Smith. With gold having been discovered at Sutter's Mill on the Sacramento River in 1848, literally thousands of gold-seekers were making the cross-country trek. Some of them opted for a more southerly route from Fort Bridger west to Salt Lake City, but many continued to pass through the Bear River Valley to the Hudspeth Cut-off north of Lava Hot Springs, Idaho. Ever the fortune hunter, it appears that Smith fell prey to the same gold fever that was driving the emigrants west past his doorstep. In 1850 he abandoned his business and joined the thousands already in the process of relocating to the California gold fields.[72]

Some deviations from the main Oregon Trail, which ran past Pegleg Smith's outpost and continued on to Fort Hall, meandered through present-day Rich County much as did the Bear River.[73] The trail blazed by J. B. Chiles in 1843 entered present-day Rich County in the vicinity of Woodruff and followed the meanderings of the Bear

River back and forth across current state boundaries, roughly joining the other trails at the north end of Bear Lake.[74] Other routes cir-
cumvented what is now Utah, however, not entering Bear Lake Valley
until southeastern Idaho.[75] Russell R. Rich, in his study of Mormon
settlements in the Bear Lake Valley, suggests another possibility.

> The Oregon Trail entered Bear Lake Valley from two different
> directions, the older of which went along the southern and west-
> ern shores of Bear Lake. Today there is a "Trails and Landmarks"
> marker stationed by the road between Fish Haven and Garden City
> in memory of the years when those hardy pioneers passed along
> the trail at this point.[76]

Rich does not refute nor confirm the validity of the marker's
contention; nonetheless, the possibility seems highly unlikely. Some
of the suppositions made on the marker are not historically accurate.
[77] Still, Bear River Valley was the logical route to enter Bear Lake
Valley, it being "one of the natural gateways from western Wyoming
and northern Utah to Snake River and the northwest," according to
George R. Mansfield. As trappers and traders had selected the route,
it made sense that overlanders would also follow the same course.[78]
Like water flowing in the Bear River, emigration along the Oregon
Trail followed the course of least resistance, and that course appears
to have been along the eastern fringes of present-day Rich County.

State and county boundaries did not exist in 1827, of course, nor
did they exist during the 1830s and 1840s. Local boundaries were
important only in a diplomatic sense. The Mexican government
made clear its displeasure with the inter-tribal treaties negotiated
between the Utes and Shoshonis by the Americans at the 1827 rendezvous. The Mexican government considered the Americans to be
trespassers, as indeed they were. Although the south end of Bear Lake
was within Mexican territory, the north end of the Bear Lake Valley
was above the forty-second parallel, beyond the international
boundary between Mexican territory and the jointly occupied
American/British Oregon territory. The United States government
did not seem any more concerned with Mexican claims to the land
below the present boarder separating Utah and Idaho than it was
with British claims to the Oregon territory. By the mid-1840s the

United States was actively coveting both areas as officials began a campaign to explore and survey the area.

Government Surveys

The first U.S. government survey of the Bear River Valley was conducted under the leadership of Major Benjamin L. E. Bonneville. Taking a leave of absence from the army in 1832, Bonneville spent the next two years exploring the region of the Great Basin while also trying his hand at the fur trade.[79] He explored northward from the Green River where, according to Washington Irving: "Crossing an elevated ridge [he] came upon Bear River . . ."[80] Following the Bear River north, as had been the custom of trappers (Bonneville was accompanied by the trapper Joseph Walker), the party camped "at the outlet of a lake about thirty miles long, and from two to three miles in width, completely embedded in low mountains, and connected with Bear River by an impassable swamp."[81]

From their campsite on Bear Lake, the Bonneville party continued north to explore the Soda Springs area and beyond. Bonneville's most noted contribution to geographical knowledge was the dispatch of a separate group under Joseph Walker to explore the Great Salt Lake and a westward route to California. While Walker is credited with the discovery of Walker's Pass through the Sierra Nevada and the charting of the major overland route to California, Bonneville received credit for physically describing the Great Salt Lake. Bonneville, however, never actually saw the Great Salt Lake, nor did he recognize the prehistoric lake of which Great Salt Lake was a remnant. Nonetheless, the early lake—Lake Bonneville—was later named in his honor. Bonneville's discoveries through his associates proved that the Great Salt Lake was a terminal lake and that no river flowed west from it to the Pacific Ocean. Trappers and mountain men already knew this: a party of William Ashley's men claimed to have skirted Great Salt Lake in the summer of 1826.[82]

Bonneville's exploration and those of subsequent government-sponsored explorers were important in publicizing information about the West. The mountain men's knowledge generally was not widely published; in fact, many trappers guarded their knowledge jealously. But two years after Bonneville's return, Washington Irving immortalized his exploits by publishing *The Adventures of Captain Bonneville in the Rocky Mountains and Far West.*

Although Bonneville received some publicity, more fell to John C. Fremont. A man uniquely capable of self-promotion, Fremont was the first surveyor to venture into the Rocky Mountains with both commission and purse. Through the help of his father-in-law, Missouri Senator Thomas Hart Benton, Fremont was given both funding and official status through the Army Corps of Topographical Engineers. Fremont presented his official report of his first expedition to the United States Senate in March 1843. Aided by the descriptive prose of his wife Jessie (Fremont dictated the narrative to her, allowing her considerable literary license), the report lent a romantic flavor to the West which the public accepted wholeheartedly. The Senate evidently felt likewise, ordering the printing of a thousand additional copies.[83]

The Fremont expedition entered the Bear River Valley from the Green River Basin much as Bonneville had done a decade before. Unlike Bonneville, however, Fremont may have found a more clearly marked route already existing. Overland travel by wagon, at least as far as Fort Hall, had been proceeding at a fairly constant pace since 1841. By 1843 more than a thousand emigrants had made the journey to either Oregon or California.[84] Fremont took note of the fact that emigrants relied on the forage of the Bear River and Bear Lake valleys to refresh their stock. He also commented upon the "attractive and fertile appearance of the Bear Lake Valley." [85] Emigrants expressed similar views about the area, one describing "excellent grass, already mowable." Another remarked how two sections of land elsewhere would not be worth trading for one section in the Bear River Valley. Nonetheless, even with the glowing descriptions of the area, overlanders continued on their way to either California or Oregon.[86] The Bear River and Bear Lake valleys remained an area traversed by overlanders and explored by surveyors, but it would not be settled by farmers for at least another fifteen years.

Fremont's expedition and subsequent report helped fuel the fires of expansionism. Fostered by the election of President James K. Polk in 1844, American notions that it was the nation's "manifest destiny" to stretch from the Atlantic to the Pacific soon led the country into conflict with the British in the Pacific Northwest and with Mexico to the south. There is little doubt that Fremont's second expedition in 1845 was part of a government plan to control the continent. Fur traders such as William Ashley had been advocating the annexation of Oregon since 1829.[87] Also it had long been the dream of Senator Thomas Hart Benton to establish American superiority throughout the continent. By 1846 with more than eight thousand immigrants arriving annually in Oregon and the west coast,[88] Great Britain capitulated and agreed to a compromise boarder along the 49th parallel. The Mexican problem was not solved so easily.

Having explored the overland route to California with his first expedition, Fremont's second venture was supposed to limit itself to the exploration of the Red and Arkansas rivers. However, he continued west in violation of orders (or perhaps in acquiescence to "private" orders from Senator Benton), and became embroiled in the California revolt, including being present when the rebels raised the Bear Flag at Sonoma on 1 July 1846.[89]

Lieutenant Joseph W. Revere brought the short-lived Bear Flag Republic under the control of the United States when he replaced the Bear Flag with the Stars and Stripes at Sonoma on 11 July.[90] This, coupled with the other campaigns of the Mexican War—those of Winfield Scott and Zachary Taylor in the Southwest and in Mexico— would, by 1848, give the United States possession of all previous Mexican territory from the 42nd parallel on the north to the Rio Grande on the south. Present-day Rich County, along with the soon-to-be-created Utah Territory, now belonged to the United States, and this prospect would bode both good and ill for the subsequent Mormon settlers of the region.

ENDNOTES

1. Mildred H. Thomson, comp., *Rich Memories: Some of the Happenings in Rich County from 1863 to 1960* (Salt Lake City: Daughters of Utah Pioneers, 1962), 18.

2. Richard Poll, et al., ed., *Utah's History* (Logan: Utah State University Press, 1989), 6–7.

3. G. B. Richardson, *Geology and Mineral Resources of the Randolph*

Quadrangle, Utah-Wyoming, USGS Bulletin 923 (Washington, D.C.: Government Printing Office, 1941) 6, 38, 39.

4. Ibid., 39.

5. George Rogers Mansfield, *Geography, Geology and Mineral Resources of Part of Southeastern Idaho,* USGS professional paper 152 (Washington, D.C.: Government Printing Office, 1927), 199.

6. Ron Hatzenbuehler, address given at Idaho centennial celebration, Lava Hot Springs, Idaho, July 1990 (copy located in Special Collections and Archives, Merrill Library, Utah State University, Logan, Utah).

7. Poll, *Utah's History,* 719.

8. Ibid., 5–22.

9. *Soil Survey of Rich County, Utah* (Washington, D.C.: Soil Conservation Service, 1980), 1–7.

10. Ibid., 23.

11. Allen D. Willard, "Surficial Geology of Bear Lake Valley, Utah" (Master's thesis, Utah State University, 1959), 52.

12. Clarence T. Johnston and Joseph A. Breckons, *Water-Right Problems of Bear River,* USDA, Office of Experiment Stations Bulletin 70 (Washington D.C.: Government Printing Office, 1899), 12–13.

13. Russell R. Rich, *Land of the Sky-Blue Water: A History of the L.D.S. Settlement of the Bear Lake Valley* (Provo: Brigham Young University, 1963), 79.

14. Richard C. Bright, *Lake Bonneville* (Lincoln: Nebraska Academy of Sciences Proceedings, 1965), 136.

15. Julian H. Steward, *Basin-Plateau Aboriginal Sociopolitical Groups,* Smithsonian Institution Bureau of American Ethnology Bulletin 120 (Washington, D.C.: Government Printing Office, 1938), 10.

16. Merle W. Wells in Brigham D. Madsen, *The Northern Shoshoni* (Caldwell, Idaho: Caxton Printers, 1980), 17.

17. Ibid.

18. Ibid.

19. Ibid.

20. An archaeological survey was conducted by M. S. Berry beginning in 1974; however, financial restraints limited the scope of the investigation. In the fall of 1992 low water in the Bear Lake uncovered the remains of a mammoth, and this find was investigated by the Division of State History. The mammoth find, coupled with the discovery by A. R. Standing and the subsequent investigation by anthropologists from the University of Utah of the Woodruff Bison Kill area, suggests that the animals were present and that Indian cultures to the east of Rich County were also active in the Rich

County area itself. See M. S. Berry, "Rich County," report on file, Division of State History, Salt Lake City, Utah.

21. Rich, *Land of the Sky-Blue Water,* 54.

22. Steward, *Basin-Plateau,* 230. See also George C. Frison, *Prehistoric Hunters of the High Plains,* 2d ed. (San Diego: Academic Press, 1991), 12.

23. Frison, *Prehistoric Hunters,* 13, 14.

24. Steward, *Basin-Plateau,* 231.

25. Ibid., 14.

26. Ibid., *Basin-Plateau,* 231.

27. Frison, *Prehistoric Hunters,* 153–55.

28. John Charles Fremont, *Memoirs of My Life, vol. 1* (Chicago: Belford, Clark and Co., 1887), 218.

29. Frison, *Prehistoric Hunters,* 153.

30. Ibid., 201.

31. M. S. Berry, "Rich County," (Salt Lake City: Antiquities Section, Utah State Historical Society, January 1974).

32. Frison, *Prehistoric Hunters,* 204.

33. Ibid.

34. Wells, *Northern Shoshoni,* 17.

35. Robert B. Butler, *When Did the Shoshoni Begin to Occupy Southeastern Idaho? Essays on the Late Prehistoric Cultural Remains from the Upper Snake and Salmon River Country,* Occasional Papers of the Idaho Museum of Natural History, no. 32 (Pocatello: Idaho State University, 1981). Butler's essays concern themselves with the issue of Shoshoni occupation and contend that the original inhabitants of the region during the prehistoric and Paleoindian periods were Fremont.

36. Rich, *Land of the Sky-Blue Water,* 6, 7. See also Philip Ashton Rollins, ed., *The Discovery of the Oregon Trail: Robert Stuart's Narratives* (New York: Charles Scribner's Sons, 1935), 85, 86.

37. Rollins, *Discovery,* 86. According to Stuart, the Arapahays were an outlaw band of the Arapahoes. See also Rollins, 162.

38. Ibid., 270.

39. Ibid., cxxxv–cxxxvi. Rollins published the letter from Ramsay Crooks, dated 26 June 1856, in which Crooks refutes John C. Fremont's claim to the discovery of South Pass. Crooks, who was a member of the Wilson Price Hunt Expedition, notes that "after several days journey came through the celebrated 'South Pass' in the month of November 1812."

40. Alexander Ross, *The Fur Hunters of the Far West,* edited by Kenneth A. Spaulding (Norman: University of Oklahoma Press, 1956), 153.

41. LeRoy R. Hafen, ed. *The Mountain Men and the Fur Trade of the Far West,* vol. 9 (Glendale, CA: Arthur H. Clark Co., 1972), 382.

42. Don Berry, *A Majority of Scoundrels* (Sausalito, CA : Comstock Editions, Inc., 1977), 8–9. Also, Thomas Hempstead, writing to his Missouri Fur Company partner, Joshua Pilcher, noted on 3 April 1822 that "Gen Ashley's company starts this day with one boat and one hundred and fifty men . . . my opinion as regards the manner that those men are employed might differ with yours, but I think it will not. they are engaged in three different ways I am told the hunters and trappers are to have one half of the furs etc. they make the Company furnish them with Gun Powder Lead etc etc, they only are to help to build the fort and defend it in case of necessity." Quoted in Dale L. Morgan, ed., *The West of William Ashley* (Denver, CO: Old West Publishing Co., 1964), 3–4.

43. Berry, *A Majority of Scoundrels,* 3.

44. Ibid., 16.

45. Morgan, *The West of William Ashley,* 23. See also Sardis W. Templeton, *The Lame Captain: The Life and Adventures of Pegleg Smith* (Los Angeles: Westernlore Press, 1965), 24.

46. Donald McKay Frost, *Notes on General Ashley, the Overland Trail and South Pass* (Barre, MA: Barre Gazette, 1960), 59.

47. Dale L. Morgan, *Jedediah Smith and the Opening of the West* (New York: Bobbs-Merrill Co., 1953), 164.

48. Morgan, *The West of William Ashley,* 149.

49. Ibid., 162.

50. "150th Anniversary of the Historic Rendezvous," *Bear Lake Magazine* 1 (1 July 1977), 2.

51. Berry, *A Majority of Scoundrels,* 174.

52. Morgan, *Jedediah Smith,* 193–201.

53. Morgan, *The West of William Ashley,* 152.

54. Ibid., 305. There is some evidence that Jedediah Smith, David Jackson, and William Sublette conducted some preliminary business in Cache Valley prior to the meeting which took place at Bear River. See George R. Brooks, ed., *The Southwest Expedition of Jedediah S. Smith: His Personal Account of the Journey to California, 1826–1827* (Glendale, CA: Arthur H. Clark Co., 1977), 35.

55. Ibid., 168.

56. Ibid.

57. Quoted in Morgan, *The West of William Ashley,* 168–169.

58. Ibid., 169.

59. Ibid., 146.

60. The HBC employed Thomas "Pegleg" Smith to trap beaver as far south as present-day Arizona, for example.

61. Berry, *A Majority of Scoundrels,* 183.

62. Warren Angus Ferris, *Life in the Rocky Mountains, 1830–1835* (Salt Lake City: Rocky Mountain Book Shop, 1940), 41, 42.

63. Berry, *A Majority of Scoundrels,* 374–394. One cannot rule out the significance of Nathaniel Wyeth in all of this. Wyeth had made an agreement with the RMFC to supply them with provisions in 1834, contrary to the RMFC's agreement with Sublette. Sublette, upon finding this out, endeavored to beat Wyeth to the rendezvous. He succeeded, and the RMFC ended up reneging on their deal with Wyeth.

As the RMFC had already dissolved, the company felt no obligation to honor the contract with Wyeth. Yet the company was also unaware of William Sublette's shenanigans. Bradford Cole points out that Wyeth did not fare as badly as many have supposed. He was able to recoup approximately $1,300 from his $3,000 cargo; the remainder was used to construct and supply Fort Hall on the Portneuf River. See Bradford Cole, "Failure on the Columbia: Nathaniel Wyeth's Columbia River Fishing and Trading Company," paper presented at the sixth annual North American Fur Trade Conference, Mackinac Island, Michigan, September 1991.

64. Hafen, *Mountain Men,* vol. 8, 347.

65. Hafen, *Mountain Men,* vol. 5, 347–359. See also John D. Unruh, Jr., *The Plains Across: The Overland Emigrants and the Trans-Mississippi West, 1840–60* (Urbana: University of Illinois Press, 1979), 20, 29.

66. Ibid., 25, 206.

67. Ibid., 159–86.

68. Templeton, *The Lame Captain,* 160.

69. Ibid., 166.

70. Ibid., 178.

71. Ibid., 184, 199.

72. Ibid. 206.

73. See map on front cover of Doyce B. Nunis, Jr., *The Bidwell-Bartleson Party, 1841: California Emigrant Adventure* (Santa Cruz, CA: Western Tanager Press, 1991).

74. William H. Goetzmann, *Exploration and Empire: The Explorer and the Scientist in the Winning of the American West* (New York: Alfred A. Knopf, 1966), 171.

75. Unruh, *The Plains Across,* 172.

76. Rich, *Land of the Sky-Blue Water,* 8–9.

77. The marker reads: "The first wagons came into the valley in 1830,

during which year they made their way as far west as Fort Washakie, Wyoming. Continued efforts were made to find passable wagon trails through the mountains to the Pacific Coast, which goal was finally reached in 1840."

The historic marker is probably referring to the wagons brought west for the Green River rendezvous by William Sublette in 1830. It seems a considerable stretch to include this area of Wyoming within Bear Lake Valley. See John E. Sunder, *Bill Sublette, Mountain Man* (Norman: University of Oklahoma Press, 1959), 85–86.

The marker continues: "At the time the entire northwest mountain area was known as the Oregon Country, and western travel was either to the Oregon or California regions. While early maps give the probable location of the Oregon Trail somewhat to the north, well marked wagon ruts and stories of Indian and early settlers of this region indicate that the first wagon migration to Oregon followed the southerly and westerly shores of Bear Lake. Leaving this valley through a canyon to the northwest, they proceeded to the upper reaches of the Bear River."

The area above the present boundary of Utah and Idaho was considered the Oregon Territory, jointly occupied, as of 1818, by the United States and Great Britain. Southern Bear Lake Valley was, however, Mexican territory. Mexico acquired all the area west of the Rocky Mountains and south of the forty-second parallel after obtaining its independence from Spain in 1820. The "well marked wagon ruts" could be a result of travel within the area by early settlers, and since the area was not settled until the 1860s, it seems improbable that early settlers would have knowledge of overland activity in the 1830s and 1840s. The marker endeavors to provide "additional color" by mentioning the 1827 rendezvous:

"Additional color is given to this belief by the fact that this area was the site of an important trappers rendezvous as early as 1827 and well marked trails were followed for many years in and out of the valley."

The marker is correct in stating that the first "wagon" into the area did arrive at the southern shore of Bear Lake. It is doubtful, however, that it entered the valley from the south, down Laketown Canyon. The terrain was simply too steep and rugged. As mentioned before, the four-pound cannon, mounted on a carriage chassis, holds the distinction of being the first wheeled vehicle to cross South Pass. It is known that the cannon was at the Rendezvous of 1827 because it was fired off upon the arrival of Jedediah Smith. But it most likely entered the Bear Lake Valley from the north.

According to the contract negotiated between Sublette, Jedediah Smith, and David Jackson with William Ashley, the party was to meet at the northwest end of Bear Lake See, Morgan, *Ashley,* 152. In all probability the caravan in 1827 followed the route of the later Oregon Trail and descended the pass in southeastern Idaho, thereafter taking the caravan either west, crossing the Bear River and then south up the west shore route, or south up the east shore of Bear Lake to the rendezvous point. The caravan likely took the east shore route because the outlet of Bear Lake which connected the lake with the river was considered an "impassable swamp" which probably inhibited travel from the east to the west around the north end of the lake. See Washington Irving, *The Adventures of Captain Bonneville, USA in the Rocky Mountains and the Far West* (New York: G. P. Putnam's Sons, 1898), 311.

This does seem like a long way around, and one wonders that they were going to meet at the north end of the lake why they did not simply hold the rendezvous at that location. Again, as mentioned, the rendezvous site had been a traditional meeting place for Indians and may have been chosen by the Indian partners rather than by the fur traders.

78. Mansfield, *Geography*, 33.

79. William H. Goetzmann, *Army Exploration in the American West, 1803–1863* (New Haven: Yale University Press, 1959), 52.

80. Irving, *Captain Bonneville*, 310.

81. Ibid., 311.

82. Morgan, *The West of William Ashley*, 148.

83. Goetzmann, *Army Exploration*, 83.

84. Unruh, *The Plains Across*, 119.

85. Mansfield, *Geography*, 3.

86. Templeton, *The Lame Captain*, 164.

87. Morgan, *The West of William Ashley*, 183–86.

88. Unruh, *The Plains Across*, 119.

89. Jack K. Bauer, *The Mexican War, 1846–1848* (New York: Macmillan Publishing Co., 1974), 169.

90. Ibid., 172.

2

"*The Snow Lies Too Low on the Mountains Here for Utah*"

THE MORMON SETTLEMENTS IN NORTHERN BEAR LAKE VALLEY

Only six months after John C. Fremont witnessed the Bear Flag Revolt in California, another group of overlanders left western Illinois on a cross-country trek destined to have far-reaching effects on the Great Basin and future Rich County. Fremont's report would play a pivotal role in the Mormon decision to settle within the Great Basin. Some of the Mormons who fled Hancock County, Illinois, in search of sanctuary for their new religion would ultimately settle the area around Bear Lake: first, at the northern end, in what is now Idaho, and later at the southern end near Laketown in what is now Utah.

The history of Mormon settlement in Rich County and Utah in general could be said to have begun in upstate New York in 1830 with the organization of the Church of Jesus Christ of Latter-day Saints. Declaring himself the recipient of visitations, revelations, and visions, Joseph Smith, Jr., the church's founder, is believed by his followers to have translated from gold plates the *Book of Mormon,* a record of the ancient inhabitants of the Americas. In addition to the *Book of Mormon,* Smith also later published his own revelations as the *Book of Commandments* and from these two works, in addition to the Bible, developed the theological framework of Mormonism.

The fledgling church grew and prospered, benefiting from a number of notable conversions, including that of Brigham Young. But from the outset the Mormon church faced opposition—not only over theological matters but also over Mormon social organization. Because of the church's politics and practices, the Mormons were successively driven from Ohio to Missouri to Illinois.[1]

It was at Carthage, Hancock County, Illinois, on the morning of 27 June 1844 that opposition to the Mormons and their prophet Joseph Smith culminated in the murders of Joseph and his brother Hyrum.[2] This tragic event set the stage for the great Mormon exodus from Illinois to the Salt Lake Valley. Preparations for the westward exodus began within the year.

Brigham Young, the new Mormon leader, planned a tentative departure date for April 1846, but continued persecution and threats of violence prompted him to move the date forward to February. Furthermore, Illinois governor Thomas Ford made clear his inability, or his unwillingness, to protect the Mormons in Hancock County and encouraged Brigham Young to move his followers west.[3]

It is possible that Joseph Smith himself had plans to relocate his followers to the Rocky Mountains.[4] But whether or not such a plan was actually being considered before Smith's death, Brigham Young and other church leaders began to seriously study the possibilities shortly after their return to Nauvoo in August 1844. John C. Fremont's report of his 1843 expedition was carefully scrutinized, and sections of it were read aloud at a meeting of the Quorum of Twelve Apostles.[5] Fremont had commented favorably on the area around Bear Lake as well as on other areas of the Bear River Valley. Though he waxed poetic about the Great Salt Lake, he was less than enthusiastic about the area around it, noting the alkaline and sandy soil.[6]

If Fremont's opinion about the Great Salt Lake Valley was somewhat less than flattering, it paled in comparison to that of Lansford W. Hastings. In 1845 Hastings published his *Emigrants' Guide to Oregon and California,* the content of which soon became well known to the Mormons. Hastings, like Fremont, noted the "more than ordinary fertility" of the Bear River Valley but claimed the land around Salt Lake was "entirely sterile and unproductive, as [was] all that portion of the country contiguous to that lake."[7] The most positive news about the Great Salt Lake Valley came from an encounter at Winter Quarters, Nebraska, with the Catholic priest Jean Pierre De Smet. De Smet painted a substantially more rosy picture of the area; but his description concerned itself more with that area north of the Great Salt Lake, particularly Cache Valley.[8]

Although the Mormons did not venture west blindly with no destination in mind, it is not certain that Brigham Young had his mind set upon the Great Salt Lake Valley when the first wagons left Winter Quarters in April 1847. More likely the decision had been made to seek out and settle the more well-reported area of the Bear River Valley. Conceivably, the destination included the Great Salt Lake Valley, the Weber River Basin, Cache Valley, and Bear Lake Valley. Also under consideration was Utah Lake Valley to the south of the Great Salt Lake, but this was later ruled out because of potential Indian problems. This was only one of the important considerations in arriving at a decision; others included fertility of the soil, climate, and altitude of the area. Answers to these questions simply could not be made prior to the departure of the Mormons. They were gradually decided upon and answered while en route to the Great Basin.

By 10 July the first caravan of Mormons into the Great Basin had committed to a route leading them away from both Bear Lake Valley and Cache Valley. With questions regarding soil fertility, Indian hostility, altitude, and climate having evidently been answered to their satisfaction, the Mormons struck southwest from Fort Bridger, following roughly the trail blazed by Lansford Hastings and the ill-fated Donner-Reed party of a year earlier.[9] Ultimately, the decision to settle in the Great Salt Lake Valley rather than in Cache Valley or Bear Lake Valley probably had to do with the practicality of agriculture. Both Fremont and Hastings mentioned the possible pursuit of agriculture below the 42nd parallel, but above the 42nd parallel agriculture was considered risky.[10] Additionally, along the trail the Mormons encountered an outbreak of sickness which some thought to be caused by high altitude and sudden temperature changes—hot days and cold nights.[11] The Latter-day Saints were certainly aware of the cold climate, for on 11 July they awoke to a quarter of an inch of ice in their water buckets.[12] Furthermore, the mountains still sported a covering of snow, and this may have caused them to seek the lowest possible elevation within the confines of the Great Basin, the valley of the Salt Lake.

Nonetheless, the decision to settle in Salt Lake Valley proved to be a good one, for although other areas of the Great Basin and Bear River Valley were probably superior in terms of the relative amount of arable land and potential irrigation water, the longer frost-free growing season in the Salt Lake Valley at least gave the Mormons a fighting chance to succeed agriculturally in the arid West. Bear Lake Valley remained a favored site along with Cache Valley to the north of Salt Lake and Utah Valley to the south. The Salt Lake settlement formed a base of operations for expansion into these other areas as circumstances permitted and as population demands required. Brigham Young fully intended to expand Mormon settlement throughout the Great Basin as is evidenced by his purchase of trapper Miles Goodyear's operation at the mouth of the Weber River in 1847[13] and his offer in November 1848 to purchase the operation of Pegleg Smith in the Bear Lake Valley.[14]

The high, cold environment in the Bear Lake Valley persuaded Young to settle farther south, but he carried on a line of communication with Pegleg Smith, and Mormons were infrequent visitors to the area.[15] After Pegleg's abandonment of his post in 1850, Brigham Young appears to have placed Bear Lake Valley on hold. As virtually all of the non-Mormon emigrants passing through the area after 1849 were more interested in gold or Oregon than in establishing farms locally, Young possibly felt little urgency in proceeding with the immediate settlement of an area which he already knew would require extraordinary effort because of the high altitude and severe winters. Additionally, he knew the Bear Lake region to be the domain of Chief Washakie's Shoshoni people. Mormons were already experiencing Indian problems in Cache Valley, and he certainly did not want to compound the situation.[16] Furthermore, after 1857 the Saints were preoccupied with the approach of the U.S. army troops.

Most of Utah's citizens looked to the Mormon church for leadership in both religious and political matters. Brigham Young had

Chief Washakie of the Shoshoni. Washakie's people frequented the areas of Bear Lake and Bear River valleys. (Special Collections and Archives, Utah State University, Logan.)

been appointed governor of the territory in 1850, but the other government officials—particularly the judiciary, land agents, and Indian agents—were federal appointees whom the Mormons considered "outsiders," and corrupt outsiders at that. Tales told of Mormon belligerence and "willful disregard of federal authority" soon reached ears in Washington, D.C.[17] Recently elected President James Buchanan dispatched a large escort force, under Brigadier General William S. Harney, to Utah on 18 July 1857 to install a newly appointed territorial governor, Alfred Cumming. News of the march, orders for which were issued in May, probably reached Brigham Young prior to 24 July when three riders interrupted a Pioneer Day celebration to theatrically announce the approaching invasion. Among the Mormon faithful the threat of military invasion by United States troops quickly escalated into preparations for a holy war.[18] Charles C. Rich, who would soon be involved in the settlement of Bear Lake Valley, having recently returned to Salt Lake City from the settlement at San Bernardino, California, because of the impending conflict with the United States Army, wrote to his friend Addison Pratt concerning the situation: "We have come to the conclusion that we dont want them and that we wont have them. . . . We will have the Kingdom of God or nothing."[19]

Brigham Young and those local leaders in charge of operations in the other settlements immediately began devising plans to thwart the government's invasion of Zion. An important part of Young's plan was to use guerrilla warfare against the federal army. The first effort was to burn Fort Bridger; then attack and burn army supply trains and run off the government's cattle.[20] In the event these activities proved unsuccessful, Young devised a plan to evacuate the settlements, move south, and put to the torch a decade of the Latter-day Saints' accomplishments by burning Salt Lake City.

Although Mormon guerilla activities combined with early winter blizzards to successfully halt the march of the army which was unable to enter Salt Lake City before the onslaught of winter, the call for evacuation south nonetheless came in March 1858. The army, now under the command of Colonel Albert Sydney Johnston, waited out the winter near the remains of Fort Bridger.[21]

While the army waited and the Mormons evacuated, Brigham

Young and newly appointed territorial governor Alfred Cumming were able to work out a degree of compromise with the help of an intermediary, Colonel Thomas Kane. Young relinquished control of the government to Cumming in exchange for the agreement that the army would be kept separate from the Mormons.

Coincident to the compromise, President James Buchanan issued a full pardon to Brigham Young and the Mormon people for any act of rebellion. When Johnston's Army entered Salt Lake on 26 June, the troops found the city deserted.[22] The army marched thirty miles southwest of Salt Lake City to a previously agreed-upon location in Cedar Valley. Here they established Camp Floyd, later changed in name to Camp Crittenden. Army troops would remain at that location, apart from main Mormon settlements, until the outbreak of the Civil War some three years later.

The Utah War made clear the uneasy relationship between the Mormons and the federal government. This uneasiness continued for at least the next thirty years. The Utah War also further impressed Brigham Young with the necessity of controlling other areas within the Great Basin. As early as 1857 he had sent scouting parties into the areas around Salt Lake City to determine possible routes into the valley which the army might take. An observation party of eleven men under the command of Marcellus Monroe left Ogden on 18 August 1857. Their main purpose was to watch for soldiers, but Monroe also scouted timber and water resources and made contact with various bands of Indians between Cache Valley and Bear Lake Valley. The party endeavored to enlist the support of the Indians should an open conflict develop between the army and the Mormons. Monroe reported on 18 August:

> Visited one Indian camp—chief's name Sagua—had a smoke with them and gave them some tobacco, all felt well. Bro. Jas. Brown [the interpreter] gave them the necessary instructions, they see it with a good spirit—they knew nothing of any importance about the soldiers.

After traveling through the southern part of Cache Valley, the party turned east to Little Bear River and ascended the canyon of the main fork. Traveling northeast through the mountains, Monroe reported:

> We changed our course to N.E. and traveled through a beau-
> tiful Country, low range of mountains, with groves of pine quak-
> ing-asp—grass and water very plentiful. in a plain Indian
> trail—[crossed] three low divides—Travelled about 30 miles and
> encamped in sight of Bear River Lake.

After again encountering an Indian band and repeating the ritual of
smoking and giving them tobacco, the party

> crossed over a ridge entered Bear River Lake Valley—This valley is
> on the S.E. side of this Lake—some 6 or 8 miles in diameter—sev-
> eral small streams running thro' it, good grass and some timber
> consisting of alder and cottonwood - This is one of the prettiest
> Lakes I ever saw—it has a beautiful sandy beach and groves of tim-
> ber around its margin in places. Followed an Indian trail around
> the lake in a northerly course—saw a mountain of sand stone—
> suitable for grinding stones. This lake, as near as we can ascertain,
> is from 5 to 8 miles wide 30 to 40 long . . . The water in this lake is
> strongly impregnated with soda—followed the lake some five miles
> . . . turned in the Kanyon leading out [across] Bear River—we
> found some good meadow land—cedar in abundance and no end
> to currents in this region—saw bear signs—crossed a ridge into
> another Kanyon—meadow land plenty—saw about 20 antelope—
> boys out after them.[23]

Leaving Bear Lake Valley, the party struck the Bear River and
traveled upstream before turning southwest and leaving Bear River
Valley over the divide near present-day Wanship. The party then followed the Weber River down the canyon. They made no contact with
the army; the information they gathered concerning Bear Lake and
Bear River valleys would be useful, however, in the years to come.

A short while later, another party left Cache Valley to explore the
Bear Lake region. An anonymous writer to the *Deseret News* noted
how a group under the direction of Bishop William Maughan left
Wellsville and traveled north into the Bear Lake Valley via Cub River
(which ostensibly received its name because of an incident involving
Maughan's group and a bear), and down the same canyon used by
the first settlers to the area six years later. Maughan's party was most
likely sent in order to determine possible roads in and out of Bear
Lake Valley, for after descending the summit between Meadowville

and Logan Canyon, they reported that "A road . . . connecting Cache and Bear Lake valleys is absolutely out of the question."[24]

The settlement of Bear Lake Valley became a matter of renewed urgency after Congress passed the Homestead Act on 20 May 1862. This act opened up the possibility that any settler could conceivably patent land within Bear Lake Valley and other areas in close proximity to Salt Lake City. In 1861 and 1862 two Mormon exploring parties journeyed into Bear Lake Valley. Utah Territorial Militia Colonel James H. Martineau, a member of the party, recorded how he was

> one of an exploring party into Bear Lake Valley, crossing the mountains at the head of Blacksmith's Fork River. In some places our trail lay along precipices, barely wide enough for a horse to pass along, and where a single false step would send one to certain death, but we had no accident. On our return by the source of the Little Bear River, we discovered a large deposit of iron ore, assaying 70 percent. Three days after our return, I started with a strong company on another tour of exploration into Bear Lake Valley, by way of Cub River, and made a thorough examination of its facilities for settlement, etc. I was historian and topographer, and made report to President Young that the Valley was suitable for settlement, it being generally supposed non-inhabitable by reason of its altitude - nearly 7000 feet above sea level. We returned by way of Soda Springs and had much difficulty and danger in swimming our horses across Bear River and other swollen, raging torrents fed by the melting snows.[25]

It is clear that Martineau's party explored at the request of Brigham Young and, given the number of routes used to enter and exit Bear Lake Valley, it is also clear that they too were looking for the best route for settlement. It is unknown if the Martineau Expedition also investigated the area of present-day Strawberry Canyon which was the route later used by Charles C. Rich to enter the valley; however, a year earlier on 17 July, Martineau, in company with G. L. Farrell and Israel J. Clark, under the command of Colonel Thomas E. Ricks, had explored "the country lying east of Cache Valley." It is assumed they entered Bear Lake Valley via Logan Canyon, for upon leaving Cache Valley, they "crossed the main range of the Wasatch mountains, explored the Bear Lake country and mountainous region east of that valley, returning by way of Soda Springs. . . ."[26]

After passage of the Homestead Act, some fear developed in Mormon circles that Bear Lake Valley might be lost to non-Mormon settlers. Some non-Mormons within the territory, in order to counter the Mormon political majority, openly encouraged non-Mormon settlers. Colonel Patrick Connor, who had been dispatched to Salt Lake Valley to establish Fort Douglas after the outbreak of the Civil War, adopted a strategy of inviting "hither a large Gentile and loyal population sufficient by peaceful means and through the ballot-box to overwhelm the Mormons by mere force of numbers."[27] Although Connor openly opposed Mormon political dominance, he probably did more to make possible the expanse of Mormon settlement in Cache Valley and Bear Lake Valley than any other single individual. Connor and his California Volunteers not only were sent to Salt Lake to monitor the Mormons but also to guard against Indian hostilities.[28] At least two settlers and one Indian died in a skirmish at Smithfield during the summer of 1860. Indian threats, both perceived and real, were common in virtually all Cache Valley settlements from Franklin in the north to Wellsville in the south.[29] James Martineau estimated that in June 1861 "about 3000 Indians entered the valley . . . with the avowed intention of exterminating the settlers."[30] By 1862 the hostile situation in Cache Valley had become acute.

The rapid encroachment by Mormon settlers upon Indian lands altered the delicate ecological balance of the valley, thereby jeopardizing the Indians' livelihood.[31] This certainly was not unique to Mormon settlers in northern Utah; the same drama had been playing itself out since the founding of Jamestown, Virginia, in 1607 and would continue through the nineteenth century. As wild game disappeared and as more and more of the land came under the plow, Indians often retaliated by stealing cattle and horses. Their resistance to white intrusion is understandable; as Newell Hart has written, for them "not to have resisted an invasion would have been unnatural on their part." As the "bones of their . . . ancestors . . . were entombed in [these] lands . . . their historic choice was to either keep the homeland or deposit their massacred bones alongside those of their forebears."[32]

Unfortunately for the Indians in northern Utah, the Shoshonis indeed laid "their massacred bones alongside those of their fore-bears." On 21 January 1863 Colonel Connor began mustering his troops for a march northward from Salt Lake City to Cache Valley. The march was staggered to mislead the Indians of the smallness of the force being sent against them; on 24 January another 220 cavalry troops left Salt Lake City under Connor's personal command.[33] On 29 January Connor's troops engaged the Indians at their winter camp on Beaver Creek (renamed Battle Creek) near the Bear River, south-west of present-day Preston, Idaho. The Battle of Bear River ranks as one of the worst Indian massacres in the history of the western United States, with some accounts placing the number of Indians killed—many of them women and children—as high as four hun-dred.[34]

The horror of the episode was not lost on Cache Valley settlers, but the massacre at Bear River was probably down-played by the settlers in the aftermath because of the advantages it opened up for them.[35] Nonetheless, through his "near annihilation of the Northwestern Shoshones," wrote Newell Hart, Colonel Connor, who was promoted to the rank of general for his exploits at Battle Creek, inadvertently opened up a "big land boon for the Mormon settlers, though it was certainly not his intention to so favor them."[36]

Utah Indian Superintendent James D. Doty reported that the massacre "struck fear into the hearts of savages hundreds of miles away from the battle field."[37] And the lessening of Indian tensions no doubt played a part in Brigham Young's decision to call together an historic meeting in Logan the summer following the massacre. Charles C. Rich was called to Salt Lake City from his Centerville home to accompany church president Young. Evidently Young did not reveal the purpose of the meeting until they were at the home of Ezra Taft Benson in Logan.

> Now what I am about to say you will do well to keep to yourselves [he told those present]. We have in our minds to settle Bear River Lake Valley; I for one would like to have a settlement there. As yet I have said nothing to anyone except Brother Benson. Now if you will keep this matter to yourselves nobody will know anything about it, but otherwise it will be telegraphed to old Abe Lincoln by

Mormon Apostle Charles C. Rich, leader of the first Bear Lake settlements. (Special Collections, Utah State University, Logan.)

some of these [Army] officers, and then it will be made a reservation of immediately to prevent us getting it.[38]

Brigham Young had his mind made up not only concerning the
necessity of settling Bear Lake Valley but also whom he would call to
lead the expedition. Reportedly, Brigham Young opened the informal
meeting by telling Rich how "Brother Benson thought you would like
to go there. I never had a feeling about it, but Brother Benson and me
had a talk on the subject and he thought you would be pleased to go."
Rich, who had only recently returned from California, was not over-
joyed at the prospect. He replied: "So far as pulling up stakes and
moving my entire family, I would rather not do it." Undaunted by
Rich's initial refusal, Young turned his eyes away from Rich and used
what was probably one of his favorite ploys for convincing uncoop-
erative colonizers. "I will tell you what I would do," he said. "I would
rather have my family altogether." Rich tried once more. "Mine are
all together now," he said. The Logan meeting adjourned with Young
clearly of the opinion that there was unanimity among those present.
"We have said yes, that we will settle that valley; that is sufficient. . . .
We calculate to be kings of these mountains. Now let us go ahead and
occupy them." [39]

Historian Leonard J. Arrington notes that even though Rich was
opposed to the calling, he "knew he would soon have the unpleasant
task of uprooting his families once more." Charles C. Rich already
had been an active participant in both missionary and colonization
efforts, having returned from the church's European Mission just one
year prior to his "assignment" to settle Bear Lake Valley. In the 1850s
he also had made a valiant effort to settle San Bernardino Valley,
California.

The same devotion which prompted Rich to sell his California
holdings and move back to Utah when the Latter-day Saints were
called to return to defend the Utah holdings during the Utah War
also mandated that he accept Brigham Young's call to settle Bear Lake
Valley. Although the massacre at Bear River had virtually eliminated
Indian hostility in Cache Valley, the land around Bear Lake was still
the territory of Chief Washakie's people. The relationship between
Brigham Young and Washakie was one of mutual respect. Not wish-

ing to jeopardize this friendship or create an Indian uprising in Bear
Lake Valley which might give General Connor an opportunity to
intervene and disrupt Mormon plans to colonize the area, Rich
approached Washakie. Details of this historic meeting are sketchy and
exist only in the oral tradition. It is not entirely clear whether Rich
negotiated the terms with Washakie prior to leaving Cache Valley for
Bear Lake Valley or whether the "treaty" was later finalized at Bear
Lake.[40] According to most sources, Washakie was perfectly willing to
allow Mormon settlers into the Bear Lake Valley.[41] One wonders,
however, if Washakie would have been as receptive to the proposal
before the massacre at Bear River. A practical man, Washakie realized
the potential dangers and the ultimate futility of resisting white
settlement; as a friend of Brigham Young, he also realized that he
stood a better chance of negotiating with the Mormons than he
would with the likes of General Patrick E. Connor. Therefore,
Washakie permitted the Mormons to settle within the valley, but he
retained that portion of the Valley at the south end of Bear Lake for
the exclusive use of his people.

Charles C. Rich and the first group of settlers arrived in the Bear
Lake Valley on 18 September 1863, taking four days to travel from
present-day Franklin, Idaho, north to the Bear River and then east
approximately to the confluence of Mink Creek and the Bear River.
From Mink Creek the company headed east through a natural pass
later known as Emigration Canyon.[42] The company decided to settle
the west side of the valley because of the availability of water and timber.[43] Rich reported back to Brigham Young, giving a "favorable
description of the country[,] water[,] soil, temperature[,] grass and
timber."[44] Additional families soon joined the settlement. Among the
first group of settlers to arrive in the spring of 1864 was Frederick T.
Perris, a friend of Rich who also had left the colony at San
Bernardino. Perris surveyed the initial townsite at the west end of the
valley which, though the spelling would be corrupted, was named in
his honor.[45] St. Charles (and later Rich County) was named in honor
of Charles C. Rich. Other communities also were established and surveyed, including Fish Haven, Bloomington, Liberty, Montpelier,
Ovid, and Bennington. The surveying of these communities was
directed by Charles's son, Joseph C. Rich. By fall 1864 nearly seven

hundred Mormons had immigrated into the valley.[46] In the spring of 1864 Brigham Young guided a group of immigrants into the Bear Lake Valley. Heber C. Kimball, George A. Smith and John Taylor accompanied this party.

Solomon F. Kimball, a son of Heber C. Kimball, later described difficulties encountered by the group:

> On Monday morning, May 16, 1864, at 8:30 o'clock, this little company drove out of Salt Lake City on its journey. It consisted of six light vehicles and a baggage wagon . . . They reached Franklin, Idaho, on the afternoon of the third day. . . . There were no houses between Franklin and Paris, Idaho, consequently the program was to drive directly through to Paris in one day if possible.

Taking the same route as had the first settlers the year before, the company turned east to Mink Creek and "reached the foot of the big mountain which divides Cache Valley from Bear Lake Valley." At this juncture, their journey turned interesting.

> The mountain was so steep that all were compelled to walk except Apostle Smith who was so heavy that it would have been dangerous for him to undertake it, as he weighed not less than three-hundred pounds. The mounted men soon had extra horses harnessed and hitched to singletrees, and President Young and others, who were too heavy to help themselves, took hold of these singletrees with both hands and were helped up the mountain in this way.

Coming to the aid of the company, Charles C. Rich and other settlers started up the opposite side of the pass with several ox-teams. Hooking several yokes to Smith's wagon, they hauled it up the mountain,

> but before he reached the summit his wagon was so badly broken that he was compelled to abandon it. Everybody had a good laugh . . . , it being the second vehicle broken down under his weight that day. With careful management under the supervision of President Young and council, the brethren managed to get him onto the largest saddle horse that could be found and another start was made.[47]

After crossing the summit, the company became mired in mud,

and Kimball remarked that "to see that presidential procession wad-dling through the deep mud was enough to make any living thing smile." The mud was three feet deep in places, miring the wagons to their hubs and the horses to their sides. Most had to abandon their wagons and walk. Just as the road appeared to improve, a horseman from the rear "brought word that Brother George A. Smith's horse had given out, and that they were obliged to build a scaffold in order to get him onto another one." Once they reached the bottom of the canyon, the company rested and fed their horses before continuing on, not reaching Paris until 3 o'clock in the morning.[48]

Brigham Young's presence, nonetheless, brought a jubilant feel-ing to the community. In his address before the congregation outside of Charles C. Rich's log cabin, Young emphasized cooperation and reiterated that Rich was leader of the colony. The church president also called attention to the probable geographic location of the Bear Lake communities: "As to whether we are in Utah Territory or Idaho Territory, I think we are now in Idaho," announced Young. And then with a gesture towards the surrounding hills he added, "the snow lies too low on the mountains here for Utah."[49] Young's casual statement about the climate and geography reinforced the Saints' uneasy feel-ing about agricultural development north of the forty-second paral-lel.

Following President Young's address, similar messages of hope, faith, and courage were added in turn by George A. Smith, John Taylor, and Heber C. Kimball. Ever on the lookout for soldiers and other unwelcome white "interlopers," Kimball had written his son in November of the previous year:

> We are making a settlement in Bear Lake Valley; some one hun-dred families will be there this fall. Brother Charles C. Rich is the leader of the company; it is one of the best places in the moun-tains—we want to keep out the Devils if possible; they have troops all about as laying snares and traps. Never mind. God rules, and he will take care of his people.[50]

Only white Mormon settlers were visible to Kimball the follow-ing spring. In addition, Rich's first correspondence to Salt Lake City made no mention of any military troops or other white settlers.[51] The following year, Rich did find the Soda Springs area bustling with both military troops and freighters preparing to depart for the Montana mines.[52] The major problem of the Bear Lake settlement was not having unwanted settlers but convincing enough settlers to come and colonize the area. The Saints were blessed the first year with an unusually mild winter which allowed them the luxury of hauling logs from the nearby foothills to construct approximately thirty crude dwellings. Some of the initial settlers left during the first year, but the deceptively mild first winter convinced the majority to stay, perhaps giving them a false impression of the severity of the climate. However, the second winter in the Bear Lake Valley convinced them of the realities and the potential problems of farming at high altitudes north of the forty-second parallel.

The summer of 1864 foreshadowed an early winter. An early summer frost froze virtually all of the vines, corn, and vegetables. A second frost in the fall destroyed the wheat crop before full maturity. By January, three and a half feet of snow blanketed the valley floor.[53] In virtual isolation, cut off from both Salt Lake City and Cache Valley, the settlers made due with the scant provisions on hand. The previous year, Rich had managed to secure provisions through the Cache Valley tithing office, but during the winter of 1864–65, communication with the world outside the Bear Lake communities was virtually impossible.[54] Franklin Young left the colony between storms in November to mill grain in Cache Valley. The return trip took sixteen days and required that a party be dispatched from Bear Lake to rescue Young and his meager cargo. By January the snows stopped Charles C. Rich from fulfilling his obligation at the territorial assembly; even in April, Rich's attendance at general conference in Salt Lake City required him to snowshoe the forty miles from Paris to Franklin.[55]

The winter of 1864–65 served notice to the Latter-day Saints that the settlement of the Bear Lake Valley would not be an easy matter. Understandably there was a great deal of dissatisfaction throughout the various settlements as the immigrants fought to survive. By spring a number of the settlers petitioned to be relieved of their calling. Rich responded to his dissatisfied partners by addressing them on matters of responsibility. His comments serve as a true memorial to the Mormon ideal of being "called" to settle.

> Brethren—in the fall of 1863 President Young called me into his office and said, "Brother Rich, I want you to go up to Bear Lake Valley and see if it can opened for settlement; and if it can, I want that you should take a company there and settle it."
>
> That was all I needed. It was a call. I came up here, with a few brethren; we looked over the valley; and, although the altitude was high, the snows heavy, and the frosts severe, there was plenty of water for irrigation purposes and plenty of fish in the lake and streams. So, with a company, I came here and settled with my family.
>
> There have been many hardships. That I admit . . . and these we have shared together. But if you want to go somewhere else, that is your right, and I do not want to deprive you of it. If you are of a mind to leave here, my blessing will go with you. But I must stay here, even if I stay alone. President Young called me here, and here I will remain till he releases me and gives me leave to go.[56]

Rich's plea for community spirit and maintaining a respect for one's calling did not fall on deaf ears. Many responded as Rich might have expected by staying with the settlement. Still, others packed their few belongings and headed for the warmer climate of Cache Valley. Historian A. J. Simmonds noted that many of the initial settlers to Weston, Idaho, came from the dissatisfied ranks of Bear Lake settlers.[57] In her study of the Bear Lake settlement at Bennington, Charlotte M. Wright mentioned the disaffection of Evan M. Greene:

> Over the rough winter, seven of the family's cows froze to death, along with one of their horses. Evan's son Admanzah died, as did Rhoda [his daughter] and her new baby. In the spring, the family asked permission of Charles C. Rich to leave. In this case, Rich granted it, and the stricken family moved to Cache Valley.[58]

The "called" colony was an important part of Mormon settlement within the Intermountain West. Although not all settlements were called, the Bear Lake colony was an indisputable example of a "called" colony.[59] Bear Lake Valley did not enjoy widespread popularity. During the few early successful agricultural years, families moved in. Families moved out when severe winters or grasshoppers began plaguing the area. Statistics reveal that in 1863 and 1864 when the call went out, only eighteen percent of the Bear Lake Valley immigrants came from Cache Valley; the remaining eighty-two percent emigrated from other Utah communities.[60] These statistics imply that Cache Valley settlers were less inclined to relocate to Bear Lake Valley and more inclined to relocate within the newly formed communities in Cache Valley. Families from older Utah communities where arable land was more at a premium were more willing to relocate in Bear Lake Valley. Still it appears that often an actual "call" was necessary to provide the motivation.

A higher percentage of those settlers who immigrated to Bear Lake Valley after the initial call came from Cache Valley. This might suggest that the arable lands which opened up following the massacre at Bear River were quickly taken up by the excess population already living in Cache Valley.[61] Furthermore, those families who moved into the Bear Lake region from Cache Valley tended to have been only short-term residents in the Logan area before moving on. Thirty-one percent of this later group of settlers came from other communities within the territory. They tended to be second-generation settlers: either children at the time of the Mormon exodus from Nauvoo, children of early arrivals in Salt Lake Valley, or individuals born in Utah. Many of these second-generation Utahns initially settled south or north of Salt Lake City where the familiar scenario of scarce land and irrigation water was being played out.

In the years following 1865, there also was a high number of foreign-born immigrants to Bear Lake Valley. Many of these individuals and families, prior to the completion of the transcontinental railroad, came across the Mormon Trail with one of the wagon train companies, pausing only long enough to regroup in Salt Lake City before heading north to the Bear Lake Valley.

The Perpetual Emigration Fund, initiated during the 1850s to help aid the foreign poor in their trip to Utah, was expanded after 1860 when Joseph W. Young successfully crossed from Salt Lake City to Florence, Nebraska, with an ox-train and managed to return to Salt Lake City in only one season. He later preached an effective sermon, calling attention to the fact that oxen could make the trip both

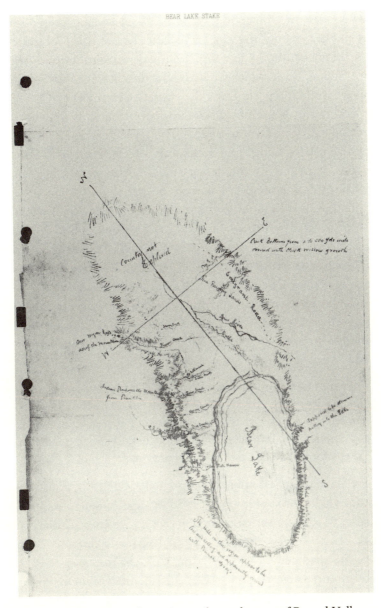

Early map of Bear Lake Valley prior to the settlement of Round Valley, ca. 1864. The writing at the southwestern tip of Bear Lake makes reference to the "low, rolling" hills being covered with "bunch grasses." (Church of Jesus Christ of Latter-day Saints Archives, Salt Lake City.)

ways and return in as good a shape as if they were purchased in the east and driven only one way. It thereafter became the procedure for each colony within the territory to provide wagons, supplies, provisions, and ox-teams which would rendezvous in Salt Lake City sometime in April for the trip east.[62] Between the years 1861 and 1868, the last year of the operation, 20,426 European emigrants were brought into the territory.[63] These people, along with emigrants from the states, all needed homes and livelihoods. With the increased pressure on land in the older settlements, some of them were either sent or moved north into the Bear Lake colonies.

Those who immigrated into the Bear Lake valley came by one of several routes: by way of Emigration Canyon via Soda Springs, directly from Franklin, or via Ogden to Huntsville over the Wasatch Range and down into Round Valley. None of the routes was looked upon as being particularly good. The Franklin Road was too steep, the old Emigration Road and Soda Springs route too long, and the Huntsville route barely more than a trail. Joseph C. Rich, who had initially surveyed and constructed the Huntsville route, wrote in 1868:

> Having just made the trip from Salt Lake City to Bear Lake Valley, I consider myself posted in regard to the manner of reaching this point; and, for the benefit and guidance of future pilgrims bound for this locality, I will give a little history of the trip and how it can be performed on the most round-about route.[64]

The territorial assembly appropriated $500 for the construction of the road in 1866. Additionally, $450 was appropriated to reimburse Charles C. Rich for the construction of a bridge crossing Blacksmith Fork River.[65] In 1865 Brigham Young had made clear his desire to have the road constructed. Writing to Rich, Young applied some good-natured arm-twisting: "We will be quite willing to visit Bear Lake Valley whenever I can hear that the new road up from Ogden Kanyon is completed, but not before, so that if the Saints want a visit from us, they must go to work and fix the road." [66] This outlay was to no avail, however, for the winter of 1868 brought heavy snows and landslides, leaving the road impassable.

During the summer of 1869, when Brigham Young again visited

Bear Lake Valley, the unreliability of the Huntsville route prompted his suggestion that a road be built through Logan Canyon.[67] By fall of the same year, the road was well underway, the construction being carried out cooperatively between the settlers of Cache County on one side of the mountain and those of Rich County on the other. The *Deseret Evening News* reported:

> The enterprising inhabitants of Cache and Rich counties have nearly completed a most commendable undertaking in the way of building up this northern portion of the territory. I allude to the new road which is now being made to connect the above named counties by a nearer and much easier route than that betwixt Franklin and Bear Lake. This new road will run through Logan Kanyon. When it is completed, which, it is expected will be within three weeks from now, it will only be a comfortable day's drive, about forty miles, from Logan to St. Charles, Rich County. This is not, however, the only advantage to be derived from the opening of this new road for the Kanyon abounds with timber of the very first quality. In view of these advantages, Bro. Hezekiah Thatcher, with his usual enterprise, has already sent for a steam sawmill, which will be put in operation as soon as practicable.

The author of the piece, pen-named Monsterio, appended a postscript to his letter implying that the Cache Valley settlers would be obligated to take the road as far as Rick's Spring:

> Since writing the above I have learned that Bishop Peter Maughan intends, in a few days, to go up the Kanyon to personally superintend the making of the road, and had made a call upon all the Bishops of Cache Valley with all their forces to assist him, that the road may be completed in a few days to Rick's big spring, where they expect the citizens of Bear Lake to meet them.[68]

The type of effort being made by Peter Maughan in Cache Valley was likewise being made by Charles C. Rich in Bear Lake. Citing correspondence between Rich and Brigham Young, Leonard J. Arrington writes that "Rich told Young that he would call for mass participation in the road construction and then they would apportion the work out 'to the different settlements, according to their strength and place a captain over each company.'"[69]

Almost constant effort was required to keep the Logan-to-St. Charles route open. Yet it was much shorter than any other option and was destined to become the major route between Bear Lake and other Utah settlements. In 1880 the Logan Canyon road was altered on the Bear Lake side to descend into Garden City rather than traversing the ridge north into St. Charles.[70]

Reliable transportation routes were of paramount importance to the continued success of the Bear Lake settlements. Every able-bodied man was expected to contribute time or money towards the upkeep not only of the roads in and out of the valley but also of the roads within the valley itself.[71] The territory of Utah contributed funds for the upkeep of roads within the Bear Lake Valley until it was determined that the majority of the settlements were really in Idaho. It was actually no secret that most of the Bear Lake settlements were in Idaho. As mentioned, even Brigham Young had alluded to the fact in 1864. Members of the territorial assembly must also have known the settlements' location, for an act passed in 1866 reads:

> All that portion of the Territory bounded south by Summit and Morgan Counties, west by Cache County, north by latitude forty-two degrees north, and east by the summit of the divide between the waters of Bear River and the tributaries of the Green River is hereby made and named Richland County, with the County Seat at St. Charles.[72]

The exact geographical location of the forty-second parallel was unknown. That boundary would not be determined absolutely until a federal survey was completed in 1872 under Daniel G. Major.[73] So the Bear Lake settlers took advantage of the lack of a definitive survey by refusing to be part of Idaho until such proof was furnished. Even after their incorporation into Idaho Territory's Oneida County, and later into Bear Lake County (in 1875), Mormon settlers continued to look south to Salt Lake City rather than north to Boise City for all but governmental appropriations. Ecclesiastically, the Latter-day Saints of northern Bear Lake Valley would be grouped with the Saints of southern Bear Lake Valley, and, ultimately, Bear Lake Stake would extend as far south as Evanston, Wyoming.

ENDNOTES

1. See Joseph Smith, Jr., *History of the Church of Jesus Christ of Latter-day Saints, with an introduction and notes by B. H. Roberts,* 7 vols.(Salt Lake City: Deseret Book Co.,1966); hereafter referred to as Smith, *CH.*

2. Ernest H. Taves, *Trouble Enough: Joseph Smith and the Book of Mormon* (Buffalo: Prometheus Books, 1984), 208–9. See also Smith, *CH,* 6:561–631.

3. Smith, *CH,* 7:398.

4. See, Smith, *CH,* 7:547. See also Leonard J. Arrington, *Great Basin Kingdom: An Economic History of the Latter-day Saints, 1830–1900* (Cambridge: Harvard University Press, 1958) and Richard H. Jackson, "Myth and Reality: Environmental Perception of the Mormons, 1840–1865: An Historical Geosophy (Ph.D. dissertation, Clark University, Worcester, Mass, 1970), 60, 90–93. Brigham Young also mentioned the needless death of the prophet when he stated: "If Joseph Smith, jun., the Prophet, had followed the Spirit of revelation in him he never would have gone to Carthage ... Joseph intended to go West ..." Cited in, Stanley P. Hirshson, *The Lion of the Lord: a Biography of Brigham Young,* (New York: Alfred A. Knopf, 1969), 79.

5. Arrington, *Great Basin Kingdom,* 41.

6. Jackson, *Myth and Reality,* 72.

7. Lansford W. Hastings, *The Emigrants' Guide to Oregon and California* (Princeton: University Press, 1932), 78.

8. Hiram M. Chittendon and Alfred T. Richardson, eds., *Life, Letters and Travels of Father Pierre-Jean De Smet, S.J., 1801–1873,* 4 vols. (Cleveland: Arthur H. Clark Co., 1905), 4:1404–05.

9. The Mormons encountered several knowledgeable individuals along the trail, including guide and trapper Moses "Black" Harris and Jim Bridger. Both gave accounts of the areas around present-day northern Utah which may have influenced the Mormons' decision to opt against the higher elevations of Bear Lake and Cache valleys. Bridger's descriptions of the area seem somewhat imprecise as recorded by William Clayton. See George D. Smith, ed., *An Intimate Chronicle: The Journals of William Clayton* (Salt Lake City: Signature Books, 1991), 349. Howard Egan, who also commented on Bridger's description, was less kind in his assessment of the trapper: "From his appearance and conversation, I should not take him to be a man of truth," wrote Egan. "In his description of Bear River Valley and the surrounding country, which was very good, he crossed himself a number of times. He said that Harris knew nothing about that part of the country. He says there is plenty of timber there; that he had made sugar for the last

twenty years where Harris said there was no timber of any kind." See Rich, *Land of the Sky-Blue Water,* 15.

10. Jackson, *Myth and Reality,* 78–83.

11. Leonard J. Arrington, *Brigham Young: American Moses* (New York: Alfred A. Knopf, 1985), 141.

12. Smith, *An Intimate Chronicle,* 355.

13. Ibid., 355.

14. Rich, *Land of the Sky-Blue Water,* 15.

15. Sardis W. Templeton, *The Lame Captain: The Life and Adventures of Pegleg Smith* (Los Angeles, Westernlore Press, 1965), 182–95.

16. Edward W. Tullidge, *Tullidge's Histories, Northern Utah and Southern Idaho,* 2 vols.(Salt Lake City: Tullidge, 1890), 2:74.

17. Clifford L. Stott, *Search for Sanctuary: Brigham Young and the White Mountain Expedition* (Salt Lake City: University of Utah Press, 1984), 22.

18. Ibid., 25, 26.

19. Charles C. Rich to Addison Pratt, 7 October 1857. Cited in Leonard J. Arrington, *Charles C. Rich* (Provo: Brigham Young University Press, 1974), 218–19.

20. See J. Cecil Alter, *Jim Bridger,* rev. ed. (Norman: University of Oklahoma Press, 1962), 273–81. According to Alter, the Mormons may possibly have purchased Ft. Bridger twice from Bridger's partner, Louis Vasquez, apparently without the knowledge of Bridger.

21. Stott, *Search for Sanctuary,* 34.

22. Alter, *Jim Bridger,* 272.

23. "Report of the Party of Observation, consisting of eleven men under the command of M. Monroe, started from Ogden City, Aug. [18]57. Records of the Utah Territorial Militias, microfilm, Division of Special Collections and Archives, Utah State University, Logan, Utah.

24. *Deseret News,* 23 June 1869.

25. Edward W. Tullidge, *Tullidge's Histories* (Salt Lake City: Juvenile Instructor Press, 1889), Supp Biographical Appendix, 74–75.

26. Ibid., 363.

27. Arrington, *Charles C. Rich,* 248.

28. Ibid., 247.

29. Tullidge, *Tullidge's Histories,* Supp Appendix, 74. See also Brigham D. Madsen, *The Shoshoni Frontier and the Bear River Massacre* (Salt Lake City: University of Utah Press, 1985), 171–74.

30. Tullidge, *Tullidge's Histories,* Supp Appendix, 74. Newell Hart places the number more reasonably at 1000. See Newell Hart, *The Bear River*

Massacre (Preston, ID: Cache Valley Newsletter Publishing Co., 1983), 25.

31. Madsen, *Shoshoni Frontier,* 12–13.

32. Hart, *Bear River Massacre,* 1.

33. Madsen, *Shoshoni Frontier,* 180.

34. Hart, *Bear River Massacre,* 183–84. Between 250 and 300 is more accurate.

35. See transcriptions of letters and firsthand accounts of settlers in Hart, *Bear River Massacre,* 129–38. See also typescript of firsthand accounts of the massacre culled from the *Journal History of the Church of Jesus Christ of Latter-day Saints,* manuscript, Department of Special Collections and Archives, Merrill Library, Utah State University, Logan, Utah (hereafter referred to as JH).

36. Hart, *Bear River Massacre,* 185. Only recently has the Battle of Bear River come to be known as the Bear River Massacre. As the battle occurred during a time when the eastern half of the United States was preoccupied with fighting the Civil War, it received only scant publicity.

37. Ibid., 2.

38. The 23 August 1863 meeting is discussed in Arrington, *Charles C. Rich,* 249.

39. Arrington, *Charles C. Rich,* 249.

40. It is not clear whether any actual documentation exists regarding the agreement between Rich and Washakie. Previous writers on the history of the region, Russell R. Rich and Leonard J. Arrington, disagree whether the meeting took place after the first company arrived at Bear Lake or before the company left Cache Valley. Arrington, who had access to the personal correspondence of both Brigham Young and Charles C. Rich, which correspondence is contained in the LDS Church Archives and is restricted to most researchers, cites his source of information as a letter to Brigham Young from Charles C. Rich dated 18 September 1863. As Washakie was a not infrequent visitor to Cache Valley and was possibly visiting the settlements to obtain a feeling for his people's safety following the incident at Bear River, it is likely that Rich may have encountered him there. On the other hand, with more than 200 of his fellows having been recently slaughtered in Cache Valley, it was perhaps the last place he would have wanted to be. See Arrington, *Charles C. Rich,* 250.

Russell R. Rich, whose research was done in the 1940s and 1950s, also had access to some unique documents in church archives which are now unavailable to most researchers. Rich cites and prints a letter from Charles C. Rich's son Joseph C. Rich as his main source of information about the event. Joseph was particularly close to his father and may have been more closely involved in the day-to-day operations of the Bear Lake settlements than was Charles. Rich's letter, taken from Andrew Jenson's manuscript history of Bear Lake Stake is herein printed: "When father was called upon to settle this valley, he held a council with Washakie and his Indians, in 1863, in this valley, and obtained their consent to settle this valley, which was claimed by them as their summer hunting and fishing ground, the Indians at that time not being on reservations. On father's part, he agreed that when the settlers raised crops, they would give the Indians such provisions as they were able to, when they should visit the settlements and they, in return, would not molest the settlers nor steal their animals." See Rich, *Land of the Sky-Blue Water,* 62.

41. Rich, *Land of the Sky-Blue Water,* 62.

42. JH, 18 September 1863.

43. Arrington, *Charles C. Rich,* 252.

44. JH, 18 September 1863.

45. Arrington, *Charles C. Rich,* 255.

46. Ibid., 255.

47. Solomon F. Kimball, "President Brigham Young's First Trip to Bear Lake Valley," *Improvement Era* 10 (February 1907): 296–300. See also JH, 19 May 1864.

48. Kimball, "Brigham Young's First Trip," 298.

49. Ibid.

50. JH, 8 November 1863.

51. Arrington, *Charles C. Rich,* 252.

52. Ibid., 255.

53. Rich, *Land of the Sky-Blue Water,* 44.

54. Leonard J. Arrington, "The Mormon Tithing House: A Frontier Business Institution," *The Business History Review,* March 1954, 28:48.

55. Journal of Thomas Sleight, 28 March 1865, typescript, Department of Special Collections and Archives, Utah State University, Logan, Utah.

56. Arrington, *Charles C. Rich,* 264.

57. In Lars Fredrickson, *History of Weston, Idaho* (Logan: Utah State University, 1972), 2.

58. Charlotte M. Wright, "Bear Lake Blizzard: A History of Family and Community Conflict in Bennington, Idaho, 1864–1915" (M.S. thesis, Utah State University, 1986), 2.

59. Much scholarly effort has been devoted to the Mormon plan of settlement in the Intermountain West. The traditional viewpoint has been that individuals were "called" to settle various locations at different times and that the settlement of the area was a well-planned and ordered phenomenon. While allowing that called or "corporate" communities were part of the

settlement of the Intermountain West, Charles M. Hatch also notes how "Migration to the *corporate communities* has come to symbolize the willingness of Mormons to sacrifice private aspirations while joining with fellow Saints and church leaders in building the Kingdom of God. It is natural for historians to characterize this symbol as reality for Mormon people. Yet the resulting stereotype obscures the role of free choice in its failure to distinguish the corporate needs of the church from the private needs of individuals and families." See Charles M. Hatch, "Creating Ethnicity in the Hydraulic Village of the Mormon West" (M.S. thesis, Utah State University, 1991) 22.

A. J. Simmonds also has objected to "the calm assumption that Brigham Young was in charge of everything that went on in all of the Mormon colonies in the Great Basin. It seems that every other biographical sketch that I pick up indicate[s] the subject of the biography was *sent* by Brigham Young to settle whatever town it was. That just can't be the truth. Brigham Young didn't sit like some traffic cop at the intersection of State and South Temple and direct people where to go. See A. J. Simmonds, "Looking Back," *Herald Journal,* 27 December 1992.

60. Statistics are taken from a comparison of biographies contained in Edith Parker Haddock and Dorothy Hardy Matthews, comp., *Bear Lake Pioneers* (Salt Lake City: DUP, Bear Lake County, Idaho, 1968).

61. The population of Cache Valley grew considerably during the early 1860s. Basing his population figures on the muster roles of the Cache Valley Brigade of the Nauvoo Legion, A. J. Simmonds postulates that the population of Cache Valley increased 97 percent between 1861 and 1865. "An indication of just how restricted Cache settlement was in the 1860s is that no new irrigation canal was constructed in Cache Valley between 1860 and 1864. While there was probably some enlargement of existing systems during those years, the numerical increase in the valley during that time placed enormous pressure on the arable land that had been brought under cultivation in 1859 and 1860." See A. J. Simmonds, "Looking Back," *Herald Journal,* 17 January 1993.

62. Gustive O. Larson, *Prelude to the Kingdom, Mormon Desert Conquest: A Chapter in American Cooperative Experience* (Francestown, NH: M. Jones Co., 1947), 216–17.

63. Ibid., 227.

64. JH, 7 May 1868. Rich continues with his travelogue, noting with some humor the great difficulty undertaken to reach the Bear Lake settlements:

> The distance from Salt Lake City to Paris, Rich County, on the Huntsville road, is about 125 miles, this valley lying a little east of north from your city.
>
> Travel north about thirty-five miles to the mouth of Weber

Canyon, where you can purchase, for one dollar, a ticket signed "J. C. Little", which ticket, with the assistance of a good team, strong wagon and sound constitution, will take you through Weber Canyon. A great amount of work has been done on this road, and were it not for a few hundred thousand full grown boulders that still adorn the track, you might feel some reverence for your ticket, notwithstanding the loss of your greenback.

The last eight miles has been in an easterly direction. At Mountain Green settlement the road bears north east seven miles over a low chain of hills that divide Weber and Ogden Valleys. I passed over snowdrifts and in fording the south tributary of Ogden River found it high, even to run over the wagon box.

At Huntsville, sixty miles distant from the south settlement in Bear Lake the road to Rich County was reported to be impassable for teams, in consequence of snow and a land slide up the canyon that had slid a portion of the road into the river, completely daming[sic] it up; and some enterprising individuals had taken advantage of this freak of nature, and were erecting a saw mill at the dam. Not being able to make the trip on this route, the only alternative is to strike west twelve miles, down Ogden Canyon, at the mouth of which a kind-hearted man charges you only a dollar and a half for the damages.

The road down this Canyon has not been fixed this spring, and was pretty rough, though generally, it is in splendid condition. The gatekeeper says the scenery in the canyon is worth the price of travel, and from his honest looks I would not judge him capable of misrepresentation.

65. JH, 21 Feb. 1868.

66. Arrington, *Charles C. Rich,* 274.

67. JH, 20 June 1869.

68. JH, 17 October 1869.

69. Arrington, *Charles C. Rich,* 274.

70. Ibid., 274.

71. Ibid., 274.

72. JH, 10 January 1866, 2.

73. Arrington, *Charles C. Rich,* 272.

3

*"Nine Months Winter and the Balance . . .
Pretty Cold Weather"*

LIFE AND SETTLEMENT
IN RICH COUNTY,
1864–1896

The federal survey of 1872 did little more than complicate matters for an already complex Rich County. There was no practical reason to separate the northern half of Bear Lake Valley from the south. Nor was there any geographic logic for including Randolph and Woodruff within Rich County along with the Bear Lake settlements of Garden City and Laketown. The settlements at Randolph and Woodruff in the Bear River Valley were more closely associated with southwestern Wyoming than they were with the Bear Lake Valley. The longitudinal and latitudinal lines of surveyors seldom made any geographic sense, however. Because Bear Lake straddled the forty-second parallel, half went to Utah and half went to Idaho. And because Randolph and Woodruff lay west of thirty-four degrees from Washington, D.C., they remained in Utah, separated from the Bear River Valley towns of Wyoming. The early history of Laketown, Meadowville, Round Valley, and Garden City cannot be separated from the early history of Onieda County, and later Bear Lake County,

Idaho. Similarly, the settlement of Randolph and Woodruff cannot be understood fully without discussing Uinta and Lincoln counties, Wyoming.

Rich County consists of two distinct geographic areas: Bear Lake Valley and Bear River Valley. In the Rich County portion of Bear Lake Valley are located Laketown and Garden City. The Laketown area also includes the communities of Round Valley and Meadowville. The Bear River Valley lies south of Bear Lake Valley and includes the communities of Randolph and Woodruff. The Bear River Valley is approximately three and a half miles wide with a gentle slope towards the river. Running from present-day Cokeville, Wyoming, on the north, the valley stretches fifty-five miles south to include Saleratus Creek.

Overcoming the geographic impediments of Rich County required a concerted effort on the part of its settlers. Whereas in Cache Valley only a few miles separated the major settlements of Logan, Hyde Park, Smithfield, and Richmond, as much as forty miles separated the Rich County settlements of Garden City, Laketown, Randolph, and Woodruff. Laketown and Garden City had more in common with the Idaho settlements at Fish Haven, St. Charles, and Paris than they did with the county seat at Randolph.

The western states are full of geographic peculiarities such as Rich County. In carving the West into territories, Congress considered geography very little. And considering the scarcity of arable land and irrigation water resources in the West boundaries based solely upon natural geography would likely have been most irregular. Brigham Young had based his conception of the State of Deseret largely on geography. Young's Deseret, in addition to present-day Utah, included virtually all of present-day Nevada, most of Arizona, northwestern New Mexico, the western half of Colorado, the southwestern corner of Wyoming, the southeastern corner of Idaho, and parts of California and Oregon. In a larger sense, the proposed State of Deseret was bounded by the major mountain ranges and river drainages which have since defined the Great Basin: the Sierra Nevada, the Cascades, the Tetons, and the Colorado Rockies. Brigham Young's proposal made sense geographically. Its boundaries naturally placed the drainages of the Colorado, Green, and Bear rivers within the State of Deseret. These rivers have since engendered considerable debate, adjudication, and compromise between the several western states which now share water drainages. Today, for instance, the Bear River heads in Utah, flows north to Wyoming, crosses state boundaries again into Utah and then into Idaho, before turning south and finally emptying into the Great Salt Lake, less than eighty miles from its source in Summit County, Utah. Geographic considerations would have placed the Bear River entirely under the control of one territorial government and also have naturally placed Bear Lake entirely within the boundaries of one territory. But the State of Deseret encompassed far too great an area to ever be allowed by the federal government. As discussed earlier, this was particularly true given the uneasy relationship between the government and the Mormons during the 1850s. In the Compromise of 1850, Congress created the territories of Utah and New Mexico as well as granting statehood to California. Furthermore, between 1850 and 1868 the federal government redrew the territorial boundaries, incorporating much of the territory of Utah into the state of Nevada and the territories of Colorado, Wyoming, and Idaho. Boundaries were determined by federal survey, not by natural geographic considerations.[1] And once the natural geographical boundaries were disallowed, no method existed for equally carving out the territories except according to the federal survey system. Although it made little sense to split Bear Lake in half, for example, the boundaries of the western territories, with few exceptions, were defined and described according to abstract government survey lines.

The federal system of land surveys dates back to 1785 when Congress, under the Articles of Confederation, debated how to dispose of the public lands. The southern states used a system based loosely on geography. The New England states adopted a system of mapping into townships those lands which were to be sold. The southern system produced a tangle of indecipherable property descriptions bounded by creeks, swamps, rocks and trees. In contrast, the more orderly New England system used a system of description based on the township, a rectangular piece of land six miles square. The township took into account all the land within the township, including the marginal lands. The New England system came to be viewed as more egalitarian. And although considerable debate took place, Congress eventually adopted the township method in 1796. New territories were surveyed and bounded accordingly.[2] The Northwest Ordinance, passed by the Congress in 1787, continued to provide the framework by which settled areas could become territories and ultimately petition for statehood. Under provisions of this ordinance, Utahns petitioned Congress six times between 1849 and 1887.[3]

In Rich County a renewed push for settlement south of the forty-second parallel anticipated the federal survey of 1872. By 1868 the tracks of the Union Pacific Railroad had reached Evanston, Wyoming, less than ten miles east of the Utah border. A year later, the tracks would be linked with those of the Central Pacific at Promontory Summit, Utah, making transcontinental travel possible. The railroad also made areas of Bear River Valley more accessible to settlers but increased the risk that those settlers would not be Mormon. Mormons were urged to stake claim to the areas in the proximity of the railroad. In some cases, members were called by church leaders to settle particular areas; in other cases, they came of their own choice. During the years 1870 and 1871 settlement took place at Randolph and at Woodruff, twenty-two miles from Evanston, Wyoming. Settlers later moved into the Garden City area and began diverting the waters of Swan Creek south to irrigate their fields and orchards.

Laketown

Settlement began in Rich County at the northern end of Bear Lake Valley because the settlers perceived that the best agricultural land, building materials, and water resources existed there. Furthermore, the Shoshoni chief Washakie had granted permission to settle the northern part of the valley but insisted that the southern part of the valley be left vacant for the use of his people. The agreement with the Shoshoni was short-lived. Only a year after the settlements of Paris and St. Charles, settlers began moving into southern Bear Lake Valley. The earliest settlement in Rich County, Utah, took place in the vicinity of present-day Meadowville and at Round Valley. The early settlers included Ephraim Watson, Joseph Moore, Robert

Laketown looking east, ca 1913. (Utah State Historical Society, Salt Lake City.)

Beers, William Busby, John Oldfield, George Braffet, George W. Russell, Zacharias Anderson, John C. Marley, William Morley, and Luther Reed.[4]

Little information exists as to why this group disregarded the counsel of Charles C. Rich and broke the agreement with Washakie by pushing into southern Bear Lake Valley. Luther Reed had been stationed at Goshen, Utah County, during the Utah War in 1857. In 1864 he received an assignment to join an exploratory expedition into Bear Lake Valley, ostensibly to construct a saw mill. According to early accounts, Reed "came alone with his company. They traveled by way of Mink Creek in Cache Valley. A half dozen or so men rigged with wagons and supplies."[5] The original settlers into southern Bear Lake Valley resembled a military expedition more than a settlement expedition. The expedition came without families and appears not to have been associated with settlers in northern Bear Lake Valley. After entering Bear Lake Valley by way of Emigration Canyon, the group went directly to the Laketown area. Their move was a bold one, considering that the area was jealously guarded by the Shoshoni. But it was not as bold as might have been expected.

In August 1864 Chief Washakie traveled through Cache Valley on his way east to hunt buffalo. Mormon settlers were instructed to pro-

vision the chief with flour and beef. Washakie and his people were
not expected back for at least a year.[6] With the Indians out of the picture, fall 1864 was an opportune time to try to settle the southern
part of Bear Lake Valley.

The settlement of Laketown was considered an absolute necessity if the Mormons were to continue with their plan of settling as
much of the Intermountain West as possible before non-Mormons
could gain a toehold in the region. Heber C. Kimball mentioned the
importance of settling Bear Lake in order to "keep out the devils,"[7]
and the settlement of Round Valley and Laketown were the first crucial steps towards this goal. The agreement with Washakie, however,
impeded this goal. Although Brigham Young often urged the
Mormon people to feed rather than fight the Indian, and part of the
agreement made between Washakie and Charles C. Rich had been for
a portion of the Mormon's crops in exchange for the privilege of settling the valley's north end, the reality of the situation was such that if
the Mormons did not find a way to expand settlement into southern
Bear Lake and Bear River valleys, non-Mormon settlers would; or as
Young feared, the government might make an Indian reservation out
of the entire area.[8]

Brigham Young's fear was well grounded. In July 1863 Utah
Superintendent of Indian Affairs James D. Doty negotiated treaties
with several of the tribes having interest in Utah lands. The treaty
with the Eastern Shoshoni defined the boundaries of their "homeland" on the north to the Snake River, on the east by the Wind River
Mountains, and on the south by the Uinta Mountains. The western
boundary, however, remained "undefined" according to the treaty,
"there being no Shoshonees [sic] from that district of country present; but the bands now present claim that their own country is
bounded on the west by Salt Lake." Given the vagueness of the document, the Eastern Shoshoni actually claimed the entirety of northern
Utah. The one provision that gave settlers the possible right of ownership was contained in the statement that the United States was willing to compensate the "bands of the Shoshonee nation" for any
"agricultural and mining settlements."[9] If Mormons could establish
themselves in Bear Lake Valley and come to some agreement for
compensation, such as Charles C. Rich did when agreeing to provide

provisions and a share of Mormon crops to the Indians, then the possibility increased of averting the inclusion of Bear Lake Valley into an Indian reservation. Summarizing the 1863 treaty, historian Grace Raymond Hebard wrote that the document "granted to the Government the right to use the lands of the Shoshones for roads and travel, for military and agricultural settlement and for military posts thereon; to establish ferries over the rivers and to erect houses and to found settlements at stated points from time to time as the country might develop, and to operate telegraph and overland stage lines as well as a railroad."[10]

Joseph W. Moore was appointed presiding Mormon Elder in the southern Bear Lake settlements in 1864.[11] A logical choice to lead the expedition into southern Bear Lake Valley, Moore had been involved in numerous Indian battles in Utah, most specifically during the Walker War, and had also been enlisted as one of Brigham Young's bodyguards at the time of the leader's first visit to Sanpete County.[12]

No more than a dozen or so men accompanied Moore in 1864, but the group founded three separate settlements the first year. It had been customary in northern Bear Lake Valley to keep the number of settlers at each location as large as possible and the number of settlements to a minimum in order to better safeguard families. Initially, however, families were not involved in the Laketown area; the settlements at Round Valley could only have consisted of a few individuals each. The first settlement, in the vicinity of Meadowville, was later abandoned.[13] The settlement then moved to the south end of Round Valley and split into three groups, at Sly Go, Pottawattamie, and Mud Town. During the harsh winter of 1865, survival dictated that the settlers congregate at Mud Town, located between Big Spring and present-day Meadowville.[14] A dozen cabins dotted the landscape the following spring. Towards late fall Washakie and his people returned from their year-long buffalo hunt, and problems between the Indians and the residents of Mud Town flared. Although possibly exaggerated, some estimates of the Indian army amassed at Round Valley place the number as high as three thousand.[15] Most distressing to the settlers in the northern settlements was Washakie's threat to annihilate not only those settlers at Round Valley but also those in the other villages. By January 1866 the Mud Town residents were forced to flee to the safety of the fort at St. Charles.[16]

Charles C. Rich attempted to appease Washakie and called upon Ira Nebeker, E. N. Austin, and Amos Wright to accompany him to the Indian encampment. In the midst of these negotiations, a white presence was continued in the area as Luther Reed, George W. Russell, George Braffet, and John C. Marley returned from St. Charles to winter at Sly Go and Chimney Town.[17]

Local tradition records that Charles C. Rich met with Washakie in 1866 and arranged a truce whereby the Mormon settlers were allowed to settle the southern part of the valley. Explaining that the white settlers were as numerous as the waves on Bear Lake and as impossible to stop, Rich appealed to Washakie's sense of practicality.[18] Although Washakie's people had played no part in the battle at Bear River, the massacre by the military of his western cousins in January 1863 was no doubt still on his mind. Furthermore, to Washakie, whose people had never been numerous and by 1865 were fewer than two thousand, the whites must have indeed seemed as relentless as the waves of Bear Lake.[19] Earlier another Indian chief, while viewing the seemingly endless waves of migration along the Oregon Trail, remarked how he would move his people to the east because he could not imagine that any white people were left there.[20]

Saddened, Washakie took Charles Rich atop the hills overlooking Bear Lake and gave him the right to settle all the land as far as he could see in all directions. Reportedly, Washakie then implored Rich to contact the United States government to find a place where his people could go. As Indian agent for the area, Rich would have been the likely choice to intervene on behalf of the Shoshoni people.[21] As a Mormon apostle, however, it is unlikely that he cut a very wide swath with the bureaucracy in Washington. By 1868 the creation of the Uinta Wind River Reservation diminished the Indian problems in Bear Lake Valley. Nonetheless, the Shoshoni people continued to gather in the Bear Lake Valley, but in much smaller numbers, until at least 1872.[22]

Whether the settlement of southern Bear Lake Valley was a planned event on the part of Brigham Young and other Mormon leaders or whether Joseph W. Moore, Luther Reed, and the others acted of their own accord, the end result was the same. Aided by the able Amos Wright, Charles C. Rich accomplished for Bear Lake Valley precisely what Colonel Connor had accomplished for Cache Valley at the Bear River Massacre—the removal of the Shoshoni and the expansion of white settlement. The means to his ends, however, were significantly more benign.

In 1867 Luther Reed and others, along with Edwin G. Lamborn, constructed a fort at the present site of Laketown.[23] Reed had returned to Utah County the previous season for his wife Elizabeth and their two children. Lamborn also brought his family. This is the first hint of the settlement of families at Laketown.[24] In 1869 the settlement was being directed by John Oldfield. The settlers called their settlement Ithaca after the city in New York.[25]

As a result of Indian threats during previous years, the original settlers at Sly Go, Chimney Town, Mud Town and other locations in Round Valley abandoned their claims and moved to the Laketown fort. By 1868 Round Valley was depopulated.[26] After Indian hostilities abated, however, new settlers moved into Round Valley, bringing their families with them.

The new settlers moving into Round Valley in 1869 founded the town of Meadowville. These settlers were among the first to immigrate into Bear Lake Valley via Ogden and Blacksmith Fork canyons. Most of the original settlers stayed for only one year before returning to Salt Lake City.[27] Among those who stayed or later returned to establish a permanent settlement would be the family of Heber C. Kimball. The Kimball family came to have a long association with the town of Meadowville.[28]

In June 1869 Brigham Young, Wilford Woodruff, and a company of church leaders visited the new settlement in southern Bear Lake Valley.[29] Young's tour through Bear Lake Valley, coupled with the new influx of settlers to Round Valley, brought about another tense situation with the Shoshoni the following summer. Lewis L. Polmanteer, one of the new arrivals in Meadowville, explained in a letter to Salt Lake City:

> On or about the 16th Inst. Sagwich a Chief of the Shoshona Tribe and who talks good english—came to my house at Round

Valley Rich Co. and after obtaining something to eat earnestly begged me to accompany him to the camp of some Two Thousand Shoshona and Ute Indians to explain to them the object of President Young and Party's visit to Rich County. I went as requested and on my arrival had an interview with some Twentyfive Chiefs and Braves of the Shoshona Tribe. After a sullen pause of a few minutes one of the Indians asked 'What the hell does all this talk mean'? I asked him what talk? He answered 'the talk about Brigham Young Coming here with Two Thousand men to use us up'. I replied that such was not the Case—that Prest. Young and party was at Soda Springs on their way to this County in some Thirteen vehicles and accompanied by some (9) nine females He said 'that did not look much like fighting.' [30]

Oral tradition records the event in Laketown as involving Washakie's people.[31] Polmanteer makes it clear, however, that Washakie was not involved. Being a man of his word, Washakie made no further demands on the settlers after his agreement with Charles C. Rich to allow settlers into Laketown in 1867. Utah Superintendent of Indian Affairs J. H. Head began urging his superiors as early as January 1868 to set aside the Wind River area for the use of Washakie's people. In a letter to T. G. Taylor, Head wrote how "Washakie, the principal chief of Shoshonies is extremely anxious that the valley [Wind River] be set apart as a reservation."[32]

Until after 1870 the Laketown settlement remained within the confines of the fort. In 1869 Charles C. Rich appointed David P. Kimball to assume control of the Laketown settlement from John Oldfield. Oldfield, according to the manuscript history of Laketown, was never formally appointed.[33] He and others of the original expedition to southern Bear Lake Valley left the area after 1869.

Of the original settlers, William Morley, William Busby, John Marley, and Ephraim Watson remained to be enumerated as Laketown residents in the 1870 census.[34] The 1870 census shows John Oldfield as a resident of Millard County.[35] Joseph W. Moore also ended up in Millard County. He was listed as a resident of Fish Haven in 1870.[36] Moore later served as bishop in Bennington, Idaho, until about 1880 before moving to Millard County, and ultimately to Grand County.[37] George W. Braffet is listed as a resident of

Kimballville, the name originally applied to Meadowville.[38] Luther Reed moved to Bennington, Idaho, and there helped construct a sawmill.[39] The 1870 census lists him as a resident of Fish Haven.[40] Sometime after the enumeration of the 1870 census, he returned to Round Valley to inspect the mill which he had helped construct on Big Spring. There Reed fell into the icy waters, contracted pneumonia, and died.[41]

No record exists for Robert Beers, George Russell, or Zacharias Anderson following their exit from Laketown.[42] It is possible that these men may have died between 1866 and 1870.

Notwithstanding the departure of many of the early settlers, southern Bear Lake Valley grew considerably following 1869. The population of Laketown by the early 1870s approached two hundred individuals. Interestingly, Laketown and the other Rich County communities grew phenomenally during their first decade; the population then reached a plateau by 1884 and thereafter remained relatively static.[43] In 1883 Laketown residents issued a plea for new settlers, stating that opportunities existed "for the poor who are industrious to come here and make for themselves homes, rude in structure and design though they may be yet withal their own . . . [and] all things considered," the plea concluded, "we think our peoples condition . . . will compare very favorably with that of our friends . . . in the lower valleys."[44]

Whether above or below the forty-second parallel, the climate of Bear Lake Valley was severe. Reporting Bear Lake still frozen over and snow deep enough that one could walk over the tops of fences, one resident of Laketown offered a twenty-five-dollar reward "to any man woman or child who [could] successfully predict the exact ushering in of spring. Here in this valley," he noted, "we usually have nine months hard winter and the balance . . . pretty cold weather."[45] Agricultural communities in Bear Lake Valley were at the mercy of nature. And nature was often a cruel master.

It required tremendous perseverance and a fair amount of experimentation to succeed at agriculture in Rich County. Initially, successes at the Laketown settlement were few, and a fair amount of cooperation was necessary to achieve even those. William Howard, an early settler in Rich County, remarked how "public improvements

[were] the greatest instigators of industry that [could] be gotten up in a newly settled country. . . . They enhance the value of every man's property," he added, "and pride will not let many sit still."[46] But cooperation did not come easily at Laketown. When David P. Kimball arrived at the Laketown settlement in 1869, he found a disorganized group meeting in a log cabin.[47] This crude structure served the community for some fifteen years as both school and church.

Cooperative efforts were difficult to undertake without a stable population. As with the settlements at the north end of Bear Lake Valley, out-migration in Laketown often exceeded in-migration. A correspondent from Laketown writing to the *Deseret News* reported that "the migration fever [had] somewhat abated. For a while it seemed as if half the town would venture in search of a more congenial climate."[48] The widely dispersed population also made cooperative enterprises more difficult. Southern Bear Lake Valley was fragmented into three separate communities: Laketown, Meadowville, and Round Valley.

For all practical purposes, the earliest recorded history in southern Bear Lake Valley took place in Round Valley. It was here that Luther Reed, George Braffet, and others first came in search of a suitable mill site; and it was the settlement of Round Valley that infuriated Washakie and created the situation in which the initial settlements were abandoned and then resettled. Broadly speaking, it was the effort by Reed and others which ultimately led to the removal of Washakie and his people to the Wind River Reservation and made possible the resettlement of Round Valley, the settlement of Laketown, and the push into the Bear River Valley. The history of Laketown, Round Valley, and Meadowville is so inextricably linked that to speak of them separately is very difficult. Yet separate they were. And each of the three communities clung tenaciously to its own identity. Each settlement had its own prominent families; each was organized into separate wards of the LDS church, and each operated as an independent school district.

The physical distance between the three communities, which complicated travel and communication, effectively separated them, but in some matters cooperation among the three was in their best interests. Probably nowhere was the cooperative spirit of the settlers in Bear Lake Valley better exemplified than in the construction of irrigation systems. Permanent settlements were always located with an eye towards the diversion of water to farm land. Community construction of irrigation works was played out in each of the Great Basin Mormon settlements since the first such undertaking on City Creek in the Salt Lake Valley.[49] Similarly, when Joseph C. Rich surveyed the site for Laketown in July 1867, he did so knowing the necessity of irrigation water.[50] The settlers of Meadowville and Round Valley constructed small ditches as early as 1868.[51] The south ditch at Laketown was completed in 1872. But beyond these smaller enterprises, the Laketown system was slow to materialize. The settlers of the three communities cooperated in constructing a dam on Big Spring in about 1880 which brought water to a portion of the irrigable land.[52] With water still insufficient for their needs, the group undertook to extend the canal, but as late as 1888 the *Deseret News* wryly noted the scarcity of irrigation water in Laketown. Allowing that plenty of water existed, the newspaper elaborated:

> A few years ago, at great expense, a ditch of several miles length was built, and, through some mismanagement some of the survey stakes were lost, and the work was done apparently with the view of making the water run up hill, which it stoutly refused to do.[53]

Beyond the engineering difficulties in bringing water to Laketown, development was also retarded by a climatic wet cycle which began shortly after settlement. A resident of Laketown commented in 1884 that never even "during the experience of the oldest inhabitants has there been so much snow upon the ground as at present."[54] Two to three feet of snow covered the valley with drifts up to eight feet deep. This kind of precipitation, occurring for a ten-year period from the mid-1870s through the mid-1880s, made supplemental irrigation in some cases unnecessary. It became fashionable during the wet cycle, which extended to about 1888, for settlers to assume that they were somehow responsible for the increased rainfall. This idea was perpetuated by scientists who argued "that climates in the west are becoming moister; . . . rainfall is increasing steadily."[55] The *Deseret News* noted how "a good sized stream of water" ran perpetually into Bear Lake. Even "during the summer and fall it overflow[ed], preventing . . . farmers from cutting hundreds of tons of good hay on the bottom lands."[56] The canal supplying water to Laketown and Meadowville took more than ten years to finish.[57] In 1888 two companies were formed which divided the water from Big Spring in Round Valley and the water flowing from Laketown Canyon. The Laketown District Company retained exclusive right to a third of Big Spring and the Laketown Company claimed another third plus all the issuance of Laketown Canyon. The remaining third of Big Spring became the right of Meadowville.[58]

The canal, however, served the needs of Laketown better than her Round Valley neighbors. By 1889 the canals and ditches conveying water from Big Spring water had raised the level of the ground water in both the Round Valley and Meadowville communities. The small log school house built at Round Valley had to be placed on skids and moved to a higher location.[59] Bishop Joseph Kimball of Meadowville convened a meeting in 1889 to discuss the best method for moving the homes in that community. There were eighteen homes, a church, and a school building which needed to be moved. The townsite was moved a mile north and a new survey conducted.[60] The uprooting, however, eventually doomed the small community.

Irrigation programs were conducted in all Mormon settlements in Utah. Even in southern Bear Lake Valley, where cooperation seemed less zealous, they were carried out. Mormons had fostered a spirit of cooperation since before their arrival in Salt Lake City. While in Jackson County, Missouri, Joseph Smith had embarked on a cooperative experiment known as the United Order which endeavored to bring about economic equality through a common ownership of property.[61] Under the plan, known as the Law of Consecration and Stewardship,[62] excess property was consecrated to the church and a portion was then given back to individuals consistent with their needs. As everything upon the earth was viewed as God's property, individual church members were considered stewards of the property entrusted to their care.[63] This early social experiment carried out in Missouri and elsewhere met with little success. But Mormon leadership continued clinging to the idea of cooperative living. The Mormon cooperative movement in Utah began at Brigham City in 1864 under the leadership of Lorenzo Snow.[64] After the initial success of the Brigham City Cooperative, a churchwide organization, the Zion's Cooperative Mercantile Institution, was implemented.[65] Brigham Young sermonized at the October 1868 conference, saying that "We have talked to the brethren and sisters a great deal with regard to sustaining ourselves and ceasing . . . outside trade."[66] Part of Young's plan was to halt the inroads being made by non-Mormon merchants in Utah. Until his death in 1877, trading with outside, or "gentile," merchants was an excommunicative offense.[67]

In Rich County, trade with non-Mormon merchants was a luxury not enjoyed without travel outside the community. Even though non-Mormon merchants did not operate in Bear Lake Valley until at least the mid-1880s, settlers were dependent upon acquiring goods wherever goods were available. Significant trade occurred between the northern settlements of the valley and non-Mormon merchants at Soda Springs.[68] In the southern valley, settlers traded at Evanston or Kemmerer throughout the 1870s. Still, Charles C. Rich returned from the 1868 LDS general conference with the conviction that cooperatives should be established. He convinced the settlers of both Paris and St. Charles to establish cooperatives in 1868.

Laketown residents were slow to follow suit, however; it would be twelve years before a cooperative store appeared at Laketown. Once incorporated, the store, under the proprietorship of Joseph Irwin, proved extremely profitable. From humble beginnings with virtually no capital and shares worth only five dollars, the cooperative was doing over $12,000 business annually by 1891 with shares valued at forty dollars.[69] With the success of the cooperative movement, Brigham Young encouraged the establishment of United Orders in communities throughout Utah. United Orders continued in some places until about 1883. A United Order was established at Laketown on 27 May 1874 by Mormon Apostle Wilford Woodruff. Bishop Ira Nebeker was installed as president, William P. Nebeker as vice-president, William B. Gibbons as secretary, and Nathaniel M. Hodges as treasurer. The board of directors consisted of John Marley, Edwin Lamborn, and Moroni Pickets.[70]

Neither in Laketown nor any other Utah community did the United Order experiment achieve great success. Federal legislation such as the Edmunds Act in 1882 proved disruptive to Mormon communities.[71] Furthermore, the United Order concept was difficult to live. Private property and free enterprise were deeply entrenched in the predominantly English and "yankee" American Mormon settlers who were less willing to give up private land holdings and the possibility of future financial success for the more indeterminate good of the community.

The free enterprise spirit, not the cooperative spirit, accounts for one of the most important events in the building up of Laketown. This occurred with the emigration of Nehemiah Weston and his wife Roseana Gifford in 1870. The couple left England in July 1870 after disposing of all their land and personal property, bringing with them thirty thousand dollars in capital. Nehemiah not only used his fortune to establish himself at Laketown, buying land and cattle, but he also helped establish the community by investing in machinery. Hiring millwright A. O. Williams, Weston reconstructed the sawmill below Big Spring.[72] Many of the original Laketown homes, along with those at Meadowville, were built from lumber sawed at Weston's mill. In partnership with George Robinson, Weston also harnessed the waters of Spring Creek to run a gristmill. Furthermore, Weston bankrolled the area's first blacksmith, N. O. Wahlstrom, by putting up the money to buy the machinery and tools necessary to operate the business. The first threshing machine to operate in southern Bear Lake Valley also came as a result of Weston's investment, and the machine reportedly was used to thrash grain as far away as Huntsville in Weber County.[73]

Through his generosity and community spirit Weston did much to foster the Laketown settlement. Although Laketown never achieved Brigham Young's prediction of a population of five thousand,[74] it became a thriving, close-knit community which LDS church historian Andrew Jenson characterized as "one great family."[75] In actual fact, the population of Laketown nearly approached an extended family—many of those who persevered and stayed in Bear Lake Valley were descendants of Nehemiah Weston.

The finances at the disposal of Weston were the exception rather than the rule in Laketown where most settlers arrived with little or no cash. A short cash supply persisted until the end of the century, but as one Laketonian remarked in 1884, "We need have no fear of

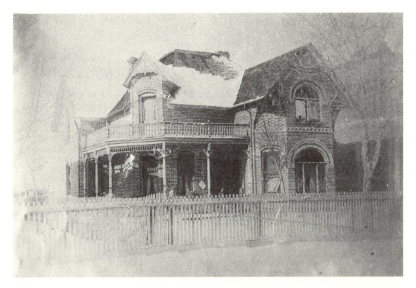

The Laketown Hotel, operated by Mrs. Ann Kearl. (Courtesy Eldon Mattson.)

starving this season, plenty of wheat and potatoes and plenty of fat cattle on the range for beef for our own use. . . . All we lack is cash."[76] Bernice Weston Sims recalled that when the first creamery was built, it not only alleviated the need to churn butter and make cheese at home, but that "after the produce was subtracted, Father received [the balance]. This was probably the first cash he received for produce."[77]

With both a creamery and gristmill to process local produce, Laketown was self-sufficient in many ways. Only two commercial business establishments, Robinson Brother's Mercantile, which competed with the cooperative store, and Kearl House, a hotel run by Ann Kearl, operated in 1897.[78] Most Laketown residents, at least until the introduction of the automobile, relied on their own gardens and farms for most of their food. As Bernice Weston Sims recalls:

> We canned all our vegetables from the garden and the apples and plums from the orchard . . .
>
> The flour and cereal for family use was obtained by carting the wheat we raised to be ground by the Old Mill in Old Mill Canyon.
>
> All of the dairy products came from the dairy herd. When I

was small I remember Mother churning our butter in a large round churn. It looked like a short barrel set on its side on a small stand on the table. The handle from the front turned the paddles inside, splashing the cream around until it began plopping with chunks of butter. The buttermilk drained from a spout in the bottom. At first the cream was skimmed from the pans of milk cooling on the basement floor. Later a separator was used until a creamery came to town.

[Father] hauled whey . . . from the creamery to help feed the pigs he raised, butchered and cured for the family's use. We kids pulled tons of weeds from the garden and fed those to the pigs and the chickens who furnished our eggs and chickens for the table.[79]

Laketown settlers often sold or bartered their excess produce at Evanston or Kemmerer, Wyoming. As noted in the *Deseret News* of 1887: "A great amount of produce is being hauled per team from Bear Lake to Almy and Evanston, where the granger finds a good market and their teams load back with coal which they purchase at a nominal figure."[80]

Longtime Laketown resident, Ray Lamborn, recalled the freighting process:

Our vegetables and things that we raised during the summer, why we took 'em to Kemmerer or Evanston, Kemmerer was the best bet.

We usually had a spike horse or an extra team to go up Laketown Canyon. Laketown Canyone [sic] that was up the Mill Canyon that's a dirt road. From then on up and then by Kearl's Spring is six miles up. . . . Usually the first day's trip from Evanston or to Kemmerer would be about fifteen miles above Sage. There was a spring there where there was a nice place to camp. It was level and it had willows and brush which you could use for the fire and there the spring for water. We always tried to make it at that particular place. Our campout would be our bedding that we took along with us, a few quilts scattered on the g[r]ound, and then our grub box which we always took to furnish our grub for those four days that we were out. We'd got to Kemmerer, oh, around noon the next day and try and sell our load, about noon the next day we'd try to get started home with a load of coal and a sack of sugar and maybe a pair of overshoes and overalls that we bough[t] from the J. C. Penny's store . . . He had a little dry goods store, and he was a good man to do business with, so we always went to the J. C. Penny's store and bought a few things before coming back and maybe we came back with ten to fifteen dollars from our load.[81]

Although it was the first and oldest settlement in Rich County, Laketown never achieved the commercial success of Randolph. Whereas Randolph was within thirty miles of the Union Pacific railroad station at Evanston, Laketown was an additional day's travel. Laketown's isolation not only hindered its commercial development but also its political development due to the geographical isolation from the county seat at Randolph. Both Laketown and Garden City remained more closely tied to the Idaho Bear Lake settlements of Paris and Fish Haven than to the Bear River settlements at Randolph and Woodruff. In some respects, this has been an enduring characteristic in the history of Rich County.

Randolph

The first wave of Mormon settlers into the Bear River Valley arrived near the present site of Randolph on 14 March 1870 under the direction of Randolph H. Stewart.[82] The settlement was later named in his honor. The company included Wright A. Moore, Joshua Stewart, William West, Wallace Young, Frank Robbins, Waldron Kennison, Robert Pope, Charles Pope, T. Pope, and William A. Pearce.[83] Others may have accompanied the first arrivals as well.

After Indian tensions abated in Bear Lake Valley, making possible the successful settlement of Laketown, the door was opened for Mormons to push into neighboring Bear River Valley. Stewart and company left St. Charles, traveled by sled along the west shore of the lake, past Laketown, up Laketown Canyon, then east to Sage Creek. The group may have chosen to depart in the early spring in order to take advantage of the frozen ground and remaining snow. The road between Fish Haven and Laketown was practically nonexistent. Stewart and company were among the first to attempt travel up Laketown Canyon. Without the benefit of a road, travel by sled was a far more practical mode of transportation. After they arrived at Sage Creek the wagon boxes were evidently set again upon axles and the group continued their eighteen-mile trek to Little Creek on wheels.

Another company of settlers from Salt Lake City soon joined the group. Randolph, and later Woodruff, are unusual because they were settled from two different directions. The Salt Lake City group traveled up Big Cottonwood Canyon then north to Huntsville. From Huntsville they followed the road to Bear Lake Valley as far as Millcreek Canyon. At Millcreek Canyon the settlers turned east, crossed the Bear River Range, and then roughly followed the meanderings of Big Creek out of the mountains to Stewart's settlement. The Salt Lake contingent included William Howard, William Pead, Levi O. Pead, John Arrowsmith, Harvey Harper, William Bowthorpe, and Edward Bailey.[84]

The settlers dug two small ditches on the north bank of Little Creek the first year and, on a small scale, immediately began farming the lands situated around the townsite. By September 1870 the settlers had made a rough survey and established the Randolph precinct. Approximately twenty houses were built during the first year, including the home of Randolph Stewart. Stewart's house holds the distinction of being the first residence constructed in Randolph.[85]

Joseph C. Rich resurveyed the townsite the following spring, and new settlers "learning of good opportunities for obtaining land . . . flocked in from all parts of the country."[86] The new arrivals in 1871 included one of the families of Apostle Wilford Woodruff. Partially as a result of his interest and enthusiasm for the area, Randolph grew dramatically.[87] Woodruff settled the family of his plural wife Sarah Brown and the family of his son Wilford, Jr., on a twenty-acre parcel of land in Randolph. The group left Salt Lake City on 19 July 1871.[88] Woodruff's diary reveals the circumstances which greeted the new arrivals, as well as detailing the efforts required in settling the area.

> 24 We Moved on to our 20 Acre lot and pitched our camp and broke up about 3 Acres of New land with two teams. We had a pleasant Camp on a small trout Brook. Through a mistake of the boundaries given us we ploughed 85 yards west of our line.
> 25 We hunted a while for our horses then ploughed North and South and Burnt Sage Brush in the Evening.
> 27 We ploughed 2 Acres.

Apostle Wilford Woodruff, who settled the family of his plural wife Sara Brown Woodruff along with son David, and his family, at Randolph in 1872. The town of Woodruff is named in his honor. Wilford Woodruff served as the fourth president of the Church of Jesus Christ of Latter-day Saints from 1889 to 1898. (Special Collections and Archives, Utah State University, Logan.)

28 Horses gone again. Hunted untill 2 oclok and found them then ploughed 2 Acres and draged till night.

29 I went fishing trout with Bishop and Frank Robins. I Cought 17 trout 4 of which weighed 17 lbs. [A] large trout Broke My Fishing Rod which I had owned 31 years. I hooked more large trout to day than I Ever had in all my life but lost the largest of them. While I was fishing the Boys ploughed 2 acres and sowed Oats and Barley and draged the ground.

30 Sunday I met with the people and spoke to them about one hour, then met with the Teachers in Afternoon and Entered into arangements to Enter the land. I spent the night with Brother Arrow Smith.

May 1, 1871 A Pleasant Morning. I have a severe Cold sore throat and head Ake. We planted Potatoes and Peas.

2d We went into the Canyon and got a load of Posts timber and explored the timber Canyon. We tied up our Horses at night one span and went to Bed.

3d All our Horses are gone this Morning those tied to the post and all But we found them again and went to the Canyon and got Posts and Poles.

May 4 1871 We went to the Canyon and got poles.

5 I spent the day Choreing. Made shave horse. Planted [.] Acre of Corn. Made 2 long waggon Reads. Wilford and Keets are in Canyon Cutting pole.

6 I went to the Canyon. Got 2 loads of poles. 16 M The boys had cut 300 poles and 100 Post timber.

7 Sunday I met with the Saints at Randolph and as I had spoken 2 Sundays I requested them to speak. They did so. I followed them and gave instruction to the Saints.

8 We made 22 Posts and Put up 20 Rods of fence.

9 In Company with Frank Turnbow and Wm Cahoon and Brother Trowbull I went fishing trout. We caught about 10 lbs in all. At 3 oclok we put 2 teams on a Breaking Plough and Broke about one Mile of Ditch for water to our farm.

10 We cleaned out our water ditch got the water into our lot and Came away and left it running. I was so tiered out I Could hardly Stand up. We hitched to our waggons and drove to Woodruff on our return Home and spent the night with Bishop Lee.[89]

The presence of an LDS church apostle at Randolph was a powerful argument in favor of settlement. John Snowball, an early settler, estimated that only sixty-three families lived in Randolph during the fall of 1871.[90] This number had increased to ninety by January 1872. Indeed, through his presence and promotional work and in his efforts to organize and oversee the construction of the canal coming off the southern bank of Little Creek, Woodruff became a major advocate for the settlement of Randolph.[91]

With the possible exception of his allotting more time for fishing, Woodruff's experiences at Randolph mirrored those of other settlers. Houses needed to be built, fields plowed, and crops sown. In keeping with the tradition of Mormon settlements throughout the Intermountain West, the settlers began constructing a meetinghouse on 15 February 1871.[92] The small eighteen feet by twenty-four feet, one-room log structure served as both a school and chapel until 1875. In March 1875 William Tyson, who had helped lay the logs for the first public meetinghouse, began laying the rock foundation for a new building. It measured a spacious thirty feet by fifty-five feet and sported fourteen-foot ceilings. The settlers finished the building in time to hold their Christmas feast there.[93]

The construction of the new meetinghouse required the cooperative efforts of the entire community, and cooperation appeared to come easier in Randolph than it had at Laketown. The residents of Randolph established a cooperative store far earlier than did Laketown's citizens. By the fall of 1872 a cooperative store capitalized at three hundred dollars, with shares valued at five dollars each, was in place. A tithing house was also erected during the same year.[94] The Deseret News noted that the cooperative store "is in a lively condition. It is run on a small capital, and in consequence of it being turned over several times in six months, the dividend being declared every six months, the dividend is very large."[95]

Part of the reason for the quick turnover may have been in the popularity of one particular commodity.

> The store opened at the residence of A. E. Pearce who was made manager. The business prospered for a time, but the second year a 40 gallon barrel of whiskey was brought in and sold by the mea-

sure. The people of the town, most of whom were stockholders, objected to the whiskey part of the business . . . [96]

The above may have been one reason why the *Deseret News* remarked that "some of shareholders are pleased with the large dividend"; others were not.[97] Cooperation was an easier pill to swallow if individuals had the chance of a return on their investment or perhaps a small sip of whiskey. "When," asked the author of the *Deseret News* article, "shall we all be able to see alike?"[98]

Whether or not they were Mormon, not all settlers saw alike. Though a majority of Randolph settlers voted in favor of Wilford Woodruff's suggestion of establishing a United Order, the vote was not unanimous. The Randolph United Order was established during Woodruff's trip, a day earlier than the one at Laketown. The apostle also established United Orders at Woodruff and in the northern Bear Lake settlements. [99]

Wilford Woodruff became a voice in favor of United Orders throughout the Mormon settlements. He also sought to improve the agricultural economy through his involvement with the Deseret Agricultural and Manufacturing Society. Woodruff was an inveterate dabbler in agricultural experimentation and through the society imported hundreds of non-native plants and seeds. According to historian Thomas G. Alexander, Woodruff promoted all kinds of exotic ideas.[100] During one of his trips to Randolph, he introduced salmon fry into Big Creek, and this experiment was also tried in other Bear River tributaries.[101]

Woodruff also may have been involved in convincing Archibald McKinnon and George A. Peart to bring with them a number of young fruit trees from Salt Lake Valley in June 1871. The fruit trees proved no more successful, however, than had the transplanting of salmon into the Bear River drainage. The trees were planted along the banks of little creek, but, "as the creek over-flowed in the winter and the ice was over a foot thick around the trees, this proved the end of the fruit orchard."[102]

Agriculturally, Bear River Valley proved even more difficult than Bear Lake Valley. William West, one the initial settlers accompanying Randolph H. Stewart in 1871 and later bishop of the Randolph Ward, recalled that there were frosts every day of the year. West remembered a frost in June 1873 which killed the leaves on all the cottonwood trees.[103] Small quantities of grain were raised the first year and in subsequent years. Olavus Jacobson raised and hand flailed 175 bushels of oats in 1872; but, according to the manuscript history of the Randolph Ward, the amount of grain raised locally would remain insufficient for the settlers' needs for the first fourteen years.[104]

By 1873 the LDS church historian recorded how "a great many of the settlers got discouraged because of the frosts and went away."[105] In 1876 David Woodruff, his mother Sarah, and family traded their cattle and holdings in Randolph for "a home and forty acres of land near the Bear River at Smithfield in Cache Valley."[106] By 1877 the number of local families had dipped to a low of fifty-one from the estimated high of ninety families in January 1872.[107]

In August 1880 Mormon church president John Taylor responded to the climatic hardships being endured by the settlers at Randolph by blessing the "land, water and labors of the people." Taylor "prophesied that the Lord would temper the elements."[108] Some eight years later a writer to the *Deseret News* recalled the event

> when President John Taylor and party paid Randolph a visit in their tour through Bear Lake Stake, after dismissing the meeting and when people were on their feet and leaving the building, President Taylor stood up and called the people back, and blessed them and their lands in the name of Israel's God, and prophesied in the name of the Lord, that we would raise grain for our sustenance.[109]

Mormon settlers clung to the hope which the prophecy provided. And this hope helped make possible the survival of the Randolph settlement. With typical Mormon optimism, the writer of the *Deseret News* article noted:

> Just think of a whole settlement buying bread and potatoes for fourteen years . . . We had to do this, but our bright day is dawning. President Taylor's prophesy is being fulfilled; we can see it, and can see it more and more as the years roll on.[110]

Whether by blessing or coincidence, the return of a wet cycle during the 1880s did improve circumstances. Sam Brough allegedly grew seventy bushels of oats to the acre, but Brough's crop was still the exception rather than the rule.[111] Small grains were not successfully cultivated for some time in the Bear River Valley. As the climate moderated during the 1890s and early part of the twentieth century and as irrigation projects were completed to bring water to new lands, the farms and ranches in Randolph gradually increased their yield of oats and barley.

The early settlers generally accepted the fact that most years the cultivation of small grains would be a dismal failure. Equally as dismal was the prospect of horticultural and garden crops. The settlers came to realize that an option to the risky prospect of farming was to utilize the area's natural vegetation in the production of livestock. This was made more evident when in 1887 a hail-storm destroyed virtually all the grain crops.[112]

Livestock production was not unique to Rich County or to the Bear River Valley; it had been an integral part of farming operations in most Mormon settlements. Neither was the use of the area's natural forage an idea unique to the Mormon pioneers. The cattle industry had been pressing west along with the railroad throughout the previous decade. Some of the area adjacent to the Mormon settlements at Randolph and Woodruff was already being used by large cattle operators at the time of the Mormons' arrival.[113]

Horses and other livestock accompanied the first settlers into Randolph during the early spring of 1870. In December of that year William Tyson introduced the first sheep to the area.[114] The grasses surrounding Randolph supported both beef and dairy cattle as well as sheep. Furthermore, as the native grasses were naturally occurring plants, already acclimated to the severe winters and early frosts, they formed a dependable source of forage for the settlers' livestock. The grasses provided good-quality graze during the spring and summer and could also be cut and dried for winter feed. During years of light snowfall, the grasses would dry and cure standing, making it possible to range livestock the year round.

Livestock operators in and around Randolph also benefited from the close proximity of the railroads. Randolph was a day's ride from the Union Pacific Railroad at Evanston. After 1883 and the comple-

Interior of Will Jacobson's Store, Randolph, ca. 1913. (Courtesy Mildred Jacobson.)

tion of the Oregon Shortline Railroad, Randolph was only eighteen miles south of Sage Junction.

Many in Randolph expressed disappointment when the Oregon Shortline selected a route away from the Mormon Bear River Valley settlements, departing instead from Granger, Wyoming, and roughly following the route of the old Oregon Trail. Writing to the *Deseret News* in January 1876, William Howard revealed his expectation that the valley would be blessed by a railroad the following summer.[115] The rails never materialized. Still, Randolph grew to become the center of commercial activity in Rich County.

In the twenty years between 1877 and 1897 Randolph nearly doubled in population.[116] From Robert Pope's first private store in 1871 which bartered mostly in butter, Randolph could boast of two mercantiles by 1892.[117] Robert and Peter McKinnon established their two-tiered brick store in 1892 in competition with William and O. J. Spencer's store which had opened a year earlier. In addition, Randolph also included a barbershop, a brick kiln, two lime kilns, three hotels, a harness and saddlery shop, a blacksmith shop, a cheese factory, a dress-making shop, a carpentry shop, two water-power mills and one steam mill for sawing lumber and processing grain, and a newspaper.[118]

Randolph's location made it the most accessible community within Rich County, and as such, it became the center of county government after 1872. It had easy access to Salt Lake City via the Union Pacific Railroad, and, therefore, was less isolated than was Laketown. Furthermore, located as it was amid the plentiful water supplies of Big and Little creeks, Randolph held the most promise for agricultural success. Land ownership around Randolph was also less questionable; the very railroad which made Randolph an attractive site made her neighbor, Woodruff, ten miles farther south and ten miles closer to the railroad, less attractive.

Woodruff

Land ownership was always dubious whenever settlement preceded a land survey. There were always contested claims whenever patents for land were being proven. In Randolph these disputes were settled because the lands around it were within the public domain. In contrast, the lands in and around Woodruff were difficult to patent. The townsite, though favorably located on Woodruff Creek, was situated within section sixteen of the township, a section reserved for the funding of schools.[119] Furthermore, much of the area adjacent to the townsite fell within lands granted to the Union Pacific Railroad at the time of the construction of the transcontinental line.[120] The settlement of Woodruff initially was fraught with difficulties. Not only would ownership of the land require its purchase at a higher price than public land, but some of the land was already in use as open range at the time of the Mormon settlers' arrival. Loran Jackson, a rancher in Bear River Valley, noted:

> The first settlers that actually come into this country wasn't Mormons. They brought cattle herds from out of Texas and fetched them here. There was the B.Q. [Beckwith and Quinn] down north, which went nearly to Cokeville, Wyoming, and this Ford ranch or known to me in the early days as the Crawford and Thompson. There was the Whitney up there in Almy.[121]

The buildup of the large ranches such as Jackson noted occurred at approximately the same time as the Mormons' arrival. Their resources, however, far exceeded those of the Mormon settlers, and they were able to expand their operations, eventually overshadowing those of the Mormons. A. C. Beckwith had been a prominent figure in the mercantile business in Wyoming since at least 1866 when he began his business at Fort Phil Kearney. Following the westward advance of the railroad, Beckwith later moved his operation to Cheyenne, Wyoming, and then to Echo, Utah. In 1872 he took up residency in Evanston, Wyoming, but continued conducting his business operations from Echo.[122] In 1875 he had joined forces with A. V. Quinn and expanded into the livestock business, establishing the Succor Ranch some fifty miles north of Evanston.[123]

Another early figure in the cattle industry of the Bear River Valley was William Crawford, after whom the Crawford Mountains were named. Crawford opened a commercial packing house at Evanston in the early 1870s to supply meat to crews of the Union Pacific Railroad. By 1872 he had joined forces with William Thompson and moved over five hundred head of cattle on the range east of Randolph. During the severe winter of 1876 virtually the entire herd perished. During the ensuing years, Crawford and Thompson pooled their resources together with those of two other Evanston businessmen, E. S. Crocker and Harvey Booth. The four constructed the first irrigation canal from Bear River in 1878. However, during the process of trying to determine the rights on the new canal, a misunderstanding developed between the foursome. William Crawford disappeared from a dance at Evanston in February 1893. Although his body was never recovered, it was assumed that he had been taken from Evanston and thrown in the burning slag heap at the mine at Almy. Two years later Harvey Booth was murdered in a barn belonging to the company. Neither murder was ever solved.[124]

Charles Crawford continued to direct the affairs of his father's business. Beckwith and Quinn also continued to operate throughout the period, and other large ranches developed in the Bear River Valley as well. Large-scale livestock operations were beyond the financial reach of most early Mormon settlers at Woodruff. Only the Mormon settlers' willingness to face drought and killing frosts year after year eventually enabled them to make the land their own. The Mormons stayed; the others left. Their faith and conviction enabled them to persevere.

When George, Arbury, and I. V. Eastman first entered the Woodruff area along with William Longhurst and William Walton, they caused little concern for the large ranchers.[125] The actual owners of the ranches were most likely absentee owners. Those on the land realized that in 1870 the land they were using was not theirs to bicker over. The Eastmans wintered in 1870–71 with the family of a man they called Indian Jim.[126] History records nothing more of the generous "Jim"; if any might have had reason to be upset about the Mormons settling at Woodruff, it would have been he. But not since the uprising of Washakie in Laketown in 1866 and the subsequent show of force by the Shoshoni in 1870 had area Indians seriously obstructed Mormon colonization efforts. During the early years of settlement, a small Indian population remained in Bear River Valley. Robert Pope traded butter to the Indians at Randolph for fish,[127] and occasional skirmishes developed between the settlers and Indians.[128] But gradually, as occurred elsewhere throughout the western United States, the Indians were pushed farther and farther from the line of settlement. After 1875 the quarrel over the land around Woodruff was among white settlers, not between whites and Indians.

Many of the immigrants to Woodruff were young, either new arrivals to Utah, or second-generation Mormons from communities where the population had outgrown the available land and water. Many came from Bountiful, Utah.[129] Those who settled in Woodruff between 1871 and 1872 included the families of Peter Cornia, John Cox, William Stiff, Joseph Tolman, Adniah Tolman, Charles Dean, Artimus Putnam, William Reed, Charles Walton, and Richard Warrick. In 1871 the ward manuscript history reported thirty families living in the vicinity of the Woodruff townsite.[130] A year later, the Salt Lake Daily Herald reported the number of area families to be sixteen.[131] The all-too-familiar scenario played out in Bear Lake Valley and Randolph was also played out in Woodruff. Many settlers became discouraged with the prospects of farming because of the cold temperatures. The ward manuscript history notes that settlers either left or turned to stock raising.[132]

The usual pattern of Mormon settlement was for the settlers to live within the townsite and farm the outlying areas. This pattern did not work well in Woodruff. Although the early settlers concentrated their efforts on building up the town, the LDS church historian noted that "as early as 1874 they commenced to move out upon their farms and ranches."[133] The result of this migration was an even greater lack of enthusiasm for cooperative enterprises than had been the case at Laketown and Randolph. The settlers did cooperate in constructing a log schoolhouse in 1872.[134] Thirty "scholars" attended regularly.[135] The settlers also established a cooperative store in 1875 which was capitalized at a paltry $231.83. After a few years, the store at Woodruff failed.[136] This may have been due in part to Woodruff's being in close proximity to Evanston, Wyoming, and the retail outlets available there. It may also have been due to a general lack of enthusiasm on the part of the Mormon settlers or to a higher than normal percentage of non-Mormons in the vicinity of Woodruff.

In his swing through the Bear River and Bear Lake Valley settlements, Wilford Woodruff convinced the Mormons in Woodruff to form a United Order. On 28 May the following officers were appointed to head the new organization: William H. Lee, president; Peter Cornia, vice-president; William Longhurst, secretary; and John Cox, treasurer. The directors were Richard Bee, Samuel Bryson, and Arbury E. Eastman.

In June 1877 William H. Lee traveled to Salt Lake City with the evident purpose of attracting new settlers to the area. The success of the Woodruff United Order of which Lee was president would depend upon the ability of Woodruff to attract a stable and faithful population. Furthermore, Charles C. Rich had appointed Lee to act as bishop of Woodruff in 1871. His duties, as was the case with all bishops in early Mormon settlements, was to look after both the temporal and spiritual needs of the people.[137] The *Deseret News* noted Lee's visit on 15 June 1877.

> Bishop Lee of Woodruff is in town and reports all well in the regions of the upper Bear. . . . There is plenty of room for fifty more families. Water, land and timber are plentiful, and here is an opportunity for some of the unemployed of Salt Lake to make a home and achieve independence.[138]

Although the number of families had increased to twenty-six by 1877, up from a low of sixteen in 1872, still more people had left the town than were living in it.[139] A writer to the *Bear Lake Democrat* noted that only a few had stayed in the settlement; "the balance have moved from 3–6 miles from town for their own convenience." Even Bishop Lee had left the settlement and moved to his ranch. But, noted the *Democrat,* he said "he will move back." The lure of making a profit in the cattle trade, coupled with the disheartening risks of raising crops, led some, if not most, of the Woodruff settlers to concentrate on building up their ranches instead of building up the townsite. "We all want to get rich too fast," stated the *Democrat,* "which causes some division. All think that after they have built themselves up, they will then look towards the building up of the settlement."[140]

The spring of 1884 arrived cold and wet, which left all the "stockmen . . . looking for hay, [and the] grass men looking for cash." Hay was selling for seven dollars a ton.[141] This was part of a four-year cycle which the Indians warned the early settlers about during the deceptively mild winter of 1872. As foretold, the winters of 1876, 1880, and 1884 were "deep snow years."[142] During one of these cycles, a settler noted that "There are three or four men in the settlement that have more hay than they need, but on account of the scarcity they ask extortionate prices." Even when offered two loads next summer for one load now, the "hay" men refused to cooperate.[143] The *Bear Lake Democrat* took special interest in the fact that the large cattle company of Beckwith and Quinn had ranged their stock all winter near Bridger Creek. The combination of tall, dried grasses and windswept plains had enabled the company's cattle to survive in fine shape. The writer looked forward to the next season when the Mormon settlers could "buy the railroad land, we then can have more settlers to help build up the country."[144]

But the railroad dealt the Mormons a crushing blow the next season. As the Mormon settlers expanded more and more into the livestock market, they increasingly came into competition with the large cattle companies. The key to success in the livestock business centered around numbers. A successful livestock enterprise needed large areas of rangeland to accommodate ever-increasing numbers of cattle. The

Mormon settlers were new to the business; the older, established cattle operators were not. Whoever controlled the railroad lands would also control the cattle trade in the Bear River Valley.

At an LDS priesthood quorum meeting in 1884, Bishop Lee rehearsed the counsel given to him by President John Taylor, who "wished to have the land secured between this place [Woodruff] and Randolph." Taylor advised the settlers not to let the lands fall into the hands of "gentile ranchers." Quorum members John Cox and Charles Dean agreed. "Brother Dean thought it would be well to secure the land and Brother Cox said if we did not we would in time regret it."[145]

The Mormon settlers were doubtless aware of their precarious hold on the land. The railroad subsidy was immense—far too immense for the Mormon settlers to purchase. But the settlers desired very little of the whole. They had for some time leased sections of the land from the railroad at twenty-five cents an acre. Doubtless, the sections which the Woodruff settlers had utilized were among the best. However, the railroad was not interested in selling small quantities of its subsidy; it was interested in selling it all and advertised to that effect in the Evanston newspapers. The only ones financially capable of buying entire townships were the Wyoming cattle companies.

In a newspaper story of 21 September 1885 headlined "Woodruff Lands Gobbled Up By Evanston 'Cattle Kings'" the *Deseret News* devoted two columns to the subject. Written by "a citizen of Woodruff," the article claimed that the citizens had "lately been the victims of misplaced confidence." The people of Woodruff had long ago, the author stated, applied to the Union Pacific offices in Omaha, Nebraska, to buy the land and were told that "they could go on making improvements, and whenever the time came for the land to be sold they should be notified and have the first chance to purchase." Although the settlers had continually paid their rent, the "non-'Mormons' . . . who occupied land in the valley not only refused to pay the rent required, but were allowed to hold their claims without doing so." The episode also began to take on religious overtones, as the *News* article summarized:

It . . . would indicate that there is some truth in the report that has since been circulated by parties in Evanston, that the agent who had the selling of the land was really determined that "Marmons" should not purchase it.[146]

The entire ordeal dampened the plans of the Woodruff settlers. The manuscript history of the Woodruff Ward tersely records:

In 1885 the Bear River Land and Cattle Company was organized, and Smith, North and Sessions bought all the railroad lands in the vicinity of Woodruff. A large amount of this land had been used and leased by the settlers . . . with the promise . . . that those settlers should have the privilege of purchasing, when the lands were placed for sale. . . . Several petitions were signed by the people and sent to the railroad officials, and considerable money [was] wasted in trying to [protect] the rights of the settlers, but contrary to all agreement the land was sold to the above company, this unpleasant circumstance acted as a hinderance to the building up of the settlement and many sought new homes elsewhere.[147]

Negotiations continued for nearly a year. On 8 August 1886 Bishop Lee mentioned having talked with the cattle company that had purchased the railroad lands. Getting no satisfaction from the railroad, the Mormons tried to convince the "cattle kings" to part with some of the land. Bishop Lee reported that "no definite conclusion was reached."[148]

Although the settlers of Woodruff blamed the railroad and the cattle companies equally for the loss of the land, they could not help but be impressed and a little awed by the cattlemen's operations. A writer to the *Salt Lake Herald* noted: "Messrs Beckwith and Quinn of Evanston have the finest ranch in Wyoming, situated between Cokeville and Randolph. They have 15,000 acres under fences, a great part of this land is seeded down to lucerne and timothy. Their business is immense.[149]

Aside from the railroad lands which the settlers had used and which appeared to be lost, the settlers began laying plans to acquire the state lands around Woodruff. Anson Call reported on 5 July 1886 that he had visited with the land commissioner and made arrangements "to secure the land."[150] Call, John Cox, and Charles Dean had tentative hopes for action. A month later, they urged all settlers "holding land to try and [ascertain] their rights." A committee including Charles Dean and Samuel Bryson was appointed to investigate the matter further.[151] The purchase of these lands would prove as impossible for the Woodruff settlers as was that of the railroad lands. Still, the settlers were intent on ensuring that the town survived. In the midst of a controversy between cattlemen and sheepmen, which the *Salt Lake Herald* noted was causing "a bitter feeling to exist," the residents of Woodruff became "determined [to build] up a large city." If they could attract enough settlers interested in farming on a smaller scale, perhaps, they reasoned, they could counteract the divisiveness of the past few years and hold the land for "hearty" Mormon families. The newspaper continued "to effect this desirable object, [the town] has set apart one section of land, and divided the same into eight acre blocks, which is to be sold at government prices. This is to induce settlers to locate here."[152]

Few, if any, new settlers came to take advantage of Woodruff's offer. Following statehood in 1896, nearly fifty-five thousand acres of state lands were surveyed in Rich County; forty-nine thousand of these acres were school lands. As of 1897 no state land in Rich County had been purchased.[153] But the State Land Board noted:

> The small number of sales made during the year will be accounted for when it is understood that no State Lands can be sold until they are first appraised . . . , the Board deeming it but fair to the settlers on school lands in the various counties, that the lands in each county in the State be appraised before sales should commence in any.[154]

In 1899 state lands in Rich County and elsewhere were offered for sale. Much to the disappointment of the Woodruff settlers, they could not afford the price. The Woodruff manuscript history recorded:

> In July several thousand acres of range land lying west [of Woodruff] was purchased from the State by the Neponset Land and Live Stock Company. This proved a great harm to Woodruff, as the people thereby were deprived of their common stock range.[155]

In 1905 the state land board reported that since statehood, the state had transacted only two land sales in Rich County, but these totaled more than ten thousand acres.[156] Although more than fifty thousand acres of state land remained in Rich County, the best was taken first. Those the settlers had long used as public grazing lands, like the railroad lands before, had been gobbled up by the non-Mormon ranchers.

Through no fault of their own, the Mormon settlers in Woodruff had been ineffective in their attempts to control the future of their community—both the railroad lands and state school lands had been bought out from under them. Still, the Mormon settlers remained confident. To those who stayed, the hardships they were enduring were simply a continuation of hardships they had endured since 1870. And by the 1890s, the prospects for prosperity were looking up. Construction on a new meetinghouse commenced in 1893 under the supervision of Bishop John Baxter, Wesley K. Walton, Joseph H. Neville, Savannah Putnam, and Byron Sessions. The new church was completed and dedicated in August 1897.[157] A school district was organized in 1897, and construction began on a new two-story schoolhouse during the same year.[158] In 1899 an irrigation corporation was formed under the leadership of George A. Neville, Anson C. Call, and Chaplain Walton; the corporation was capitalized at twenty thousand dollars.[159]

Most of the businesses in Woodruff were operated by Mormons. Up until 1897, according to the Randolph *Round-Up*, H. H. Cook had covered the "mercantile field so thoroughly that no thought of competition [had] ever entered the mind of anyone."[160] With a growing population that had reached nearly six hundred citizens, John Baxter opened a general store in December 1897. The store's stock was later taken over by Peter McKinnon when McKinnon was made local bishop after Baxter received a call to become the first stake president of the newly organized Woodruff Stake.[161]

Through perseverance, the Mormons gradually regained control in Woodruff. The large cattle operators suffered several setbacks during the 1880s because of severe weather. The smaller farmers and ranchers were better prepared to survive the "deep snow years." They had less invested and, generally speaking, were able to find enough hay to feed their stock. By the early 1910s, Loran Jackson remembers that most of the big ranchers had either abandoned their land or sold out at reduced prices to the Mormons.[162]

The establishment of Woodruff exemplifies the difficulty in settling the Bear River Valley. The climate was unpredictable, the environment severe. As long as the land returned a profit to the corporate cattle industry, it stayed; but when conditions became unprofitable, most of the early, large ranches disappeared. Waiting in the wings were the patient settlers, mostly Mormon, who had come to the Bear River Valley not just to turn a profit from the land but to make homes for their families. Although ranches of large acreage continued to be found in the Bear River Valley, the ownership of the land came increasingly under the control of the descendants of Mormon settlers.

As the Woodruff settlers regrouped in the Bear River Valley, so too did the rest of Utah. Decades of tension eased between Mormons and non-Mormons, and between Mormons and the federal government. Old wounds healed slowly, but the process was well under way in January 1896 when Utah entered the union as the forty-fifth state.

Garden City

Garden City was never settled by non-Mormon ranchers. Situated on a narrow, one-mile-wide strip of land stretching from the mountains on the west to the lake shore, it was viewed by Mormons as being less crucial than the larger area of Round Valley to the south and Bear River Valley. In Bear River Valley, non-Mormon cattle ranchers were already threatening to dominate the region in 1870 and did dominate the region throughout the 1880s and 1890s. No immediate threat existed in "Little Valley," the name applied to the Garden City area until 1878. In comparison to Round Valley and Bear River Valley, Little Valley included only a small amount of irrigable land and acreage for grazing.

As the northernmost settlement in Rich County, it seems incongruous that Garden City was the last town settled since it is the closest to the older Mormon settlements of Paris and St. Charles and is practically next door to Fish Haven, Idaho. It would seem natural for the Garden City area to have been settled first. Yet Garden City was not

Logan Canyon Road looking east towards Garden City, ca. 1930. (Special Collections, Utah State University, Logan.)

settled until after both Laketown and Bear River Valley; over a decade separates the settlement of Garden City from that of Laketown.

Mormons had settled Fish Haven and began utilizing the waters of Swan Creek by 1864. In that year, Phineas Woolcott Cook arrived at Fish Haven and planted and reaped a small crop of grain. Later that fall, he reportedly joined in the pilgrimage to Round Valley with the intention of erecting a mill. Cook did not stay long at Round Valley but returned to erect his mill on Swan Creek the following spring.[163]

Snellen M. "Cub" Johnson was already at Swan Creek when Cook arrived in 1865. Johnson had constructed the first two log cabins there in the fall of 1864.[164] Whether or not he was interested in using the waters of Swan Creek is unknown. Very little if any farm land existed in the vicinity of Swan Creek; therefore, it is doubtful that Johnson had settled there to farm. It is not clear if Cook bought Johnson out or if Johnson left of his own volition. Johnson, his families, and brothers eventually settled in the vicinity of South Eden on Bear Lake's east side.[165] Phineas Cook's name would come to be associated with the sawmills and gristmills established at Swan Creek.[166] Cook was a consummate entrepreneur. He built the first gristmill on

Swan Creek using two large stones set in a frame. He later upgraded the mill by purchasing a set of burrs in Salt Lake City for five hundred dollars. Additionally, he erected a sawmill on Swan Creek and eventually purchased a picker and two carding machines for the processing of wool.[167]

In 1870 Fish Haven, the closest town to Cook, had a population of fifty-four.[168] The Fish Haven settlement contained only a small amount of arable farm ground, most of which was settled by 1870. The area around Swan Creek contained practically no farm ground, but the area to the south included nearly a thousand acres. If Cook could find a way to convince farmers to settle the land, he would have a dependable wheat supply for his gristmill, wool for his carding machines, and a market for lumber. So intent was he in his desire to have the land settled that he put up five hundred dollars for the construction of a canal from Swan Creek into Little Valley. Cook and his sons commenced work on the canal in 1877. The announcement of the availability of land with a dependable water source drew settlers to the area almost immediately. The canal, however, did not deliver any water until the following year. Despite that setback, a townsite was surveyed in 1877 and at least four families took up residency: Alma and Sarah Peck, William and Mary Dustin, William Spencer, and Wright M. and Helen Moore.[169]

William Dustin is credited with building the first cabin in Garden City, presumably out of lumber sawed at Cook's mill. Much to the disappointment of Cook, the first structures erected at the new townsite were not built there, nor did they use any lumber from his sawmill. Alma Peck and Wright M. Moore not only moved their families from Randolph in 1877 but also their houses. One can only imagine the difficulty of moving entire buildings twenty-seven miles over rutted roads and down Laketown Canyon. Most likely the structures were dismantled and moved one log at a time. The task must have required numerous trips with a horse and wagon.[170]

Belleview was the first suggested name for the newly surveyed townsite. The survey of the area did not exactly conform to the more traditional surveys of Woodruff, Randolph, and Laketown. In those communities each block contained ten acres. In Garden City each block contained eight acres. The streets in the other Rich County settlements were eight rods wide; in Garden City, streets were surveyed from four to six rods wide.[171] The original Garden City survey included two streets running north and south with each lot containing two acres. The original townsite extended five blocks north and south from the main road.[172]

The change in the survey was most likely made to accommodate the way in which the land was to be disposed of. The founding of Garden City essentially was a financial proposition on the part of Phineas W. Cook. The survey of the townsite proceeded according to his specifications rather than according to those previously used at Laketown, Randolph, and Woodruff which were the same as those used in surveying the early settlements of northern Bear Lake Valley. They were suggested by Charles C. Rich and were carried out by his son Joseph. They roughly conformed to the specifications of other Mormon settlements in the Intermountain West.[173] The land to be irrigated from Swan Creek, however, was to be disposed of in a manner which would bring a return on Cook's investment. By making the streets narrower and decreasing the size of the blocks by two acres, Cook could divide the land into more lots.

On 5 February 1877 the first meeting of the Swan Creek Irrigation Company was held. The names of individuals and families wanting land were recorded at this meeting.[174] The land was to be divided equally among those in attendance. Working from the supposition that the canal could deliver water to about eight hundred acres, the company divided the land into forty, twenty-acre lots. A three-dollar tax was levied on each lot for the completion of the canal, and lots were drawn on 26 March 1877.[175] In June the county court authorized the creation of the Swan Creek Precinct. The name later was changed to Garden City.[176] Phineas Woolcott Cook was in business.

Garden City was a fitting name for the new community. Among all the Rich County communities, Garden City most successfully cultivated the more tender garden crops. In his ten years on Swan Creek, Cook observed how frost was less severe there.[177] Crops of tomatoes, cucumbers, squash, and corn were grown in Garden City, while the successful cultivation of these crops elsewhere in Rich County, particularly in the Bear River Valley, was doubtful. Some even claimed the climate was suitable to the growth of sugar cane.[178]

Wright M. Moore was appointed to preside over the new settlement in 1877. Robert Calder succeeded Moore in May 1879. The settlers constructed a small log building during that same year which, as had been the custom in the other settlements, served as a school, church, and social hall.[179]

The original canal, which extended south of Swan Creek seven miles, was enlarged in 1878 and again in 1889. The canal extended south to Beers Valley.[180] The original canal brought water only as far as the Garden City limits. Soon new homesteads began taking shape south of town. Harmon Potter and William Dustin both acquired land near the vicinity of present-day Pickleville. In 1889 Emanuel Bisbing bought the Potter and Dustin lands as well as other lands in the vicinity.[181]

By the early 1890s land to the south of Garden City was consolidated once again as Nathanial M. Hodges purchased the Bisbing holdings. The Hodges Ranch eventually came to include most of the land between Garden City and the summit at Meadowville, from the Cache County line on the west to the shore of Bear Lake. The ranch included lands which later became some of the best recreational property in Rich County.

Recreation, however, in the 1890s was a luxury limited to Saturday afternoon baseball games and occasional dances. In the minds of the nineteenth century settlers, the land's purpose was to support agriculture and ranching. In 1902 Hodges established his own irrigation company and gradually extended and enlarged the canal from Swan Creek.[182] The Hodges Ranch included over nine hundred acres.[183] In addition to ranching, Hodges also erected a sawmill between Meadowville and the summit of Logan Canyon. The area became known as Hodge's Canyon, and the lumber was used not only by the ranch but also by hired men who bought smaller parcels of land from Hodges and constructed their own homes.

Hodges lost the sawmill to fire in the early part of the twentieth century, and much of his property was sold soon after he suffered a debilitating stroke in 1915.[184] However, Hodge's efforts to bring the southern part of Little Valley under irrigation became a lasting legacy.

The history of Garden City is not one of large ranches and livestock but rather one associated with smaller, specialized operations such as the cultivation of the raspberry introduced by Theodore Hildt in 1910.[185] Additionally, Garden City, more than Laketown, became most strongly associated with Bear Lake itself. The eastern terminus of the Logan Canyon Road ended at Garden City practically eye level with the lake. It was here that the recreational industry first started, and for early boating and swimming enthusiasts, the names of Garden City and Pickleville became synonymous with the blue waters and sandy beaches of Bear Lake.

ENDNOTES

1. In surveying Salt Lake City in 1847, Orson Pratt established a base and meridian at the southeast corner of Temple Square. This base and meridian was used as the basis for making longitudinal and latitudinal readings by subsequent federal surveyors from 1850 onwards. Pratt's journal records how "One block of ten acres was reserved for a temple. The latitude of the northern boundary of the temple block, I ascertained by meridian observations of the sun, to be 40 deg. 45 deg. 45 min. 44 sec. The longitude, as obtained by lunar distances, taken by the sextant and circle was 111 deg. 26 min, 34 sec., or seven hours, 25 min. 46 sec. west of Greenwich. Its altitude above the level of the sea was 4300 feet, as ascertained by calculations deduced from the mean of a number of barometrical observations taken on successive days." See *Journal of Orson Pratt from the* Millennial Star, *1849,* Utah State Historical Society Library, Salt Lake City, Utah.

2. Paul W. Gates, *History of Public Land Law Development* (Washington, D.C.: U.S. Government Printing Office, 1968), 121–26.

3. Richard D. Poll, et al., ed., *Utah's History* (Logan: Utah State University Press, 1989), 243.

4. Laketown Ward Manuscript History, 1864; Historical Department of the LDS Church, Salt Lake City Utah, (hereafter referred to as LTMH). John C. Marley and William Morley were evidentally brothers, and spelling varies according to the source. The manuscript history of Laketown uses the spelling included here.

5. Bear Lake Valley Pioneer Histories, nd, np, typescript, Special Collections and Archives, Utah State University, Logan, Utah. See also Elizabeth P. Astle, "Life Story of Ellen Jane Bailey Lamborn," 7, typescript, Special Collections and Archives, Utah State University, Logan.

6. Brigham Young to bishops Peterson and Thurston in Weber Valley and to Bishop Peter Maughan in Cache Valley, 26 August 1864. Brigham Young Collection, Special Collections and Archives, Utah State University, Logan.

7. *Journal History of the Church of Jesus Christ of Latter-day Saints,* manuscript, Department of Special Collections and Archives, Merrill Library, Utah State University, Logan, Utah (hereafter referred to as JH), 8 November 1863.

8. At a meeting on 23 August 1863, Brigham Young stated: "Now what I am about to say you will do well to keep to yourselves. We have in our minds to settle Bear River Lake Valley; I for one would like to have a settlement there. As yet I have said nothing to anyone except Brother Benson. Now if you will keep this matter to yourselves nobody will know anything about it, but otherwise it will be telegraphed to old Abe Lincoln by some of these [Army] officers. and then it will be made a reservation of immediately to prevent us getting it." The 23 August 1863 meeting is discussed in Leonard J. Arrington, *Charles C. Rich* (Provo: Brigham Young University Press, 1974), 249.

9. Charles J. Kappler, ed. *Indian Affairs: Laws and Treaties,* 4 vols. (Washington, D.C.: GPO, 1903), 2:650.

10. Grace Raymond Hebard, *Washakie, an Account of Indian Resistance of the Covered Wagon and Union Pacific Railroad Invasions of Their Territorys,* quoted in Frances Birkhead Beard, *Wyoming from Territorial Days to the Present,* 3 vols. (Chicago: The American Historical Society, 1933), 1:235.

11. LTMH, 1864.

12. Andrew Jenson, *Latter-Day Saint Biographical Encyclopedia: A Compilation of Biographical Sketches of Prominent Men and Women in the Church of Jesus Christ of Latter-day Saints,* 4 vols. (Salt Lake City: Western Epics, 1971), 3:460.

13. Job Baker, one of the original settlers to the area, died in 1864; after his death the remaining settlers left to relocate at one of the other settlements. As Washakie's people were away for the buffalo hunt and would remain absent for another year, Baker's death was probably not due to Indian hostilities and may well have been from contagious disease. At least the other settlers may have thought his death was from such. According to Andrew Jenson's field notes, the name Chimney Town was used at that time because all that remained visible were the chimneys of the former structures. See Manuscript History of Garden City Ward, Rich County, Utah, 1864, Historical Department of the LDS Church, Salt Lake City, Utah (hereafter referred to as GCMH).

14. LTMH, 1864.

15. *Bear Lake Pioneers,* 896.

16. Information on the conflict between the settlers at Round Valley

and Chief Washakie is taken from Arrington, *Charles C. Rich*, 268–69. See also Russell R. Rich, *Land of the Sky-Blue Water*, 55; and LTMH, 1866–67.

17. LTMH, 1866–67.

18. Russell R. Rich, *Land of the Sky-Blue Water: A History of the L.D.S. Settlement of the Bear Lake Valley* (Provo: Brigham Young University, 1963), 55; and Arrington, *Charles C. Rich*, 269.

19. Brigham D. Madsen, The *Shoshoni Frontier and the Bear River Massacre* (Salt Lake City: University of Utah Press, 1985), 4.

20. John D. Unruh, *The Plains Across: The Overland Emigrants and the Trans-Mississippi West, 1840–60* (Urbana: University of Illinois Press, 1979), 119.

21. Arrington, *Charles C. Rich*, 268.

22. Rich, *Land of the Sky-Blue Water*, 54, 56. Although the Wind River Reservation was set aside in 1868, Washakie refused to go on the reservation until 1872 because of enmity between the Shoshoni, the Sioux, and the Cheyenne, who claimed the same area of the Wind Rivers. See Frances Birkhead Beard, *Wyoming From Territorial Days to the Present* (Chicago: American Historical Society, 1933), 1:235. It is known that Washakie still frequented the Bear Lake and Bear River Valley areas as late as 1872. O. S. Lee, a resident of Summit County, reported seeing Washakie and his people at Woodruff and Randolph in July 1872. Washakie was returning from the Wind Rivers after an unsuccessful hunting season. Lee reported that Washakie's "herders" had been repeatedly attacked by the Cheyenne and that two men had been killed. In retaliation, Washakie stole thirty head of horses from the Cheyenne. Lee further related that "Washakie is coming down to Bear Lake to fish. He designs passing into Cache county afterwards, and may visit Salt Lake . . . he says he will be Indian for another snow, when he will turn white man." This last statement probably meant that Washakie intended to go on the reservation the following year. See *Salt Lake Herald*, 12 July 1872,[3].

23. LTMH, 1867.

24. Astle, "Life of Mary Jane Bailey Lamborn," 7.

25. LTMH, 1869.

26. Ibid., 1869.

27. Mildred H. Thomson, comp., *Rich Memories: Some of the Happenings in Rich County from 1863 to 1960* (Salt Lake City: Daughters of Utah Pioneers, 1962)0, 125.

28. For a period of time during the 1870s, Meadowville was known as Kimballville. Other settlers who came to Meadowville in 1869 included Josiah Tufts, Isaac Kimball, Bordette Folsom, Charles Henry Alley, Joseph Kimball, William Cottrom, Joshua Eldredge, Joseph U. Eldredge, Solomon

Kimball, Jedidiah Kimball, Moses Gibbons, Lewis Palmanteer, George T. Judd, William T. Edgar, Elthanan Eldredge, Jr., David H. Kimball, Manassa Williams, Joseph Moffatt, Newell Kimball, Henry Graw, Hyrum S. Groesbeck, and Moroni Pratt. See Thomson, ed., *Rich Memories,* 125.

29. Scott G. Kenney, ed., *Wilford Woodruff's Journal, 1833–1898,* Typescript, *9* vols. (Midvale, UT: Signature Books, 1983–1991), 6:479–80. Woodruff recorded on 15 June 1869: "We arose at 4 oclok Cooked our trout for Breakfast then drove over the Mountains to Round Valley. Visited the Great Spring at its head then drove to the Settlement Called the Last Chance & Nooned, then drove across the South [west?] side of the Lake to Swan Creek, Fish Haven, to St. Charles & spent the night."

30. Polmanteer continues: "I then referred them to the uniform good and kind treatment the Indians had always received at the hands of the President and that they should know better than to believe any such stories-They admitted that such was truly the case One young man stating that when the 'Mormons' first came to this Country he was but a boy and from that day till now they had always received the best of treatment from the 'Mormons' I referred them then to several instances where they had killed 'Mormons' and had driven off much of their stock and yet President Young would counsel mercy & forbearance towards them, which they frankly admitted." Affidavit of Lewis L. Polmanteer, 18 June 1870, Historical Department of the LDS Church, Salt Lake City, Utah. Polmanteer was an early settler to the Meadowville area in 1869. See Thomson, *Rich Memories,* 125.

31. Louise Delina Cheney Willis who, in 1869 at age nine moved with her parents to Laketown, recalled: "In the summer of 1870, parts of two tribes of Indians, numbering, some said, three thousand or more, mostly warriors, came and camped on the south shore of Bear Lake. Their object in coming was to prevent . . . the white people from settling here, as this part of the valley they had retained [by treaty] as their hunting ground." Willis then recounts the same scenario involving Charles C. Rich, Amos Wright, and Ira Nebeker, stating that the Indians were given supplies and "they left for the Wind River country in Wyoming." See, Thomson, *Rich Memories,* 78–79. See also Reed Eborn, Interview with Ray Lamborn, "Growing up in Laketown," 3 May 1975, 28, typescript, Special Collections and Archives, Utah State University, Logan.

Both Cheney and Lamborn assumed that the Indians in 1870 were Washakie's people; but, as Polmanteer makes clear, the Indian army entering Round Valley in 1870 was under the direction of Chief Sagwich. Furthermore, the Indian army included both Shoshoni and Ute Indians. Since the 1820s Utes had participated in annual gatherings at Bear Lake. See Morgan, *The West of William Ashley,* 168–69. Furthermore, it is known that several Shoshoni bands also shared the Bear Lake Valley. Brigham D. Madsen states that Chief Bear Hunter's people "occasionally met with Washakie . . . in Round Valley." Bear Hunter was killed at the Battle of Bear River in January 1863. Thereafter, many of the western bands were led by Chief Sagwitch. See Madsen, *The Shoshoni Frontier*, 6–8.

32. J. H. Head to T. G. Taylor, 1 January 1868, Correspondence from the Superintendent of Indian Affairs, Utah Territory, 1851–1880, microfilm, reel six, Special Collections and Archives, Utah State University, Logan.

33. LTMH, 1869.

34. U.S. Decennial Federal Census, Utah Territory, 1870. Only William Morley and William Busby are listed in the index to the censuses of 1850, 1860, and 1870. See J. R. Kearl, Clayne L. Pope, and Larry T. Wimmer, *Index to the 1850, 1860 and 1870 Censuses of Utah: Heads of Households,* (Baltimore: Genealogical Publishing Co., 1981). The actual census, however, plainly lists Ephraim Watson and John Marley as also being heads of households at Laketown.

35. See Kearl. *Index to Censuses.*

36. Census 1870. Moore, as well, is not listed as a Rich County resident in Kearl, *Index to Censuses.*

37. Jenson, *Latter-day Saint Biographical Encyclopedia,* 3:460.

38. Census 1870. Braffet is not listed by Kearl, *Index to Censuses.*

39. Astle, "Life of Mary Jane Bailey Lamborn," 7.

40. Census 1870. As with many of Reed's compatriots who first entered Round Valley in 1864, he is not listed by Kearl, *Index to Censuses.*

41. Thomson, *Rich Memories,* 77.

42. For some time, however, Robert Beers must have been a prominent figure in the area. His name is attached to the area south of Garden City, known as Beer's Valley. See Thomson, *Rich Memories,* 32.

43. LTMH, 1898. The church historian lists the population at two hundred.

44. JH, 29 May 1883, 6.

45. JH, 14 March 1894, 4.

46. *Deseret News,* 11 January 1876. Quoted in JH, 11 January 1876.

47. LTMH, 1869.

48. JH, 16 April 1894.

49. Orson Pratt recorded on 24 July 1847 how they "commenced planting . . . potatoes; after which we turned the water upon them and gave them quite a soaking." See *Journal of Orson Pratt,* 74.

50. LTMH, 1867.

51. "Report of the Special Committee of the United States Senate on the Irrigation and Reclamation of Arid Lands," Report of Committee and Views of the Minority, 4 vols (Washington, D.C.: GPO, 1890), 2:94.

52. Thomson, *Rich Memories*, 128.

53. JH, 5 June 1888, 3.

54. JH, 22 February 1884.

55. Samuel Aughey and C. D. Wilber, "Agriculture Beyond the 100th Meridian or a Review of the U.S. Public Land Commission," quoted in Gates, *History of Public Land Law Development*, 434. See also *First, Second, and Third Annual Reports of the United States Geological Survey of the Territories for the Years 1867, 1868, and 1869* (Washington, D.C.: Government Printing Office, 1873), 236–37.

56. LTMH, 1884.

57. Ibid., 1888.

58. Ibid., 1888.

59. Thomson, *Rich Memories*, 109.

60. Ibid., 129.

61. Joseph A. Geddes, *The United Order Among the Mormons (Missouri Phase): An Unfinished Experiment in Economic Organization* (Salt Lake City: Deseret News Press, 1924), preface.

62. *The Doctrine and Covenants of the Church of Jesus Christ of Latter-day Saints* (Salt Lake City: Deseret News Company, 1883), 42:32.

63. Geddes, *United Order Among the Mormons*, 31–32.

64. Dean L. May, "Mormon Cooperatives in Paris, Idaho, 1869–1896," *Idaho Yesterdays*, 21 (Summer 1975): 30.

65. Arrington, *Great Basin Kingdom*, 249.

66. *Journal of Discourses by President Brigham Young, His Two Counselors, and the Twelve Apostles* (Los Angeles: Gartner Printing and Litho Co., 1956), 12:301. Young asked for the approval of the congregation. The vote was unanimous, and in several cases members were disfellowshipped for trading outside of the Mormon network. See A. J. Simmonds, *The Gentile Comes to Cache Valley: A Study of the Logan Apostasies of 1874 and the Establishment of Non-Mormon Churches in Cache Valley, 1873–1913* (Logan: Utah State University Press, 1976), Appendix G, biography of John F. Reed.

67. The cooperative store proved profitable for shareholders. Although initiated in an attempt to thwart non-Mormon merchants, the idea changed after John Taylor took over the church presidency in 1877. Zion's Cooperative Mercantile Institution competed freely with non-Mormon merchants during the last twenty years of the nineteenth century. Local

cooperative stores, such as the one at Laketown, operated in much the same spirit as their free-enterprise counterparts.

68. This was true especially in the Laketown area, where the entire population was Mormon. In the northern valley, settlers could travel to Soda Springs which had an active trade—mostly non-Mormon merchants operating between there and the Montana gold fields. In Laketown the problem became trade in general. There was no mercantile outlet in Laketown. Those needing commodities which could not be produced locally were forced to trade outside the community. Throughout the 1870s most trade was conducted at either Evanston or Kemmerer, Wyoming. See Eborn, interview with Ray Lamborn.

69. LTMH, 1880.

70. JH, 27 May 1874.

71. While attempting to establish a branch of the United Order at Sunset, Arizona, Wilford Woodruff commented how "the Government . . . was using every means in its power to enforce the . . . anti-polygamy law with the evident intent . . . to break us up as an organized community." Kenney, ed., *Wilford Woodruff's Journal*, 9:463.

72. Williams had also been involved in the first construction of the mill on Big Spring with Luther Reed in 1865. See Thomson, *Rich Memories*, 76–77.

73. For a discussion of the life and times of Nehemiah Weston, see Samuel Weston, "Weston Family History," 6–7, typescript, Special Collections and Archives, Utah State University, Logan.

74. JH, 17 September 1884, 9.

75. LTMH, 1898.

76. JH, 20 August 1894, 7.

77. Mary Evelyn Izatt, interview with Bernice Weston Sims, "Ranching Life Style, Rich County, Utah," 27 May 1973, 1–2, typescript, Special Collections and Archives, Utah State University, Logan.

78. *Roundup*, Randolph, Utah, 23 July, 1897. Quoted in LTMH, 1897.

79. Izatt, interview with Bernice Weston Sims, "Ranching Lifestyle, Rich County, Utah."

80. Manuscript History of the Randolph Ward, Rich County, Utah, 1887. Historical Department of the LDS Church, Salt Lake City, Utah (hereafter referred to as RMH).

81. Eborn, interview with Ray Lamborn, 19.

82. Stewart was born in North Carolina on 20 July 1834, and along with his family was among the first immigrants to Utah in 1847. He served as bishop of Randolph for ten years before moving his family to Emery County

and ultimately to Moab, Grand County, where he was appointed bishop in 1881. He died in November 1909. See Steven L. Thomson, Jane D. Digerness, and Mar Jean S. Thomson, *Randolph—A Look Back* (n.p., 1981), 117–18.

83. RMH, 1870.

84. Ibid.

85. Ibid.

86. Ibid.

87. Ibid., 1871.

88. Thomas G. Alexander, *Things in Heaven and Earth : The Life and Times of Wilford Woodruff, A Mormon Prophet* (Salt Lake City: Signature Books, 1991), 225.

89. Kenney, ed., *Wilford Woodruff's Journal,* 7:15–17.

90. RMH, 1871.

91. Ibid.

92. Ibid.

93. Ibid., 1875.

94. Ibid., 1872.

95. *Deseret News,* 14 March 1876.

96. Thomson, *Rich Memories,* 138.

97. Thomson, *Randolph—A Look Back,* 16. Although the cooperative store experienced success early on, difficulties continued to be experienced. After the discontinuation of whiskey sales, the cooperative store changed hands several times. Finally "Too much 'credit' ruined the business, and ZCMI sent their attorney who closed the store, sold the ground, goods, and mortgage to Olavus Jacobson." See Thomson, *Rich Memories,* 138–39.

98. *Deseret News,* 14 March 1876.

99. Kenney, ed., *Wilford Woodruff's Journal,* 7:182.

100. Alexander, *Things in Heaven and Earth,* 208.

101. Kenney, ed., *Wilford Woodruff's Journal,* 7:278.

102. Thomson, *Randolph—A Look Back,* 3.

103. Manuscript History of Bear Lake Stake, 9 September 1894, Historical Department of the LDS Church, Salt Lake City, Utah (hereafter referred to as BLSMH).

104. RMH, 1871.

105. Ibid., 1873.

106. Alexander, *Things in Heaven and Earth,* 225.

107. BLSMH, 11 November 1877.

108. RMH, 1880.

109. Thomson, *Randolph—A Look Back,* 23.

110. Ibid.

111. *Deseret News,* 12 November 1878.

112. RMH, 1887.

113. Willa T. Kennedy, interview with Loran Jackson, 15 July 1975. Typescript, Special Collections and Archives, Utah State University, Logan.

114. RMH, 1870.

115. *Deseret News,* 11 January 1876.

116. A comparison is made between the figure of 450 given in the BLSMH, 1877, and the figure of 800 given in *Roundup* (Randolph, Utah), 23 July 1897.

117. For information on Pope see RMH, 1871. For information on the other two mercantiles see *Roundup* 23 July 1897.

118. In addition to McKinnon and Spencer, the following individuals also profited from living in Randolph: Archibald McKinnon, Jr., blacksmith, inventor of the McKinnon Haystacker, "hundreds of which are in use in this and adjoining areas"; Lemuel McKinnon, harness maker; George Webb, carpenter, builder and contractor; John Snowball, proprietor of the Randolph Hotel; Sarah Tyson, proprietor of Tyson House; Edward South, barber; Samuel Brough, brickmaker, and W. S. Muir, owner of cheese factory on Otter Creek. See *Roundup,* 23 July 1897.

119. There had long been a concern over the setting aside of public lands for educational purposes. The Morrill Act of 1862 granted public lands to states and territories for the establishment of agricultural colleges. The Utah Agricultural College at Logan was established under this and succeeding laws in 1888. When Utah was granted statehood in 1896, it received a generous grant of the public lands within its border—a full fourteen percent. "The largest addition," notes historian Paul W. Gates, " was the doubling of the school lands to four sections in each township—2, 16, 32, 36." Nearly six million acres were set aside for public schools. Some of this acreage was included within the Woodruff townsite. See Gates, *Public Land Law Development,* 314.

120. According to Gates, "The Union Pacific Railroad . . . was given a 400-foot right-of-way through the public lands and 10 (20 under the Act of 1864) odd numbered sections of land for each mile of railroad it constructed from Omaha on the Missouri River, to the western border of Nevada. . . . To prevent persons anticipating the railroad in selection of its land, the acts provided that the two companies [the Union Pacific and the Central Pacific] should locate their routes within 2 years. When informed of the routes, the Secretary of the Interior was to withdraw all lands from

entry of any kind for a distance of 15 miles (25 under the Act of 1864) from the line. This meant that a solid area 30—later 50—miles extending from Nebraska to California would be withdrawn from all entries." See ibid., 364. At least a portion of Woodruff precinct fell within this area.

121. Willa T. Kennedy, interview with Loran Jackson.

122. Beard, *Wyoming from Territorial Days to the Present*, 182–84.

123. Ibid., 315–18. Quoting C. G. Coutant, Beard states: "During the year 1877 a selection of twenty-three sections of land was made—14,720 acres—extending along Bear River on either side. This land was taken up and settled upon by Mormons several years before. Their attempt at farming proved a decided failure and they abandoned it, Mr. A. C. Beckwith buying out their rights." See Beard, *Wyoming From Territorial Days to the Present*, 316.

124. Information on William Crawford and the Ford Ranch is taken from the following sources: Elizabeth Arnold Stone, *Uinta County: Its Place in History* (Glendale, CA: Arthur H. Clark Co., [1924]), 185; Thomson, *Rich Memories*, 16–18, and Kennedy, interview with Loran Jackson.

125. Manuscript History of Woodruff Ward, Bear Lake Stake, Rich County, Utah, 1870, Historical Department of the LDS Church, Salt Lake City, Utah (hereafter referred to as WMH).

126. Historical Record, Woodruff Ward, Bear Lake Stake, Rich County, Utah, 1900, 109, Historical Department of the LDS Church, Salt Lake City, Utah (hereafter referred to as HR).

127. RMH, 1871.

128. Thomson, *Randolph—A Look Back*, 9–11.

129. JH, 11 January 1972, 4. One who came to Woodruff from Bountiful was George Eastman. He came by a rather circuitous route. He was fifty-five years old when he arrived in Bountiful in 1869. Converted to Mormonism, Eastman left Maine and traveled to the Mormon city of Nauvoo, Illinois. He did not follow Brigham Young west in 1846, remaining in the midwest. Eastman settled in Iowa for a ten-year period before returning east to Maine where he stayed until his eventual immigration to Utah. See HR, 1900, 109.

130. WMH, 1871.

131. Quoted in JH, 11 January 1872, 4.

132. WMH, 1872.

133. Ibid., 1874.

134. Ibid., 1872.

135. JH, 11 January 1872, 4.

136. WMH, 1875.

137. Ibid., 1870.

138. Quoted in JH, 15 June 1877.

139. BLSMH, 11 November 1877.

140. *Bear Lake Democrat* (Montpelier, Idaho), 24 March 1884.

141. Ibid.

142. Thomson, *Randolph—A Look Back,* 11.

143. RMH, 1876.

144. *Bear Lake Democrat,* 24 March 1884.

145. HR, 1884, 45.

146. *Deseret News,* 21 September 1885.

147. WMH, 1884.

148. HR, 8 August 1886, 60.

149. Quoted in JH, 3 November 1886, 6.

150. HR, 5 July 1886, 59.

151. Ibid., 8 August 1886, 60.

152. Quoted in JH, 3 October 1887, 5.

153. *Second Annual Report of the State Board of Land Commissioners of the State of Utah for the Year Ending December 31, 1897* (Salt Lake City: Tribune Job Printing Co., 1897), 8.

154. Ibid., 10.

155. WMH, 1899.

156. *Second Annual Report,* 24.

157. WMH, 1893.

158. Ibid., 1897.

159. Ibid., 1899.

160. *Roundup,* 23 July 1897.

161. WMH, 1898. McKinnon, who later erected a brick building adjoining Baxter's original store, was unsuccessful in the mercantile business. He later sold his building and the stock back to Baxter, who attached his original structure to McKinnon's and went back into business. See John M. Baxter, *Life of John M. Baxter: Being a Brief Account of His Experiences as a Pioneer, Missionary, Bishop, and Stake President* (Salt Lake City: Deseret News Press, 1932), 114.

162. Kennedy, interview with Loran Jackson.

163. GCMH, 1864. It is possible that Cook was beaten to the punch in Round Valley by Luther Reed, who was also intent on erecting a mill.

164. Ibid., 1864.

165. Thomson, *Rich Memories,* 32. It is doubtful that Cub Johnson sim-

ply abandoned his property. The improvements were most likely sold to P. W. Cook. Johnson was not easily intimidated. Several instances are recorded where Johnson was involved in violent confrontations with other Bear Lake settlers. See Justice of the Peace Docket for Laketown, Rich County, Utah, 7 February 1873, and 23–29 March, Special Collections and Archives, Utah State University, Logan.

166. GCMH, 1864.

167. Thomson, *Rich Memories,* 36.

168. Census, 1870.

169. GCMH, 1877.

170. Ibid.

171. Ibid.

172. Ibid.

173. Arrington, *Charles C. Rich,* 267.

174. Among the names recorded were: Alonzo Cook, Henry Howland Cook, Robert Calder, Wright M. Moore, James Furney, Amasa C. Lindford, Marion Thomas, Issac F. Odekirk, Miner Wilcox, William Dustin, James Hansen, S. Nelson, Heber Odekirk, Joseph Lindford, Adelbert C. Rich, Edward Haddock, Frank Wilcox, Alma M. Peck, Harley Mowery, Jr., and Hyrum B. Simmons. See GCMH, 1877.

175. GCMH, 1877.

176. Ibid.

177. Ibid.

178. JH, 26 July 1879, 8.

179. GCMH, 1878.

180. Thomson, *Rich Memories,* 32.

181. The Garden City Ward History records that the land south of Garden City was owned "principally by outsiders." (GCMH, 1878) For a discussion of how the land changed hands, see Thomson, *Rich Memories,* 70.

182. Thomson, *Rich Memories,* 70.

183. JH, 7 May 1894. A higher figure of two thousand acres is also mentioned. See Thomson, *Rich Memories,* 51.

184. Thomson, *Rich Memories,* 51, 71.

185. Ibid., 48.

4

"Like an Emerald Among the Mountains"

RECREATIONAL ACTIVITIES AT BEAR LAKE AND RICH COUNTY

It is doubtful that anyone who has ever looked upon the waters of Bear Lake for the first time has failed to be impressed. Warren Angus Ferris crossed the divide between Cache and Bear Lake valleys in 1832 and later wrote how "one of the most agreeable prospects imaginable, saluted and blessed our vision. It was the Little Lake . . . fifteen miles long and about eight in breadth."[1]

In 1871 United States Geologist F. V. Hayden described the lake as being "set like an emerald among the mountains." Hayden, who had seen much of the western United States, thought Bear Lake incomparable: "Not even the waters of Yellowstone Lake present such vivid coloring," he wrote.[2]

Though waxing far less poetic, early Mormon explorers to the region were also impressed. Marcellus Monroe, commander of a detachment sent from Ogden in 1857 to guard against the possible intrusion of Johnston's Army through Bear Lake country, observed Bear Lake to be "one of the prettiest Lakes I ever saw—it has a beautiful sandy beach and groves of timber around its margin."[3]

On their journey, Monroe's party met with numerous Indian

groups at or near Bear Lake. The Bear Lake area had been a favorite Indian retreat for centuries prior to the arrival of white settlers. Descriptions of what these Indian gatherings may have been like do not exist. The earliest available description comes after the arrival of white trappers and traders. In 1827 and 1828 rendezvous were held at the south end of Bear Lake. With the exception of there being white trappers and traders present, and the accompanying availability of liquor, these occasions probably differed little from earlier Indian gatherings at Bear Lake. For hundreds of years prior to the great rendezvous of 1827 and 1828, Indians had congregated on the shores of Bear Lake to dry meat, prepare skins, and recreate. Indian groups likely used other favored sites within Rich County as well, such as the Monte Cristo region west of Woodruff. Prior to the coming of white men, it is certain that Shoshoni Indians used this area as a summer camping ground and fall hunting area. Because of the abundance of feed, many forms of wildlife were plentiful. The Squaw Butte–Squaw Flat area about ten miles southeast of Monte Cristo was the central campsite for hunting parties.[4]

Most gatherings or festivals occurred in the fall or late summer after a major hunt, animal drive, or harvest. Religious ceremonies were also observed at times.[5] That the Shoshoni attached great importance to Bear Lake Valley is confirmed by Chief Washakie's insistence that Mormon settlers refrain from settling the southern part of the valley. However, the north and south portions of Bear Lake Valley were equally appealing to early Mormon settlers, and they soon reneged on the agreement with Washakie.

The severe climate of Rich County made settlement difficult. While acknowledging this, Joseph C. Rich also saw the great potential of Bear Lake Valley. He declared to his future wife Ann Eliza Hunter after returning from his first trip there:

> Only men with plenty of hair on 'em are tough enough to stand the climate of Bear Lake, but what a country! Streams full of fish; the most beautiful lake on earth; wild game; grass up to a horse's belly; timber in the mountains; fine locations for townsites; everything![6]

But even in the midst of hardship, settlers still found room for a few social diversions. Mormons had always valued social activities. One of the earliest structures built in Mormon communities was the meetinghouse, which served the educational, spiritual, and social needs of the settlers. Dramas and theatricals were common events in most communities. The dramatic association at Woodruff, led by Wesley K. Walton, was responsible in large measure for the erection of the public meetinghouse in that community as early as 1873. The community soon outgrew the old log structure, however, and erected a new meetinghouse in 1884; a stage was added to the building in 1888.[7]

The settlers at Randolph also outgrew the confines of their original public building. One account states that "at an overcrowded dance in the old meeting house some one suggested that they build an adobe meeting house large enough for meetings, school and amusement purposes." As the men had grown "tired of standing outside waiting for their turn to dance," they subscribed nearly two hundred dollars immediately.[8] Also at Randolph, Isaac Smith formed a People's Opera House Company in 1912. The group built an impressive two-story brick building that included a balcony, stage, and dance floor. The opera house changed ownership several times, finally becoming the property of the LDS church. The church renovated the building and restored it to its original purpose, staging numerous plays and musical presentations both local and vaudevillian, until the structure was condemned and torn down in 1936.[9]

Barn dances were common in early Laketown. Dances as well as theatricals, were held in the lofts of the Kearl barn, now located on the Johnson property in Meadowville, and at a barn on the Mattson Ranch in Meadowville.[10] Ray Lamborn recalled that his grandfather Weston's barn was also used on certain occasions.[11] According to Lamborn, the Kearl barn was the principal place for community gatherings because the school and meetinghouse, completed in 1884, was filled with benches and desks and lacked sufficient room. Although they had the bottom of the barn "full of horses or cows . . . they had a dance hall upstairs," Lamborn related. "It didn't smell to[o] much like a perfumed place," but it served the community's needs.[12]

The Kearl barn was supplanted after the turn of the century by the upstairs portion of Robinson's Mercantile in Laketown. Community plays and recitals were held there along with traveling shows which came infrequently through the area. During the 1920s the community erected an amusement hall. The plan, according to Lamborn, was opposed by George Robinson, who at that time was bishop of Laketown. Although suggesting that Robinson may have opposed the amusement hall's construction for business reasons, Lamborn also allowed that the bishop did not want to see the town burdened with a huge debt: "He knew how hard it was to get the money when they figured the cost of a building like the amusement hall."[13] The community spent roughly twelve thousand dollars on the construction of the building; however, the figure does not account for the amount of labor which the community contributed.[14] Lamborn states that

> Alf [Kearl] done the cutting and the town went back and got the lumber, which was mostly red pine. It came down Hell's Holler country.... They've got some red pine in there. They'd go back in ... and haul it out. Of course all the rough work was that way, so the main part of the building didn't cost them too much. It was done by donation.[15]

Dancing also served as a major form of recreation at Garden City. Local musicians such as George D. Lutz, Charles H. Pope, George Whittington, C. H. Hansen, and Rose Lutz Pope provided music for the dances. Ensembles likely consisted of one or two fiddles and possibly a piano.[16]

In their isolation, the people of Rich County had to be satisfied with whatever musical talent could be cultivated within the community. Joseph Robinson became disenchanted with the music (a harmonica duet) at a Pioneer Day gathering at Laketown in 1890. He called a meeting and convinced fourteen of his fellow townsfolk to purchase instruments and form a brass band.

> Luther B. Reed went to Evanston ... and brought the instruments home. The first night after they were distributed the men serenaded the town and made all the noise they could. It was said that all the dogs in town left and one lame ox ran away and when he came back his lameness was gone.[17]

Laketown Brass Band. (Courtesy Clayton Robinson.)

The Laketown Brass Band improved over the years to the point that they played for most community gatherings. A professor Hayden of Montpelier, Idaho, took an interest in the group, traveling the forty-plus miles to Laketown once a week to give music lessons. Eventually a band wagon was built and uniforms purchased, giving the brass band from Laketown an air of real professionalism.[18]

Music and dance were important aspects in virtually all the Mormon settlements. Church president John Taylor considered dancing to be a harmless, athletic exercise which added "to the grace and dignity of man."[19] Brigham Young also supported the idea of dancing as a recreational pastime. Historian Nels Anderson writes:

> They say that Brigham Young never started a caravan forth to set-
> tle the desert that he did not send musicians along. . . . Although
> he was himself anything but a merry-maker, Brigham always went
> to the dance and the theatre, always taking two or three wives
> along. . . . He considered the dance and the theatre as much a part
> of religious life as worship. For this reason the recreational func-
> tions in the Mormon community are always opened and closed
> with prayer.[20]

In addition to being opened and closed with prayer, dances in Bear Lake Stake were also expected to conform to other requirements. The president of Bear Lake Stake, William Budge, issued the following rules:

> 1 - Dances shall be conducted under the direction of the bishop who will be responsible for the manner in which they are conducted.
>
> 2 - Dances shall be opened and closed with prayer and not held after 12 P.M.
>
> 3 - Waltzes and other round dances will not be countenanced in our assemblies.
>
> 4 - Persons dancing out of their turn shall be considered violators of good order and may be requested to retire, and may be ejected.
>
> 5 - We will not use liquor in our assemblies nor suffer any person intoxicated.
>
> 6 - Swinging with one arm around the lady's waist shall not be permitted.
>
> 7 - To swing a lady more than once against her will shall be considered ungentlemanly; to swing more than twice under any circumstance shall be considered disorderly and requested to retire.
>
> 8 - Club dances, gotten up to make money, will not be countenanced unless specifically ordered by the Stake Presidency or Bishop.[21]

President Budge and other church leaders considered dancing acceptable only if it adhered to the standards imposed by the community. When dancing led to "profligate and intemperate habits," noted President John Taylor, it was not acceptable.[22]

Intemperance was something which Mormon settlers liked to think was not a part of their communities. An examination of the justice of peace docket for Laketown, however, reveals that alcohol related crimes were not uncommon. Furthermore, several church leaders were disfellowshipped for reasons related to alcohol.[23] The coming of the Oregon Shortline Railroad to Montpelier, Idaho, in 1882 increased the availability of alcohol in Bear Lake Valley. Although the railroad did not greatly affect the settlements at

Laketown and Garden City, it did bring a substantial influx of non-Mormons to the northern part of the valley. In Montpelier, the railroad workers established themselves at or near the railroad tracks, segregating themselves from the original Mormon settlers. Historian Earl F. Passey, later bishop of Randolph, wrote:

> For several years after 1883 two almost separate communities comprised Montpelier. The old fence built along the present site of Sixth Street, was kept up to mark the bounds of the two communities, and one [had] to stop to open the gate [in order to pass] from one community to the other.[24]

The railroad brought a new affluence to Montpelier. It also brought some of the vices characteristic of railroad towns. The Laketown community, ignoring the problems with alcohol in their own community, responded to the newer alternative forms of entertainment to the *Bear Lake Democrat:*

> We see . . . glaring advertisements announcing that there is a "first class" saloon and a "first class" Billiard Hall in Montpelier. Let us hope that our good people will not believe a word of it and that the "first class" part of any such an institution among the Latter Day Saints will always be that it cannot exist among them for want of patronage and support. Our young men and young women will do well to shun such [amusements]. They savor of hell and ruin, in this world and the world to come.[25]

Although Mormons in Bear Lake Valley looked upon the railroad as a corrupting influence, in actuality the prosperity which resulted from railroad accessibility made those in the southern part of the valley covetous of their northern neighbors. Railroads were the single most important means of transportation during the last quarter of the nineteenth century and beginning of the twentieth century. "No better spot can be found in the world as a health and pleasure resort than Garden City," remarked the editor of the *Roundup* in July 1897, "its one drawback being its distance from the railroad."[26]

Bear Lake residents realized early the potential value of their area for recreational purposes. But publicizing the fact and convincing others to come there were two different matters. Joseph C. Rich acted as area publicist during the early years of settlement. The main reason

for publicity was not to convince people to come for a healthful afternoon on the beach but to convince people to come to settle the area.
Joseph Rich happened upon a good idea when, in the summer of
1868, he began publicizing the story of the Bear Lake Monster. Rich
never claimed to have seen the monster himself, yet asserted that
some of the most respected members of Bear Lake Valley had. In
Rich's own words, the story was a "wonderful first class lie." [27] But in
the minds of those who had seen it, it was not.

According to the editors of *Bear Lake Magazine,* Rich took the
opportunity of using the story in order to "give publicity and attention to the remote settlements at Bear Lake."[28] As correspondent to
the *Deseret News,* Rich had the perfect outlet.[29] His story was not very
successful in its original intent. It did not bring droves of settlers to
Bear Lake Valley. However, the story proved to be enduring, continuing to surface periodically year after year.[30]

Like his story, Rich was also a durable part of the Bear Lake
region. Along with his father, Charles C. Rich, he settled in Paris,
Idaho, in 1863. Joe Rich was well suited to the tasks of publicist for
Bear Lake Valley; he not only was a consummate storyteller but also
had the rare ability to brag without being boring. In 1894 Rich con-
ceived of the idea of launching a steamboat on Bear Lake. Having
already gone broke during an earlier decade in a sailboat venture,[31]
he turned to the power of the press to promote his new enterprise.
Never shy about using the pronoun "I," Rich stated:

> I have built the first steamboat in Southern Idaho and will have it
> ready to launch about May 15 at Hot Springs. I want all my friends
> and all my foes to come and see me on that day. I want them to
> come and bring with them on that day all the victuals they expect
> to eat, and if convenient, put in a sack of potatoes or flour or a
> chunk of meat for me. All are invited, saints, sinners, friends, and
> foes, Democrats, Republicans, Populists, Mormons, Gentiles; also
> Bishops Price and West.[32]

Receiving, as it did, quite a lot of advance publicity, the launching
of the steamboat, modestly christened the *Joseph C. Rich,* was
expected to also launch the Bear Lake area into the tourist business. A
meeting was held at Garden City in March 1894 to consider where

the best resort areas would be around the lake. Consideration was given to Garden City, Fish Haven, and Laketown. Those in attendance visualized the new steamboat replacing poverty with prosperity by bringing "hundreds of pleasure seekers into our midst."[33]

The *Joseph C. Rich* was not ready to be launched in May, however. The townspeople all showed up—friend and foe, Mormon and gentile, and in all probability bishops Price and West. But the *Joseph C. Rich* refused to run. The steamboat was actually not a steamboat at all; it was a gasoline-powered paddle boat. The boat was constructed at Bear Lake, but Rich had sent east for the engine. Through some oversight, the manufacturer had sent the wrong engine. Rich and his helpers—practically the entire population of Rich and Bear Lake counties had turned out to offer suggestions at one time or another—could not figure out how to connect the engine to the paddles. Finally, in desperation, the manufacturer was contacted and a representative was sent west to look the situation over. Upon arriving, the representative announced that the engine was wrong and immediately wired east for a replacement. The new engine was shipped in by rail to Montpelier, but the maiden voyage of the *Joseph C. Rich* had been postponed until mid-August.[34] By then, much of newness had worn off. The gas-powered steamboat was more a novelty than a success, and, like the promotional story of the Bear Lake Monster, did not change Bear Lake Valley's poverty to prosperity. After a few years Rich sold the paddleboat to Joe Stock of Fish Haven.[35] During the early part of the century, Stock ran excursions across the lake during the summer months from his Fish Haven resort to Joe Rich's Hot Springs Resort.[36]

Most of those using Bear Lake prior to the turn of the century were the settlers themselves. Dr J. W. Hayward, who was born at Paris, Idaho, in 1879, recalled how once each summer an outing was held at Bear Lake in which all the people from the nearby communities would turn out to participate. "We would have our clothes half off by the time we got there so we could swim longer. . . . The boys would swim in one part of the lake and the girls in another," Hayward recalled.[37]

Ray Lamborn reported that the lake was also an important part of his boyhood summers. "We went to the lake quite a lot, that was two miles down and two miles back . . . we'd swim and play in the sand there until we got good and sun burnt."[38] Lamborn and his Laketown friends also used the frozen lake to ice skate upon during the winter.

Both Lamborn's and Hayward's were youthful remembrances of recreation at Bear Lake. Except for Independence Day and Pioneer Day celebrations, adults had little time for a leisurely afternoon at the lake shore. Survival often dictated that the recreational activities of adults also had to serve other functions. The members of the Randolph Ward Relief Society made thirty-one quilts in 1915 and sold them for a dollar each to raise money for the construction of the local Relief Society building.[39] Furthermore, the recollections of the descendants of Rich County pioneers are full of references to "mother's busy hands." Women baked bread, sewed, mended clothing, canned fruit and vegetables, and dried cut flowers. Though these tasks were expected of women in pioneer society, they also served a recreational function. Particular pride usually was taken by women in at least one of their tasks. For some it was the perfect loaf of bread; for others it was the flowers that adorned the entrance to their home; still others specialized in embroidery or quilting. Although most women had to be masters of many trades, each found a certain niche at which to excel.

Although women in early Mormon settlements also helped plant and harvest crops, the farm was principally the domain of men. Men often augmented their labors on the farmstead by hunting and fishing—activities which offered not only a diversion to farm work but also provided food for the table. A good deal of the time spent in Randolph by Apostle Wilford Woodruff was spent "fishing trout." Woodruff, however, unlike some who accompanied him on his forays, could afford recreational time. It is unlikely that Bishop Stewart, who often accompanied Woodruff, had much spare time away from his other personal, civic, and church duties; but just as unlikely would have been his refusal to accept an invitation to go fishing with an LDS church apostle.[40]

Fish and game were plentiful in both the Bear River and Bear Lake valleys. The redoubtable Joseph C. Rich claimed to have seined

"96 big trout" from Fish Haven Creek in 1864. Rich pitch-forked "1800 pounds . . . divid[ing] [them] with the people of Paris."[41]

As late as 1897 the Randolph newspaper, *Roundup,* maintained:

> Game is still very plentiful throughout the country, deer, elk and antelope can be found by the hunter, sometimes in large bands numbering as high as a thousand; bears and mountain lions are found in the hills, while ducks, geese and prairie chickens can be found in great number; the sage hen, however, predominates . . . trout are plentiful in every creek in the county and the size which some of the Bear Lake trout attain surpasses belief.[42]

Community leaders in Rich County made efforts to preserve the abundant wildlife in the area. John Snowball became the county's first game commissioner in 1883.[43] As early as 1866, the county court had passed a resolution to prohibit fishing from 10 April to 23 May for a distance of eighty rods on each side of all streams emptying into Bear Lake.[44] This action was to ensure that fish would have an opportunity to spawn unmolested; however, since many Bear Lake settlers had come to depend on the easy availability of fish during their spawning runs, the ordinance was later rescinded. Not until 1898 did county commissioners pass another ordinance to protect the fishery in Bear Lake. Big Spring Creek in Round Valley was set aside as a fish reserve in February of that year.[45]

Gradually, natural patterns that had been in equilibrium for thousands of years were altered with the arrival of white settlers. The tall-grass meadows were surveyed, plowed, and fenced. The mountain timber was felled and used to construct cabins and corrals: the wild game was hunted and gradually supplanted by grazing stock. Fish, which once used the streams for annual spawning runs, were harvested or found the streams themselves dammed and diverted into irrigation canals or mill-races. Still, in Rich County the process of subjugation was less intense and thorough than in other, more populated, Mormon settlements. Wild animals that disappeared from those areas of Utah survived longer in the rugged area of Bear River Valley. Grey wolves, for instance, still made meals of Rich County sheep and livestock in the 1920s. The last bounty known to have been collected on a grey wolf in the county was claimed by Frank Kennedy

Fred Feller with one of the last grey wolves taken in Rich County. Feller began his career as an expert trapper while still a teenager. (Courtesy Allen Feller.)

in November 1920.[46] Thus, although Bear Lake and the landscape of Rich County underwent change, the area still remained one of abundant potential.

There were numerous attempts, some more successful than others, to take advantage of Rich County's natural beauty by developing a recreational industry. Arguably the first such enterprise was Joseph C. Rich's resort at Hot Springs on Bear Lake's east shore.[47] After Rich sold his unsuccessful paddleboat to Joe Stock at Fish Haven, Stock's resort became the most popular early resort on Bear Lake.[48]

The advent of the automobile made the Bear Lake region more accessible. Although the east side of the lake was still remote, other resorts began appearing on the west shore. Around 1913 Mr. and Mrs. Clarence Booth began a resort on Swan Creek. They purchased some beachfront property from the Cook estate and experimented for a year or two by setting up some tents on the lake's shore. After several years of some success, the Booths began erecting cabins. Adopting the name Lakota for the resort, they also built a swimming pool, heated by a large coal-fired boiler. The area was a popular spot for Bear Lakers, and at least one lifelong romance was kindled in the heated waters of the Lakota pool.[49]

About the same time that the Booths were expanding at Lakota, businessman James W. Niel of Kemmerer, Wyoming, purchased some acreage from the Hodges Ranch, south of Garden City and began the Ideal Beach Amusement Company. James's brother Archie operated the resort along with John Wilson. The company purchased several dozen rowboats and canoes from Old Town, Maine, shipping them by rail to Kemmerer. Forty-one cabins were erected and by 1918 concessions, including a carousel, had been added. Dancing remained one of the most popular aspects of the resort, which included a dance pavilion in addition to a "first-class" lodge and restaurant.[50]

From 1914 to 1918 the resort business at Bear Lake flourished. The popularity of Ideal Beach and Lakota was the result of an economic upswing which preceded American involvement in World War I and carried through to the end of the war. The outbreak of war in Europe in 1914 created an almost overnight market for American food and fibre, resulting in increased prosperity for farmers—a general prosperity that had not been experienced since at least the 1880s. Since the Panic of 1893, the economy of the country had been sluggish and erratic. Although industry began recovering during the early part of the twentieth century, agricultural prices remained depressed.

Technological advances, which enabled farmers to produce more than they ever had been able to before, deepened the agricultural depression by creating produce surpluses. With the coming of the world war in 1914, however, the demand for American farm surpluses effectively ended the depression. Agricultural production, thereafter, expanded even further. The result was that both farmers and businessmen acquired extra spending money. Some of this extra cash was spent on recreation, and the tourist trade around Bear Lake experienced good times. When the war in Europe ended in November 1918, the tremendous surpluses created by American technology and expanded farming operations again sent agricultural prices plummeting. In rural areas such as Rich County, other businesses dependent upon a healthy farm economy also suffered. The farm depression of the 1920s resulted in less discretionary money being available to farmers and businessmen. The recreational industry around Bear Lake suffered as a consequence.

Another problem experienced by the resorts in the 1920s was the declining level of Bear Lake. Decreased precipitation after 1918 led to severe drought by the summer of 1919. As a result, irrigators below Bear Lake, who were dependent upon the flow of the Bear River, began exercising their right to the stored waters of Bear Lake to augment the flow of the river.

It had been thousands of years since the Bear River and Bear Lake were actually connected. However, during stages of high water, Mud Lake to the north and the main body of Bear Lake did merge, which allowed the waters of Bear Lake to mingle with those of the Bear River through Mud Lake.[51] Such periodic anomalies were not lost on those observing the rise and fall of Bear Lake. The Malad correspondent to the *Salt Lake Tribune* suggested in 1888 that with very little effort Bear Lake could be used as a natural reservoir.[52] This was the first written suggestion of such a thing. The correspondent's recommendation dovetailed with a project underway at Bear River Canyon between Cache and Box Elder counties. The project's sponsor, John R. Bothwell, was then engaged in raising capital to construct two canals at the head of Bear River Canyon to convey water to lands in Box Elder County. After the letter in the *Tribune* cued him to the possibilities of using Bear Lake for a reservoir, Bothwell visited the area and determined that such a plan was feasible. As early as 1889 Bothwell began constructing a dam across the outlet of Bear Lake and installing some wooden headgates. A small yet significant amount of work must have been carried out during 1889 because in August that year the *Millennial Star* reported that the level of Bear Lake would soon be raised ten feet. It was further reported that a seven-year-old Scandinavian boy had drowned in the excavated outlet.[53]

Within a few years, Bothwell himself was drowning in a sea of financial troubles. The completion of the Bear River Canal would eventually fall to Bothwell's successors, who assumed charge of the project in the 1890s.[54] Relatively normal precipitation resumed, and the flow of Bear River for the next decade was more than sufficient to fill the canals at Bear River Canyon. The Bear Lake reservoir idea waned.

The idea again surfaced in 1902 as increased demand for electric power prompted the Telluride Power Company of Colorado to explore the possibilities. The development of new technologies was making hydroelectric power more efficient, and Lucien L. Nunn of Telluride Power became interested in using Bear Lake as a storage reservoir. Nunn explained how he became

> impressed with the urgent need for reliable and continuous water suppl[ies] for the development of power in the territory. . . . In this way [I] became familiar with the power possibilities of Bear Lake [and proposed to appropriate] all of the unappropriated waters of Bear River, to be stored in Bear Lake, and released for power, irrigation, and other beneficial purposes."[55]

Nunn mustered whatever help he could to push the project through. However, opposition to the reservoir plans had been mounting in Bear Lake Valley and on the upper reaches of Bear River ever since John R. Bothwell first proposed the idea over a decade before.[56] Knowing the area residents to be predominantly Mormon, Nunn called upon the First Presidency of the LDS church in July 1902 to ask their advice and support for the project.[57] Church leaders, however, took no public stand on the issue.

By 1911, the Telluride company had succeeded in excavating the

Camp Lifton on Bear Lake's North Shore showing barge used to dredge channel to the pumps, ca. 1920. (Special Collections, Utah State University, Logan.)

Dingle Canal, connecting Bear River with Mud Lake. It had also installed headgates at the outlet canal. After storing twenty-five thousand acre-feet of Bear River water in Mud and Bear lakes, the company began releasing water during the fall to feed their power plant at Grace, Idaho. A total of some forty-one thousand acre-feet was released, which lowered the lake level from 5,923.4 feet to 5,921 feet.[58] Thus began, innocently enough, the sometimes erratic decline in the level of Bear Lake.

With the incorporation of Utah Power and Light Company (UP&L) in 1912, the Bear Lake waterworks and the hydroelectric operations of Telluride Power were consolidated. By 1917, UP&L had installed a pumping system on the north shore of Bear Lake, which enabled the company to more precisely control the flow of the Bear River. Two years later, during the height of a drought, the company started the Lifton pumps for the first time.[59]

Prior to the "replumbing" of Bear Lake, it is doubtful that the level of the lake fluctuated drastically from year to year. Certainly periods of low precipitation caused the lake to drop, but once the main body of the lake fell below the natural outlet, only evaporation lowered it further. It is clear that by 1911 the Telluride Power Company had the capability to raise and lower the level of the lake by as much as two feet. But drastic reductions in the lake's level were not possible until the installation of the Lifton pumps.

For the Booth family at Lakota, the Stocks at Fish Haven, and the Niels at Ideal Beach, a stable lake level was a predictable part of their businesses until 1919. By 1929, however, the level of Bear Lake had fallen some fourteen feet, not only because of downstream irrigation but also because of withdrawals by UP&L for hydroelectric purposes. LDS Church Historian Andrew Jenson noted that "the taking out of the water of the lake for industrial and farming purposes [has] practically destroyed the resorts at Fish Haven and Ideal Beach." Jenson maintained that because of the deeper water in the vicinity of Lakota, that resort fared better than did the other two.[60] In 1922 the LDS church began operating a Young Women's Mutual Improvement Association program at Lakota. A lodge was dedicated by LDS Church President Heber J. Grant on 11 July.[61]

In 1929 Bear Lake area residents met at Montpelier to discuss what to do about the disappearing waters of Bear Lake. In truth, there was little that the citizens of Bear Lake Valley could do. Utah Power and Light had effectively established control over the lake and the river, and the legal right to the waters stored in Bear Lake belonged to farmers in Idaho and Utah. By 1927 UP&L was operating five power plants on the river, while storing water behind four different reservoirs in addition to Bear Lake. The roles of Lucien L. Nunn and UP&L, as historian Max R. McCarthy explains,

> were important to the further economic development of the area; both the man and his work deserve the attention of history. But, the principal achievement was the establishment of an integrated system, involving both the generation of electric power and its efficient distribution over considerable distances to high-demand market areas.[62]

Rich County was not one of the "high-demand market areas" and thus did not benefit much from Utah Power and Light's activities. Rich County residents took local initiative to supply the county with electricity.[63] The lake's decline, coupled with depressed farm prices during the 1920s, checked the advance of recreational development. Parallel to the nation's economy, the level of Bear Lake continued to decline during the 1930s. In 1934 the lake reached its lowest recorded level as the worst drought in history gripped the country. While the summer of 1934 scorched the Midwest, creating the Dust Bowl, low water yields, low crop yields, and low prices for farm commodities during the Great Depression also characterized the Intermountain West. Recreational business at Bear Lake would not fully recover for over another decade.

The Great Depression of the 1930s gave way to World War II. The outbreak of war in Europe in 1939 brought new vitality to the economy and rekindled demand for American food and fibre.[64] The economic rebound was dampened, however, by the prospect that the United States would be drawn into the conflict. In December 1941 that fear was realized when the Japanese attacked Pearl Harbor.

Prior to America's entry into World War II, Farrell Spencer of Logan took over operations at Ideal Beach and began restoring the resort to its past glory.[65] Garden City resident Maon Pulley became a partner in the Ideal Beach venture for a short time. Pulley had cut his teeth in the recreational business at Garden City and Fish Haven, leasing Joe Stock's resort during the 1930s. After his marriage to Maurine Jacobsen, the couple began operating the old Frank Early store at Garden City in 1947.[66]

The aftermath of World War II was a period of unique prosperity for Americans. In general, workers enjoyed higher wages during the 1950s which, coupled with the strong post-war economy, gave them greater buying power. Additionally, many government programs that were part of President Roosevelt's New Deal during the Great Depression continued after World War II. These programs gave American workers greater power in dealing with the owners of factories by guaranteeing their right to organize.[67] The farm sector also benefitted from New Deal programs. The subsidies paid to farmers during the Great Depression were continued after the war. These subsidies were designed to balance supply and demand and to ensure that agriculture would not slide back into a post-war depression. The end result was an increase in the standard of living for both wage earners and farmers. As incomes rose, individuals found themselves in possession of more free time. Having more leisure time resulted in Americans looking for new ways to recreate.

In Rich County the increased interest in recreation brought renewed activity to the lake shore. In addition to the buildup of Ideal Beach and Lakota, the west shore of Bear Lake also included Gus Rich's resort and Blue Water Beach.[68] In 1958 the Pulley family opened the Bear Lake Motel.[69] A number of private lakeshore cabins also began appearing in the late 1950s and early 1960s. Val and Karen Siddoway began developing recreational property as early as 1952 at the southeast corner of the lake. They sold their first lot for three hundred dollars; by the late 1970s a lot was selling for more than twenty thousand dollars. Until he realized its recreational potential, Siddoway, a rancher and sheepman, did not attach much value to the land. The burrs along the shore made it difficult to even use the land for "lambing" operations. Siddoway was "quite surprised when residents of Utah's Wasatch Front came and actually offered him money for the 'wasteland.'"[70]

Although Joe Stock had sold his resort at Fish Haven, Idaho, to Reed Budge and Dick Chambers in 1945, he retained ownership of much of the land around the resort. In 1950 Stock ran an ad in the *Paris Post* which read: "Bear Lake is Booming, Here is your chance to secure an ideal lake-view, Drive-in spot. Cabins and Boats—230 foot lake frontage by 264 in length. One of the most ideal lake-view spots. Contact J. P. Stock, Fish Haven."[71]

As recreational activity steadily increased, state and federal agencies began taking an interest in the Rich County region. Their involvement is another legacy of the post-World War II period. In trying to regulate and maintain the quality of life in the post-war United States, government became inextricably linked to the lives of Americans through its involvement in the economy and in the society.

As early as 1941, Rich County state senator Alonzo F. Hopkin proposed that the state take steps to control the waters of the Bear River and Bear Lake. Hopkin introduced legislation into the Utah Senate at the same time that similar legislative proposals were introduced in Wyoming and Idaho.[72] Hopkin's name was synonymous with Rich County politics. He was first elected to the Utah House of Representatives in 1933, and a year later he ran successfully for the state senate. Hopkin served seven consecutive four-year terms in the state senate representing Rich and Morgan counties where he was also involved in family ranching operations. Although elected as a Democrat, he was a community advocate who crossed the line between political parties and was often unanimously elected from the district in which he served. Hopkin made his home on his Woodruff Ranch from 1932 until his death in 1961.[73] Although Hopkin's bill to better control the waters of the Bear River and Bear Lake, died in committee during the 1941 session, it set the stage for similar legislation passed in 1955 which created the Bear River Compact and the Bear River Commission. The joint compact among Utah, Idaho, and Wyoming was signed into law by President Eisenhower in 1958. The purpose of the compact, as outlined in the agreement, was

> to remove the causes of present and future controversy over the distribution and use of the waters of the Bear River; to provide for efficient use of the water for multiple purposes; to permit additional development of the water resources of Bear River; and to promote interstate comity.[74]

Under the original compact, all water in Bear Lake below the level of 5,912.91 feet constituted a reserve for irrigation. Utah Power and Light was prohibited from depleting the lake solely for power generation below that level. They could, however, utilize the water released for irrigation to generate power as it meandered downstream past their hydroelectric plants. Any waters above the level of the irrigation reserve could be used by UP&L to generate electric power.[75]

Fluctuations in the lake's level became a concern to scientists and fish and game officials studying the lake. The earliest scientific enquiry at Bear Lake was done by George Kemmerer, J. F. Bovard, and W. R. Boorman in 1912. They reported large populations of blue-nosed trout and Williamson's whitefish. More recent scientists speculate that the blue-nose was a unique form of Utah cutthroat and that Williamson's whitefish was the mountain whitefish. The Utah cutthroat is thought to be extinct, and the mountain whitefish is now rare in Bear Lake. Three years later, J. O. Snyder collected specimens from Bear Lake and identified three endemic species: the Bonneville whitefish, the Bear Lake whitefish, and the peaknose cisco.[76]

For the next several decades, little research was done at Bear

Placing car bodies in Bear Lake to improve fish habitat. (Utah State
Historical Society, Salt Lake City.)

Lake. The government programs which followed World War II, however, enabled researchers in Utah to again study Bear Lake. In 1951
Congress passed the Dingle-Johnson Bill, which provided federal
funds to states for fisheries research. The Utah State Department of
Fish and Game received the funds, and William F. Sigler, a faculty
member at Utah State Agricultural College (now Utah State
University), set in motion the very first Dingle-Johnson project in the
country.[77] From humble beginnings in a war-surplus trailer set up at
Swan Creek, the project eventually grew into Utah State University's
Bear Lake Laboratory. Sigler, the project's "founding father," wrote in
1962:

> Ideally, research can make us knowledgeable enough to forecast
> the potential uses and most rewarding development patterns for
> this resource [Bear Lake]. If we can realize this ideal quickly
> enough we shall be able to recommend management procedures
> that will maximize its value over time. But the diverse pressures on

Bear Lake are mounting more rapidly all the time, and the pace of our research will have to quicken. . . . The future must build upon the past and we have to understand the lake's beginnings, evolution, and current status before we can effectively plan ahead.[78]

No amount of research or planning could have prepared Rich County and the Idaho portions of Bear Lake Valley for the recreational boom of the 1970s. In the course of a few years, five major developments appeared along the lake. In 1970, Brian Swinton, a thirty-one-year-old Harvard Business School graduate from Salt Lake City, launched the Sweetwater enterprise. Swinton and associates purchased the property of Ideal Beach plus an additional 5,500 acres of "mountain, valley and lake shore properties," which at one time constituted the Hodge's Ranch. Additionally, the Sweetwater resort included

a fully contained sewer and culinary water system sufficient for extensive growth at its location. . . . Six lighted tennis courts, an all-season outdoor swimming pool . . . a 9-hole golf course . . . riding and ranch facilities, condos, individual building lots, trailer sites, cluster housing, time share facilities at Bear Lake, Jackson Hole, San Diego, Park City and now houseboats on Lake Powell.[79]

Winter recreation was also offered at Sweetwater, including snowmobile rentals, cross-country ski trails, sleigh and toboggan runs, and the "delightful pastime of simply enjoying the winter scenery of Bear Lake from windowed and balconied rooms warmed by an open fireplace."[80]

Sweetwater was the first development at Bear Lake and appeared to epitomize the recreational and leisure-time industry. Other developments soon followed. The Nebekers, the pioneering family on Bear Lake's remote east shore, began developing recreational property on a small scale in the early 1970s. By 1977 the great grandchildren of Ira Nebeker—Sidney, David and Mary Winters—had founded Bear Lake Sands. With both a sewer and water system in place, prospects for development appeared good, and within two years all the original lots at Bear Lake Sands were sold.[81] The Nebekers planned to develop an additional ninety lots at South Eden and sixty others in Idaho to the north.[82]

Access was the major drawback to east-shore development. Throughout the "boom" years of the 1970s, the east shore was accessible only by the dirt road around the lake. By 1979 the plans laid by Bear Lake Sands two years before had not materialized; the east shore still appeared much the same as it had when Hyrum and Aquilla Nebeker first established their farms and ranches there in the 1880s. The bulk of the recreational development, including a boat harbor and tennis courts, was sold to Homco Investment Company of Salt Lake City in July 1979.[83] With its easier accessibility, the west shore of Bear Lake was more attractive to developers. Outside of Sweetwater, the largest recreational enterprise in Rich County was that at Swan Creek. In a broad sense, Swan Creek Village was a legacy of Phineas Cook—a legacy which Cook certainly could not have imagined when he settled the area in 1864. But Phineas, like his great-great-grandson Vaughn R. Cook, was an inimitable entrepreneur. It had been the elder Cook's vision and ambition that brought about the establishment of Garden City in 1877. And it was Vaughn Cook, working through the Cook Family Trust, that enabled Swan Creek Village to purchase the property north of Garden City.

Vaughn R. Cook continued as secretary and public-relations director for the company, while Scott W. Bennett acted as president. Newell Dalton became general manager in January 1978.

By May 1978 some 650 acres had been enclosed by a three-rail fence, a sewage system was nearing completion, lots were being sold, and plans to develop the shoreline, complete with a boat harbor, were beginning. According to company president Scott Bennett, Swan Creek Village sought to become "the finest destination resort on Bear Lake."[84]

Each of the several developments on Bear Lake were striving for the same distinction, although each tried to capitalize on its own unique idea. Logan businessman Ted Wilson began developing Bridgerland Estates on a bench above and away from the lakeshore, in order "to give his owners more space, more privacy, beautiful views of the lake and more good mountain living."[85]

Much of the property of Bear Lake West, located just across the Idaho border, was also away from the lakeshore. To compensate for the lack of beachfront, Patrick O'Keefe merged his facilities with those of Dick Harlan at Fish Haven, thereby giving Bear Lake West owners access to the water. Harlan had purchased the Fish Haven resort from Reed Budge and Richard Chambers in 1953. While Harlan was conservative in his development, building only twelve new lakeside condominiums, O'Keefe and associates created a whirl-wind of activity.[86]

In 1970 O'Keefe and his partner Dennis Bullock bought options on four hundred acres of land belonging to Les Kimball of St. Charles. The two then formed a stock company and sold fifty thousand shares at twenty cents each. Bear Lake West planned and constructed a nine-hole golf course, restaurant, and clubhouse. By 1978 Bear Lake West was operating over sixteen hundred acres of recreational homesites.[87]

With most new facilities catering to the needs of their members, the only public access on the west shore was at Bluewater Beach. In the 1970s the state of Utah began negotiations with Wendell Johnson of Laketown to purchase his property on the south shore. Owning one of the largest livestock operations in northern Utah, Johnson had used the brush and groves of cottonwoods on the south shore of the lake as shelter for his cattle during calving season. He initially refused to sell the land. The state threatened to impose eminent domain, and late in 1977 a deal was finally struck.[88] By summer 1978 the area had been designated a state park and christened Rendezvous Beach. Much remained to be done at the park, but over the summer the state installed a chain-link fence, portable toilets, and picnic tables. Further improvements such as the acquisition of culinary water and sewage treatment facilities would have to wait for the generosity of the state legislature.[89]

In December 1978 the state announced that the Division of Parks and Recreation would spend $1.4 million on improvements at Rendezvous Beach. The state awarded a contract to Valley Engineering of Logan, Utah, to study the best alternatives. Priorities included "electric, water and sewage facilities to accommodate 8,000 people," showers and restrooms for fifty campground units, the surfacing of roads, and the construction of maintenance buildings.[90]

The need for improved facilities was obvious during the park's first season. More than eighty thousand people visited the park that year, and the "dusty roads, make-shift chemical toilets and minimum amount of culinary water" were a drawback. The state made arrangements the following year to utilize the water and sewage facilities of neighboring South Shore Development Company east of the state park. By 1980 most of the proposed improvements had been made at a cost of more than one million dollars.[91]

Rendezvous Beach State Park complemented the already existing Bear Lake Marina located one and a half miles north of Garden City. The state constructed the marina in 1965–66. The largest on Bear Lake, the marina could accommodate all sizes of boats, and, as a result, the lake witnessed a proliferation of larger sailboats and cabin cruisers. The lake's level was nearly full during the marina's first year of operation. Lake levels remained fairly constant over the next decade with only brief droughts occurring. High lake levels enabled boaters and recreationists to take full advantage of the resources offered at the state marina. Beginning in 1986, however, the level of Bear Lake began dropping, and by 1990 low water had left the Bear Lake Marina high and dry. By 1991 Bob Murray, co-chairman of the Citizens for the Bear Lake Marina, estimated that marina usage had declined by at least sixty-five percent.[92] Smarting under the economic impact of this decline, citizen groups began championing the idea of extending and expanding the state marina in order to accommodate the sometimes erratic water levels. In 1994 the state legislature appropriated over 2.5 million dollars for that purpose. The state marina now will remain usable to a lake elevation of 5,903 ft, the lake's lowest historic level.

With the immense snowpacks of the early 1980s, it was hard to imagine that the Bear Lake Valley drainage system would again experience drought. In 1980, with the high lake levels, it appeared that Bear Lake Valley was on the verge of becoming a recreational mecca. The early successes of Sweetwater, Bear Lake West, and other developments brought new developers to the area. In 1979 *Bear Lake Magazine* editorialized:

> Garden City may become one of the largest cities in northern
> Utah. Developers indicate increasing interest in land sales as the
> nation seems to be in the throes of uncontrollable inflation and a

Young recreationists on Bear Lake's west shore, ca. 1910. (Courtesy Scott Christiansen.)

steady growing energy crunch encourages residents, particularly those within a 200-mile radius, to vacation closer to home. [93]

With snowmobiling, cross-country skiing, and plans to build a downhill ski resort, developers began comparing the potential of Bear Lake to that of Lake Tahoe, Nevada. In the minds of many, it was only a matter of time before the recreational industry, fueled by Wasatch Front investment capital, transformed Bear Lake Valley into an ultramodern, leisure playground. Many in Bear Lake supported the idea; activity at Sweetwater and Bear Lake West increased the tax base significantly. Furthermore, for some who had struggled to make a living at agriculture for years, the recreational land boom was the proverbial gold at the end of the rainbow.

Not everyone was ecstatic over the development at Bear Lake, however. Scientists such as Dr. John M. Neuhold of Utah State University expressed concern over the ecological balance of the Bear Lake watershed.[94] For others, like Wendell Johnson, the concern was over the disruption of a traditional way of life. As recreational development advanced, both concerns were justified. Only community interaction and planning could forestall either an ecological disaster or a cultural clash.

The responsibility for dealing with these problems fell to the Bear Lake Commission, "a bi-state, bi-county organization . . . directed by local authorities." The Bear Lake Regional Commission came into being because of increased recreational land development in the late 1960s at Sweetwater and Bear Lake West. "This . . . brought deep concerns to local officials and citizens, thus sparking support" for the organization. Created in 1973, the commission "was formed to assist the counties in addressing problems related to impacts of growth in the two counties and specifically around Bear Lake."[95] The commission consisted of "one county commissioner from each county; one representative from each incorporated city with over 500 population in each county; and one representative of all other incorporated municipalities in the county."[96] The preservation of traditional rural values, including ranching and livestock operations, and cautious development of recreational resources were two of the commission's goals and objectives. The commission also mandated that adequate sewage and culinary water systems precede the development of recreational subdivisions. As both agriculture and recreation depended upon water, the commission also sought "to protect and expand the public water resources in the county."[97] This included Bear Lake.

Under the terms of the original compact, state legislatures of the three states involved could amend the Bear River Compact every twenty years. The Bear River Commission, the organization created as part of the 1958 agreement, approved revisions in December 1978. The state legislatures of Wyoming, Utah, and Idaho granted their approval in 1979. Under the new set of revisions, upper Bear River Valley was allowed to increase its storage right to 74,500 acre-feet.[98] As a result, the level of Bear Lake was lowered from approximately 5,914 ft, the irrigation reserve, to 5,911 ft. The additional storage for the irrigation reserve was to be held in dams above Bear Lake rather than in Bear Lake itself.[99] The revised compact would deplete Bear Lake by as much as one foot when the level of the lake was high at the beginning of the irrigation season and even more when the level of the lake was low.[100]

An erratic lake level was the main concern of developers; but the very fact that Bear Lake was being used as a reservoir at all drew the criticism of scientists. The link between Bear River and the lake through the Dingle Canal contributed a substantial amount of pollution to Bear Lake. Scientific enquiry showed that the lake was undergoing eutrophication, a process that increased organic substances and lowered oxygen levels. Scientists warned that this process "may result in the loss of several if not all of the endemic species [in Bear Lake.]"[101] Rather than opposing additional storage rights on the upper Bear River, scientists argued for even more upstream storage in order to completely bypass the use of Bear Lake as a reservoir.

In response to this, Sherman P. Lloyd, former Utah congressman and editor of *Bear Lake Magazine,* drafted an amendment to the compact. The amendment was introduced at a meeting held in Logan, Utah, in 1979, and read:

> In the distribution of the waters of the Bear River and the use of Bear Lake as the principal storage reservoir, the Bear River Compact Commission shall recognize the doctrine of multiple use; that Bear Lake is a natural lake, not directly fed by the Bear River; that Bear Lake has rare environmental and recreational qualities essential to the quality of life of past, present and future generations; that as a statement of policy, the Commission shall recognize that Bear Lake is entitled to protection against damage to its essential integrity which would result from excessive, wasteful or improper utilization of its natural waters.[102]

Not unexpectedly, the amendment was turned down by the commission. Convincing irrigators, Utah Power and Light, and the Bear River Commission that environmental issues needed to be addressed at Bear Lake was going to be a difficult.[103] Furthermore, the legal right to the waters of Bear Lake belonged to the historical appropriators. Court decisions appropriating the waters of Bear River and classifying Bear Lake as a reservoir dated back to 1922.[104] Bear Lake, however, had originally been set aside as an irrigation reservoir by director of the U.S. Geological Survey Major John W. Powell in 1889. Congress later repealed the act which had authorized Powell to withdraw potential reservoir sites from public entry because of its unpopularity with powerful western land speculators. It seems the process of surveying the western lands moved too slowly for those champions of rapid settlement. The withdrawn acres around Bear Lake were nevertheless restored in 1890. Its obviousness as a natural irrigation reservoir eventually resulted in Bear Lake's being used for that purpose. It was the first reservoir site set aside in the West by Powell.[105]

The use of Bear Lake as a reservoir did compromise its ecology. But it was not just the inflow of the Bear River and the outflow from the Lifton pumps which upset the ecology of Bear Lake. The continued settlement and development of Bear Lake Valley over the course of the previous hundred years, particularly the recent expanse of development in the 1970s, also had an impact. Citing the often made comparison between Bear Lake and Lake Tahoe, John M. Neuhold noted that the latter's population was nearly two hundred thousand people, and that realtors estimated "Bear Lake has a development potential of 21,000 recreational homesites." Allowing for five people per home, and additional service-industry people, Neuhold estimated that Bear Lake Valley could also see a population of nearly two hundred thousand.[106]

Such a scenario never materialized, however. The general economic downturn and oil shortage which was supposed to stimulate the recreational industry at Bear Lake had the reverse effect. By 1980 both the local and the national economies entered an economic recession which sent land values plummeting and slowed the pace of investment in recreational property. The situation in Bear Lake Valley was compounded in September 1981 when Bear Lake West declared bankruptcy.

Controversy had been building regarding the corporation throughout the summer. Bear Lake County, Idaho, Sheriff Larry Hardin investigated complaints against Bear Lake West earlier in April and reported that according to Idaho law the company was not operating illegally. Hardin mentioned, however, that some of those associated with the company had prior criminal records dealing with

land fraud in Arizona. A total of six formal complaints were registered against Bear Lake West in April.[107] By September, major creditors had filed claims against the company totaling $4.9 million.[108]

In addition to the impact felt directly on creditors and on those
who had purchased "undivided interest"[109] in the company, the controversy surrounding Bear Lake West's bankruptcy cast a shadow of
suspicion on the Bear Lake real estate business in general. The majority of resorts and realtors, however, continued operating in a busi-
nesslike manner. Recreational development slowed, however, and
Bear Lake did not become another Tahoe. Except for seasonal
extremes, the permanent population of Garden City and Laketown
remained about what it had been.

During the late 1970s and early 1980s, other development efforts
began affecting Rich County. The energy shortage of the 1970s
encouraged oil companies to begin searching for domestic oil supplies. The overthrust belt, extending from southwestern Wyoming
through the Bear River and Bear Lake valleys into southeastern Idaho
became a major area for exploration and development. Beginning at
Evanston, Wyoming, in the early 1970s, the growth associated with
the oil "boom" soon spread north into the Utah portion of the Bear
River Valley as drilling rigs began appearing in the vicinity of
Woodruff and in the hills east of Laketown.

ENDNOTES

1. Warren Angus Ferris, *Life in the Rocky Mountains, 1830–1835* (Salt
Lake City: Rocky Mountain Book Shop, 1940), 41.

2. F. V. Hayden, *Preliminary Report of the United States Geological
Survey of Montana and Portions of Adjacent Territories* (Washington, D.C.:
Government Printing Office, 1872), 156.

3. "Report of a Party of Observation, Consisting of Eleven Men, Under
Command of M. Monroe. Started from Ogden City Aug. [18]57." Records
of the State Territorial Militias, microfilm, Special Collections and Archives,
Utah State University, Logan.

4. Mildred H. Thomson, *Rich Memories: Some of the Happenings in Rich
County from 1863 to 1960* (Salt Lake City: Daughters of Utah Pioneers,
1961), 22.

5. Julian H. Steward, *Basin-Plateau Aboriginal Sociopolitical Groups,*

Smithsonian Institution Bureau of American Ethnology Bulletin 120 (Washington, D.C.: Government Printing Office, 1938), 237.

6. Ezra J. Poulsen, *Joseph C. Rich: Versatile Pioneer on the Mormon Frontier* (Salt Lake City: Granite Publishing Co., 1958), 162. Quoted in *Bear Lake Magazine* 3 (December 1979): 20.

7. Thomson, *Rich Memories,* 288.

8. Ibid., 140.

9. Steven L. Thomson, Jane D. Digerness, and Mar Jean S. Thomson, *Randolph—A Look Back* (n.p., 1981), 149–50.

10. *Bear Lake Magazine* 3 (June 1979): 10.

11. Reed Eborn, interview with Ray Lamborn, "Growing up in Laketown," 3 May 1975, 28.

12. Ibid. 27.

13. Lamborn notes that "all the upstairs in Bishop Robinson's store was a dance hall and a stage, so it was a fairly nice place. Of course, he didn't want to give that up . . . the town's people paid him a little you see. If he had a dance, he got a little money out of it." See Eborn, interview with Ray Lamborn, 27.

14. Laketown Ward Manuscript History, 1929, Historical Department of the LDS Church, Salt Lake City, Utah, hereafter referred to as LTMH.

15. Eborn, interview with Ray Lamborn, 27.

16. Thomson, *Rich Memories,* 38.

17. Ibid., 87.

18. Ibid.

19. Kate B. Carter, ed., "Dancing—A Pioneer Recreation," Daughters of Utah Pioneers, Lesson for April 1953 (Salt Lake City: Daughters of Utah Pioneers, 1953), 346.

20. Nels Anderson, "Dixie, a Mormon Frontier," mss. quoted in Edward J. Allen, *The Second United Order Among the Mormons* (New York: Columbia University Press, 1936), 24.

21. Carter, "Dancing—A Pioneer Recreation," 346.

22. Ibid.

23. Poulsen, *Joseph C. Rich,* 245–46.

24. Earl F. Passey, "An Account of the Settlement and Development of Montpelier, Idaho," Joel E. Ricks Seminar Paper, Utah State University, 1936, 41–42. Passey adds that the population of Montpelier grew dramatically after the coming of the railroad. In 1880 the population was 400. By 1897 the population stood at two thousand.

25. *Journal History of the Church of Jesus Christ of Latter-day Saints,*

manuscript, Department of Special Collections and Archives, Merrill Library, Utah State University, Logan, Utah (hereafter referred to as JH), 17 March 1883, 6.

26. *Round Up* (Randolph, Utah), 23 July 1897. Quoted in GCMH, 1897.

27. Poulsen, *Joseph C. Rich,* 299.

28. Ibid., 215. Quoted in *Bear Lake Magazine* 3 (1 December 1979): 22.

29. See Rich's communications to the *Deseret News* in Appendix D.

30. Fife, "The Bear Lake Monsters," 99–106. See also, A. J. Simmonds, "Utah's Mountain Lake Monsters," *True Frontier* 1 (January 1969): 37. For a later eyewitness account see *Logan Republican,* 18 September 1907, 1.

31. Rich evidentally tumbled to the idea of a sailboat after attending a family reunion at Cape Cod, Massachusetts. He "lost his shirt in the effort." See *Bear Lake Magazine* 3 (1 December 1979): 22.

32. Poulsen, *Joseph C. Rich,* 302. Quoted in *Bear Lake Magazine* 3 (1 December 1979): 22.

33. JH, 23 March 1894, 7.

34. JH, 20 August 1894, 7. The boat was reported to accommodate fifty passengers.

35. *Bear Lake Magazine* 3 (1 December 1979): 22.

36. Stock and Nathaniel Morris Hodges also may have built paddle boats about this time. Jesse Cottle, a resident of Fish Haven, recalled piloting a boat for Stock. See *Bear Lake Magazine* 3 (15 September 1979): 9.

37. *Bear Lake Magazine* 2 (15 August 1978): 13.

38. Eborn, interview with Ray Lamborn, 16.

39. Thomson, *Rich Memories,* 155.

40. Scott G. Kenney, ed., *Wilford Woodruff's Journal 1833–1898, Typescript* 10 vols. (Midvale, Ut: Signature Books, 1983–1991), 16.

41. *Bear Lake Magazine* 3 (1 December 1979): 22.

42. *Round Up,* 23 July 1897. Quoted in RMH, 1897.

43. Minutes of the Probate Court, County Book A, County Clerk's Office, Rich County Courthouse, Randolph, Utah, 5 March 1883.

44. County Book A, 5 March 1866.

45. County Book A, 14 February 1898.

46. Minutes of the County Commission, Book A, County Clerk's Office, Rich County Courthouse, Randolph, Utah, 8 November 1920.

47. *Bear Lake Magazine* 3 (1 December 1979): 22.

48. Maleta Robinson, interview with Jessie L. Cottle, 18 May 1975, 12–13.

49. Eborn, interview with Ray Lamborn, 32. Lamborn stated: "I was afraid of the girls, but Vernon Robinson wanted to go swimming so I made a date with my wife to be, to go to Lakota for swimming. They had a heated swimming pool there at Lakota."

50. Thomson, *Rich Memories,* 72.

51. See chapter 1.

52. *Report of the Special Committee of the United States Senate on the Irrigation and Reclamation of Arid Lands, the Great Basin Region and California: Utah, Nevada, California and Arizona,* 2 vols. (Washington, D.C.: Government Printing Office, 1890), 2:45.

53. JH, 12 August 1889, 12.

54. Bothwell fell into financial trouble during the early 1890s. The company formed through his promotion eventually became the property of William Garland who had been the contractor for the canals. Garland bought the company for $125,000. His business, however, also failed, and he sold the company to Salt Lake businessmen for $80,000. In 1900 the Bear River and Bear Lake Water Works was purchased by the Utah-Idaho Sugar Company for $450,000. The sugar company retained ownership of the canals and water rights, erecting a new dam in Bear River Canyon engineered by J. C. Wheelon. The sugar company also built and operated a hydroelectric plant in Bear River Canyon. In 1927 the entire operation was sold to Utah Power and Light Company which erected the present Cutler Dam downstream from the original canals. The original canals were inundated by Cutler Dam. Nonetheless, new points of diversion were given to the canals, and UP&L contracted with the irrigators to provide water during the summer season. Since 1927 some of this water has been storage water from Bear Lake. See Gary Welling, *Fielding: The People and the Events That Affected Their Lives,* (n.p., n.d.), 75–76.

55. Max R. McCarthy, *The Last Chance Canal Company* (Provo, Utah: Brigham Young University, 1987), 55.

56. *Report of the Special Committee,* 2: 46.

57. JH, 11 July 1902.

58. McCarthy, *The Last Chance Canal Company,* 61.

59. JH, 26 June 1919.

60. GCMH, 1929.

61. JH, 11 July 1922.

62. McCarthy, *The Last Chance Canal Company,* 67.

63. Permits were granted to generate hydroelectric power on Swan Creek as early as 1910. The county commission authorized the creation of the Swan Creek Electric Company in 1912. Electric power extended from

Garden City to Laketown in 1913, and in 1917 the lines were run up Laketown Canyon (Mill Canyon), electrifying Randolph. See Thomson, *Randolph—A Look Back*, 112.

The early directors and other individuals involved in the company included Edward Pugmire, Ole Transtrum, Ike Smith, George Robinson, George I. Barker, and John Weston. During the 1930s electric power from the Swan Creek Company was extended to Woodruff. The company provided electric service through the early 1960s until its absorption by Utah Power and Light Company. See Thomson, *Rich Memories*, 144, and *Paris Post* (Paris, Idaho), 6 September 1962.

64. Although the neutrality acts passed by Congress during the 1920s and 1930s essentially prohibited the United States from trading with countries where a state of war existed, the Roosevelt administration by 1940 had effectively sidestepped these laws with the lend-lease program which allowed the United States to lend or lease materials to Great Britain rather than sell them. Although the act was primarily geared towards arms and ammunition, it also extended to farm commodities. By 1940 the effects of lend-lease had helped elevate the nation's economy out of a decade of economic depression.

65. Thomson, *Rich Memories*, 72.

66. A decade later the Pulleys began construction of their own resort at Garden City, opening the Bear Lake Motel in 1958. See *Bear Lake Magazine* 3 (15 July 1979): 2.

67. Section 7A of the National Industrial Recovery Act of 1933 gave workers the right to organize into unions. It also established minimum wages for workers.

68. Agustavus Rich began operating a resort south of Ideal Beach during the late 1930s. As an officer in the military, Rich served in both world wars. Although his wife Marguerite may have carried on in his absence, it is unlikely that during the years 1941–1945 much activity took place at the resort. After World War II, Gus Rich's operation became one of the premier resorts on the west shore. See *Ogden Standard-Examiner*, 14 November, 1977, 8B.

Bluewater Beach had been owned and operated by the Naisbitt family since at least the 1930s. Preston C. Kimball purchased the property and resort in 1965. In January 1978 Kimball sold eleven acres and four hundred feet of lakeshore to Craig W. Meacham, Allan D. Mecham, and Robert Fillmore of Salt Lake City. See *Bear Lake Magazine* 1 (15 March, 1978): 10.

69. *Bear Lake Magazine* 3 (15 July 1979): 11.

70. Ibid. 3 (15 August 1979): 12.

71. *Paris Post* (Paris, Idaho), 22 June 1950.

72. *Senate Journal, Twenty-Fourth Session of the Legislature of the State of Utah* (Salt Lake City: The Seagull Press, 1941), 321. Senate Bill number 236, introduced by Hopkin, was titled: "An act providing for the organization of the upper Bear River Water Users Committee for the purpose of meeting with committees of the states of Idaho and Wyoming to divide and distribute the waters of the upper Bear River, pending the execution of a compact between said states. . . ." It was sent through the Senate Sifting Committee which killed the bill in March 1941.

73. *Salt Lake Tribune,* 16 December 1961, 1.

74. *Bear River Compact and By-laws of the Bear River Commission: Entered Into By the States of Idaho, Utah and Wyoming* (Salt Lake City, Bear River Commission, 4 February 1955), 1.

75. *Bear River Compact and By-laws,* 7.

76. William J. McConnell, William J. Clark, and William F. Sigler, *Bear Lake: Its Fish and Fishing* (Salt Lake City: Utah State Department of Fish and Game, 1957), 20.

Although Snyder supposed the whitefish to be endemic, they may have been a mixture of species. Mormon pioneers transplanted an eastern variety of whitefish into Bear Lake in 1896. Earlier in 1871, Bear Lakers experimented with the transplanting of shad, an experiment obviously not successful. See JH, 17 March 1896, 12.

This fact was apparently unknown to Snyder. William Sigler was as well apparently unaware of these pioneering attempts at propagation. See William F. Sigler, "Improving Bear Lake Fishing Forty Years Ago and Now," *Bear Lake Magazine* 3 (1 December 1979), 7.

77. John M. Neuhold, "The Bear Lake Laboratory: Science, Education and Community Resource," *Bear Lake Magazine* 3 (1 December 1979): 9.

78. William F. Sigler, *Bear Lake and Its Future* (Logan: Utah State University Faculty Association, 1962), 3.

79. *Bear Lake Magazine* 1 (15 March 1978): 9.

80. Ibid.

81. *Bear Lake Magazine,* 3 (August 1979): 5.

82. *Bear Lake Magazine* 1 (1 June 1977): 1.

83. Ibid. 3 (July 1979): 3, 5. The company purchased 265 acres on the east shore, including "the new marina to accommodate 300 slips and a full mile of beach front." The company's holdings were being overseen by Robert L. Mendenhall, who noted that eventually the company planned to offer eight hundred homesites for sale.

84. *Bear Lake Magazine* 1 (15 May 1978): 12.

85. Ibid. 1 (1 June 1977): 2.

86. Ibid. The *Paris Post* ran a story in 1951 detailing a transaction between Budge and Chambers and Frank Devenish. The *Post* claimed that Devenish had purchased the Fish Haven Resort. Perhaps the deal was never consummated and Budge and Chambers retained ownership until Harlan bought it in 1953. See *Paris Post,* 23 August 1951.

87. *Bear Lake Magazine* 2 (15 June 1978): 13.

88. For information on acquisition of the property see *Bear Lake Magazine* 1 (1 December 1977): 3. For information on Wendell Johnson's use of the land see *Bear Lake Magazine* 1 (15 May 1978): 15.

89. *Bear Lake Magazine* 2 (15 June 1978): 3.

90. Ibid. 2 (15 December 1978): 15.

91. Ibid. 3 (15 June 1979): 5.

92. Citizens for the Bear Lake Marina, "A Proposal for the Expansion of the State Park Marina at Bear Lake," 8 December 1992.

93. *Bear Lake Magazine* 3 (May 1979): 7.

94. Ibid. 4 (August 1980): 11.

95. *Rich County Land Use Guide* (Bear Lake Regional Commission, 1979), 13.

96. Ibid.

97. Ibid., 21–23. The goals and objectives of the Commission as stated in their report included:

1– The agricultural industry, particularly livestock ranching is extremely important to the economic welfare of Rich County's residents. Every effort should be made to protect and insure its continuance. Removing land from agricultural use through approving premature subdivision should be approved only where the prospects for development are high and not where land is being subdivided for speculation.

2– Outdoor recreation should be recognized as one of the county's greatest economic assets. Increasing energy costs and shortages of fossil fuels make Bear Lake and Rich County vastly more important due to the growing emphasis on regionalized recreation and tourism. Future planning must include considerations for the improvement and expanded development of existing local, state and federal recreational areas.

3– Areas of potential flooding in the county should be determined and development within these areas should be restricted.

4– Steps should be taken to protect and expand the public water resources in the county. This includes Bear Lake as well as the streams and rivers which are used for irrigation and recreational purposes. Special attention should be devoted to protecting culinary water sources. Additional culinary water sources should be developed to provide for future population increases due to oil and gas drilling and associated developments.

5– Sewerage facilities should be adequate in new subdivisions. In areas where no central sewage systems are available, other methods of sewage disposal must be approved by the Utah State Board of Health. Sewage disposal areas or dump stations should be developed at strategic locations along the county's highways for use b[y] recreational vehicle units. (21–23)

98. An acre-foot of water is sufficient to cover an acre of land to a depth of one foot.

99. *Bear Lake Magazine* 4 (25 May 1980): 15.

100. Wallace N. Jibson of the U.S. Geological Survey reported "that 70,000 acre feet of upstream storage would reduce the elevation of Bear Lake about one foot at elevation 5,919 and more [than that] amount as the elevation goes down in dry years." See *Bear Lake Magazine* 2 (15 August 1978): 13.

101. Vincent Lamarra, Chuck Liff, and John Carter, *Hydrology of Bear Lake Basin and Its Impact on the Trophic State of Bear Lake, Utah-Idaho,* excerpt quoted in pamphlet "Bear Lake," Montpelier, ID: Love Bear Lake, n.d.).

102. "The Bear Lake Letter," *Bear Lake Magazine,* 3 (15 January 1979).

103. The attempt to add an environmental clause to the Bear River Compact revision was the swan song of Sherman P. Lloyd. Lloyd died of cancer in December 1979. According to the Friends of Bear Lake, an organization with which Lloyd was affiliated: "Sherm was many things to many people. He served for 22 years as Secretary Counsel for the Utah Retail Grocers Association. He was a Congressman, State Senator, a Vice President of a Savings and Loan, a Lecturer at the University of Utah and USU. . . . In his government connected endeavors, he worked with the Department of Commerce, the U.S. Information Agency, was Chairman of the Utah Legislative Council dealing with criminal justice, and the Utah Council on Higher Education. As a U.S. Congressman, he served on many committees . . . most of all, Sherm was indeed a 'Friend of Bear Lake'. He loved the scenery, he loved the sheer beauty of the area, and all to do with the Bear Lake Valley and it's [sic] people." See "The Bear Lake Letter," *Bear Lake Magazine* 4 (19 April 1980).

104. McCarty, *The Last Chance Canal Company,* 69–90.

105. Wallace Stegner, *Beyond the Hundredth Meridian* (Cambridge, MA.: Riverside Press, 1962), 309.

106. *Bear Lake Magazine* 4 (August 1980): 11.

107. *News-Examiner* (Montpelier, Idaho), 23 April 1981, 1.

108. Ibid., 3 September 1981, A-3.

109. "Undivided interests" were common forms of real estate transactions in the recreational properties. An individual bought a small portion of the whole and was then deeded a part of the whole as a shareholder. See *The News-Examiner,* 23 April 1981, 1.

5

"Like A Slow-Moving but Unstoppable Glacier"

NATURAL RESOURCES IN THE BEAR RIVER AND BEAR LAKE VALLEYS

The oil boom that came north from Uinta County, Wyoming, into the Bear River and Bear Lake valleys during the 1970s was a continuation of a western tradition that started in the California gold fields of 1849. The discovery of gold near Sutter's Fort on the American River brought an overland stampede of eighty thousand would-be miners into California between 1849 and 1851. The California gold rush was short lived, but in the space of two years it helped transform the Mormon settlement at Salt Lake City from failure to success and enabled Brigham Young to consider plans for expansion. The gold rush also brought a significant increase in area population as merchants and businessmen, many of them non-Mormons, moved to the "cross-roads of the West" to take advantage of the overland trade. By 1851, however, the rush was practically finished. Emigrants continued to pass through Salt Lake City just as they continued to follow the meanderings of the Bear River to Fort Hall and on into Oregon, but these emigrants were largely farming families heading for permanent settlements. The search for precious metals, however, remained an enduring part of western history and both directly and indirectly affected Rich County and the rest of Utah throughout the remainder of the nineteenth century.

During the early years of settlement, Utahns were too preoccupied with establishing communities to prospect for gold themselves. Their chief interest was not in developing the region's natural resources for immediate profits but in utilizing those resources for the improvement of the settlements. Therefore, early Mormons in Salt Lake Valley, and later in the Bear Lake and Bear River valleys, harvested the mountain timber, harnessed streams and rivers to power sawmills and gristmills, and used local mineral resources in the construction of bricks and adobe. Furthermore, Mormon leaders discouraged prospecting for precious metals.[1] They nonetheless encouraged the development of more immediately useful minerals such as coal and iron.[2] Exploring parties into the remote parts of the territory were ever on the lookout for water resources, building materials, or outcroppings of other useful minerals. In his reconnaissance of Bear Lake Valley in 1861, Colonel James H. Martineau noted "a large deposit of very rich iron ore" around the summit of Monte Cristo. The ore assayed at seventy percent.[3]

Exploration parties were sent to many areas both north and south in the vicinity of Salt Lake City. Reconnaissance parties sent to observe Johnston's Army in 1857 also took note of natural resources. An observation party sent north from Weber County noted the heavy stands of "good timber" in Little Bear River Canyon. As the party traveled north towards Bear Lake Valley they noted watercourses, timber, and vegetation. Descending into the valley from the west side, the group traveled north up the east side of the lake past "a mountain of sandstone—suitable for grind stones."[4] These stones would later be used by Mormon settlers to construct the Paris LDS Tabernacle and the Laketown chapel.

A year before settlement proceeded in Bear Lake Valley, President Abraham Lincoln dispatched a company of California Volunteers under the command of Colonel Patrick E. Connor to Utah. Connor's main assignment was to guard the overland mail route against Indian attacks, but after his annihilation of the Western Shoshoni at the Bear River in January 1863, Connor had little trouble with Indian depredation. Thereafter, a good deal of his time was spent "watch-dogging" the Mormons. As discussed in chapter two, Connor was interested in attracting non-Mormon settlers to Utah in order to supplant the Mormon majority. One way to accomplish this goal would be to start a gold rush within the territory's boundaries. After word reached Connor in September 1863 of a mineral discovery in Bingham Canyon, he began promoting the territory's mineral resources. He did this by first helping the discoverer, George Ogilvie, file on the claim, and second through the publication of the *Union Vedette,* a newspaper devoted to publicizing the territory's mineral wealth.[5]

Brigham Young was concerned about the repercussions of a possible gold rush. Yet he feared not so much the invasion of non-Mormons into the area; his fear was that Mormon settlers would join in the frenzy. At the church's general conference in 1863 he remarked:

> On the bare report that gold was discovered over in these West Mountains, men left their thrashing machines, and their horses at large to eat up and trample down and destroy the precious bounties of the earth. They at once sacrificed all at the glittering shrine of this popular idol, declaring they were now going to be rich, and would raise wheat no more. Should this feeling become universal on the discovery of gold mines in our immediate vicinity, nakedness, starvation, utter destitution and annihilation would be the inevitable lot of this people.[6]

Of perhaps equal concern for Brigham Young were Indian problems caused by the gold rush. Under the terms of the 1863 Treaty with the Shoshoni, the entire area of the Wind River Valley was set aside for the Indians' use.[7] The trespassing of miners in the area created ill feelings between the miners and Chief Washakie's people. Occurring as it did in 1867 and 1868, the gold rush at South Pass City may have exacerbated the tensions between the Bear Lake settlers and Washakie during the confrontation at Laketown. The gold rush raised concerns not only in Salt Lake City and Rich County but also in the nation's capital. Utah Superintendent for Indian Affairs J. H. Head expressed to his superiors the urgency of setting aside the Wind River Reservation because of the influx of miners. Noting how the Shoshoni were friendly towards the whites, Head cautioned that "should their favorite & ancestral hunting ground be taken from them I cannot but be apprehensive that disturbances would insue."[8] As Head anticipated, the rush of miners into the area did decrease the size of the Indian claim. The Wind River Reservation, formulated at Fort Bridger in 1868, included far less land than originally had been allowed by the earlier 1863 treaty. This change was precipitated by the claims of settlers and miners during the gold rush. Despite this, the Shoshoni remained friendly.[9] Few problems developed within Utah Territory, particularly in the north, after the Bear River Massacre. As discussed earlier, the last tense situation between Indians and whites recorded in northern Utah occurred in 1870 at Bear Lake.

Still, the activities of miners were a concern for Utah settlers and the leaders of the Mormon church. On the heels of the discovery of gold at South Pass City came another strike in 1870 in southeastern Idaho only sixty miles from Bear Lake Valley. With that strike at Caribou Mountain, north of the Mormon settlement at Soda Springs, mining camps appeared to surround the Mormon agricultural settlements. Jesse "Cariboo Jack" Fairchilds, Frank McCoy, and F. S. Babcock are commonly credited with finding the placer gold at Caribou Mountain.[10] The frequency of gold strikes in the vicinity of Mormon settlements undoubtedly caused church leaders to wonder where the next strike might occur and to ask the question: if it happened at Bear Lake or in Bear River Valley, would the Mormons be numerous enough to maintain themselves as a separate settlement? Furthermore, would Mormon settlers join in the rush as Brigham Young feared? The strike at Caribou caused tremendous excitement throughout Utah. Many of the settlers at Paris, Idaho, tried their luck there.[11] The Corinne newspaper, the *Daily Utah Reporter,* noted on 12 September:

> It is not yet a week since the discovery of the rich gold diggings in Eastern Idaho became known through the towns and settlements along the roads between here and Montana. Thomas Winsett informs us that he was at Malad City when the account reached that place, and in an hour afterward there were parties of from two to ten on their way to the gold fields, and all the way down to Corinne he met people going up to try their fortunes.[12]

Since the completion of the transcontinental railroad in 1869,

Corinne had become the major starting point for freight being shipped north to Montana. Corinne also supplied the mines at Caribou. The Montana Trail had been used extensively (and profitably) by Utahns since at least 1862 to provide goods to the Montana miners.[13] Not until 1884 did a north/south railroad supplant the Montana Trail.

Railroads brought new possibilities to the mining industry of the West with their ability to transport large quantities of ore. The mining of coal reserves in Bear River Valley was made possible by their close proximity to Evanston, Wyoming, and the Union Pacific line. The mines at Almy, Wyoming, provided employment for many of the early settlers at Randolph and Woodruff. Some of the earliest miners at Almy also had direct ties to Woodruff. Joseph Fife is included in some histories as being among the initial settlers at Woodruff.[14] In 1862 Fife, his family, and the families of David and Thomas Johnson immigrated to Utah. They later moved to the Bear River Valley and became active in the mining industry. In 1872 Fife opened his own mine.[15]

James Bown, a Mormon convert from England, served as bishop of the Almy Ward upon its organization within Bear Lake Stake in 1873. Bown also rose to prominence at the Almy mines, being made foreman in 1885 at mine number three. He later became superintendent for the Union Pacific mines in 1892. After the mines' closure around 1900, Bown retired to a ranch in the Bear River Valley.[16]

Until the organization of Wyoming Territory in 1868, the coal reserves in the Bear River Valley remained part of Green River County, Utah. It was no secret that the area held abundant mineral resources. The Stansbury expedition of 1852 had designated the area of Bear River Valley as the western edge of the "Great Coal Basin."[17] It was doubtless no accident that the lines of the Union Pacific Railroad skirted these coal reserves from present-day Sweetwater County, Wyoming, to Evanston. As the railroad lines pushed west past Evanston in 1868, Congress passed the organic bill creating the Territory of Wyoming on 25 July. Much of the coal reserve was thereafter a part of Wyoming.

The exact extent of the coal deposits was unknown in 1868. But shortly after the Union Pacific line pushed past Evanston in that year,

Lime kiln probably located in Laketown Canyon. (Special Collections and Archives, Utah State University, Logan.)

two former engineers from the company located claims three miles from the tracks.[18] Although there was little coal mining in the Utah portion of the Bear River Valley, the completion of the transcontinental railroad line made more urgent the necessity of settling that portion of the Bear River Valley left to Utah.

Mormons sought to hold the country by establishing permanent farmsteads rather than by filing mining claims. The permanence of Randolph and Woodruff as well as the Bear Lake settlements depended upon a well-entrenched population. And such a population required the construction of permanent buildings which in turn required the use of the area's natural resources. Samuel Brough, who settled in Randolph in 1871, had been a brick mason in England before emigration. Bringing this knowledge with him, Brough constructed pugmills and began mixing the mud with which to make bricks. He also operated a lime-kiln to process lime rock into plaster and whitewash. The rock was hauled from the mountains ten miles west of Randolph. Brough augmented his brick and lime business with a small ranch and by working the winter months at the Almy mines.[19]

Many Randolph homes were constructed from Brough's bricks. Most, however, were frame structures made of lumber hauled from the mountains. The earliest structures were built of hand-hewn logs, but two sawmills were in operation at Randolph as early as 1875. Writing to the *Deseret News* William Howard reported, "We have got two of the old fashioned upright saw mills, one owned by J. F. Hutchinson, and the other by Howard and Harper."[20] Howard and Harper later constructed a steam-powered mill on Little Creek. In July 1878 the mill was the scene of a tragedy: an explosion killed one man as well as the child of William Howard. Howard himself was so badly scalded that he could hardly be recognized.[21]

Even with the dangerous conditions, lumber and shingle mills were profitable enterprises and essential to the early communities of Rich County. In Woodruff John Allen and John Dean began the operation of a water-powered mill in 1872. Set up in the canyons west of town, the water source proved undependable and the mill was later moved to the forks of Woodruff Creek. The mill had several different owners during its existence, but sometime in the late 1890s, S. C. Putnam traded the mill to James Kearl of Round Valley for a herd of cattle.[22] The Kearl mill operated for at least thirty years in the Laketown area.[23]

Joseph C. Rich professed to have established the first sawmill in Bear Lake Valley,[24] but in 1864 Phineas Cook erected the first sawmill in present-day Rich County at Swan Creek.[25] The need for sawmills also appears to have been one of the reasons for Luther Reed's early settlement on Big Spring at Round Valley in 1864.[26] Because of the difficulties experienced during the early years of trying to settle southern Bear Lake Valley, it is unclear how successful Reed's sawmill was. Nonetheless, his untimely death in 1870 is attributed to an accident he had while working at the mill site.[27] The sawmill at Big Spring was revamped by Nehemiah Weston a short time later. Weston hired A. O. Williams to operate the mill. Williams had been a partner of Luther Reed.

During the early part of the twentieth century, the citizens of

Nathaniel W. Hodges's steam powered sawmill at the summit between Logan Canyon and Meadowville. (Special Collections and Archives, Utah State University, Logan.)

Laketown also constructed several attractive stone buildings. The sandstone quarried out of the hills above the east shore of Bear Lake, the same observed by Marcellus Monroe's party on the reconnaissance of Bear Lake Valley in 1857, was used to construct the Laketown chapel in 1908 and the Robinson store two years later.[28]

Rich County and the adjoining areas of western Wyoming and southeastern Idaho were rich in mineral resources. Although gold and silver were found in a few isolated spots, rock-phosphate production was the most promising prospect. Rock-phosphate was commonly processed with acid to break down the raw material into phosphorous which could be used as a plant fertilizer. Phosphorous was also used in the manufacture of incendiary bombs and would eventually find a wide market as an important ingredient in laundry detergents.[29]

The Arickeree Mine, the first phosphate mine in Rich County, began operation in about 1906 and was located northeast of Randolph, just west of the Wyoming border. The mine was owned by two Massachusetts businessmen, Peter and Robert Bradley. The company employed approximately twenty men, including miners, blacksmiths, and teamsters. Most were from Rich County. The rock was hauled by wagon nine miles to connect with the railroad at Sage

Junction, Wyoming.[30] From Sage the rock was shipped west for processing at the American Agricultural Chemical Company's facilities in Los Angeles in which the Bradleys held an interest. In 1909 the mine consisted of a 450-foot-long main tunnel and a smaller tunnel of about 300 feet which followed the phosphate bed.[31]

Other mines in the vicinity of Cokeville, Wyoming, were also in operation during the early part of the century. The mining of phosphate was a laborious undertaking. At Cokeville the method used involved "breaking of the rock by overhead stoping." A stope was a dug-out portion of the main tunnel.

Given the danger and amount of labor required, profits were insufficient for the Bradley brothers to continue their operations at the Arickeree which closed down after operating a few years. The mine at Cokeville suffered a similar fate. Phosphate production was further slowed when, in 1908, the Secretary of Interior placed over 4.5 million acres of phosphate lands in Idaho, Utah, and Wyoming in reserve.[32] A survey of the area was conducted by the U.S. Geological Survey in 1909. The survey showed extensive deposits of rock-phosphate, stretching from the Crawford Mountains in Bear River Valley to Laketown and on through the Bear Lake Valley at Paris, Montpelier, and over the pass into Soda Springs. In 1921 the Anaconda Company began operating an underground mine at Soda Springs. The ore was shipped north for processing at the company's plant in Montana. The Conda Mine holds the distinction of being the oldest continuously operated mine in the western states.[33]

Even though ninety percent of the rock-phosphate in the United States (sixty percent of the world's known supply) was found in the four western states of Utah, Idaho, Wyoming, and Montana,[34] profitable exploitation of the resource remained a recurrent problem. Beginning in 1937, the four states which contained the western phosphate fields began holding annual conferences to determine the best way of exploiting their geologic resources. Attended by the governors of the four states, Department of Interior officials, scientists and industrialists, the first conference was marked by a concern for national security. World events in Europe and Asia had brought to power aggressive, fascist regimes in Germany, Italy, and Japan. Characterizing those in attendance as the "guardians of our national security and possibly of international peace," H. A. Morgan of the Interior Department expressed his concern that unfriendly foreign powers might try to acquire the vast phosphate reserves in the western United States.[35]

The paranoia was not entirely unfounded. The Italian dictator Mussolini had already successfully invaded Ethiopia in 1935. During the summer previous to the conference, Japan had invaded China, capturing Peking in July 1937. In 1936 Germany had occupied the Rhineland in violation of the Versailles Treaty, and in March 1938 Hitler's troops invaded and annexed Austria. It appeared even to the most casual observer of world events that the world outside of the United States was chaotic and unpredictable.

The western phosphate reserves were safe from foreign intrigue, however. In fact, during the course of American involvement in World War II, from 1941 to 1945, very little phosphate mining occurred in the West. Following the war, the western states again met in conference to discuss how to capitalize on their phosphate reserves. G. G. Davidson of the Department of Interior addressed the group and asked for proposals to find a way to profitably mine the rock-phosphate. The *Salt Lake Tribune* noted:

> If anyone has the answer to the question posed by the interior department official let him step forward and be acclaimed the modern Moses to lead us to the promised land of economic balance and health.[36]

The "modern Moses" in this case turned out to be the Monsanto Chemical Corporation which began construction of a processing plant north of Soda Springs in 1951.[37] Two things contributed to the revitalization of the phosphate industry. One was the integration of mining and processing begun by Monsanto and J. R. Simplot in southeastern Idaho and by the San Francisco Chemical Corporation at Leefe, Wyoming. By combining the two operations, the corporations eliminated the cost of transportation and processing at distant plants. The second boon to the phosphate industry was the development of surface, or open-pit, mining. Underground mines such as the Arickeree in Rich County were limited in the amount of rock which could be produced. Open-pit mines, such as operated at Soda

Springs and at Beckwith Hills, just across the Utah border in southwestern Wyoming, were mechanically mined and could produce much more raw material.

Even though the mines in Rich County did not lend themselves to surface mining, the San Francisco Chemical Company reopened them in the 1954. The largest of these, the Cherokee, produced possibly the richest rock-phosphate in the West. The rock was processed at the Leefe, Wyoming, plant, also owned by the San Francisco Chemical Company.[38]

Even with improved production and processing methods, the phosphate industry in Rich County and at neighboring Leefe experienced economic setbacks during the mid-1960s. Ironically, the improved technologies which made surface mining possible and increased the efficiency of processing plants also increased the supply of phosphate products and lowered the price. Furthermore, the environmental concerns raised over phosphate use in laundry detergent decreased the demand for the product. The San Francisco Company was absorbed by Stauffer Chemical Company in the mid-1960s.[39]

Phosphate mining in Rich County suffered from the same market forces affecting other commercial enterprises. The up-and-down pattern of the phosphate industry is characteristic of most mining and mineral operations. Similar forces came to bear on the production of domestic oil in the United States during the mid-1970s. Throughout the 1960s, the United States and other western industrialized nations had become increasingly reliant on inexpensive foreign oil. The often cutthroat competition among international oil producers allowed the United States to prosper using cheap foreign sources of oil. Inexpensive foreign oil caused the development and production of domestic reserves to stagnate. The creation and unification of the Organization of Petroleum Exporting Countries (OPEC) during the 1960s gradually altered the relationship between the foreign oil producers and the United States, the world's largest oil consumer. Beginning in 1970 OPEC announced substantial increases in the cost of crude oil. Furthermore, because of the United States' pro-Israel position during the Arab-Israeli War in 1973, OPEC members imposed an oil embargo on the United States and some other western nations.[40] The result was an energy crisis in the United States that lasted throughout the 1970s and sent the nation into an economic recession.

The increased cost of crude oil drove up energy costs and made the production of domestic oil once again profitable. As Americans waited in line to pay what many considered exorbitant prices at the gasoline pump, oil companies began redeveloping old oil fields and exploring for new ones. One area that received particular attention was the overthrust belt, the geologic structure extending from Sweetwater County, Wyoming, through Rich County and on into southeastern Idaho.

The presence of oil along this geologic structure had been known to exist for over a century. The occurrence of "oil springs" in the vicinity of South Pass was recorded by fur trappers as early as 1826.[41] Wyoming governor John W. Hoyt in his 1878 annual report called attention to White's Oil Springs east of Evanston:

> To the railroad crossing of Bear River in Uintah County; along the railroad near Green River Station and then . . . into Utah . . . there are indications of very large deposits of crude petroleum. The present price of petroleum, coupled with the cost of transportation, does not afford a powerful stimulus to the enterprise, but there is no doubt of the value of the deposit.[42]

Prior to the second decade of this century, kerosene, used primarily in lamps, was the main usable by-product of oil. With the advent of automobiles, however, the demand for refined oil and gasoline skyrocketed. Considerable development of oil in Wyoming began around 1910 with the greatest activity taking place in the central part of the state at Casper. This early "boom" did not reach into southwestern Wyoming or into Rich County, Utah; however, beginning in the mid-1970s, seismic crews began moving into the area of Evanston to search for promising spots to drill test wells, and by 1980 a new oil and natural-gas boom was underway. Crews sank the first test well in Rich County fourteen miles east of Laketown in the late 1970s.[43] Rich County Sheriff Thad Mattson stated, "If the oil people are right and the data we get from them accurate, oil discoveries in our little county could be the biggest in the country. The forgotten county could be remembered for a hell of a long time."[44]

As home base for the "roughnecks" operating the drilling rigs, Evanston became an overnight "boom" town. The population shot upwards from four thousand to seven thousand in the course of a few months. Uinta County officials estimated that the population could double again by 1985. All of the usual problems associated with unexpected growth plagued Evanston: housing shortages, increased crime, water and sewage problems. Wrote one commentator:

> Like a slow-moving but unstoppable glacier, the drilling crews are moving along the geologic overthrust belt . . . Evanston has been the easiest place to see this impact. Mobile homes are crammed into every square foot of open space. Truck sales lots are on graveled parking. Four-wheel drive half-tons with oversize wheels and bearded drivers growl up and down the streets. Now, that impact is coming to Woodruff. Randolph may be next, then Laketown.[45]

As the oil and gas boom spread northwest from Wyoming into Utah, the towns of Rich County also began experiencing growing pains. For some, the change was not welcome. Said one local farmer: "I've had it. These people come into our small towns, like them because they're so much different than the smokey, nervous cities they left behind. Then they go to work to change the small town to be like the places they came from."[46]

The irony of the situation was that Rich County communities had been trying to attract other people to the area for a century before the oil and gas boom. Excess population had never been a problem before. But while the lure of prosperity which the boom offered seemed attractive, the boom, like recreational development at Bear Lake, also threatened to disrupt over a century of tradition. Anne Stuart Walmsley, a retired school teacher from Woodruff, summarized:

> We're a stalwart, strong people here in Woodruff, and we don't resent growth—as long as its done right. I like my sleepy village the way it is, of course, but at the same [time] I know there's no real opportunity here for the young. Many young people who

once lived in Woodruff would like to come back, if there's work. So change can work both ways.[47]

Exploration and development of wells and test sites continued along the overthrust belt. The most significant early well tapped in Rich County was found twelve miles north of Randolph on Hogback Ridge. American Quasar Petroleum Company drilled the well which flowed an estimated 22.4 million cubic feet of natural gas.[48] This phenomenal success prompted Quasar and other companies to drill other wells, but fifteen dry holes resulted in the Hogback Ridge area after the initial discovery.[49] With each hole costing between two million and eight million dollars, it took major successes for the oil companies even to break even. But with oil prices peaking at $45 per barrel in 1981, oil companies could afford a few dry holes.[50] Development and exploration continued in Rich County. Oil companies began developing the infrastructure to process and market the newly found energy resources. In 1980 Mountain Fuel Supply Company began the construction of a twenty-inch steel pipeline from Hogback Ridge past Randolph and Woodruff to connect with the company's main supply line east of Coalville, Utah. The seventy-two-mile pipeline brought additional employment to Rich County as well as holding the promise of natural-gas service to the communities in the Bear River Valley.

Continuing to broaden the scope of exploration, Hunt Energy Company arranged with the states of Utah and Idaho to begin taking seismic readings below the surface of Bear Lake. A great deal of public concern was generated over the prospect of natural-gas development below Bear Lake. To set preservation-minded citizens at ease, the oil companies championed the idea of directional drilling. The process involved the actual drilling rig being constructed on shore. Drilling was accomplished by "drifting" the drill at an angle out into the lake bed. But as geologist Howard R. Ritzma elaborated, the method was "a tricky, difficult and very expensive operation."[51]

Idaho awarded drilling leases to Hunt Energy along with the right to conduct sonar experiments in its half of the lake. In the Rich County half of Bear Lake, however, leases remained in limbo until at least 1986.[52] By 1986 the mining of natural gas from the depths of

Bear Lake had turned far less attractive. In the aftermath of the OPEC embargo, per barrel prices for crude oil had soared to $36, peaking at $45 in late 1981. By 1987 crude oil prices had plummeted to a figure even lower than before the embargo. Ten-dollar barrels of oil made any further exploration and development of area wells unprofitable. As oil companies began closing up shop, economies experienced a slump in the western boom towns which they had helped create. Bill Cayce, a Denver, Colorado, oil company executive, explained: "when it comes to oil exploration [it] is very price-driven. That's been the big reason for the downturn in exploratory activity levels." As oil exploration ceased, Evanston and other towns along the overthrust belt saw drastic declines in population. At neighboring Vernal, Uintah County, Utah, where the emphasis had been on oil-shale development, hundreds of homes stood vacant. A home selling for seventy thousand dollars in 1984 could be bought for only slightly more than half that amount in 1987. Vernal's main street was witness to the closure of almost every third business.[53]

In hindsight, the reluctance of Laketown, Woodruff, and Rich County, in general, to completely buy into the energy boom proved beneficial. Compared with other localities along the overthrust belt, Rich County communities had less adjustments to cope with because less helter-skelter development had taken place. In part this was due to timing. At the moment the boom appeared poised to enter Rich County, the price of oil dropped and the boom quieted to a pop. Moreover, civic leaders and community activists held the onslaught of the boom at bay until they and not the oil companies decided how best to proceed. Although the oil boom conflicted with the century-old traditions of Rich County, it did hold the hope of bringing economic development to the county, a hope which could not be ignored. Along with recreational development, which also threatened to overpower the county with its meteoric speed, energy development continued. But it continued at a more orderly pace. In spite of flirtations with energy and recreational prosperity, Rich County remained rural and primarily agricultural. Yet the potential remained. Today the county enjoys unique diversity in its potential for both energy development and recreational development while maintaining the traditions of its agricultural base.

ENDNOTES

1. When asked if men should "go to the Mountains to hunt for gold and silver," Wilford Woodruff offered the following advice at Paris, Idaho, in 1870: "No. Stay at home & raise grain. . . . Let no man who finds gold in these Mountains use any of it for his own use but use it for the building up of the kingdom of God." See Scott G. Kenney, ed., *Wilford Woodruff's Journal 1833–1878, Typescript* 10 vols. (Midvale, UT: Signature Books, 1983–1991), 6:553.

2. Coal was discovered as early as 1849 at Coalville in Summit County and in 1854 in Sanpete County. Coal production was limited, however, by a lack of transportation facilities, although by 1863 it was being delivered to Salt Lake City from Coalville by ox-team for forty dollars a ton. See Thomas G. Alexander, "From Dearth to Deluge: Utah's Coal Industry," *Utah Historical Quarterly* 31 (Summer 1963): 235.

The Pioneer Iron Company was formed by Brigham Young in July 1852 with the hopes of utilizing the iron ore in the vicinity of present day Cedar City, Utah. A colony had been established there for that purpose two years previously, and considerable work had been undertaken to build the necessary refineries. The furnaces proved inefficient, however, and the enterprise was abandoned. See Gustive O. Larson, "Bulwark of the Kingdom: Utah's Iron and Steel Industry," *Utah Historical Quarterly* 31 (Summer 1963): 249–50.

3. Edward W. Tullidge, *Tullidge's Histories* (Salt Lake City: Juvenile Instructor Press, 1889), Supp Biographical Appendix, 2:74–75.

4. Report of the Party of Observation, Consisting of Eleven Men, Under Command of M. Monroe. Started from Ogden City, Aug. [18]57. Records of the Utah Territorial Militia, microfilm, Special Collections and Archives, Utah State University, Logan.

5. Leonard J. Arrington, "Abundance from the Earth: The Beginnings of Commercial Mining in Utah," *Utah Historical Quarterly* 31 (Summer 1963): 199–201. Utahns could incorporate into mining companies only with great difficulty. Arrington writes: "Despite the urging of Acting Governor Amos Reed . . . the territorial legislature failed to pass laws permitting the general incorporation of mining . . . companies, and the following spring, on May 3, 1864, the group organized the West Jordan Mining Company and incorporated under the laws of the State of California. This may or may not have given the company a legal existence in Utah, but in any case, the procedure had the backing of the army."

6. Sermon of Brigham Young, 6 October 1863, *Journal of Discourses*, vol 10, 271. Quoted in Arrington, "Abundance from the Earth," 205.

7. Charles J. Kappler, ed., *Indian Affairs: Laws and Treaties,* 11 vols. (Washington, D.C.: GPO, 1903), 2:650.

8. J. H. Head to T. G. Taylor, 1 January, 1868. Correspondence from the Superintendent of Indian Affairs, Utah Territory, 1841–1880, microfilm, Special Collections and Archives, Utah State University, Logan.

9. Although the Shoshoni remained friendly, that was not the case with other Indian tribes of the western plains. Numerous skirmishes developed from western Colorado through the Dakotas. Major battles took place, massacres occurred, and the period from 1865 through 1880 was violent. The most famous battle directly attributable to the activities of miners took place on the Little Big Horn River in southeastern Montana on 25 and 26 June 1876. The Massacre of General George A. Custer and his troops is well documented, and the list of books published on the subject almost endless. See Mari Sandoz, *The Battle of the Little Bighorn* (Lincoln: University of Nebraska Press, 1978). For a view of the battle from the Indian perspective see Dee Brown, *Bury my Heart at Wounded Knee: An Indian History of the American West* (New York: Bantam Books, 1979), 277–84.

10. Elaine S. Johnson and Ellen Carney, *The Mountain: Cariboo and Other Gold Camps in Idaho* (Bend, OR.: Maverick Publications, 1990), 20.

11. Journal of Thomas Sleight, 21 May 1871, typescript, Special Collections and Archives, Utah State University, Logan.

12. Johnson and Carney, *The Mountain,* 82.

13. See Betty M. Madsen and Brigham D. Madsen, *North to Montana: Jehus, Bullwhackers, and Mule Skinners on the Montana Trail* (Salt Lake City: University of Utah Press, 1980). See also A. J. Simmonds, "The Cache Freighting Trade to the Montana Mines," *Valley Magazine,* 24 December 1976, 4. Simmonds notes that a great deal of surplus produce was shipped north from Cache Valley. The Cache Valley route traveled north past Franklin, Idaho, and rejoined the main stem of the Montana Trail at Marsh Valley. There is also some evidence that settlers in Rich County also sent freight north to Montana and to Caribou. See Ezra J. Poulsen, *Joseph C. Rich—Versatile Pioneer on the Mormon Frontier* (Salt Lake City: Granite Publishing Co., 1958), 226–32. Additionally, the members of the Randolph Ward periodically sent livestock which had been donated as tithing to Paris and St. Charles, Idaho. It is assumed that if tithing stock was being sent north to Bear Lake Valley, then privately owned stock as well must have been driven there. Some stock undoubtedly was bartered for flour or wheat. But some of the stock was also being sent out of the area to be sold. See Tithing Record, 1877–1883, Randolph Ward, Rich County, Utah. Historian's Office, Church of Jesus Christ of Latter-day Saints, Salt Lake City, Utah (hereafter referred to as RTR).

14. Elizabeth Arnold Stone, *Uinta County: Its Place in History* (Glendale, CA: Arthur H. Clark Co., [1924]), 185.

15. Ibid., 126.

16. Ibid.

17. Ibid., 121.

18. Ibid., 122.

19. In describing his grandfather's brick business, Lewis Longhurst wrote in 1962:

He first built two pugmills, each having a pit about ten feet square and three feet deep behind it. The pits had dirt walls and a board floor, and were filled with one-half top soil and one-half red clay; water was run in on the dirt mixture, making the mud with which to build the bricks.

The pugmills were made of 2-inch planks—a box about four feet square and five feet high, with a plank floor. A log was secured upright in the center of the box, with paddles attached around it; then a large pole, perhaps twenty-five or thirty feet in length, was fastened horizontally to the top of the upright log. A horse was hitched to the smaller outer end of the horizontal pole; it walked around and around the pugmill. As the horse walked around the pugmill and mud pit, the paddles turned, thus mixing the mud to the desired consistency. A hole was cut, about a foot square, at the bottom of one side of the pugmill. As the horse circled around, the mixed mud was squeezed out through the hole onto a plank table that was at ground level; at one end of the table a hole was dug about waist deep, and grandfather stood in the hole to work at the table.

He would sand the table, and using both hands, cut off a piece of mud just big enough to make one brick, roll it on the sanded table (like kneading bread), then throw it down hard into a brick mold which held three bricks, and repeat the action twice more to fill the mold. He would next take a steel cutter with a wire and run it along the top of the mold, cutting off any surplus mud. Then, those three bricks were ready to be carried out on the yard, tipped out of the mold, and left on the yard to dry.

To run this operation smoothly required Grandfather to mold bricks, one man to shovel mud from the pit into the top of the pugmill, a horse to turn it and two boys to carry bricks, empty them from the mold, return, wet and sand the mold, and take it back to the table. . . .

When the bricks were dry enough to handle without crumbling, they were . . . hauled . . . to the kiln and stacked . . . up on edge, in tiers four bricks high, followed by a "checker" tier laid on top, and the holes filled with slack coal. Another four-course layer of bricks would go above that, a "checker" layer, slack coal, and so on, until it reached a height of twelve to fourteen feet, approximately twenty feet square; this took about

100,000–150,000 bricks. See Steven L. Thomson, Jane D. Digerness, and Mar Jean S. Thomson, *Randolph—A Look Back* (n.p., 1981), 87–89.

20. Thomson, *Randolph—A Look Back,* 14.

21. Manuscript History of the Randolph Ward, Rich County, Utah, 1878. Historical Department of the LDS Church, Salt Lake City, Utah, (hereafter cited as RMH). Della S. McKinnon recorded the event in great detail:

The boiler in the shingle mill exploded, killing instantly, Chris Hanney, the engineer and Willie Howard, the 7 year old son of William Howard. Parley Pead was severely scalded. He was packing shingles some distance from the boiler.

John and William Corless, who were unloading timber, narrowly escaped death from the flying debris. Something had gone wrong and Mr. Howard and Hanney were making the repair when the explosion occurred. A part of the boiler weighing about 1,000 pounds landed in a field about 90 rods away. . . . Mr. Howard and Hanney were not only scalded, but their skin was blown full of dirt and sawdust, and their clothing torn from their bodies. Mr. Hanney seemed to get full force of the explosion as nearly every bone in his body was broken.

Mr. Howard . . . was at death's door. His eyes, ears and mouth were blown full of dirt . . . and in removing the dirt the cooked skin came off with it. . . . Willie Howard . . . was killed by a part of the smoke stack which came down cutting the back part of his head off." See Mildred H. Thomson, comp., *Rich Memories: Some of the Happenings in Rich County from 1863 to 1960* (Salt lake City: Daughters of Utah Pioneers, 1962), 170.

22. Woodruff Centennial Committee, *The First Hundred Years In Woodruff* (Springville, UT: Art City Publishing Co., 1972), 98.

23. Reed Eborn, interview with Ray Lamborn, "Growing up in Laketown," 3 May 1975, 26–27.

24. *Bear Lake Magazine* 3 (1 December 1979): 22.

25. Manuscript History of Garden City Ward, Rich County, Utah, 1864, Historical Department of the LDS Church, Salt Lake City, Utah (hereafter referred to as GCMH).

26. See "Bear Lake Valley Pioneer Histories," typescript, Special Collections and Archives, Utah State University, Logan. See also Astle, "Life Story of Ellen Jane Bailey Lamborn," 7.

27. Thomson, *Rich Memories,* 77.

28. Ibid., 82. See also Eborn, interview with Ray Lamborn, 28–29.

29. Hoyt S. Gale and Ralph W. Richards, "Phosphates: Preliminary Report on the Phosphate Deposits in Southeastern Idaho and Adjacent Parts of Wyoming and Utah," in C. W. Hayes and Waldemar Lindgren, *Contributions To Economic Geology, Short Papers and Preliminary Reports,*

United States Geological Survey, Bulletin 430 (Washington, D.C.: Government Printing Office, 1909), 461–62.

30. Thomson, *Rich Memories,* 19–20.

31. Gale and Richards, "Preliminary Report on the Phosphate Deposits," 516.

32. Ibid., 457.

33. Richard L. Day, *Trends in the Phosphate Industry of Idaho and the Western Phosphate Field, Pamphlet no. 155* (Moscow, ID: Idaho Bureau of Mines and Geology, 1973), 7.

34. *Journal History of the Church of Jesus Christ of Latter-day Saints,* manuscript, Department of Special Collections and Archives, Merrill Library, Utah State University, Logan, Utah (hereafter referred to as JH), 24 May 1938, 2.

35. JH, 8 October 1937, 4–5.

36. *Salt Lake Tribune,* 7 September 1948. Quoted in JH, 7 September 1948, 2–3.

37. JH, 15 July 1951.

38. Day, *Trends in the Phosphate Industry,* 13–14.

39. Ibid., 15.

40. Dimitri Aperjis, *The Oil Market in the 1980s: OPEC Oil Policy and Economic Development* (Cambridge, MA: Ballinger Publishing Co., 1982), 1–4.

41. Dale L. Morgan, *The West of William H. Ashley* (Denver: Old West Publishing Company, 1964), 94.

42. Frances Birkhead Beard, *Wyoming from Territorial Days to the Present,* 3 vols. (Chicago: American Historical Society, 1933), 1: 297.

43. *Salt Lake Tribune,* 24 October 1979, D-6.

44. Ibid., 23 July 1979, C-1.

45. Ibid., 7.

46. *Bear Lake Magazine,* 4 (25 May 1980): 8.

47. Ibid.

48. Ibid. 2 (15 September 1978): 8.

49. Ibid. 5 (June 1981): 2.

50. *Salt Lake Tribune,* 28 June, 1987, 4 F.

51. Howard R. Ritzma, "Directional Drilling," *Bear Lake Magazine* 2 (15 September 1978): 7.

52. *Bear Lake Magazine* 3 (1 April 1979): 5. See also *Salt Lake Tribune,* 21 November 1986, 20–B.

53. *Salt Lake Tribune,* 28 June 1987.

6

"New Country and Untried Climate"

THE AGRICULTURAL HISTORY OF RICH COUNTY

Agriculture was the first and most important pursuit in Rich County. Despite the advances in mining, oil and gas exploration, and recreation, Rich County has remained predominantly agricultural during the entirety of its 130-year history. And although other areas colonized or settled by Mormons in Utah have since outgrown their agricultural roots, almost all were settled originally because of their agricultural potential. Brigham Young decreed early that his people should direct all of their energies to agricultural pursuits. It was Young's opinion, wrote natural historian Walter P. Cottam, that agriculture formed "the basis of a permanent society."[1] Young further noted:

> As you are located in a new country and untried climate . . . we recommend that you begin to plant and sow such seeds as soon as the snow is gone in the spring, so that we might know by experiments whether it is possible to ripen grain in the valley before the summer drouth shall demand the labor of irrigation.[2]

Mormons sought the most promising oases within the Great

Basin in which to establish agricultural settlements. Initially these settlements were confined to areas known to be below the forty-second parallel. One of the main reasons for choosing the Salt Lake Valley for the initial settlement, as opposed to Bear Lake Valley, Cache Valley, or areas of Bear River Valley, was its supposed milder climate. Both Lansford P. Hastings and John C. Fremont were optimistic about the possibility of farming certain parts of the Great Basin.[3] The Mormons in Salt Lake Valley proved their optimism to be well-founded. Nonetheless, in establishing their agricultural settlements, Utahns had little precedent to build on. By and large, the agricultural successes of early Utahns were built upon trial and error. The determined settlers experimented with a great variety of plants, different times for sowing seed, and different methods of irrigation. Still, the "new country and untried climate" made their experiments difficult. And as settlements moved farther north, these experiments became even more precarious.

The first to experiment with farming in Bear Lake Valley was the trapper and trader Thomas "Pegleg" Smith. In a letter addressed to the *Missouri Adventurer* at Saint Joseph, Smith wrote. "I shall soon have a large farm in operation."[4]

As discussed in chapter one, Smith set up his trading post near present-day Dingle, Idaho. Calling the outpost Big Timber, Smith kept a few milk cows, some pigs, and chickens. In addition, he tilled and planted several acres to garden and cereal crops. Like the Mormons in Salt Lake Valley, Smith's operation suffered from frost and crickets in 1848. Unlike his Salt Lake valley neighbors, however, his operation was not providentially visited by hungry seagulls, and after the "wheat grew to two feet in height, [it] was destroyed by crickets, which also ate most of the vegetables."[5] Smith was a fair-weather farmer, and after his initial experiment failed, he abandoned the idea completely. Not so the settlers who eventually followed him into Bear Lake Valley. They too failed a good share of the time, but with continued trial and error, they eventually established a working agricultural system.

Spring came early to Bear Lake Valley in 1864. Marianne Sleight recorded that the frost had gone from the ground by 11 April. She and her husband William commenced plowing, and ten days later

Hay mowing crews moving out on the meadows near Woodruff. (Courtesy Carl Gunn.)

planted wheat, but a storm on 5 May left five inches of new snow on the ground. Five days later the Sleights sowed several acres to oats followed with the planting of squash and corn on 16 May. The schedule of planting followed by the Sleights during the first season at Bear Lake succeeded. That fall Marianne recorded that although "not much grain matured here this year, mine did and was cut before the frost came, and some excellent potatoes were raised here. Some corn matured. We had plenty of green corn."[6]

William and Marianne had inadvertently stumbled onto one of the most important aspects of farming in Rich County. It was necessary to plant grain crops as early in the spring as possible to ensure their maturity before the hard, fall freeze. The hard winter which followed the first year of settlement magnified that fact. The severe winter of 1865 covered the valley with three to four feet of snow. The snow cover persisted throughout April, so planting was postponed until about the middle of May. Marianne Sleight managed to plant a small portion of her garden on 9 May—some corn and potatoes—but she noted in her diary the bitter cold.[7] Between 12 May and the end of the month William sowed two acres of wheat and several acres of oats. Marianne recorded frosts about every other day throughout May. Even with the cold, the garden sprouted and grew. On 5 June, however, Marianne recorded: "Sharp frost this morning[;] everything is cut to the ground." What little was left growing above ground was further decimated on 15 June by a hailstorm.

The summer of 1865 was more severe than most. But following the cold spell of June, the weather gradually warmed, and typical of the Bear Lake climate, turned hot in July. Although no mention is made in her brief diary, Marianne and others in the Paris settlement must have been amazed at the rapid recovery of their gardens between 5 June and 24 July. The potato vines blackened by frost in June reemerged from the ground, and on Pioneer Day the settlers enjoyed a few new potatoes and one or two squash. But William, who recently had returned from a trip to Cache Valley, noted how the vegetation at Bear Lake appeared to be at least a month behind that at Logan.[8] Cache Valley had evidently escaped the hard frost of 5 June.

For the Bear Lake settlers, the first fruits of their gardens were inconsequential compared to the wheat growing in their fields. Wheat formed the basis of their survival. With planting postponed a month later than the previous year, hard frosts around the first of September froze the milky heads of the maturing wheat crop. The lack of provisions for the following winter and the fear that the previous growing season was typical caused some settlers to pull up stakes and seek warmer, more hospitable regions. But the season of 1865 was not typical. The heavy snows of the previous winter were the exception, not the rule. The next several seasons brought successful harvests for those who stayed in Bear Lake Valley. The settlers learned from both their failures and successes. The necessity of early planting prompted them to adopt the practice of fall plowing, which enabled them to begin working and planting their fields as soon as the frost had left the ground. In his visit to Bear Lake Valley in 1870, Brigham Young rehearsed the procedure for the settlers.

> When you can have your ground plowed in the fall, and sow a grain that will mature early, there will be no trouble in harvesting as good crops [here] as we do elsewhere in this country.[9]

The determination of the early settlers at Paris and other locations in the north carried over to the settlements in southern Bear Lake Valley. The isolation of these early settlements demanded that they become as self-sufficient as possible. The early settlers attempted the cultivation of most garden crops. Furthermore, they continually experimented with plantings of fruit trees, berries, and currents. It appears that a much more diverse agriculture was carried out in Bear Lake Valley than is currently practiced. Nehemiah Weston's orchard, for instance, produced bushels of apples and pears.[10] On Bear Lake's east shore, Phoebe and Hyrum Nebeker farmed and gardened, growing diverse quantities of vegetables. Their daughter Luella Nebeker Adams recalled the landscape at their South Eden Home:

> There was a large orchard south of the house, with a wonderful assortment of fruit: transparent, red astrachan, wealthy, and duchess apples; all kinds of plums; apricots, large and juicy; dark, juicy cherries; a great variety of small fruit, dark cherry and white currants, gooseberries, dewberries, and an abundance of raspberries. . . . People from long distances came to marvel at and to enjoy our fruit. They could not believe that such wonderful fruit could be raised in the Bear Lake Valley.[11]

Their location at South Eden, being at the foot of the canyon and adjacent to the lake, may have been responsible for the Nebekers' success. But beyond this, the settlers had learned from past experience how to improve their chances. Late frosts could be discouraged by keeping the ground wet through frequent irrigation. Marianne Sleight discovered this in 1865 when the first hard frost of September had been preceded by a rainstorm—the wheat was saved because of the wet soil. Unfortunately, a second hard frost followed a week later after the ground had dried.[12]

At South Eden the Nebekers planted rows of poplars to act as windbreaks, protecting their orchards from cold spring winds, the time when fruit trees are most susceptible to damage. Vegetables as well benefitted from the protection of the poplars. Sweet corn, peas and beans were all grown at South Eden. Furthermore, Luella added that "Mother's tomatoes were always the pride of the family. A great deal of time and labor was required to have ripe tomatoes every year." Phoebe started the plants inside each year in March after going into the canyon to collect the rich, humus soil. "The seeds were planted in boxes in March," according to Phebe's daughter, "then the plants were transplanted into cans later on." The tomatoes were evidently protected in canisters until all threat of frost was past before the plants were transplanted a third time into the garden. By August the plants were beginning to bear fruit, for which, wrote Luella, "Mother felt repaid for her effort. She enjoyed showing to people the patch and gave them away in great quantities to relatives and friends."[13]

Agricultural success in Bear Lake Valley required some extra effort on the part of settlers, but it was not an impossible proposition. It also required that the settlers develop a keen sense of observation. They had to observe the seasons closely to know when to plant, and they had to observe the locations of their different fields to know which crops would mature best at which location. At Laketown, the Lamborns took note of the peculiarities of their land. After the death of his brother, Edwin Lamborn married William's widow Eunice as a plural wife. Caring for his brother's two daughters, Edwin also fathered a second family with Eunice. John, Edwin's son from his first marriage, recalled that the two families resided on different sections of land but noted that the potatoes for both families were always raised at the north field. "You could raise potatoes in the north field where you couldn't out in this south field, so they always had a batch of potatoes alongside of ours."[14]

Not all of the efforts of the Laketown settlers succeeded. No amount of observation or preparation could prepare the settlers for all of nature's offerings. Hard winters, late springs, droughts, and pestilence were beyond their control. Only their faith in the divine calling of their leaders and their firm belief in an interactive God held out hope for avoiding natural calamities. Brigham Young had said that the settlement of Rich County, "accompanied as it is by the faith and prayers of the Saints and the blessings of the land by the priesthood [would] produce a modification of the elements."[15] The importance of prayer and faith in the lives of Bear Lake farmers was reinforced during the 1868 season. Crickets continued to pay periodic visits to the Great Basin, affecting settlements throughout Utah and southeastern Idaho.[16] In the Bear Lake Valley the plague of

Haying with push rakes in Woodruff. (Courtesy Carl Gunn.)

grasshoppers was particularly hard felt because of the recent establishment of the settlements. But similar to the experience of the Salt Lake Valley settlers of 1848, the prayers of Bear Lake settlers were also answered in miraculous fashion. Oral tradition records that a huge wind swept down upon the grasshoppers and lifted them out into Bear Lake where they gradually washed ashore, forming giant windrows of dead insects. Joseph C. Rich noted the scourge in his customary earthy, literary style:

> We thought ourselves isolated . . . from . . . the ravages of those pestiferous critters. About a week ago, however, they made their appearance in the south end of the valley, and destroyed all the crops at Round Valley and Swan Creek. Stone walls, nettles, dirt covered houses, stink bushes and bachelors seem to be about the only thing they hold sacred. There was not room for all to light on the ground, so one swarm of a few hundred million eased themselves gently into Bear Lake, which resulted in an extensive grasshopper casualty. There [sic] bodies will not be recovered.[17]

The feeling that God was indeed on their side and would intervene on their behalf gave the Mormon settlers added reason to persevere. By 1871 some settlers from Bear Lake Valley and additional settlers from Salt Lake Valley had relocated to Bear River Valley, southeast of Laketown. Prayers notwithstanding, the climate at

Randolph and Woodruff had yet to moderate. The settlers in Bear River Valley had to depend upon the successes of Laketown farmers and those in other Bear Lake settlements for their wheat and potatoes. It took at least fourteen years for farmers in the Bear River Valley to develop successful farming methods.[18] The method developed in the Bear River Valley resulted in most of the settlers' energies being directed towards livestock raising rather than the cultivation of cereal crops. An examination of the tithing record for the Randolph Ward during the late 1870s and early 1880s sheds light on the precarious nature of the settlers' relationship with the climate in Bear River Valley. Even more so than at Laketown, timing was everything at Randolph. The tithing record for the ward notes the successes and failures of crops in the valley and how they relate to the severity of the climate during any given year.

Between 1877 and 1883 the settlers of Randolph continued to experiment with plantings of wheat and barley and for the three years 1877, 1878, and 1879 produced small quantities.[19] In 1878, a bumper year for grain production at Randolph,[20] tithes amounting to $2.88 worth of barley and $23.00 worth of wheat as well as $156.00 worth of oats were donated by the Randolph settlers. In 1879 the settlers evidently felt assured of a successful wheat crop and cut back their plantings of oats considerably. Seventy-eight dollars worth of wheat was donated as tithes in 1879 compared to only $52.00 worth of oats; no barley was donated in 1879.

Those years were characterized by relatively mild winters and early springs, which allowed the settlers to sow their wheat early enough to assure maturity. The winter of 1880, however, was one of the "deep snow years," which delayed spring planting. Consequently, the tithing record for 1880 lists no barley and no wheat but both were given lines in the ledger. Although the settlers certainly realized that oats mature much faster than wheat or barley and that they were a much safer bet in the high cold climate of Bear River Valley, wheat was a much more profitable and desirable crop. Only twenty-two dollars worth of oats were tithed in 1880. After three successful years, the settlers tried to plant wheat in 1880, only to have the crop fail completely.

The following year the settlers again returned to the safer crop of oats, having largely abandoned barley. Tithes of wheat amounted to only $9.00; $154.00 of oats were donated. With favorable growing conditions prevailing during the 1881 season, many settlers returned to the more profitable and desirable crop of wheat in 1882. Tithes for oats dipped to $120.00 in 1882, but although the ledger still showed a line for wheat, none was donated.

The ledger for the following year, however, omits lines for any other cereal crop except oats. After the failures of the wheat crops following 1879, the settlers had evidently decided to cut their losses and concentrate on raising oats. In 1883 tithes amounting to $233.00 worth of oats were donated. The tithing record for the Randolph Ward is interesting in several other respects. Lines were supplied in the ledger for all the possible commodities which might have been donated, including cash, merchandise, stock, vegetables, hay, and fruit. Not surprising, although fruit was listed as a category during all six years of the ledger, none was donated. Vegetables, probably potatoes, and other root crops, were practically nonexistent except for the bountiful year of 1878 when $24.00 worth was contributed. [21]

Irrigation

Successful crops required not only a cooperative climate but also timely irrigating. Irrigation in the Bear River Valley began shortly after the Mormons' arrival in 1870. The settlers at Randolph dug two small ditches from the north bank of Little Creek in 1870 to irrigate a small amount of land in the vicinity of the settlement. The settlers in Laketown likewise constructed a ditch to irrigate the lands in the vicinity of the fort built there in 1869. The Laketown south ditch was finished in 1872. Meadowville settlers, who reoccupied the area in 1869, began using the waters of Big Spring in 1872. Also, Round Valley pioneer George Braffet, who was among the original settlers into southern Bear Lake Valley, constructed two ditches from a spring bearing his name in 1868. Cottonwood Creek, flowing from the southwest into Round Valley, was also tapped as an irrigation source in 1868.[22] Most of these early irrigation efforts lacked sufficient water to irrigate all of the settlers' lands. Therefore, larger, more reliable projects were undertaken in the Bear Lake and Bear River valleys.

Insufficient irrigation water has been a recurring problem

throughout the history of Rich County. To counteract it, the settlers of Laketown, Round Valley, and Meadowville cooperatively constructed a larger network of canals in 1888 to completely harness the waters of Big Spring and Laketown Canyon. The settlers at Randolph constructed the lower ditch between 1877 and 1881 to convey water from Big Creek to meadowlands below the settlement.[23]

Water development was an endless effort, and the citizens of Rich County continually sought ways to increase their late-season supply. The construction of reservoirs throughout the western states occurred after passage of the Newlands Reclamation Act in 1902. The Newlands Act brought the federal government into partnership with the western states to develop dams and improve irrigation systems,[24] and this partnership between state and federal agencies has continued to the present day. Further water development at Randolph began in 1936 when the state approved the construction of Big Creek Reservoir. The reservoir on Big Creek received the number-one priority from the county commission when it issued its "wish list" to the federally financed Public Works Administration.[25] Preliminary work on the project moved slowly and was postponed indefinitely after the outbreak of World War II in 1941. In 1944 a larger reservoir planned for construction on the Woodruff Narrows of the Bear River convinced most irrigators that smaller projects were impractical. Nonetheless, a smaller reservoir was constructed on Little Creek to the north of Big Creek a number of years later.

The key to irrigation in the Bear River Valley, however, was to harness the potential of the Bear River. Several large canals were constructed to convey water from the Bear River; these included the Crawford and Thompson Canal, the Beckwith Canal, and the Chapman Canal. In 1902 after the founding of the Neponset Land and Livestock Company, Evanston bankers and businessmen George F., A. O., and W. O. Chapman petitioned the General Land Office to withdraw public lands for the construction of a canal and reservoir in Utah.[26] The Neponset Reservoir would not be completed until 1924,[27] but after its completion the reservoir stored Bear River water conveyed to that point by the Chapman Canal, which headed on Bear River north of Evanston.[28] The reservoir acted as a distribution point for the lands irrigated by Neponset's successors, A. W. Crane and the

Deseret Land and Livestock Company. A large shallow reservoir, Neponset now inundates over one thousand acres of land.[29]

The Randolph/Woodruff Canal is also a major appropriator of Bear River water. Between 1885 and 1891 the canal was completed from Woodruff, where it tapped the Bear River two miles east of town, to Sage Creek. The canal was flumed across the various intervening streams. It cost $22,000 to build, and at the time of its completion was supposed to supply water to thirty-eight thousand acres.[30] Currently, the Randolph/Woodruff Canal irrigates slightly more than ten thousand acres.[31]

As a way to finance large irrigation projects such as the Randolph/Woodruff Canal, Rich County was organized into districts. Under a law passed by the Utah Territorial Assembly in 1884, the county was organized into six different irrigation districts: Randolph, Laketown, Meadowville, Garden City, Bear River Stream, and Woodruff.[32]

The Woodruff Irrigation District was organized in January 1891 with John Baxter elected as chairman and S. C. Putnam as secretary. Anson Call explained that "there was an opportunity to procure stock to the amount of three thousand dollars in the proposed canal which was to pass through this district in its extension to Otter Creek."[33] Call, along with Samuel Bryson and Peter Cornia, had been engaged in studying the prospects of the canal since 1884 when they met with Bishop John M. Baxter and other representatives from Randolph to survey the route for the ditch.[34] At the 1891 meeting, a two-cent per acre tax was levied against all stockholders for ditch work.[35]

In addition to Bear River water, Wesley K. Walton and others in the vicinity of Woodruff used Woodruff Creek as an irrigation source as early as 1874. By 1879 the Woodruff South Ditch was completed. Forty different irrigators diverted water from the Walton and South Woodruff ditches. During seasons of heavy snowfall, Woodruff Creek in conjunction with the small creek originating in Birch Canyon to the north could irrigate six to seven hundred acres. John Snowball estimated that an additional fifty-four hundred acres was irrigable in the area if supplemental water were to be available.[36] In 1899 Woodruff citizens organized an irrigation corporation to further develop the waters of Woodruff Creek. George A. Neville was elected

Woodruff Narrows Dam, 1995. (Courtesy Blair Francis.)

president; Anson Call, vice president; and Chaplain Walton, secretary. The corporation was capitalized at twenty thousand dollars.[37] The officials of the new corporation immediately began formulating a plan to construct a dam on Woodruff Creek about a half mile above the town.[38] Ezra Brown recounted the history of the development of the Woodruff Creek Reservoir, noting that in 1901 the water users of Woodruff Creek surveyed a reservoir site and had specifications prepared. The site became known as Lone Pine Reservoir, and the specifications called for the construction of a dam forty feet high with a spillway running "around the north end of the dam." The dam was specified to be around three hundred feet across the top and about fifty feet at the bottom. Brown gave no indication as to who drew up the original specifications, but his terms "around" and "about" give the impression that the plans were far from exact. Furthermore, a twelve-inch pipe was placed at the bottom of the dam which, according to Brown, "was entirely too small to carry the flood waters of spring time." The dam failed during the spring of 1902. Undaunted, the Woodruff irrigators began a new dam the following summer, only to be again frustrated by its complete failure the next spring.

After being knocked down twice in as many attempts to erect the dam, the Woodruff citizens abandoned the idea until 1923. In that year "the water right[s] of Woodruff were asked to be determined by the State Engineer." Ezra Brown noted that the "determining of the water right, no doubt, had much to do with uniting the people for a move to increase the water supply."[39] Cooperative Extension Service Agent for Rich County W. R. Smith offered to contact L. M. Winsor, an engineer who had experience in constructing this type of dam.[40] A town meeting was called in which Winsor explained the method whereby he felt the irrigators could construct the dam over a period of years without going into massive debt. Ezra Brown explained Winsor's plan:

> Mr. Winsor gave us a plan where by we would use the wash . . . around the old dam, that was made years ago, for the spillway. The spillway should be built of rock and cement. After putting in a good bowl for the water to land in after going over the spillway; the spillway is raised each year as the earth dam goes up. By this plan the people of Woodruff have been able to raise the dam, each year, as their time and means permits and still at the end of each year's work have their work left in safety for the spring time floods.[41]

Work began on the new dam in 1926. A foundation was put in and the dam and spillway raised about fifteen feet. The following year another five feet was added, and in 1928 the dam was raised six additional feet. The goal was to raise the dam to a height of forty feet. An initial assessment of one dollar an acre was made in 1926. During succeeding years the assessment went as high as $2.50 an acre; but, in concluding his remarks in 1928, Ezra Brown noted: "We have not bonded ourselves and are not in debt. This work had its inception from our Extension Agent . . . and was put in motion by L. M. Winsor . . . who gave us his service at times when he would have been resting from his regular duties."[42]

The Cooperative Extension Service played an important role in promoting agriculture in Rich County. Congress created the Extension Service under the Smith-Lever Act of 1914. In conjunction with the more usual objective of promoting new, scientific farming principles, the Extension Service also had special programs for homemakers and youth. The 4–H program endeavored to involve young men and women in various clubs; these included sheep clubs, beef clubs, clothing clubs, forestry clubs, and others. Programs began in 1925 with fifty 4–H club members. By 1937 there were more than two hundred involved from Garden City to Woodruff.[43] Mrs. Helen Wamsley was actively involved in 4–H and as a home demonstration agent in Rich County.

The amount of storage at Woodruff reservoir was small in comparison to that of Neponset, but it was of inestimable value to the irrigators of the district as a series of dry years during the 1930s followed the reservoir's completion. During the 1930s plans were made to construct a similar series of reservoirs on the left hand fork of Woodruff Creek in Birch Hollow.[44] The irrigators hoped to use funding from the federal government through the Public Works Administration.[45] The outbreak of World War II postponed the construction of the dams. Additionally, in 1941 a question of who owned the water right to the Birch Canyon drainage became an issue,[46] and the problems were not resolved until 1951 when the reservoir on Birch Creek was finally completed. Ten years later, plans were laid for a second reservoir on Birch Creek, which was completed in September 1970.[47] Both reservoirs are plumbed into the canals owned by the Woodruff Irrigation Company, and they provide water to approximately forty-five hundred acres.

A larger storage project on the narrows of the Bear River, twenty miles north of Evanston, began taking shape in the late 1940s. Initially, most irrigators from Otter Creek in the north to Woodruff in the south felt that the new reservoir would make all other storage facilities unnecessary.[48] The Rich County Water Users Association was created in 1946 to help formulate plans for the project. L. B. Johnson, one of the vice-presidents for the organization, is credited with spearheading the project to completion. Other members of the water users association included J. Earl Stuart, president; Ben Weston, vice-president; H. H. Frederick, secretary; Charles W. Pope, treasurer; and Raymond Rees, director from Woodruff.[49]

Although the Woodruff Narrows Reservoir was located in Wyoming, most of the land which benefited from the project was located in Utah. The original reservoir, dedicated in September 1962, was built fifty feet high and was capable of impounding twenty-eight thousand acre-feet of water.[50] Financing for the project came from the irrigation companies involved, which contributed $610,000, and a $380,000 low-interest loan from the Utah Water and Power Board. Grants were also secured from the Utah Department of Fish and Game, Wyoming Department of Fish and Game, and the U.S. Soil Conservation Service.[51]

Storage at Woodruff Narrows Reservoir was limited by the provisions of the original Bear River Compact, agreed to by the states of Wyoming, Utah, and Idaho, and signed into law in 1958. The original compact allowed that additional storage rights above Bear Lake could be developed by the several states; and it was under this provision that Woodruff Narrows Reservoir was built. As early as 1970 negotiations began to amend the compact to allow additional storage above Bear Lake. In 1979 changes to the Bear River Compact were approved by the Bear River Commission, and the amended compact became law on 8 February 1980. During that year, Woodruff Narrows Reservoir was enlarged to provide an additional twenty-five thousand acre-feet of storage.[52]

Woodruff Narrows Reservoir supplies a reliable source of water to the canals below. Two of these canals originate in Wyoming: the Francis-Lee Canal provides water to five hundred acres of land in Wyoming and Utah, and the Bear River Canal irrigates lands only in Utah although the water right originates in Wyoming.[53] Incorporated in 1879, the Bear River Canal has one of the earliest rights on the river.[54] The canal currently supplies water to 1,660 acres of land. After crossing the Wyoming-Utah border the Bear River supplies an additional eleven canals with irrigation water. The earliest Utah water right on the Bear River belongs to the Crawford-Thompson Canal. Constructed in 1872 by partners William Crawford and William Thompson, the canal company's appropriation dates from 1873.[55] The Crawford-Thompson Canal commences about two miles east of Woodruff on the east bank of the river and supplies water to slightly over four thousand acres of land. The Crawford-Thompson is also one of the longest canals in Rich County, running north from Woodruff nearly twenty miles to Otter Creek. The Dykins Canal, named after rancher and former sheriff of Randolph John W. Dykins,

also taps Bear River's east bank and conveys water northward; it irrigates approximately eleven hundred acres of meadowland between
Woodruff and Randolph. Many of the canals in Rich County are
named for the original ranchers and livestock companies that first
constructed them. The Beckwith and Quinn Canal, which begins on
the east bank of Bear River about five miles northeast of Randolph
and roughly follows the meanderings of the river across the state line
into Wyoming, was named after cattle kings A. C. Beckwith and A. V.
Quinn. The Beckwith-Quinn Canal supplies water to over fifty-six
hundred acres in Utah and Wyoming. The Enberg Canal runs from
the east bank of the Bear River about seven miles northeast of
Randolph and conveys water to lands which were formerly part of
the old Enberg Ranch. Similarly, the Rees Land and Livestock Canal
conveys water from the east bank of the river three miles east of
Woodruff to a small section of land owned by that company. Rees
Land and Livestock also holds stock in several other irrigation companies to irrigate their extensive holdings in Utah and Wyoming.

Other canals that utilize the waters of Bear River and bear the
names of stockmen in the area include the Neville, which begins
downstream from Woodruff Narrows Reservoir across the Utah border, and the McKinn Canal, which takes off the west bank of the river
about five miles northeast of Randolph and provides water to
approximately fifteen hundred acres of meadowland to the north.

Other streams and tributaries of Bear River are also used for irrigation in the Bear River Valley. A small amount of land is irrigated by
Sage Creek, but the Randolph and Sage Creek Irrigation Company
takes water from the west bank of the Bear River four miles south of
Randolph and carries it north about twelve miles to the Six Mile
Creek drainage. Approximately five hundred acres are irrigated by the
Six Mile Creek system, which includes a small reservoir located about
four miles west of the point where Bear River crosses the state line
back into Wyoming. The Otter Creek area north of Randolph is irrigated by canals which tap both banks of the creek and convey water
to lands situated along the drainage. The Rich County-Otter Creek
Irrigation Company provides water to about thirteen hundred acres
of hay pasture; however, the company is responsible for a complicated network of canals which stretch over twenty miles in length.

Within its valley, the Bear River and its tributaries water over fifty thousand acres of land in Rich County. In contrast, only about fifty-six hundred acres are irrigated within the Rich County portion of the Bear Lake Valley. The largest irrigation sources within Bear Lake Valley are Big Spring and Swan Creek.[56] Swan Creek Spring is one of the most prolific and dependable in Utah.[57] The Rich County *Round Up* claimed in 1897 that Swan Creek had an unlimited supply of water. This was after the original canal had been enlarged and extended in 1888. The editor of the newspaper wrote that "it is a pity to see such a large volume of water rushing to the lake without serving man in some form."[58] Some of the water from Swan Spring is used as culinary water for the community of Garden City as well as by residents northward to the Idaho state line.[59] The largest user of Swan Creek water is the Hodges Irrigation Company. Named for Nathanial M. Hodges, whose ranch at one time extended the distance from Garden City to Meadowville, the Hodges Canal services approximately one thousand acres.[60] Much of the old Hodge's Ranch was purchased in 1969 by Sweetwater Resorts and is used as recreational property today.[61] Two other companies also use the waters of Swan Creek. The Swan Canal and the Swan Creek Canal Company jointly irrigate more than twelve hundred acres.[62] The Swan Creek Canal flows south, and the Swan Canal flows north. The construction of the Swan Canal required excavation through solid rock to bring water across the Idaho border to Fish Haven. Much of the work was accomplished through the vigorous activity of Alexander Sims.

Raspberries

Most of the irrigation water in Rich County is used for meadows, pasture, and hay. Some of the waters of Swan Creek, however, empty into furrows and irrigate some of the tastiest raspberries grown anywhere in the world. Wild berries and currents were native to the area and grew in great abundance. An exploration party to Bear Lake Valley in 1857 traveled north along the lake's east shore, then "turned in the Kanyon leading out Across Bear River—we found some good meadow land—cedar in abundance & no end to currants in this region." The group also witnessed Indian women gathering berries

and choke-cherries.[63] Pioneer settlers to Bear Lake Valley also experimented with all kinds of fruit, berry, and current plantings.

Although many kinds of berries, including raspberries, were
grown in individual gardens, the Hildt family is credited with the
commercialization of the crop. Carl (Charles) and Gottleibin Hildt
immigrated to Utah from Germany in 1881 after converting to the
Mormon faith. They were the parents of eleven children. They settled
at Garden City and filed a homestead claim on land west of town.
The Hildts "produced large quantities of fruit and vegetables which
they hauled and sold to the mining camps and towns."[64] Carl and
Gottleibin's oldest son, Theodore, began experimenting with raspberries in 1910. He planted about a quarter acre of "native" berries
which were reportedly "so soft that they had to be picked right into
the bottles." Their taste, however, made them favorite delicacies from
Logan to Kemmerer, Wyoming. In 1924 Theodore and his wife
Elizabeth replaced the quarter acre of native berries with an additional half acre of Cuthberts. The Cuthberts were also known as
"shippers" because of their firm texture. The shift to this variety permitted the Hildts to begin shipping their produce fresh.[65] In 1935
farming operations were turned over to Theodore's and Elizabeth's
oldest son, LaVoy. LaVoy was joined in the business following World
War II by his brother Ivan. The families expanded their acreage and
continued experimenting. Arlo and Mattie Hildt Price became
involved in the business after their marriage, and in 1980 the Hildt-
Price Company was raising raspberries on sixty-five acres of land.[66]

Fruit horticulture is particularly labor intensive. It is perhaps the
one area of agriculture in which mechanization does not work.
Raspberries form each year on new shoots, or canes, and at the conclusion of the season, old canes must be cut out and new canes
thinned. All of this work must be done by hand. Additionally, berries
have to be harvested by hand. Some of this work has been alleviated
through the introduction of a pick-your-own policy. Hundreds of
people make the migration to Garden City to pick raspberries each
season. In 1980 Lowell Gibbons and Drew Cook sold most of their
twenty acres of raspberries in this manner. Gibbons began cultivat-
ing raspberries in the mid-1950s after he became frustrated with having to lease public lands for his ranching operation. Gibbons felt that

raspberries were the best cash crop available to Bear Lake farmers. Even given the amount of labor required, raspberries bring a handsome return on an investment. When the Hildts first began shipping berries in 1935, a case sold for about seventy-five cents. In 1976 a case sold for eleven dollars, and since then, depending upon availability, the price has risen to fifteen dollars or higher.[67]

Dry-farming

Even with continued development of water resources, a shortage of irrigation water still existed in Rich County. This was particularly true during the early part of the twentieth century before the construction of storage reservoirs. Thousands of acres of fertile soil existed in the county for which no water right was available. With increased water storage, some of this land was brought into production. There was some land in the county, however, which was not irrigable under any circumstance. As the scientific concept of dry-land farming gained acceptance throughout the western United States, some of this land was brought into production. The first dry-farming in Rich County actually predates by at least a decade the wide acceptance of the practice. Wet periods often allowed farmers to mature grain crops with little or no irrigation. It was only a matter of time before some farmers began trying to cultivate a crop where no water existed for irrigation. In 1894 farmers in Laketown and Meadowville began "utilizing the land above the canal for raising grain."[68] The experiment was probably short-lived as drier conditions prevailed after 1894, but the idea had been shown to work. Utah led the way in dry-farm agriculture through experiments conducted by the Utah Agricultural College at the Nephi Experiment Station in Juab County. William Jardine, a scientist at the college, noted at the first dry-farming congress held at Denver, Colorado, in 1907 that the "work already done in Utah in an experimental way . . . has aided in the development of the dry farming industry probably as much or more than the work done by any other state."[69] Director John A. Widtsoe of the Agricultural Experiment Station at the college was a major advocate of the practice, and in 1911, after his appointment as president of the college, he published a pioneering work on the subject.[70]

Thrashing with stationary thrasher. (Courtesy Larry Vernon.)

Because of the great amount of arid land in Utah, the state took an avid interest in the promotion of dry-farming. The state legislature appropriated funds to the college to launch several dry-land experimental farms in 1903. By 1906 the federal government also began promoting the practice, and by 1908 Congress was debating the pros and cons of dry-farming. Western senators, such as Utah's Reed Smoot, championed the notion of increasing the size of a homestead from 160 acres to 320 acres. In 1909 Congress passed an Enlarged Homestead Act. The act made it possible for farmers to patent twice as much land in the customary five year period.[71]

Even a doubling of the entry still made dry-farming a risky venture. Climatic conditions needed to be just right, and the principles of summer fallowing and resting the land every other year needed to be followed religiously. As a general rule, the larger the block of land, the more successful the dry-farm. To augment their homesteads, Hyrum and Aquilla Nebeker began purchasing hundreds of acres of state land in the northeastern part of Rich county in 1910. At one time the Nebekers controlled or owned the entire east shore of Bear Lake and all the area extending north and east from South and North Eden canyons. Over fifty thousand acres of land is currently farmed in the vicinity.[72]

Fred and Phebe Smith were two who homesteaded part of the area about twenty-five miles north of Randolph. Phebe brought her seven children out to the dry-farm in 1925. "It wasn't very much a home," she told Willa Kennedy in 1975, "we had two rooms and a lean-to that we had to live in."[73] In time, Fred and his sons constructed a better house. Still, the proving up of the homestead required them to live on the land five months out of the year for three years. "We had to haul our water in barrels for a mile and a half from Rabbit Creek Spring," Phebe noted. "We would go down every day and get the five barrels of water and dip it up into the troughs for the horses, because we couldn't spare the horses to go down there and drink." Phebe explained the process of preparing the land for planting.

> They plowed with a plow and five head of horses. Two of them plowing, and then the other would be picking brush, and then we'd have to burn all this brush. The rocks came up, too. All the children were out helping gather up the rocks, and then finally we'd get the crop planted in the spring . . . then the same thing went over again the next year.[74]

The Smiths eventually acquired 640 acres of dry-farm land. But at best, forty bushels of wheat to the acre could be realized from dryland. Prior to the depression the Smiths received as much as $1.35 a bushel for their wheat. In 1932, however, their grain crop brought only twenty-five cents per bushel. Furthermore, as Phebe explained, the procedure was to allow half the land to remain fallow every other year in order to soak up the winter moisture. That meant that on any given year only 320 acres were in production. The difficulty of making a living on a small dry-farm prompted many in the western states to abandon their claims. The Smiths, however, persisted in their efforts even though Fred and the older sons contracted their labor each summer to haul hay. In her husband's absence, Phebe remained at the homestead. "I'd stay with the little ones out on the farm because I had chickens and pigs and cows and everything to tend, and I would keep the younger children on the farm, and the older ones'd go with him to put up this hay.[75]

Haying

Agriculture required an extraordinary amount of labor before the end of World War II. Horse power was the choice of most farmers until the 1940s. "Nearly all the ranchers had a band of horses," noted J. Earl Stuart.[76] Horses were raised as a cash crop as well as for work on the ranch and farm. Bernice Weston Sims recalled that the horses used during hay season were used for nothing else; the rest of the time the horses were turned out to graze on the foothills. When hay season came around, they were rounded up, fed grain and hay, and put in condition to operate the mowers, rakes, and other haying machinery.[77] A great deal of effort was put into breeding good work horses. J. Earl Stuart remembered as a child when the people of Woodruff bought a registered stallion named Mastik from Paris, France: "As scarce as money was in those days, they paid thirty-six hundred dollars for this horse, and that's where the foundation stock of Woodruff work horses came from"[78]

Along with horses, dozens of farm hands were needed at harvest time. Stuart remembers the "haying season last[ing] all summer." Whereas the season now lasts maybe ten days, Stuart recalled: "In those days, a lot of the times those larger ranches went for six weeks putting up hay."[79] Loran Jackson recollected that what now takes the labor of three or four men required the labor of a sixteen-man crew. Jackson, who began ranching around 1910, recalled those early times.

> When I first started out haying . . . we pitched it on the hay rack with an ordinary hand pitchfork, and we pitched it off the hayrack with the pitchfork and stacked it . . . Then came the hay loader. We had the hay loader, which was attached to these hay racks from the rear and was driven by self-power. One man drove the team on the hay rack right in the middle of the wind row . . . Then you had to have two men in back there to pitch the hay up into the front half of the hay rack, and had to have another man up there to tromp it down.[80]

Jackson characterized the operation of the next technological breakthrough in hay machinery, the boom derrick, as "the hardest work that a human being ever done." Attached to the derrick was a Jackson fork, which was operated by hand. Jackson continued:

> Then it went from the Jackson Fork, to the net. They took the hay in with a push rake [horse powered, with the horses harnessed in back of the rake] and there was a big steel net set there, and they pushed the hay on with the push rake, took the two sides up and hooked them in a big hook, and then they took it up on these boom derricks. Then it went from there to the overshot derrick which pushed the hay up on these teeth on the bottom and it'd go on up them slides [Beaver slide?]. Then they got to these other mechanical derricks. It went from the mechanical derrick into the farm hand of that line where the derrick was put on a tractor. Now it's coming to a point of stockhand machines—I've bought me one of them now [1975]. I decided I couldn't handle that labor anymore, and we're going to put it up with the self stacked mechanical machine, and feed out by mechanical machine.[81]

Ranchers and farmers like Loran Jackson whose memories go back to the horse-power days seldom recall them with any romantic nostalgia. J. Earl Stuart's reminiscence is typical:

> When I think of getting on a tractor and starting it up and going to mow now, and enjoying the fact that your horses didn't get tired or didn't get sore necks, or didn't get bothered by flies and mosquitoes, and so forth; when I think of what a change there is nowadays, makes me wish I was born about forty years later, because I really went through a lot of this that was far from being pleasant.[82]

Although mechanization and technology have revolutionized agriculture in Rich County, they have also decreased the population base of the county. No longer are hundreds of men needed to outfit hay crews or man the thrashing machines or care for the corrals full of horses. Bernice Weston Sims remembers what it was like cooking for the men in a haying camp:

> We would take a sheep camp . . . and I was to use that for my bedroom and keep all the food, the perishables in there because the cabin leaked. . . . We'd have to cook steak for breakfast, so I'd have to get up about 5:00 in the morning in order to have it ready. In

those days you couldn't buy bread even if you went to the store . . .
I had to bake my own bread and I baked bread every other day[,]
so after breakfast I'd have to get all the bread dough set, ready to
raise. I cooked for about 15 men. The problem was some of them
were growing boys. They ate more than the men did. I'd try to
cook enough at noon so I could reheat it for dinner at night, and
wouldn't have to go through the whole process again. It was a hard
job to get enough cooked for one meal, never mind two.

He [Dad] always killed a beef just before we started haying.
There was a lean-to on this shack full of sawdust and they had put
up ice in the wintertime so we kept the beef in there. . . . I'd have to
get Jesse [Early] at night or in the morning before he left to cut me
off some roasts[,] and I usually had a roast for dinner. Then probably for supper too, because we had the biggest meal at noon. I
always made cake, everyday one or two cakes, puddings, potatoes,
boiled potatoes and gravey. We brought potatoes in by the hundred pound sack.[83]

Livestock and Ranching

Livestock came to form the basis of the economy in both the
Bear River and Bear Lake portions of Rich County. Other crops such
as dry-land grain and raspberries also contributed to the agricultural
success of the region. Furthermore, beginning in 1926 and lasting
through about 1940, L. B. Johnson, E. B. Fairbanks, and Mrs. P. J.
Quealegy operated a fur farm. The Wyuta Fur Farm was located on
L. B. Johnson's ranch; at its peak it produced about six hundred fox
pelts a year.[84] The fur farm constituted only a part of L. B. Johnson's
enterprises. Johnson also raised grain crops, turkeys, and hogs, as well
as ranging cattle and sheep on his seventy-five hundred acre farm.[85]

Livestock had been an important part of the area's economy since
its founding. Wilford Woodruff reported in 1871 that Charles C. Rich
had about fifteen hundred acres northeast of Montpelier, Idaho, and
that it was some of the finest ranch land he had ever seen.[86] As discussed earlier, large ranching operators from Evanston, Wyoming,
moved into the Randolph and Woodruff area in the mid-1870s. The
operations of Beckwith and Quinn, Crawford and Thompson, Booth
and Crocker, and the Whitney Ranch were gradually supplanted
between 1890 and the early 1900s by other ranching enterprises. After

Working cattle near Woodruff. (Courtesy Carl Gunn.)

the disappearance of William Crawford in 1893, and the declaration of his death, Byron Sessions was appointed receiver for the estate. Sessions was vice-president of Smith, North and Sessions Company, also known as the Bear River Land and Livestock Company.[87]

Legal difficulties plagued the Crawford estate. William was survived by a very large family, and after legal issues were finally resolved, the estate was divided between the heirs. Additionally, the district court placed a writ of attachment on Crawford's land because of a fifteen thousand dollar debt owed to Crawford's partner William Thompson.[88] The matter eventually resulted in a sheriff's sale of a portion of Crawford's estate. Orlando North of Bear River Land and Livestock Company was the high bidder at the sale and acquired nearly four thousand acres of land.[89] A large portion of the Crawford and Thompson lands was also purchased by David Rees in February 1907.[90] Rees Land and Livestock eventually acquired additional acreage in the Bear River Valley in both Rich County and neighboring Wyoming, and it remains in business today as one of the area's major livestock producers.

Another important livestock enterprise today in Rich County is the Deseret Land and Livestock Company whose holdings comprise much of the land in the southern half of the county. After the death of A. C. Beckwith, George F. Chapman was appointed trustee of the estate. He along with A. O. Chapman and W. O. Chapman formed the Neponset Land and Livestock Company.[91] Much of the land associated with Beckwith and Quinn was purchased by Neponset. Over five thousand acres, however, was sold at a sheriff's sale in May 1901 to Thomas W. Jones for about $4,000.[92] The huge land holdings of Beckwith and Quinn had made it necessary for them to mortgage some of their land, and after acquiring a large share of the Beckwith holdings, the Neponset Company also had to mortgage land. The Neponset Company was heavily indentured to Commercial Trust and Savings of Chicago, Illinois, and although the livestock company survived until at least 1916, it began selling off portions of its land to other companies. The Deseret Land and Livestock Company purchased some of their land directly from Neponset in 1916, but at that time the bulk of Neponset's holdings became the property of W. A. Crane.[93]

Between 1917 and 1928 Deseret Land and Livestock eventually acquired most of the old Beckwith and Quinn property. The land acquired by Thomas W. Jones at the sheriff's sale in 1901 along with an additional six thousand acres owned by Jones was purchased by Deseret from Jones's estate in 1917.[94] Additionally, in 1928 the Deseret Company purchased the holdings of W. A. Crane. A smaller amount of Crane's land was purchased by the Woodruff Grazing Land Association.[95] Much of the association's land was subsequently lost to foreclosure during the Great Depression.

After the demise of Beckwith and Quinn, Crawford and Thompson, and other large livestock operations, most of the land still remained under the control of a large company. Deseret Land and Livestock differed from the earlier companies in several ways, however. First, Deseret Livestock was engaged in sheep raising rather than cattle; second, whereas the cattle barons were non-Mormons, the owners and major stockholders of Deseret were all members of the Mormon church. Third, Deseret was a cooperative stock company, mostly self-reliant and without the financial ties to eastern capital that had supported the earlier cattle companies. The Deseret Livestock Company incorporated in 1891 and was an amalgamation of the sheep bands of several Utah families. Included were the holdings of the Moss, Nelson, Hogan, Ellis, Noble, Atkinson, and Pace families. Many of these people were neighbors and prominent Davis County, Utah, families. The names of William Moss and John E. Hatch figure prominently in the history of the company. Prior to the incorporation of the Deseret Livestock Company, the Hatch-Moss Sheep Company ranged approximately twelve thousand head of sheep in southern Rich County. The Hatch-Moss enterprise shared the range with other companies, including the Three-Slope Company, South Bountiful Sheep Company, Nelson and Company, and the company of Joseph E. Moyle. In order to safeguard his company's summer range, William Moss began considering plans to purchase railroad land in the county. He approached the other companies with the idea of jointly purchasing twenty-nine sections of land and consolidating their sheep bands into one company. Thus the Deseret Livestock Company was formed.[96]

The influx of thousands of sheep into Rich County each summer created tension between the settlers around Woodruff and the sheep companies. It also created tension between the large cattle interests and the sheep companies. The *Salt Lake Herald* reported in 1887 how the "cattle interest is being severely damaged in this and adjacent counties by the encroachment of sheepmen upon their ranges."[97] The Rich County Commission responded to the encroachment of sheep by passing an ordinance in 1897 which required that each head of sheep in the county be licensed, that licenses cost ten cents per head, that the county clerk would issue all licenses, and that failure to abide by the ordinance would constitute a misdemeanor punishable by one hundred days in jail or a fine of one hundred dollars or both. John E. Hatch of Deseret Livestock objected strenuously, stating that his company would "have to go out of business." Ed Chapman of Neponset Land and Livestock also objected to the "unjustness of the law," noting that if sheep were to be licensed then horses and cows should be assessed the same fee. County Assessor Sam Weston spoke in favor of the ordinance, stating that he had canvassed the county and found two-thirds of the residents in favor of the proposition. The ordinance passed on 15 July 1897.[98]

In August 1897 Sheriff D. W. Marshall inquired of the court how to proceed in serving notice on sheep owners. The "court ordered him to present notes to all sheep herders and if they fail to sign notes

Sheep became of ever increasing importance to livestock men during the early 1900s. (Courtesy Kris Limb.)

to arrest them for misdemeanor under the ordinance."[99] The following June, the county court met again to reconsider the ordinance. It opted to change the ten cent per head portion of the ordinance to a sliding scale and base the ordinance on a similar one used in Cache County. The new ordinance required sheep owners with more than five thousand head to secure a $250.00 license plus pay $50.00 for each additional one thousand animals. The scale decreased in increments until owners with fewer than five hundred head were required to secure only a ten dollar license.[100] Sheep owners were reluctant to comply even with the new ordinance. Sheriff Marshall and Commissioner John Kennedy reported that they had traveled throughout the county and had actually found very few of the owners with their sheep licenses. The sheriff was again ordered to issue the licenses, although he was allowed to enter protests from the sheep owners on the back of the license.[101] There is no indication that the county ever collected any money from the sheep ordinance. In June 1899 the county attorney offered the opinion that the ordinance was probably unconstitutional.[102] The sheep ordinance not only was designed to discourage extensive sheep-raising interests among the large property owners in the county but also to discourage the use of open range by transient sheep herds. Much of the land area in Rich County remained part of the public domain. In 1905 Congress created the Forest Service and transferred forest lands from the General Land Office within the Interior Department to the Department of Agriculture. One of the first things mandated by the Forest Service after the transfer was the removal of sheep from the forest reserve. At the outset, only a small amount of land was affected in Rich County; but by 1909 nearly 7.5 million acres had been set aside as national forest land in Utah.[103] Of more importance in Rich County was the public land which did not meet the requirements for administration under the Forest Service. Much of this land was used by grazers who either owned adjoining parcels of land or who brought their livestock (most often sheep) into the county for summer range. Until 1934 there was no provision for leasing or controlling the use of these public lands by grazers. The sentiment in most areas of Utah was that such land should be available for the use of residents of the county in which the land was located. Beginning in 1922, Utah led the way to have the remaining unreserved public lands placed under federal protection and restricted to the use of local residents who would sign long-term leases with the government. In 1934 Congress passed the Taylor Grazing Act, which placed all the remaining public lands under the United States Grazing Service within the Department of Interior. The Taylor Act was based almost entirely on earlier legislation proposed by Utah Congressman Don B. Colton.[104]

More than a quarter of the total land area in Rich County ultimately came to be included within the provisions of the Taylor Act. Today more than 170,000 acres in the county are administered by the Bureau of Land Management (BLM), the successor to the Grazing Service. This land is leased primarily to grazers, but in 1976 Congress also mandated that the public lands under the jurisdiction of the BLM be used for recreation and other multiple-use purposes.[105]

Grazing leases on BLM lands are granted to both individuals and corporations such as the Deseret Land and Livestock Company. Prior to passage of the Taylor Act, these lands were used on a first-come first-serve basis. The Deseret company's holdings in 1890 were in excess of seventeen thousand acres, including twenty-eight thousand head of sheep. By 1899 the company's livestock assets had grown to nearly fifty-six thousand head of sheep. With the outbreak of World War I in Europe in 1914 and the entry of the United States into the war in 1917, the years between 1914 and 1918 brought a huge demand for wool and agricultural products in general. The Deseret Livestock Company experienced its strongest growth during that period. By the mid-1920s, after the purchase of the Crane and Jones property, the company controlled 225,000 acres of land.[106] Deseret Livestock Company used its holdings in Rich County and neighboring Uinta County, Wyoming, mostly for summer range. The company acquired the Iosepa Agricultural and Stock Company, a large ranch in Tooele County owned by the Mormon church, around 1915 for use as winter range.[107] The trailing of sheep from northeastern Utah to the west desert during the fall had long created a problem for tax assessors in Rich County. It seemed that by the time the Rich County Assessor got around to valuing the livestock in the county, most of the sheep had already been removed to their winter range. Beginning in 1883 the county clerk was authorized "to make demand on the county court of Tooele County for one half of the tax collected on sheep wintered in that county."[108] Similar authorizations were made for Box Elder County.[109] By 1893 the west desert had become a favorite winter range for several large operators, including Deseret Livestock, T. W. Jones, Erickson Brothers, Wrathall and Mander, A. G. Nygreen, and Sutton Brothers. The clerk was again instructed to demand payment from Tooele County for one-half the taxes.[110] By 1902 the county had reached an agreement with neighboring Uinta County, Wyoming, but not with Tooele County. The problem was not a matter of the sheep owners refusing to pay their taxes (although they could not be expected to pay taxes twice); the problem was one of cooperation between the two counties. The sheep owners involved in the Deseret Livestock Company had already learned the benefits of cooperation; but it would be some time before county governments did likewise.

This predicament remained throughout the prosperous years prior to and during World War I. Despite the recession which plagued agriculture, particularly wool producers, following the close of World War I, the Deseret Livestock Company held its own during the 1920s.[111] Beginning in 1929, however, as economic depression spread throughout the nation, financial problems became evident in the company's operations. Wool prices dipped even lower after 1929, falling from twenty-nine cents per pound to thirteen cents in 1932.[112] The company was forced to acquire loans from the Wasatch Livestock Loan Company and to cut employees' wages. The company's loans were later refinanced with and transferred to the federally supported Agricultural Credit Corporation.[113]

The federal government played an integral part in supporting efforts to confront the agricultural depression in Rich County. Through the restructuring of Deseret Livestock's finances, the Agricultural Credit Corporation helped avert an economic catastrophe for the company. The federal government was also involved with other ranchers in Rich County during the Depression. In 1935 after suffering through the worst drought in recorded history, local cattlemen sold 5,815 head of cattle under the Emergency Cattle Purchasing Program. The 236 livestock producers received only a little over seventy thousand dollars for the cattle, or about twelve dollars a head; but according to County Agent E. L. Guymon:

> The Emergency Cattle Program has virtually saved a large per cent of the cattlemen in Rich County. Had it not been for this program approximately 5,000 cattle would never have reached a market due to lack of flesh. Besides this, prices would have been depressed until the cattle that were in fair condition would hardly have paid their way to market. Also, leinholders have been saved from taking a complete loss on approximately 2,000 head.[114]

A host of other federally financed programs, including rodent control, weed eradication, development of stock wells, dairy and beef cattle improvement, and drought relief also benefited Rich County farmers and ranchers during the years of the depression. The outbreak of World War II brought renewed prosperity to the farming sector within the United States. Prices for agricultural products rose dramatically, particularly prices for wool and livestock. The Deseret Livestock Company largely retired its debt during the early 1940s as its total worth approached two million dollars by 1946.[115] With the resignation of James H. Moyle in 1929 and the death of William Moss in 1933, many of the original founders of Deseret Livestock company were gone by end of World War II. Nevertheless, the company stayed under the control of the original families: Ralph J. Moss remained as company foreman, and Henry D. Moyle assumed the directorship of the company after his father's resignation. Ralph J. Moss passed away in 1949, and in 1953 Salt Lake City businessmen Ken Garff and David L. Freed, with backing from various Utah bankers and entrepreneurs, formed a syndicate and bought controlling interest in the company. The syndicate controlled the Deseret Livestock Company for the next twenty years. Livestock production remained the primary interest of the company, but the owners also expanded into other areas. During the 1970s the owners offered to sell their land in Rich and neighboring counties to the Utah State Division of Wildlife. The proposal was turned down by the state legislature in 1974, and the company was thereafter sold to Hong Kong businessman Joseph E. Hotung. The Garff interests, however, retained the mineral rights on the Rich County and Uinta County, Wyoming, lands, and during the oil boom of the 1970s leased the oil exploration rights to American Oil Company. No oil or natural gas was found, however. In 1979 Hotung sold the sheep, and four years later the entire company was purchased by the Mormon church which retains ownership today.[116]

Dairy Industry

Although large livestock interests have been historically important, the majority of residents in Rich County operated much smaller enterprises. Individual ranchers and farmers kept some sheep and some cattle. Most of the smaller operators raised both beef and milk cows. The earliest dairying activity occurred in Bear Lake Valley and was a response to the cooperative movement encouraged by the Mormon church in the late 1860s and early 1870s. Thomas Passey was selected to manage a dairy cooperative in Nounan Valley north of Montpelier, Idaho, in 1876. The company began operation with two hundred head of cows which were turned over to the cooperative by individuals in exchange for certificates of stock in the company. By 1883 the cooperative was milking fifteen hundred head and producing two hundred thousand pounds of butter a year. Creameries began appearing in many of the communities in the Bear

Ernest McKinnon, master cheese-maker, at work in the Rich County Creamery. (Courtesy Nathell Hoffman.)

Lake and Bear River valleys around the turn of the century. The community at Paris, Idaho, constructed the Pioneer Creamery in 1901.[117]

J. Earl Stuart recalled how most "every farm had a little flock of cows. They didn't have any large spread . . . like they do in these dairies today, but nearly every ranch had a few . . . I guess it was the only way they made their cash."[118] Stuart's family purchased the Woodruff Creamery in 1903 and operated the business for about twelve years.[119] During this time, J. Earl worked at the family business and recalled that after they had collected the milk and separated it, the farmers would "take the skim milk back and feed it to their pigs and their calves."[120] Stuart maintains that some of the ranchers turned a better profit from milking cows than they did from their beef operations: "Price for beef wasn't very good, but they had these cows and they milked the cows and got their pay every month."[121]

Milk trucks such as this one made daily rounds to the farms in Rich County to pick up milk for delivery to the creameries. (Courtesy Nathell Hoffman.)

A creamery was begun at Randolph in 1902 after some of the residents purchased the building constructed by H. J. Faust a year earlier. The original building burned down around 1906, and a second creamery was started by Ike Smith, Arthur G. Barton, John Woolsey, and Robert McKinnon. The operation was later sold to the Mutual Creamery Company in 1916.[122] At the same time, Mutual Creamery also purchased the original Laketown Creamery, constructed in 1907, and the creameries in Woodruff and in Paris, Idaho. "For years," Laketown resident Ray Lamborn remembered, "I had stock in the Mutual Creamery."[123]

The Bear Lake Cooperative Dairymen's Association was formed during the Depression years of the 1930s. The cooperative purchased and assumed control of several creameries owned by the Mutual Company in Bear Lake Valley. In 1938 the communities of Woodruff and Randolph created the South Rich Dairy Cooperative and separated from the Bear Lake group. Individuals involved in the creation of the South Rich Creamery Cooperative were Aden W. Thornock, Frank Frazier, Edwin C. Hoffman, Carlos Cornia, Lewis Longhurst,

Shelby Huffaker, Alma Argyle, and Raymond Spencer. Bear Lake Cooperative member L. L. Cook of Garden City was instrumental in helping the South Rich group complete its building. Ernest McKinnon worked at the plant for many years as the master cheese-maker. The South Rich Creamery Cooperative Association purchased the operations of the Mutual Creamery Company in 1942. The coop-erative continued to function until the early 1960s, gradually expand-ing to become a feed store and supplier of gas and oil products.[124]

With the closing of the Randolph Cooperative Creamery, the dairy industry in Bear River Valley largely disappeared. Dairying remained important within the Bear Lake region, but the large dairies were mostly located in the Idaho portion of the valley. Dairies in Rich County were converted to beef-cattle operations, or sheep and wool producing operations. In 1990 Rich County reported having fewer than five hundred milk cows out of a total of forty-five thousand head of cattle. At present in northern Utah, Rich County is second only to Box Elder County in sheep production. The almost total changeover to sheep and beef production in Rich County is supported by the amount of grass hay produced in which the county surpasses all oth-ers—harvesting thirty-three thousand acres in 1989. Farms and ranches in Rich County are also on average the largest in Utah. Of the 166 farms in Rich County, sixty are larger than one thousand acres. The median size of the majority of Utah farms is still less than one hundred acres. The average sized farm in Rich County is in excess of three thousand acres.[125] Rich County farms have progressively grown in size over the years. In 1880 the average farm in the county con-tained 135 acres. By 1900 the average had increased to 582 acres. During the next twenty years, average farm size in Rich County rose dramatically to over eleven hundred acres.[126] The number of farms in the county remained static throughout the forty-year period. The increase in the size of the farms was probably due to new lands being brought into production in the northeastern part of county under the Enlarged Homestead Act and through the purchase of state lands for dry-farming. There has, nonetheless, been a gradual trend in consoli-dation of farmland over the last thirty years. In 1959 there were 227 farms reported in Rich County compared to 166 in 1989.[127]

Successful livestock and farming operations in Rich County have been the net result of the experiences of settlers over the last 130 years. Their willingness to experiment and to accept failure as part of the experimental process proved the practicality of agriculture at high elevations. Furthermore, the faith and religious conviction of the predominantly Mormon settlers played no small part in the establishment of a working agricultural system in Rich County.

ENDNOTES

1. Walter P. Cottam, "Is Utah Sahara Bound," *University of Utah Bulletin* 37 (19 February 1947): 5.

2. Richard H. Jackson, "Myth and Reality; Environmental Perceptions of the Mormons, 1840–1865: an Historical Geosophy," (Ph.d. diss., Clark University, 1970), 231.

3. Landsford W. Hastings, *The Emigrants' Guide to Oregon and California* (New York: DaCapo Press, 1969), 78, and Jackson, *Myth and Reality,* 72.

4. Sardis W. Templeton, *The Lame Captain: The Life and Adventures of Pegleg Smith* (Los Angeles: Westernlore Press, 1965), 183.

5. Ibid., 184.

6. Journal of Thomas Sleight, typescript, 52–53, Special Collections and Archives, Utah State University, Logan.

7. Ibid., 56.

8. Ibid., 57.

9. Leonard J. Arrington, *Charles C. Rich, Mormon General and Western Frontiersman* (Provo: Brigham Young University Press, 1974), 272.

10. *Journal History of the Church of Jesus Christ of Latter-day Saints,* manuscript, Department of Special Collections and Archives, Merrill Library, Utah State University, Logan, Utah (hereafter referred to as JH).

11. Luella Nebeker Adams, *Phebe Almira Hulme Nebeker* (Salt Lake City: n.p., 1955), 50.

12. Journal of Thomas Sleight, 58.

13. Adams, *Phebe Almira Hulme Nebeker,* 50, 51.

14. Reed Eborn, interview with Ray Lamborn, "Growing up in Laketown," 3 May 1975, 6. See also Elizabeth P. Astle and Mary P. Stucki, "Life History of Ellen Jane Bailey Lamborn," typescript, Special Collections and Archives, Utah State University, Logan.

15. Leonard J. Arrington, *Charles C. Rich* (Provo: Brigham Young University Press, 1974), 272.

16. A correspondent from Malad, Idaho, to the *True Latter Day Saints*

Herald (Plano, Illinois) noted in February 1868 how "our crops were taken by grasshoppers. Malad Valley, Cache Valley, Round Valley and Bear Lake Valley, all suffered more or less." See *The True Latter Day Saints' Herald,* 1 March 1868, p. 78.

17. *Deseret News,* 27 July 1868, quoted in Russell R. Rich, *Land of the Sky-Blue Water: A History of the L.D.S. Settlement of the Bear Lake Valley* (Provo: Brigham Young University, 1963), 70.

18. *Deseret News,* 18 September 1888.

19. Tithing Record, 1877–1883, Randolph Ward, Rich County, Utah, in Historian's Office, Church of Jesus Christ of Latter-day Saints, Salt Lake City, Utah (hereafter referred to as RTR).

20. Eight thousand bushels of grain reportedly were produced by the farmers at Randolph. See Manuscript History of the Randolph Ward, Rich County, Utah, in Historical Office, Church of Jesus Christ of Latter-day Saints, Salt Lake City, Utah (hereafter referred to as RMH), 12 November 1878.

21. A surprising amount of cash was donated, particularly after 1880. In 1880 only $26 was contributed, but in 1881, 1882, and 1883 an average of $177.00 was received in cash donation. See RTR. This probably reflects the wages earned at the Almy coal mines where some of the Randolph and Woodruff settlers were employed during the winter months. It might also reflect cash acquired through the selling of surplus livestock at the Almy mines or the selling of surplus in the gold fields at Caribou Mountain fifty miles north of Soda Springs, Idaho, or further north along the Montana Trail into the gold fields of southwestern Montana.

22. *Report of the Special Committee of the United States Senate on the Irrigation and Reclamation of Arid Lands, the Great Basin Region and California, Utah, Nevada, Arizona* (Washington, D.C.: GPO, 1890), 2:94.

23. The Randolph Ward History records that the ditch was constructed in 1877. However, a report submitted by John Snowball to the Senate Special Committee on Irrigation states that the ditch was not in use until 1881. See RMH, 1877; and *Irrigation and Reclamation of Arid Lands* 2:94.

24. Paul W. Gates, *History of Public Land Law Development* (Washington, D.C.: GPO, 1968), 654–56.

25. RMH, 1936, and County Book B, Rich County, Utah, 21 February 1935, 256, in Clerk's Office, Rich County Courthouse, Randolph, Utah. (hereafter referred to as County Book).

26. *Annual Report of the Commissioner of the General Land Office to the Secretary of Interior for the Fiscal Year Ended June 30, 1903* (Washington, D.C., Government Printing Office, 1903), 162.

27. Reservoir file, Utah Division of Water Rights, Salt Lake City, Utah.

28. "Working Paper: Irrigation Conveyance System Inventory Summary, Bear River Basin, Idaho, Utah, Wyoming, for Bear River Basin Type IV Study," April 1976, 99–135 (hereafter cited as "Irrigation Conveyance Systems").

29. Rich County Land Use Guide, 74.

30. RMH, 1885.

31. Irrigation Conveyance Systems, 97.

32. Laws of the Territory of Utah, twenty-sixth session Utah Territorial Assembly, 13 March 1884, 127–33.

33. Woodruff Irrigation District minutes, 20 January 1891, Office of the LDS Church Historian. Salt Lake City, Utah (hereafter cited as WID).

34. Historical Record, Woodruff Ward, Bear Lake State, Rich County, Utah, 28 September 1884, 46.

35. WID.

36. *Irrigation and Reclamation of Arid Lands* 2:94.

37. Manuscript History of Woodruff Ward, Bear Lake Stake, Rich County, Utah, 1870. Historian's Office, Church of Jesus Christ of latter-day Saints, Salt Lake City, Utah, (hereafter referred to as WMH), 1899.

38. *Deseret News,* 14 June 1899.

39. Annual Report of Extension Work, 1928, Rich County, "Cooperative Extension Work in Agriculture and Home Economics," State of Utah, 15, (hereafter referred to as County Agent's Report).

40. L. M. Winsor holds a number of distinctions in early twentieth-century Utah history. He was the first engineering graduate from Utah State University and the first county agent in the United States. Winsor's activity as a county agent actually anticipates the creation of the extension service by three years. He was sent to the Uinta Basin in 1911 after graduation. The Smith Lever Act which created the Cooperative Extension Service was not passed until 1914. Winsor had also been involved in the construction of several small dams in Utah, particularly the Enterprise dam in Washington County, Utah. See Luther M. Winsor, *Life History of Luther M. Winsor* (Murray, UT: R. Fenton Murray, 1962).

41. County Agent's Report, 1928.

42. County Agent's Report, 1928, 15.

43. County Agent's Report, 1937.

44. County Agent's Report, 1939.

45. County Agent's Report, 1937, 25.

46. County Agent's Report, 1941, 33.

47. Woodruff Centennial Committee, *The First Hundred Years in Woodruff* (Springville, UT: Art City Publishing Co., 1970), 68.

48. County Agent's Report, 1944.

49. County Agent's Report, 1946.

50. *Fifth Annual Report of the Bear River Commission,* 1962, 17–18.

51. *Paris Post,* 6 September 1962, 1.

52. *Bear River Commission Report,* 1985–86, 25.

53. "Irrigation Conveyance Systems," 101.

54. *Irrigation and Reclamation of Arid Lands* 3:531.

55. Ibid.

56. See "Irrigation Conveyance Systems," for information on this and the previously mentioned canals and ditches.

57. *Rich County Land Use Guide,* 35.

58. *Roundup,* 23 July 1897.

59. *Rich County Land-Use Guide,* 35.

60. "Irrigation Conveyance Systems."

61. *Bear Lake Magazine* 1 (15 March 1978): 9.

62. Irrigation Conveyance System Inventory Summary, Bear River Basin, Idaho-Utah-Wyoming for Bear River Basin Type IV Study (n.p. 1976).

63. "Report of a Party of Observation, Consisting of Eleven Men, Under Command of M. Monroe. Started from Ogden City Aug. (18)57." Records of the State Territorial Militias, microfilm, Special Collections and Archives, Utah State University, Logan.

64. Mildred H. Thomson, *Rich Memories: Some of the Happenings in Rich County from 1863 to 1960* (Salt Lake City: Daughters of the Utah Pioneers, 1962), 64.

65. Ibid., 48.

66. *Bear Lake Magazine* 1 (1 August 1977): 4.

67. Ibid. 2 (15 July 1978): 7.

68. JH, 8 September 1894, 10.

69. Dry Farm Congress. *Proceedings of the Trans-Missouri Dry Farming Congress,* January 24, 25, 26, 1907, 32.

70. John A. Widtsoe, *Dry-Farming: A System of Agriculture for Countries Under A Low Rainfall* (New York: Macmillan Co., 1911).

71. Gates, *Development of Public Land Law,* 503.

72. *Bear Lake Magazine* 3 (15 August 1979): 6–9.

73. Willa Kennedy, interview with Phebe Smith, "Dry Farming in Rich County," 24 April 1975, typescript, 3, Special Collections and Archives, Utah State University, Logan.

74. Ibid., 4–5.

75. Ibid., 7.

76. Willa Kennedy, interview with J. Earl Stuart, 27 May 1975, typescript, 7, Special Collections and Archives, Utah State University, Logan.

77. Mary Evelyn Izatt, interview with Bernice Weston Sims, "Ranching Life Style, Rich County, Utah," 27 May 1973, typescript, 4, Special Collections and Archives, Utah State University, Logan.

78. Kennedy, interview with J. Earl Stuart, 8.

79. Ibid., 3.

80. Kennedy, interview with Loran Jackson, 15.

81. Ibid., 15.

82. Kennedy, interview with J. Earl Stuart, 4.

83. Izatt, interview with Bernice Weston Sims, 2–4.

84. Steven L. Thomson, Jane D. Digerness, and Mar Jean S. Thomson, *Randolph—A Look Back* (n.p., 1981), 217.

85. *Rich County Reaper,* 31 October 1941.

86. Scott G. Kenney, ed., *Wilford Woodruff's Journal, 1833–1898,* typescript, 9 vols. (Midvale, UT: Signature Books, 1983–1991), 30 June 1871, 21.

87. Deed and Mortgage Record, Rich County, Utah, Book E, p. 243; record in the Assessor's Office, Rich County Court House, Randolph, Utah (hereafter referred to as D and M).

88. D and M, Book E, 85.

89. Ibid., Book H, 71.

90. Ibid., Book H, 345–48.

91. Grantor's Index, Rich County Utah, Book 6a, Randolph, Utah; record in Recorder's Office, Rich County Court House, Randolph, Utah.

92. Miscellaneous Record, Book 1, 3 May 1901, 37–38; record in Recorder's Office, Rich County Courthouse, Randolph, Utah.

93. D and M, Book L, 401.

94. Ibid., Book M, 18.

95. Ibid., Book P, 511.

96. Jean Ann McMurrin, "The Deseret Live Stock Company: The First Fifty Years, 1890–1940" (master's thesis, University of Utah, 1989), 37–40.

97. JH, 3 October 1887, 5.

98. County Book A, 30 April 1897, 319.

99. Ibid., 9 August 1897, 329.

100. Ibid., 8 June 1898, 343.

101. Ibid., 9 August 1898, 348–9.

102. Ibid., 2 June 1899, 363.

103. Gates, *Development of Public Land Law,* 579–81.

104. Robert Parson, "Prelude to the Taylor Grazing Act: Don B. Colton and the Utah Public Domain Committee, 1927–1932," *Encyclia: The Journal of the Utah Academy of Sciences, Arts, and Letters,* 68 (1991): 209–32.

105. Ibid., 217.

106. McMurrin, *The Deseret Livestock Company,* 92.

107. Ibid., 77.

108. County Book A, 4 June 1883, 109.

109. Ibid., 15 January 1884, 116.

110. Ibid., 232.

111. Prices for wool fell 289 percent between 1920 and 1921. See McMurrin, *The Deseret Livestock Company,* 81.

112. McMurrin, *The Deseret Livestock Company,* 81.

113. Ibid., 83.

114. County Agent's Report, 1935, 18.

115. McMurrin, *The Deseret Livestock Company,* 93.

116. Ibid., 95–97.

117. *Bear Lake Magazine,* 2 (15 July 1978): 8.

118. Kennedy, interview with J. Earl Stuart, typescript.

119. *Woodruff—The First Hundred Years,* 440.

120. Kennedy, interview with J. Earl Stuart, 6.

121. Ibid., 5.

122. Thomson, *Randolph—A Look Back,* 100.

123. Eborn, interview with Ray Lamborn.

124. Thomson, *Randolph—A Look Back,* 100–101.

125. *1992 Utah Agricultural Statistics, Utah Department of Agriculture Annual Report, Enterprise Budgets* (Salt Lake City: Utah State Department of Agriculture, 1992,) 52–69.

126. *1969 Statistical Abstract of Utah* (Salt Lake City: University of Utah, 1969), 194.

127. *1969 Statistical Abstract of Utah,* 192.

7

"Still Look to the Future in Faith"

RELIGION AND LIFE
IN RICH COUNTY

The predominantly Mormon farmers of Rich County sought an idyllic life and at times approached it. Generally hard-working and passionately religious, the settlers came to epitomize the motto of "industry" later inscribed on the Great Seal of the State of Utah. There was a good deal of cooperation and community identification in early Rich County. Long hours were spent creating a society which the settlers hoped would fill both their spiritual and temporal needs. Under the rigors of frontier society, the spirit often had to carry the settlers through times when temporal pursuits failed them as well as through times of sorrow. Early Round Valley settler Merlin Eastham Kearl lost two of her children to diphtheria in one night. Of her husband James it was said: "He could ride hard, work hard, bury his dead, and still look to the future in faith."[1] Faith and conviction of purpose played an integral part in the development of Rich County. Devastated by the death of his young wife Marianne in 1865, Thomas Sleight later paid tribute to the difficulties experienced by her and other early women settlers in Bear Lake Valley.[2] Sleight remarked:

Just imagine a woman brought up in circumstances in Europe, or in the States, living in a log cabin, having ground for the floor, scant clothing, and hungry children, with frozen wheat poorly ground for bread, and a haggard husband, all sitting around a homemade table to make a meal of that article to keep the lamp of life burning.[3]

With few creature comforts to sustain them, settlers placed much of their lives in the hands of providence. Their religious beliefs fostered a closely knit society which looked to their church for guidance. During the early years, the Mormon church for all practical purposes provided both religious and civil guidance. Communities were organized into wards or branches and placed under the direction of a bishop or presiding elder. Although Charles C. Rich was the acknowledged leader in Bear Lake Valley, the area settlements were further grouped together into a sort of stake organization in 1869. David P. Kimball was appointed to preside over the Bear Lake settlements as stake president, with the assistance of Joseph C. Rich and James H. Hart.[4] In 1874 David P. Kimball was released from his position, and Charles C. Rich assumed control. Perhaps the very reason that Kimball was chosen in the first place proved his undoing. The organization of the Bear Lake settlements into a cohesive, religious community required domineering leadership. Demanding and energetic, Kimball brooked no excuse for laziness. Although details are sketchy, Kimball evidently issued a royal tongue-lashing to some of the Saints who did not measure up to his expectations. He spared no words, including the profane, and was reprimanded by Apostle Rich and relieved of his duties. Shortly thereafter, Kimball left Bear Lake Valley.[5]

From 1874 until 1877 Charles C. Rich reassumed leadership, functioning in the capacity of stake president without the benefit of counselors. In 1877 a reorganization took place, and the Bear Lake Stake was officially created. William Budge was appointed stake president, a position he would occupy for nearly thirty years. Budge converted to the Mormon church in his native Scotland and served several missions throughout Europe before immigrating to the United States with his wife, Julia, and their infant son in 1860. The family settled in Farmington, Davis County, where William married his second wife, Eliza Pritchard. In 1864 he and his families left Farmington and settled in Providence, Cache County. Four years later, William married his third wife, Ann Hyer, and two years after that was appointed presiding bishop of Rich County. Budge was supposed to look after the temporal needs of the settlers and was put in charge of "all tithing business in that section of the country."[6]

With the organization of Bear Lake Stake in 1877, Budge was placed in charge of a huge ecclesiastical district stretching from Star Valley, Wyoming, to Soda Springs, Idaho, and south to include all of the Bear Lake and Bear River valleys. With the exception of the present Rich County communities, the remainder of Bear Lake Stake was in either Wyoming or Idaho. Budge was assisted in his duties as stake president by James H. Hart, first counselor, and George Osmond, second counselor.[7] He served through one of the most tumultuous periods in Mormon history.

In 1862, two years after William and Julia's emigration, Congress passed the Anti-Bigamy Law. The law made polygamous marriages a punishable crime within the U.S. territories. While some members of Congress and much of the nation were comparing polygamy to slavery and referring to them as "the twin relics of barbarism," Utah Mormons claimed that the practice of polygamy was protected by the First Amendment to the Constitution. The debate lingered for over a decade with no one ever being successfully prosecuted under the law's provisions. Congress proposed other measures to strengthen the 1862 law and in 1874 passed the Poland Act. The Poland Act was in some ways milder than other anti-polygamy bills brought before Congress. The earlier Cullom Bill, for instance, not only sought to toughen existing anti-bigamy laws but also to virtually revamp the territorial government in Utah.[8] Many Mormon polygamists breathed a sigh of relief with the defeat of the Cullom Bill and the passage of the Poland Act, because the latter allowed the Mormons to continue to appoint probate judges within Utah, and therein resided the Mormon method of using the law in their favor. That luxury lapsed with the passage of the Edmunds Act in 1882 and the Edmunds-Tucker Act of 1887. From then on, court officials became federal appointees removed from Mormon church influence or control.

At Woodruff, a noticeable conflict developed between Mormons and non-Mormons at the time of the Edmunds-Tucker Act. Perhaps because of its close proximity to the mining and railroad towns of Almy and Evanston or because of the conflict between Mormon farmers and non-Mormon cattlemen, Woodruff for a brief period following 1888 came to be politically dominated by gentiles or non-Mormons. In 1872 the community cooperatively erected a meeting-house for both worship and school.[9] But as the community grew during the first decade of its existence, a proposal was made to construct a new building. Like the original, the new public building was to be used as both a church and school.

The settlers in Woodruff subscribed twelve hundred dollars in 1884 for the new buildings construction.[10] After its completion, a squabble developed between the LDS bishopric and the school board over ownership of the property. According to the Woodruff ward history, in 1884 the school board was composed of "one LDS, one gentile Liberal and one Mormon Liberal."[11] The two "Liberals" claimed that because the building had been used as a school and constructed under that pretense, it was a school, and therefore rightfully belonged to the district. Many Mormons in Woodruff disagreed and sued the school district in federal court. In 1890 Judge Henderson of the First District Court at Ogden, Utah, ruled in favor of the school district, and the meeting house became its property.[12]

This was the first wave of troubled waters between the Mormon settlers and their non-Mormon counterparts. Political turbulence became common throughout Utah in the 1880s. Utahns had shunned political affiliation along national lines, preferring to divide according to religious affiliation: the People's party representing the views of Mormons and the Liberal party representing those of non-Mormons. The passage of the Edmunds-Tucker Act exacerbated the situation. The act reaffirmed the illegality of polygamy and gave federal marshals and judges greater leeway in the pursuit and prosecution of offenders.[13]

In Woodruff, as the rift between Mormon and non-Mormon settlers widened, a petition to remove William H. Lee as bishop circulated through the community. Circulated by the "Band of the Loyal League," the petition sought Lee's removal because of his plural marriages.[14] Furthermore, in addition to being bishop of Woodruff, Lee was also the president of the People's party.[15] A Woodruff historian at the time editorialized that some of the "bitterest enemies of the Church [are] residing in Woodruff" and noted that "Deputy Marshals find comfortable quarters" there.[16]

By 1888 four Mormons, including Bishop Lee, had been fined and imprisoned for cohabitation.[17] With the arrest of Lee and the other members of the community, excitement in Woodruff was hard to suppress. Lorinda Allen pleaded with her Relief Society sisters "not to speak against the principle of Celestial Marriage[,] if we can't understand it[,] don't condemn it."[18]

But polygamy was being condemned not only by non-Mormons in Woodruff but also by the entire country. Federal authorities were resolute in their opposition and cited the Mormon practice of polygamy as the chief reason for the denial of statehood to Utah. Furthermore, as renewed efforts for statehood mounted, Liberal party members wanted Mormons disfranchised. In 1888 the Journal History of the LDS Church commented on the political climate in Woodruff: "Politics are running high in this country and especially in this precinct. At a recent primary to choose delegates to the county convention the vote stood 13 to 16. The Liberals succeeded in electing all but one representative.[19]

Woodruff precinct was the lone stronghold for the Liberals in Rich County. In Randolph, Laketown, and Garden City, the People's party consistently elected an overwhelming majority of candidates and overshadowed the success of the Liberal party at Woodruff. At a county convention held in Randolph, the People's party prevailed by sending Ira Nebeker, Edwin Spencer, and Acquilla Nebeker to the state convention; Judge Joseph Kimball of Laketown was elected to the territorial assembly. Nevertheless, arrests for cohabitation also occurred in Laketown and Randolph; in 1891 federal marshals arrested Nils O. Wahlstrom and Edwin Lamborn of Laketown.[20] A year earlier, a similar occurrence took place in Randolph. The *Deseret News* reported:

> Last evening Deputy Marshal Whetstone arrived in our town, drove up to the residence of brother O. J. Spencer, and arrested

him on a charge of unlawful cohabitation. After his arrest Brother Spencer invited the marshall and his driver to remain the night. The invitation was accepted . . . [21]

The next morning Marshal Whetstone also arrested George A. Peart and by ten o'clock, with prisoners in tow, caught the train at Evanston for the return trip to the district court in Ogden.[22]

Federal marshals did not always have such easy an easy task, however. In comparison to the number of polygamists living in Bear River and Bear Lake valleys, relatively few arrests were made. "Here is the secret," wrote Paris, Idaho, resident Jesse R. S. Budge, son of stake president William Budge:

> My sister Julia who for a number of years was telegraph operator at Paris for the old Deseret Telegraph Company, was acquainted with the telegraph operator at McGammon, Idaho, which, in those days, was a sort of rendezvous for the deputy marshals, and this friend was particularly diligent in acquiring information as to their plans for making journeys to the various "Mormon" settlements. It is not known just how he would inform himself, but suffice to say he did so and thereupon immediately wrote my sister of the date when certain of the deputies intended to be at Paris.[23]

President Budge himself was arrested for unlawful cohabitation in June 1887 but was later acquitted after the prosecution was able to secure only one witness.[24] Repercussions from the practice of polygamy were particularly hard-felt in the Idaho portion of Bear Lake Valley. In 1884 the Idaho legislature passed an act designed to limit Mormon participation in politics. The act effectively disfranchised all Mormons within Idaho; bigamists and polygamists not only were prohibited from voting or holding office, but the law also targeted anyone who

> teaches, advises, counsels or encourages any person or persons to become bigamists or polygamists . . . , or to enter into what is known as plural or celestial marriage, or who is a member of any order, organization, or association which teaches, advises, counsels, or encourages its members or devotees, or any other person, to commit the crime of bigamy or polygamy.[25]

The act, in addition to prohibiting Mormons from holding

office, sitting on juries, and from voting, also included a means to assure that individuals were in compliance with the law through the administering of a oath. "If any person offering to vote shall be challenged by any Judge or Clerk of the election," read the act, one of the judges was to tender an oath to the individual, having him swear that he was neither practicing polygamists nor a member of any organization which advocated polygamy.[26]

The law effectively stifled Mormon political influence in Bear Lake County, Idaho. Nonetheless, administration of the test oath, according to historian Merle W. Wells, "proved to be more awkward for the anti-Mormons than for the Saints." When attempting to hold court in Paris, anti-Mormons found it difficult because "not enough gentiles were available to empanel a grand jury to indict the horse and cattle thieves who roamed about the country unimpeded."[27]

Populated mostly by members of the Mormon Church, Bear Lake County became the focal point for anti-Mormonism during the test oath period in Idaho. Utah officials also implemented a test oath under the provisions of the Edmunds-Tucker Act in 1887. The Utah oath, however, only disfranchised polygamists. Nonetheless, the close proximity of the Rich County communities to the Idaho Bear Lake communities, and their affiliation together within Bear Lake Stake, made them more conscious of the problems affecting their neighbors. Yet members of the Bear Lake Stake did not spend all their time trying to avoid the deputy marshals; they continued in their quest to establish their ideal society. In May 1884 the members of Bear Lake Stake began making plans for the construction of a tabernacle. Subscriptions for the construction of church buildings exacted a heavy financial toll on the members of the Bear Lake Stake, and the building of the tabernacle was postponed for a number of years. As early as 1867, Bear Lake settlers began contributing towards the construction of the Salt Lake Mormon Temple. Although cash was scarce in the newly settled area, the stake members made generous in-kind donations. The *Deseret News* reported in 1876 that "One hundred and sixty head of cattle arrived [in Salt Lake City] from the Bear Lake and Bear River Valley Country, donated by the brethren . . . to the good work of building the temple."[28]

Construction began a year later on the Logan LDS Temple, and

Bear Lake Stake Tabernacle, Paris, Idaho. (Courtesy Eldon Mattson.)

Bear Lake Stake was again expected to contribute towards its completion. The members of the stake raised over eleven thousand dollars in support of the project, "or an average of about $3.27 for every man, woman, and child in the stake."[29]

The completion of the Logan Temple in May 1884 enabled the Saints of Bear Lake to begin building their long-awaited tabernacle. Throughout the summer, sandstone was quarried from Indian Creek Canyon on Bear Lake's east shore; it was then hauled the twenty or so miles in wagons to the town square at Paris. Brick masons remained busy throughout the fall laying the foundation for the building. An assessment of $1.50 per church member was levied in order to raise the estimated $6,200 needed to complete the foundation and walls. By August the *Bear Lake Democrat* reported, "The walls of our new tabernacle begin to loom up above the surface of the ground so that they can be seen at a distance."[30] Initially, construction costs were estimated to be around twelve thousand dollars.[31] However, the building ultimately cost fifty thousand dollars before it was completed in 1889. The building was planned by architect Joseph Don Carlos Young. The *Deseret News* noted:

> All who have seen the Bear Lake Stake House unite in pronouncing
> it one of the handsomest and most substantial structures in this

region. It is built of rock, that of the walls proper being of a dark
hue, while that of the abutments and facings is red sandstone.[32]

The Paris tabernacle was the most imposing religious structure
in Bear Lake Valley and left little doubt as to the area's predominant
religion. Nevertheless, with the arrival of the railroad in 1882, making
Montpelier, Idaho, a division point for the Oregon Shortline, other
religious denominations began making an appearance. A year after
the railroad's arrival the Presbyterian church purchased property in
Montpelier for the construction of a church. The actual erection of
the building was delayed a number of years, but according to historian A. McKay Rich: "The Presbyterian Church was the pioneer evan-
gelical church in Montpelier; it exerted a powerful influence for
community betterments."[33] The Presbyterians were followed in succession by the Episcopal church in 1895 and the Roman Catholic
church in 1896.[34]

The railroad played an important role in diversifying religious
access in Bear River Valley as well as Bear Lake Valley. The railroad
town of Evanston and the mining town of Almy, Wyoming, for
instance, were predominantly non-Mormon. As Mormon church
houses were the only ones available in Rich County, non-Mormon
families whose ranches were in the vicinity of Woodruff and
Randolph were obliged to worship at Evanston. By 1871 a Methodist
Episcopal church and a Baptist church had been established in
Evanston. The Union Pacific Railroad donated land for the construction of the Methodist Episcopal church while the Baptist organization constructed a "substantial edifice on the corner of Center and
Ninth Streets."[35] Presbyterian services were also held in the town in
1871. Evanston businessman A. V. Quinn, who later became involved
with A. C. Beckwith in the cattle industry in Rich County, was among
the first trustees of the Presbyterian church in Evanston.[36] In 1884 the
Catholic church established a parish at Evanston under the leadership of a Father Fitzgerald. Mormon membership slowly spread and
increased in southwestern Wyoming, as well, although the area
remained largely non-Mormon until well into the twentieth century.
Consisting originally of only eight members, a branch of Bear Lake

Stake under the direction of William G. Burton was established at Evanston in 1872.[37]

Except at Evanston and Almy, Wyoming, Mormons were the dominant group in the area. As the communities grew, new ecclesiastical structures were built, remodeled, and added to. Although the construction of the church at Laketown in 1884 was fraught with difficulties, it is important to note that the Laketown church's construction coincided with the building of both the Logan Temple and the Bear Lake Stake Tabernacle, both of which the Laketown settlers contributed generously towards.[38] The church, began in 1884, was completed in 1888 and served the community for seventeen years. In 1905 Laketown Ward members began quarrying sandstone from Indian Creek Canyon for the construction of a new meetinghouse. The building was completed three years later and was dedicated on 25 October 1908. The old church was converted into an amusement hall, and it was used as such until 1925 when it was taken down and a new amusement hall constructed in its place. During the depression years of the 1930s the citizens of Laketown constructed a new fence around the church and amusement hall, painted the outside woodwork, planted lawns, shrubs, and trees, and laid cement walks.[39] A sound system was installed in the chapel in 1965, and an organ in 1969.[40]

At Garden City the original meetinghouse constructed in 1878 served the community for nearly fifty years. In 1929 plans were made to completely refurbish the chapel. The new edifice was dedicated by LDS Church President Heber J. Grant on 15 June 1930. Two days of celebration preceded the dedication at which over five hundred people attended.[41] In 1974 through the utmost care and annual ward spring cleanings, the church building approached a century of service to Garden City Ward members. In September 1974 Bishop Dale B. Weston approached church building coordinator Wayne Prince about the possibility of Garden City constructing a new church house. Plans were tentatively made to commence construction in April 1975. The new building was estimated to cost about a half million dollars of which the Garden City Ward members were to raise $150,000—half of which had to be in hand before construction could begin. This financial obligation, coupled with the fact that the Fish

Haven Ward across the border in Idaho also needed a new building, led church leaders to propose a consolidation. The manuscript history of Garden City Ward tersely notes that on the eve of the celebration commemorating the community's centennial, "August 24 at 3:30 pm the history of Garden City Ward came to an end."[42]

Garden City, however, still received its new church house. Merged with Fish Haven Ward, the new Bear Lake Ward church house was dedicated at Garden City on 28 August 1977. Dale B. Weston was retained from Garden City as the new bishop of the Bear Lake Ward until 1976 when he was succeeded by Arlo B. Price.[43]

Few events were more important in Mormon communities than the construction of a new meetinghouse. In 1893 the citizens of Woodruff began plans to erect a new church house, and a committee consisting of John Baxter, Wesley K. Walton, Joseph H. Neville, Savannah C. Putnam, and Byron Sessions was appointed. Under the supervision of Joseph H. Neville, who provided the brick for the building, construction started in January 1895, and the building was completed and dedicated in August 1897.[44]

The building cost approximately five thousand dollars to construct, and it served the community for many years. In 1937 the ward attempted to improve the church house, but during the hardships of the depression, the project faltered. In 1943 a renewed push began to improve the meetinghouse, and Carl G. Youngburg was appointed to construct a vestibule on the front of the chapel which would provide access to the new rooms being planned for the basement. Improvements were made to the existing chapel over the course of the next several years. Furthermore, the ward bishopric approached church leaders for their approval to add a recreation hall. Citizens of Woodruff began hauling lumber from the west mountains. Art Peck, who had previously worked to construct the county courthouse, was contacted and agreed to come from Salt Lake City to supervise the new construction. Ground was broken in April 1948.

All did not go smoothly, however. Many in the community, after suffering through more than a decade of economic depression and war, objected to what they considered extravagant expenses and the related destruction of some of the oldest cottonwoods in the Bear River Valley. Furthermore, the authors of a Woodruff Ward history record: "We employed some men from neighboring communities who agitated the workers for more pay. This soon resulted in a strike for higher wages. Being unable to meet their demands, we terminated their employment."[45]

Another group of brick masons from Salt Lake City also proved unreliable and the quality of their work questionable: "After working one day [they] went to Kemmerer and spent the following day drinking and gambling." The Woodruff citizens also terminated their employment. Skilled brick masons were not easily found in Rich County, so after hiring and firing most of those available, the citizens finally employed an Indian family that was willing to work under the community's limited finances. Arthur Peck trained the family, and they performed admirably. Still, completion of the building cost more than the small community could bear, and the presiding bishopric initially "refused to meet [their] payroll." After several meetings and a good deal of arm-twisting, Bishop W. Emerson Cox finally succeeded in convincing the presiding bishopric to bail out the ward. The new building was completed in 1949, and the ward had completely paid their debt by 1950 at which time the church was dedicated at a stake conference held in the new Woodruff chapel.[46]

As they joined their fellow members from neighboring communities in celebration of their religion and community, a great deal of satisfaction must have been in the hearts of the Mormon citizens of Woodruff. The people of Randolph, however, were only slightly upstaged by the new Woodruff church. Randolph Ward members also had sacrificed to construct their own meetinghouse.

Randolph had been the center of stake activities since the completion of the Randolph Tabernacle and the formation of the Woodruff Stake of Zion. Named for church president and early Bear River Valley settler Wilford Woodruff, Woodruff Stake was organized in 1898. Construction of the Randolph Ward meetinghouse began that same year under the direction of Bishop Archibald McKinnon. Nearly sixteen years elapsed before the building was finally dedicated. Under the guidance of Bishop John C. Gray who succeeded Bishop McKinnon in 1900 and also acted as the project's architect, the Randolph church was dedicated in July 1914.

Scrapper crews under the supervision of George A. Peart began

Workmen putting the finishing touches on the Randolph Tabernacle.
(Courtesy Nathell Hoffman.)

excavation of the basement as early as September 1898. A year later subscriptions amounting to thirty-three hundred dollars had been collected as local leaders urged "all to do their part so they could crowd the work along."[47] In response to his own plea, Bishop Gray joined the men who worked through the winter hauling logs from the mountains. Contractor Gustave Nelson of Logan began laying brick in November, but cold weather and shoddy building materials halted progress until the following spring. Nonetheless, by fall 1900 work had progressed far enough to enable Nelson to put in place the stone entrance and stone-cut window sills.

With plastering completed and the roof in place, the building was close enough to completion by fall 1904 to hold the stake conference. During the proceedings, however, Apostle George A. Smith dropped a bombshell, ordering work to discontinue "until all debts were paid."[48] Ward members were allowed to use materials already on hand to finish the basement, however, and the building continued to be used over the course of the next seven years. Ward members resumed their collection of subscriptions, and work went slowly but steadily forward. The dedicatory services on 26 July 1914 were attended by Apostle George A. Smith, Wilford Woodruff, Jr., and his daughter Lucy Woodruff Smith.

Improvements and renovations were made to the Randolph meetinghouse after its dedication. The grounds were planted to lawn in 1929, and in 1937 a baptismal font was constructed in the northeast corner of the basement. During the 1950s an addition to the west end of the building was completed to supply office space and kitchen facilities. The Randolph Ward meetinghouse served the needs of ward members as well as the needs of church members throughout Woodruff Stake. The building was often referred to as the Randolph Tabernacle; since the building could seat over seven hundred, most stake meetings were held there.[49] Woodruff Stake was organized on 6 June 1898 with John M. Baxter appointed president. Byron Sessions and Charles Kingston were appointed counselors. John M. Baxter was born in Salt Lake City and moved to Randolph in 1871 with his mother Jane and her brother Archibald McKinnon. He lived the remainder of his adult life in the Bear River Valley. In 1878 he married Agnes Smith, and their marriage partnership lasted fifty-eight years. At Randolph John became involved with William and Sarah Tyson in the mercantile business. He and Agnes would also become successful merchants, first at Randolph and then at Woodruff, after John was appointed bishop there. After Baxter's appointment as stake president, business matters were largely the province of his wife. Establishing and organizing the new Woodruff Stake required much effort, and much of John's time was spent traveling to the various communities to encourage and counsel church members. While he was away on church business, Agnes minded the store. And judging from the history records, she minded it very well. John recorded that after he arrived home from his first mission he "found himself out of debt and everything at home in good shape." Most missions were financial hardships for families, and most missionaries arrived home to find themselves deeply in debt. "Not many L.D.S. missionaries [found] conditions as favorable as I did," John recorded. "It was all due to the good management of my wife."[50]

In addition to running family businesses, Agnes Baxter was also involved in church activities. Her financial acumen made her a natural for appointment to the position of treasurer in the Woodruff Relief Society. Individual ward relief societies played an important role in the religious development of Rich County as they did throughout Utah and in stakes churchwide. The Relief Society had its beginnings at Nauvoo, Illinois, on 17 March 1842 when eighteen women were organized by church president Joseph Smith.[51] Once the Mormons had re-settled at Salt Lake Valley, the organization regrouped in 1851.[52] Relief societies were customarily established in all communities as Mormon settlement spread across the Intermountain West. In Rich County, relief societies had been established in all the various communities by 1879.

In addition to a humanitarian mission of caring for the sick, poor, and aged in the individual communities, early relief societies were also involved in gleaning wheat. After the fields were harvested, a small but substantial amount of grain remained in the fields. The society "sisters" worked to recover and store the otherwise wasted portion of the crop as a bulwark against possible future famine. Relief Society President Emmeline B. Wells inaugurated the program in October 1876.[53] By November, however, questions were being raised by the sisters in relation to the traditional division of labor within the communities: "It has always been the woman's sphere to cook the food; has it now become her place to look after and provide it also? If the women are to engage in such business, what, indeed, will be left for the brethren to do?"[54]

Women's Exponent, the Relief Society publication, attempted to answer these questions by claiming that there was certainly no fear of either the brethren or the sisters having nothing to do. The *Exponent* also reassured its readers that the grain was to be stored indefinitely, not simply for speculative purposes. Beginning in 1876, local relief societies began the process of gleaning fields and storing the grain. The process continued until World War I when the Relief Society agreed to sell over 200,000 bushels of wheat to the United States government in 1918. Clarissa Smith Williams writing in the *Relief Society Magazine* noted how the "grain that was gleaned in aprons, bought with the difficult dimes and nickels of the faithful sisters, stored in their own or hired granaries for nearly half a century" was turned over to the government. Williams added that the "whole nation—nay, the allied nations, the cause of liberty itself—stands indebted to the women of this Church for this noble and generous deed."[55]

The gleaning and storing of grain was a more difficult task in Rich County than it was in more hospitable climates. M. Isabella Horne in her trip through the Bear River and Bear Lake communities in 1878 commented on how members of the Woodruff Relief Society "were raising stock to sell for the purpose of raising money to buy wheat to store away, as it was too cold to raise much grain."[56] By 1879 President Harriet A. Lee of the Woodruff Relief Society reported that the sisters had twenty-five head of livestock "which we propose to sell next fall and buy wheat."[57] With further optimism regarding the rigorous climate in Bear Lake Valley, M. A. Pratt of Meadowville noted that "if the frost takes the grain we will save the straw, and braid it into hats."[58]

Pratt's optimism was not offered in jest. Relief Society members in Rich County went to great lengths to support their communities, church, and nation. Their motto, "charity never faileth," had been the official creed of the Relief Society since at least 1912 although in essence charity had always figured prominently into the organization's mission. During times of economic difficulties, local relief societies often stepped in to assist. During the Great Depression of the 1930s, the Relief Society became a focal point for church-sponsored relief measures.

The church itself was opposed to government relief and work programs which were part of the New Deal. J. Reuben Clark, Jr., a member of the church's First Presidency, feared that the politically "liberal" New Deal program could jeopardize the "saint's freedom to live and to work and to worship."[59] Lorena Hickock, a federal relief worker who met privately with the First Presidency in 1934, was of the opinion that "understanding or support from the Latter Day Saints of Utah" for the New Deal could not be counted on.[60] The church's response to the economic catastrophe of the 1930s was the creation of a welfare organization. Initiated in 1936 as the Church Security Program, the name was changed in 1938 to the Church Welfare Program.[61] The program was at once heralded in the conservative press but condemned in the liberal press.[62] The church estimated that the program would take eighty thousand Mormons off federal work relief. The mass exodus did not occur, but the welfare program did not fail because of a lack of effort. It failed for the same reason that federal and state relief measures failed: the depression was too widespread to be halted by piecemeal measures. Ultimately, it would be the massive industrialization of World War II which would bring about the economic reversal. Still, an extraordinary effort was undertaken by the Mormon church, particularly by its Relief Society, in its attempt to reverse the economic circumstances of local Mormons.

Relief societies were organized within wards and branches, as well as at the stake level. Each reorganization within Rich County required the re-establishment of relief societies, bishoprics, stake presidencies, and other positions of leadership. After the organization of Woodruff Stake in 1898, Apostle John Henry Smith proposed that the center of the stake be located at Evanston. To President John Baxter and others it made little sense to establish the stake's headquarters in a community that was overwhelmingly non-Mormon.[63] Baxter and Byron Sessions made a special trip to Salt Lake City and met with President Wilford Woodruff who rescinded the order and allowed the stake headquarters to remain at Woodruff.[64] The stake's tabernacle was built in Randolph, but the local membership also contributed the finances to construct an office building at Woodruff.[65]

The separation of the Rich County communities into two separate ecclesiastical units was an unfortunate necessity. The distance between Paris, Idaho—the center of activities for Bear Lake Stake—and the outlying areas of Bear River Valley and Star Valley, Wyoming, made it necessary to expand church organization. The Star Valley communities were made a separate stake in 1892. In the case of the eleven communities involved, its creation was logical. All of the communities were contained within the confines of Salt River Valley, and all were located within Lincoln County, Wyoming. In contrast, although Laketown and Garden City shared Bear Lake Valley with their Idaho neighbors, they were politically part of Utah.

In truth, the ecclesiastical division of the area made more sense than did county and state boundaries. Laketown and Garden City remained a part of Bear Lake Stake along with the other Bear Lake Valley communities of Idaho while Randolph and Woodruff became affiliated with the other Bear River Valley communities of Evanston and Almy, Wyoming. Politics by the 1890s, however, had become at least as important to community development as the church, if not more so. For Rich County, ecclesiastical separation was a setback to its political development. Woodruff Stake also included communities outside of Bear River Valley, including communities as far away as Rock Springs, Wyoming, and in present-day Daggett County, Utah. Stake President Baxter who was bishop of Woodruff before his appointment recalled visiting different communities and church members after the stake's formation. On one occasion, he wrote of a member who was in destitute condition with "two little children, one in her arms and one about two years." Their dwelling was a "cabin, with a dirt roof, containing one room, no door, window or floor.[66] The woman was nonetheless cheerful, Baxter records, in spite of her circumstances. She, like James Kearl, must also have been able to look "to the future in faith." But the future was a difficult thing to gauge. The Mormon faithful were often expected to sacrifice personal prosperity in the interests of settling new areas. This had been true in

Rich County history since Charles C. Rich forsook the comforts of his Centerville home and relocated to Bear Lake Valley. It required considerable time to become prosperous in Rich County, but some of those who persisted in their pursuits did so. Such was the case with Byron Sessions who moved to Woodruff from Bountiful in the 1870s. Sessions was deeply involved in community and religious affairs and was also one of the few Mormons who successfully competed with the early Wyoming cattle ranchers in Bear River Valley. During the mid-1880s Sessions joined forces with Orlando North and William Smith of Evanston to form the Bear River Land and Livestock Company. The company's purchase of thousands of acres of state land around Woodruff did not make it particularly popular with Mormon settlers. Sessions nevertheless continued in his church work and eventually rose to the position of first counselor in the Woodruff stake presidency. In 1900 he was called before Mormon church president Lorenzo Snow and asked to resettle his family and the families of his four sons to the Big Horn River Basin in northern Wyoming. The church had come to an agreement with the state of Wyoming to allow settlement into the area with the understanding that the Mormons would construct a canal from the Shoshone River to irrigate the land.[67] President Baxter, who accompanied Sessions to the meeting and was his close friend, recalled Sessions's selfless acquiescence to the request of President Snow:

> We returned home and Brother Sessions commenced at once to make preparations for moving. . . . He had a great task before him. He was a partner, stockholder and manager of a large land and livestock company, that owned thousands of acres of land and hundreds of cattle and horses. Four of his boys, all married men, with families, were employed by the company. Bro. Sessions dissolved partnership with this company, selling his share at a great loss. Then he, with his boys and their families, were ready to start.[68]

Sessions left Woodruff with horses, wagons, provisions, new harnesses, and all the accoutrements necessary to make a new start in the new country. The construction of the canal, however, proved more difficult than expected; and, after its completion, the irrigation water raised the alkali and spoiled the soil. Furthermore, Sessions expended all his savings on the new settlement and in the support of his boys and their families. John Baxter recalled how conditions went from bad to worse:

> It was not long until the funds he had at his command were exhausted. His horses got poisoned, and he lost all but two or three head. His wife took seriously ill and he was at her bedside for fourteen years, or until she died. He was, therefore, reduced to extreme poverty.[69]

Sessions moved in with his oldest daughter after the death of his wife May only to have his daughter pass away a short time later. Destitute and in feeble health, he left the Big Horn country and moved to Salt Lake City where he lived out the remainder of his life in a rented room. The saddest aspect of Sessions's later years was the fact that no one in Salt Lake City knew of his near-heroic deeds in the Big Horn Valley, his part in the settlement of Rich County, his successes in land and livestock in Bear River Valley, or his membership in the Woodruff Stake presidency. At his funeral on 19 January 1928 held at the Salt Lake Sixteenth Ward, Bishop Joseph H. Lake noted only that he was a very faithful ward teacher.[70]

The life of Byron Sessions is an example of the triumph and tragedy which was part of the Mormon settlement experience. In some ways, the only way to achieve prosperity in a Mormon community was to somehow avoid the call to settle new areas. Unfortunately, the only way to avoid the call was to avoid success. The ability to make a success in early Rich County was ample proof of exceptional ability. And as individuals with exceptional ability were those most sought after for undertaking the settlement of new areas, early Rich County settlers were often asked to make the sacrifice. Most were willing.

The communities of Rich County have been regrouped several times as a result of shifts in population centers during the twentieth century. In 1926, with the creation of Lyman Stake, the Wyoming communities of Lyman, Rock Springs, Green River, and others in the general vicinity were separated from Woodruff Stake.[71] In 1930 William R. Smith succeeded John M. Baxter as president of Woodruff Stake.[72] Baxter lived the remainder of his life on his Almy, Wyoming,

Entrance to what was the Ike Smith Store in Randolph. Later the building was used to show silent movies, ca. 1910. (Courtesy Nathell Hoffman.)

ranch, dying there on 17 July 1936.[73] After 1926 the communities of Randolph, Woodruff, Almy, Evanston, Hilliard, Kemmerer, Diamondville, and Cumberland constituted the Woodruff Stake. In 1974 the Woodruff Stake was dissolved and the headquarters of the stake was moved to Evanston. J. Wilburn Bowns, former president of Woodruff Stake, continued in that capacity after the reorganization.[74] Little more than a year later, Randolph and Woodruff were separated from Evanston Stake and placed in the newly formed Kemmerer Stake with Merrill R. Anderson sustained as president.[75]

The Rich County communities of Garden City and Laketown have historically been associated in the same stake since 1879. Bear Lake Stake, however, was divided in 1974 to form two stakes: the Paris, Idaho, Stake, including Garden City and Laketown; and the Montpelier Stake, containing the remaining Bear Lake Valley communities.

The legacy of Mormonism remains a part of Rich County today where over ninety-eight percent of the population belong to the Mormon church.[76] Other tenets of the faith also remain. The cooperative spirit, strong family values, and traditions rooted firmly in an agricultural past are also part of Rich County's Mormon experience. Religious life in the county has played a large part in its history. Hand-in-hand with religious development has been the development of civil government within Rich County and the associated growth of social and educational institutions. Early on, little difference existed between civil and religious leadership in Rich County; religious leaders in the communities were responsible for both the spiritual and temporal well-being of individuals. Civil government gradually assumed more and more responsibility for the county's development. Most elected and appointed county officials were, however, also Mormon church members, so the influence of Mormonism, for better or worse, remained. The Mormon church also influenced the development of education within early Utah, and we shall examine next how that influence can be seen in Rich County.

ENDNOTES

1. Mildred H. Thomson, comp., *Rich Memories: Some of the Happenings in Rich County from 1863 to 1960* (Salt Lake City: Daughters of the Utah Pioneers, 1962), 115.

2. After returning from Brigham City with a wagonload of fruit, Marianne pricked her thumb trying to dislodge the pit from a peach. She evidently contracted blood poisoning and died. See Ezra J. Poulsen, *Joseph C. Rich—Versitle Pioneer on the Mormon Frontier* (Salt Lake City: Granite Publishing Co., 1958), 199.

3. Manuscript History of Bear Lake Stake, 1900, Historian's Office, Church of Jesus Christ of Latter-day Saints (hereafter referred to as BLSMH).

4. Andrew Jenson, *Encyclopedic History of the Church of Jesus Christ of Latter-day Saints* (Salt Lake City: Deseret News Publishing Co., 1941), 48.

5. David P. Kimball, fourth son of Heber C. and Vilate Kimball, was born at Nauvoo, Illinois, on 23 August 1839. On 19 July 1869 he moved to Bear Lake Valley with 100 or so other settlers in response to a request to bolster the population of that area. David was placed in charge of the Bear Lake settlements. He invested liberally in the new settlement, building a sawmill and gristmill as well as demanding the construction of a three-pole fence from St. Charles to Laketown to separate stock range from farm ground. Although energetic, Kimball was not a shrewd manager of money and soon found himself nearly bankrupt. Solomon F. Kimball writes: "As long as he had money he gave his friends and associates the benefit of it, even when it was against his own interests to do so. Having given away to his better judgement in relation to such matters, he soon found himself in financial straits. . . . Notes were becoming due, lawsuits pending, and the beneficiaries who had helped to bring about this condition of things were among the first

to desert him." See Solomon F. Kimball, *Life of David P. Kimball and other Sketches* (Salt Lake City: Deseret News, 1918), 25.

Kimball's financial problems led him to lose his temper and also increased his appetite for whiskey. Leonard J. Arrington in his biography of Charles C. Rich relates a situation that developed in Bear Lake Valley in 1873. Although Arrington omits names, the situation doubtless involved David P. Kimball. Writes Arrington: "A high official of Bear Lake Stake was tried by Rich and the stake high council for drunkenness, personal abuse, and taking the name of God in vain." Arrington quotes from the minutes of the Bear Lake Stake High Council: "Brother _____ has no reason to think that I have not been a friend to him. I am a friend to him. Bro. _____ has no reason to feel bad on account of this decision. I believe he desires to do well, but this Stake would not be justified in sustaining [him] in such conduct. If we let such acts pass in a [high official], how can we, justly handle anyone else? Brother _____ has been very leniently dealt with. We cannot sustain or fellowship Bro. _____ if he does not stop these evil habits now. We are willing to help him, but we desire to help the kingdom of God more than anything else. When this Council met on his case they decided that he be disfellowshipped until he makes restitution for the wrong he has done. What I would do if I was in Bro. _____'s place, would be to confess my fault to the people and ask for their faith and prayers to help me to do better." See, Leonard J. Arrington, *Charles C. Rich* (Provo: Brigham Young University Press, 1974), 281–282.

Upon Kimball's release, Brigham Young spoke to the settlers at Paris, and praised him for the outstanding work he had accomplished. Young also chastised the people for their failures. Joseph C. Rich considered Kimball to be "the hardest working man I ever knew. Maybe that was his trouble," he continued. "He tried to go too fast. He expected the rest to keep up with him, and many were not able to do it. So they lagged behind, and he scolded, then they became resentful." Rich added that "Dave had his faults—same as I have. . . . But he had enough to make a man take a drink occasionally." See Poulsen, *Joseph C. Rich,* 246.

After his release from Bear Lake Valley, David P. Kimball left Utah for the Mormon settlements in northern Arizona. There he died on 22 November 1883. See Kimball, *Life of David P. Kimball,* 67.

6. Jesse R. S. Budge, *The Life of William Budge* (Salt Lake City: Deseret News, 1915), 93.

7. Jenson, *Encyclopedic History of the Church,* 48.

8. Gustive O. Larson, *The "Americanization" of Utah for Statehood* (San Marino, CA: Huntington Library, 1971), 65.

9. Manuscript History of Woodruff Ward, Bear Lake Stake, Rich

County, Utah, 1872 Historian's Office, Church of Jesus Christ of Latter-day Saints, Salt Lake City, Utah (hereafter referred to as WMH).

10. WMH, 1884.

11. The term Liberal here refers to political affiliation. Most non-Mormons who were politically active were members of the Liberal Party. Most Mormons were members of the People's party. Some Mormons, however, who opposed the practice of polygamy were referred to by other Mormons as Liberal Mormons.

12. WMH, 1884.

13. Larson, *The Americanization of Utah for Statehood*, 210–14. According to Larson, the Edmunds-Tucker Act "included provisions to destroy the Mormon Church politically and economically."

14. According to historian Gustive O. Larson, the non-Mormons in Utah organized the Loyal League "to succeed the defunct Gentile League of Utah. Its objective was to 'combine the loyal people of Utah . . . in opposition to the political and law-defying practices of the so called Mormon Church; to oppose the admission of Utah into the Union until she has the substance as well as the form of Republican government' and 'to raise money to maintain agents in Washington or elsewhere to labor for these ends'". See *The Americanization of Utah for Statehood*, 208.

15. Other leaders of the Woodruff People's party included Byron Sessions, S. Bryson, Arbury Eastman, and John Dean.

16. Historical Record, Woodruff Ward, Bear Lake Stake, Rich County, Utah, Historian's Office, Church of Jesus Christ of Latter-day Saints, Salt Lake City (hereafter cited as HR), v. 15, 8 August 1887, 35.

As attested to by a letter of support to United States President Benjamin Harrison regarding the appointment of S. V. Frazier to the office of probate judge, a great deal of opposition existed to the practice of polygamy in Woodruff. Those signing the letter included John Johnson, George Smith, R. J. Martin, Charles Reid, John S. Jones, William B. Gunn, William T. Brough, D. McAllister, Jens E. Jensen, William Crawford, John W. Dykins, Thomas Gibson, J. Witherell, William Pearce, Jacob Benzley, Jerry M. Richardson, Edward J. Hayes, Dr. Affeck, William L. Pugmire, John W. Benzley, S. L. Huffaker, B. C. Walton, Thomas Frazier, Charles Crawford, George Galbraith, James L. Smith, John Dean, H. Storm, F. Rideout, M. A. Moffatt, J. S. Moffatt, Elijah Sells, Joseph Dean, George Eastman and A. L. Eastman. See *Records Relating to the Appointment of Federal Judges, Attorneys, and Marshals for the Territory and State of Utah, 1853–1901*, microfilm, roll 5, 1889–1893 (A-G).

Some of the signatures affixed to the letter were those of original settlers of Woodruff. Stephen V. Frazier himself was an early settler to the area, though he was not an LDS church member. John and Joseph Dean, however, were born into the LDS church, being the sons of Charles Dean who settled at Woodruff in 1872. The Eastmans—A. L. and George—were among the first to settle at Woodruff Creek in 1870. Both were affiliated with the LDS church at that time. See Thomson, *Rich Memories*, 300–24.

Others supporting Frazier's appointment were non-Mormon ranchers in the area. Among them were William Crawford, Charles Crawford, J. Witherell, and John Dykins. Dykins was also appointed Deputy U.S. Marshal at Randolph. See *Records Relating to the Appointment, 1853–1901*, microfilm, roll 5, 1889–1893 (A–G).

17. The other Woodruff settlers arrested included William Reed, Savannah C. Putnam, and John Cox. See WMH, 1888.

18. Minutes of the Woodruff Ward Relief Society, 1890; LDS Church Historian's Office, Salt Lake City, Utah.

19. *Journal History of the Church of Jesus Christ of Latter-day Saints*, manuscript, Department of Special Collections and Archives, Merrill Library, Utah State University, Logan, Utah (hereafter referred to as JH), 6 August 1888, 3.

20. Laketown Ward Manuscript History, 1891 Historian's Office, Church of Jesus Christ of Latter-day Saints, Salt Lake City (hereafter cited as LTMH).

21. *Deseret News*, 1 February 1890, quoted in Steven L. Thomson, Jane D. Digerness, and Mar Jean S. Thomson, *Randolph—A Look Back* (n.p., 1981), 24.

22. Ibid.

23. Budge, *The Life of William Budge*, 110.

24. Merle W. Wells, *Anti-Mormonism in Idaho, 1872–92* (Provo: Brigham Young University Press, 1978), 110.

25. An Act to Provide for Holding Elections and Prescribing the Qualifications of Electors, and for Other Purposes, *Laws of Idaho, 1884–1885*, p. 107. microfilm, Special Collections and Archives, Utah State University, Logan.

26. Ibid., 110.

27. Wells, *Anti-Mormonism in Idaho, 1872–92*, 69.

28. Russell R. Rich, *Land of the Sky-Blue Water: A History of the L.D.S. Settlement of the Bear Lake Valley* (Provo: Brigham Young University Press, 1963), 158.

29. Ibid.

30. Ibid., 159. See also *Bear Lake Democrat*, 8 August 1884.

31. Rich, *Land of the Sky-Blue Water*, 157–63.

32. JH, 20 July 1889, 4.

33. A. McKay Rich, *The History of Montpelier from 1864 to 1925* (master's thesis, Utah State Agricultural College, 1957), 97.

34. Rich, *The History of Montpelier,* 99–100.

35. Elizabeth Arnold Stone, *Uinta County: Its Place in History* (Glendale, CA: Arthur H. Clark Co., 1924), 139.

36. Ibid., 142.

37. Ibid., 143.

38. In 1883, members of the Laketown Ward contributed $250 towards the construction of the Logan Temple; similar amounts were no doubt contributed during other years. See JH, 5 April 1883, 5.

39. LTMH, 1935 and 1938.

40. LTMH, 1965 and 1969.

41. Manuscript History of Garden City Ward, Rich County, Utah, 1930, Historian's Office, Church of Jesus Christ of Latter-day Saints, Salt Lake City (hereafter cited as GCMH).

42. GCMH, 1975.

43. Bear Lake Ward Manuscript History, 1976. LDS Church Historian's Office, Salt Lake City, Utah (hereafter cited as BLWMH).

44. Woodruff Centennial Committee, The First 100 Years in *Woodruff* (Springville, UT: Art City Publishing Co., 1970), 21.

45. Ibid.

46. The account of the construction of the Woodruff Ward Church House is taken from *Woodruff—The First Hundred Years,* 18–23. The community of Woodruff received a new church house in 1984, and the original chapel and additions were demolished. See *Uinta County Herald,* 29 June 1984.

47. Steven L. Thomson, *Randolph—A Look Back,* 143.

48. Ibid., 145.

49. The account of the construction of the Randolph Tabernacle is taken from Thomson, *Randolph—A Look Back,* 141–47.

50. John McKinnon Baxter, *Life of John M. Baxter* (Salt Lake City: Deseret News Press, 1972), 86.

51. *History of Relief Society, 1842–1966* (Salt Lake City: General Board of Relief Society, 1966), 17–18.

52. Ibid., 28.

53. Ibid., 109.

54. *Women's Exponent,* 1 November 1876, 1.

55. *The Relief Society Magazine* 5 (August 1918): 446.

56. *Women's Exponent,* 15 June 1878, 12.

57. Ibid., 15 June 1879, 10.

58. Ibid., 15 June 1878, 14.

59. D. Michael Quinn, *J. Reuben Clark: The Church Years* (Provo: Brigham Young University Press, 1983), 190.

60. Papers of Dean R. Brimhall, Box 12, folder 9, Marriott Library, University of Utah, Salt Lake City.

61. Leonard J. Arrington and Wayne K. Hinton, "Origin of the Welfare Plan of the Church of Jesus Christ of Latter-day Saints," typescript, Special Collections and Archives, Utah State University, Logan.

62. Papers of Dean R. Brimhall, Box 29, folder 1.

63. Baxter maintained that the Mormon population of Evanston was about two hundred. He also related an incident involving the Catholic priest at Evanston and Apostle John Henry Smith. When the priest inquired of Smith what all the Mormons were doing in Evanston, Smith replied, "We have just organized a new stake of Zion, and . . . we are going to Mormonize this town of Evanston." See Baxter, *Life of John M. Baxter,* 107–08.

64. JH, 16 June 1898.

65. JH, 11 February 1901.

66. Baxter, *Life of John M. Baxter,* 112.

67. Frances Birkhead Beard, *Wyoming From Territorial Days to the Present* (Chicago: American Historical Society, 1933), 1:538.

68. Baxter, *Life of John M. Baxter,* 117.

69. Ibid., 196.

70. Ibid., 197.

71. Woodruff Stake Manuscript History, 1926; Church Historian's Office, Church of Jesus Christ of Latter-day Saints, Salt Lake City, Utah (hereafter referred to as WSMH).

72. WSMH, 1930.

73. WSMH, 1936.

74. Evanston Stake Manuscript History, 1974. Church Historian's Office, Church of Jesus Christ of Latter-day Saints, Salt Lake City, Utah.

75. Kemmerer Stake Manuscript History, 1978. Church Historian's Office, Church of Jesus Christ of Latter-day Saints, Salt Lake City, Utah.

76. *Churches and Church Memberships in the United States from 1990* (Atlanta: Glenmary Research Center, 1992), 393.

8

"To Gain the Attention of Children"

EDUCATION IN RICH COUNTY

T he establishment of schools for the education of children was among the most important concerns for early Mormon colonists throughout Utah. Many of the early converts to Mormonism, including Brigham Young, came from the New England states where community education had been an important feature. These ideas traveled west with the Mormons, first into Ohio, then Missouri, and lastly to Nauvoo, Illinois, before the exodus to Utah.[1]

Even during the exodus from Nauvoo in 1846, educational organizations were put in place. Brigham Young encouraged other leaders to continue providing educational opportunities for children at Council Bluffs, Iowa. Several schools were established and maintained during the winter of 1846. George A. Smith, a member of the First Presidency, was among those most responsible for maintaining instruction at Winter Quarters. In a eulogy read before the Utah Territorial Assembly, Moses Thatcher said of Smith:

> He was ever particularly interested in the subject of education, wherein he exhibited a strikingly practical and admirable trait of his character, as an evidence of which, in 1846, when our people

were driven from their homes and were journeying towards the setting sun, it was his almost constant endeavor to organize for the young, a system of common school education, in which he succeeded admirably, and nightly around the camp fires of the weary exiles, was heard his cheering voice calling the children to come with their books, and recite what they had learned.[2]

Given the herculean effort required to sustain a school under such conditions, it is no surprise that Mormon settlers continued their efforts after arriving in Utah. Brigham Young promoted the establishment of schools at Salt Lake City and in other communities as Mormon settlement expanded within the Intermountain West. In his general epistle of 15 March 1848 Young reiterated the importance of education and instructed the Latter-day Saints to gather together

> every valuable treatise on education—every book, map, chart, or diagram that may contain interesting, useful, and attractive matter, to gain the attention of children, and cause them to love to learn to read; and also every historical, mathematical, philosophical, geographical, geological, astronomical, scientific, practical, and all other variety of useful and interesting writings.[3]

It is clear that education in Utah was to embrace much more than religion, although religious training was to be an integral part of education. In early Mormon settlements there was little difference between the sacred and the secular. The same building used for church services on Sunday often was used for school during the week and for a public dance or dramatic presentation on Saturday. Mormon doctrine, along with mathematics and history, was a regular part of most school curriculums during the early settlement period. This was particularly true in outlying communities such as those in Rich County where the population was almost wholly Mormon. "Faithfulness to Latter-day Saint thinking," remarked one historian, "was one of the requirements for school teachers in early Utah schools."[4]

Some of the first acts passed by the new legislative assembly for the territory concerned education. The University of Deseret was created to oversee the educational development of Utah's citizenry. The university trained teachers while the university's board of trustees frequently visited settlements to advise teachers and local officials on how best to operate their schools. The legislative assembly also provided for schools to be established within the various counties. The counties "were to be divided into districts and each town or city was to have one or more schools supported by local taxation."[5] Under the law, counties were to elect school trustees who in turn were given authority to impose and collect taxes for the support of the schools.[6]

The 1851 law also created the Office of the Superintendent of Common Schools. The law was amended in 1865 to allow for the election of the superintendent by the voters of the territory. The 1865 amendment to the school law also clarified an oversight in the original law which had not allowed collected tax funds to be used to pay teacher salaries or to purchase textbooks.

The territory had over a decade of school experience before the first settlers entered Bear Lake Valley in 1863. The first school at Paris, Idaho, however, opened in February 1865 during one of the worst winters ever recalled by early Bear Lake settlers. Thomas Sleight and Lewis Ricks taught seventy-five students at various grade levels in a "one room log structure with one door, few windows, and a fireplace to provide heat."[7]

As settlement expanded in the northern Bear Lake area, settlers established other schools. Likewise, as settlers began moving into Laketown, Meadowville, Round Valley, and later into Bear River Valley and Garden City, they set up schools under the best circumstances possible. The conditions were not ideal. At Laketown the old town meetinghouse was reported to be "so naturally ventilated" that Laketonians would not even ask "a respectable dog . . . be compelled to spend the chilly winter there for the sake of an education."[8] School was nonetheless carried out under the direction of R. S. Spence. "It was marvelous to us," commented one citizen, "that school teaching could be so successfully carried on under such plainly disadvantageous circumstances."[9] Historian Earl F. Passey, in his study of Rich County schools, pays tribute to Robert Spence by noting how his "reputation as an excellent schoolmaster" earned him the respect of even those in the older, more established communities: "Young people from these northern settlements were not so fortunate as to be instructed by so able a teacher in their own communities." Some students came to Laketown and "boarded out" with Laketown families in order to attend school under Spence.

> As his school grew, an assistant moved about in the crowded classroom to give aid to the anxious students. To have been a student of "Bob" Spence is today treasured as a valued experience. Those of his students who may have received from him a "Card of Approbation" for outstanding work or behavior treasure it as a memento of his great teaching.[10]

Realizing the tremendous resource which the community had in Robert Spence and the difficult conditions under which he was laboring, a citizen's meeting convened on 12 March 1883 "to take into consideration the matter of a new school house."[11] The citizens subscribed $1,010 toward the project and later contracted with Charles South of Randolph to build it.[12]

The building of the new meetinghouse did not pass without incident, however.[13] A disagreement between the contractor and the building committee over money caused construction to stop during the summer of 1884. This prompted one citizen to remark to the *Bear Lake Democrat* that "if ever the patience of a people [has been] tried, that of the Laketonians has been severely so. Whether it is the devil or some other evil influence we know not, but there is something materially wrong somewhere."[14] The residents subscribed an additional $1,690 to finish erecting the new meetinghouse, bringing the total to $2,700, and the disagreement was eventually rectified.[15] The new meetinghouse received its final coat of plaster and paint in late November 1884.

The new Laketown school served its purpose as school, church, and social hall for at least fifteen years. Around 1900 a ward meetinghouse was constructed which alleviated the need for holding church services in the building, and various barns were in use to accommodate dances and dramatic presentations. By 1914 the Laketown school trustees determined that the building was insufficient for the needs of the community and resolved to construct a new schoolhouse made of brick.[16] By 1917 the building, at least the basement portion of the two-story structure, was ready for occupancy; however, passage of new school laws within the state complicated the completion of the building. A consolidation act of 1915 created county wide boards of education.[17] These district school boards, elected by the citizenry of each county, supplanted the system of individual school trustees which had been in existence throughout Utah since territorial times. Under the law, the previous school trustees turned over all educational facilities and financial resources to the county school board. This placed a financial burden on the Laketown citizens who had taken it upon themselves to erect the new building through their own financial resourcefulness.[18]

The consolidation law of 1915 was certainly not meant to be a hindrance, and in many cases the consolidation of schools worked well. Nevertheless, the geography of Rich County made aspects of consolidation less practical. Schools had been established separately in various communities because of the distance between them. Separate schools operated in the communities of Laketown, Meadowville, and Round Valley.

In similar fashion to their Laketown neighbors, the settlers of Round Valley constructed a small public building shortly after the area was resettled in 1869. Some of those who participated in the early settlement of Round Valley also became involved in the educational organization of the community. The area was settled in 1869–70 by the families of James Kearl, John Price, Peter Allen, George Murphy, and George Earley. By 1892 the population of Round Valley had grown—mostly through natural increase—and a separate ward of the Mormon church was started and the old public building was given to the church. In 1906 the school trustees erected a new building, offering education through the eighth grade and employing two teachers.

The Round Valley School experienced its highest enrollment prior to about 1907 when as many as fifty students attended. As a result of depressed farm prices and adverse weather conditions, the population of Round Valley gradually decreased to the point that it was no longer practical to maintain the school. After the consolidation law passed, the school only operated until 1920 before it closed. Local trustees were transferred to Laketown.[19]

Similar events took shape in Meadowville. With the customary public building erected in about 1870, Meadowville became first a

branch and later a ward within the LDS church. The town was settled in 1869 by Josiah Tufts, Bordette Folsom, Charles H. Alley,
William Cottrom, brothers Joshua, Elthanan, and Joseph Eldredge,
Moses Gibbons, Lewis Polmenteer, George T. Judd, Willam T. Edgar,
Manassa Williams, Joseph Moffat, Henry Graw, Hyrum S. Groesbeck,
and Moroni Pratt.[20] The extended family of Heber C. Kimball also
figured prominently in the settling of Meadowville. The community
prospered for a number of years until the irrigation system, cooperatively completed by the communities of Laketown, Meadowville,
and Round Valley, raised the ground water level and fouled the townsite. From this point the community's destiny was reversed. After
1900 most of the population moved to other locations either in or
out of Bear Lake Valley, and the school, and later the ward, eventually merged with that of Laketown.[21] As population decreased, available land was gradually consolidated within a handful of families,
and it became impractical to continue the operation of separate
schools in Round Valley and Meadowville. A similar condition came
to exist in Bear River Valley where separate schools were maintained
at Kennedyville and at Sage Creek.

The effort was made at both Woodruff and Randolph to maintain the Mormon village pattern. The Mormon village was characterized by specific dimensions being accorded to streets and blocks,
and by the fact that residents maintained homes in the village while
farming the land on the outskirts of the village. In other words, farmers did not live on the farms but within the village.[22] In much of the
Bear Lake region, particularly the northern settlements, this pattern
was adhered to as Joseph C. Rich surveyed the settlements to comply
with the usual Mormon plan. Both Randolph and Woodruff were
also surveyed according to this pattern. But in Bear River Valley the
early interest in stock raising and the unsuccessful attempts at culti-
vating small grains led settlers to move farther and farther from the
townsites. As discussed in chapter three, settlers began moving out of
Woodruff and settling on their ranches as early as 1874. The widely
dispersed population in Bear River Valley and the lack of favorable
roads made it increasingly difficult for ranchers to maintain community ties with the larger towns of Woodruff and Randolph. To off-
set the need to travel to Randolph for church and school functions,

the communities of Sage Creek and Kennedyville were established in Bear River Valley.

The early ranchers who moved north of Randolph to establish Sage Creek included the families of Lorenzo Schenck, Melvin Schenck, Arthur McKinnon, William Jones, Deronda Nebeker, Fred Feller, August Johnson, William Hoffman, Leonard Hoffman, and Alma Argyle. School was convened at the homes of settlers themselves until 1909 when a building was erected specifically for the purpose.

The problems of geography were not completely overcome by establishing new community centers. For instance, Arthur Dean, the first teacher at the Sage Creek school, had to travel thirteen miles from Woodruff by horseback. Similarly, south of Randolph the area known as Kennedyville "covered many square miles of territory," according to local educator Earl F. Passey, "and, even by establishing a new community center, . . . the people who came there to attend school, or church . . . still faced the necessity of travelling considerable distances."[23]

Kennedyville was named after John Kennedy, Sr., who settled the area in about 1875. Gradually, LDS Church Historian Andrew Jenson noted, as the area residents "increased in number they . . . obtained permission . . . to hold meetings among themselves."[24] The small community also initiated a school program in 1885, and at a meeting in December of that year voted to change the name of the town to Argyle in honor of the residents' Scottish ancestry.[25] The first school sessions at Argyle were held in private homes, but in the late 1890s the community erected a one-room brick schoolhouse. By 1900 Argyle had a population of 111 inhabitants.

As transportation gradually improved, both Argyle and Sage Creek fell victim to progress. Although an education through the eighth grade could be obtained in both communities, the quality of that education compared to that available at Randolph was questionable. Furthermore, the communities had no available goods or services. Residents made the trip to Randolph to purchase necessary items, and as the frequency of the trips increased especially with the advent of the automobile, ties between the communities became closer. In 1915 the Argyle school closed and merged with the school at Randolph. The Sage Creek school continued into the early 1920s, but, like the school at Argyle, was also eventually consolidated with the Randolph school.[26]

The development of education in Randolph proceeded similarly to that in the other Rich County settlements. A public building was erected within a year of the original settlers' arrival. A. B. Strickland was employed as the first teacher in Randolph.[27] In 1875 the community constructed a new church building, and in 1888 a two-story brick courthouse. The original public building was used only for school after 1875.

After the construction of the county courthouse in 1888, the upper floor of the building was converted into school facilities which housed the Randolph Academy, an educational institution sponsored by the Mormon church. Mormon academies had been established at selected sites throughout Utah during the 1870s. At the behest of Apostle Wilford Woodruff, stake presidents were instructed to put into place a church board of education which would in turn begin to operate church schools.[28] The push for church-sanctioned education came about as non-Mormons within Utah began challenging Mormon domination of the common schools. As discussed earlier, the schools established in early Utah communities were imbued with Mormon theology. Following passage of the Edmunds-Tucker Act in 1887, however, the public schools throughout Utah were forced to refrain from teaching the tenets of Mormonism. Wilford Woodruff explained the church's position on the public schools in his letter to stake presidents in 1888:

> Religious training is practically excluded from the District Schools. The perusal of books that we value as divine records is forbidden. Our children, if left to the training they receive in these schools, will grow up entirely ignorant of those principles of salvation for which the Latter-day Saints have made so many sacrifices.[29]

It is fitting that one of the first settlements to found a church academy after Woodruff's letter was Randolph, a community in which the apostle had been intimately involved since 1871. Separation of church and state in educational matters did not seem to be an issue of great importance in Randolph, symbolized by the fact that the church school occupied the top floor of the center for public government in Rich County—the county courthouse. The Randolph Academy opened in December 1888 with Oluf Larson as principal. Larson was assisted between the years 1888 and 1903 by Harriet Cornia, Mary A. Thomas, and Agnes South.[30] In 1903 the Randolph Academy closed, and what few students were attending the church school transferred to the Fielding Academy at Paris, Idaho. The Fielding Academy, named in honor of Mary Fielding Smith, mother of newly installed Mormon church president Joseph F. Smith, opened in 1901. The academy at Randolph could hardly compete with the sixty-five thousand dollar building constructed at Paris. The imposing structure, which within three years included two additional stories and "magnificent stairways [leading] from the central halls," had an enrollment of nearly three hundred students. The Fielding Academy was one of the more successful schools operated by the church. It operated under church sponsorship until 1922 when it was absorbed by the state of Idaho and opened as a public high school. Virtually all the church academies remaining in operation were sold or absorbed by their respective states during the 1920s.[31]

Most of the more rural church academies did not meet the expectations of church leaders. The anticipated exodus from the public schools into the church schools never materialized. The public schools in rural Utah posed far less of a problem for the church than did those in the Salt Lake Valley. This was a fact evidentally overlooked by the church's leadership. Writes historian John D. Monnett, Jr., "Rural Utah . . . presented a much different educational picture than the Salt Lake City environment that was so familiar to church officials."[32] Monnett notes that in counties such as Rich where "amicable relations exist[ed] between church and district school and [where there were] a preponderance of Mormon teachers in the district schools, rural Mormons felt justified in sending their children to public schools."[33] Although public school teachers in rural Utah refrained from openly teaching Mormon doctrine, sprinklings of theology no doubt flavored their instruction to students.

Another hindrance to the success of the church system was the initiation in 1890 of a free school system within Utah. The church academies were not expensive by most standards, but neither were they free. Wilford Woodruff had urged that the schools "be made so cheap that [they] will be within the reach of the humblest in the land." But Mormon bishop Christian A. Madsen noted in 1892 that "the poor families of this Ward [are unable] to obtain books and requisits [sic] and pay for their tuition fees."[34] The idea of a free education was attractive to both Mormons and non-Mormons, and in areas such as Rich County with its homogeneous population, it made little difference to most residents whether children received their education at a church institution or a public institution.

Perhaps the greatest animosity over the school issue existed in Woodruff, where, as discussed in the previous chapter, a squabble developed between church officials and school trustees over ownership of the public meetinghouse.

For seven years following the district court's decision in favor of the Woodruff school trustees, the Mormon settlers at Woodruff were without an official church house, although the school building continued to be used for that purpose. Between 1893 and 1897 both a new church and a school were completed. The school became the showpiece of the community for many years. It was built of brick and contained two stories. Construction was done under the direction of Joseph F. Neville.[35]

During the first fifteen years of the twentieth century, the school system in Woodruff was also the showpiece of education in Rich County. In 1915, after passage of the consolidation act which created countywide school districts, the Woodruff precinct was the only former school district which issued a favorable report. Chairperson Sarah Cornia of the Woodruff School District reported the district to have one thousand dollars cash on hand. Salaries in the district were the highest paid in the county: $125 per month for the principal and $100 per month for teachers. The Woodruff School employed four teachers plus the principal who also taught, and the school had recently added the ninth grade to its curriculum. In Cornia's estimation, the Woodruff School would require a property tax levy of 5 mills for operating expenses.[36] The school continued to lead in education for the next several years. In 1916 a tenth grade was established at the school, and by 1919 the county board of education had renovated and partitioned the top floor of the school in order to provide

North Rich High School Band. (Courtesy Clayton Robinson.)

training in the eleventh grade. In 1922 the Woodruff School became both a grammar school and a high school, offering instruction in grades one through twelve.

Between the years 1922 and 1928 the Woodruff School grew to be the largest in Rich County. However, during the years of this ascendancy, the population of Woodruff began to decline. At the same time more modern school facilities were being constructed in Randolph. By 1927 the Rich County Board of Education began toying with the idea of consolidating the high school portion of the Woodruff School with the separate high school at Randolph. Board member Frank Frazier of Woodruff proposed in June 1927 that the two schools be joined.[37] Although public criticism caused the motion to be tabled, a year later the proposition was again brought before the board. This time the measure passed and grades nine through twelve at the Woodruff School were transferred to Randolph. In addition to the motion to consolidate the schools at Woodruff and Randolph, there was a motion to also consolidate the high school at Garden City with that at Laketown.

The creation in 1915 of countywide boards of education with the power to consolidate district schools was the end result of over thirty years of debate. The early examples of consolidation in Rich County—Round Valley and Meadowville with Laketown, and Sage Creek and Argyle with Randolph—were more a matter of convenience than of force. Other consolidation of the schools in Rich County did not pass so peaceably. Although the high-school portion of the Woodruff School merged with its counterpart at Randolph with relatively little pain, the merger between the high schools at Garden City and Laketown created a rift between the two communities which would persist for over twenty years. Following the vote to consolidate the various high schools at Randolph and Laketown, Joseph N. Cook, board member from Garden City, organized a public meeting to coincide with the next regular meeting of the board of education. The county courthouse in Randolph was packed with Garden City residents who opposed consolidation, and the afternoon was spent in several hours of "somewhat heated discussion."[38] As a result of the public outcry from Garden City, the board voted unanimously to rescind the order to consolidate. During the next session of the board, however, the identical motion was entertained and passed. In the view of the Garden City community, the vote to consolidate the high schools was somewhat prejudiced. Those in the southern part of Rich County had favored consolidation; the citizens of Woodruff were not opposed to the merger with Randolph. The high school at Randolph was completed between 1915 and 1918 and was constructed specifically for the purpose. It did not include any grades below the seventh. Randolph maintained a separate grade school. The high school facilities at Randolph were far superior to those at Woodruff. The latter community was using the renovated top floor of the Woodruff School for high-school classes, and it did not compare to the new high school in Randolph.

In contrast to the differences between the school facilities at Woodruff and Randolph, there was little difference between the two schools in Bear Lake Valley. Both schools were constructed between 1915 and 1918. If anything, the school at Garden City was superior to that at Laketown, and it was considered to be one of the best in the district. By 1917 students at the Garden City School were receiving instruction through the eleventh grade. The Laketown School, more-

over, had some serious drawbacks in its construction. After surveying the school, officials at the state Department of Public Instruction
remarked:

> The Laketown School . . . has a poorly planned and constructed
> entrance. . . . The main floor is heated by a hot-air furnace whereas
> the basement has heatrolas. The installation of the heating plant is
> not entirely satisfactory, in that it involves heat losses and does not
> lend itself to temperature control. . . . There is no provision for fire
> protection, artificial lighting, or satisfactory ventilation.[39]

Furthermore, the Laketown School had difficulty attracting enough
students to make the high school practical. "As the school term of
1916–17 approached," noted Earl F. Passey, "arrangements were made
to offer instruction to students of the tenth grade if as many as eight
students desired such instruction." As late as 1923 the board of education tabled a motion to add the eleventh grade at Laketown until
it could "ascertain the probable number who would attend."[40]

But the cards were stacked against Garden City residents in their
bid to have the high school established there. After the inauguration
of the board of education in 1915, the county had been divided into
five precincts with one board member from each precinct. Woodruff
and the surrounding area constituted one precinct while Randolph
literally was divided (the dividing line extended through the middle
of the county courthouse) into two precincts: the north which
included part of Randolph and the Sage Creek area, and the south
which included the other part of Randolph, extending south to
include the settlement at Argyle. The remaining two precincts were
at Garden City and Laketown.

The motions to consolidate the high schools in the county, made
in 1927 and passed in 1928, were not separate motions. On both
occasions, the main motion to consolidate Woodruff High School
with Randolph was substituted with an alternative motion by
Laketown board member George H. Robinson to also include the
consolidation of the two high schools in Bear Lake Valley. The vote
on the substitute motion was the same in both instances: the
precincts in Bear River Valley, because they favored the merger of
their two schools, voted in favor of the motion. Laketown precinct

also voted in favor of the motion; only Garden City precinct opposed the motion.

Even though Garden City opposed consolidation, the merger occurred in 1928, and students from Garden City were transported to the Laketown School. The name of the school was then changed to North Rich High School. Similarly, after the merger of the Woodruff and Randolph schools, the name of the school was changed to South Rich High School. From 1928 through the years of the Great Depression each of the four communities in Rich County maintained a school for grades one through eight, while grades nine through twelve were taught at either South Rich or North Rich high school. While South Rich High School had its own separate facility, the building designated North Rich High School also housed the Laketown students in grades one through eight.

At the beginning of the 1930s the board of education began considering ways to upgrade the school facilities in the county. Priorities were North Rich High School and Randolph Elementary School. Several building bond issues were presented to the voters during the early 1930s, but the price tag of over sixty-five thousand dollars was evidently too high in the midst of the depression, and the voters turned them down. In 1934 the county board of education reduced the bond to ten thousand dollars to be used only in the construction of the new Randolph elementary school. The school board further sought the aid of the federal government and obtained a grant from the Federal Emergency Relief Administration for approximately $10,000. This time the bond issue passed by a wide margin and construction began on the Randolph school within the year.

Between 1944 and 1948 the issue of new school facilities became even more urgent—in February 1944 LaVon Sprouse of Garden City awoke in the early morning to find the Garden City school engulfed in flames. The fire completely destroyed the building.[41]

After the Garden City fire, the county was scoured for desks, books, and extra supplies, and the school moved into the local LDS ward chapel. The destruction of the Garden City school opened up the possibility of further consolidation, and district superintendent Earl F. Passey implored the communities to consider a merger of their elementary schools.[42] The Garden City residents preferred to have the

Students in front of entrance to old South Rich High School, Randolph.
(Courtesy Nathell Hoffman.)

lower grades remain within the community rather than joining with the students at Laketown even though it meant moving into the old, long vacant Garden City school building.

As discussions began taking place concerning the fate of the Garden City students, the proposal was made to construct a new school at Garden City which would be large enough to accommodate all the students within northern Rich County. Why, asked Clarence Cook of Garden City, build only a small elementary school at Garden City when both a high school and elementary school could be built more practically? This proposition would have eliminated the school at Laketown. Once again the matter of consolidation created substantial tension within the two communities.

The Laketown community was not about to relinquish the school to Garden City. The Laketown precinct which included all of the Round Valley area contained many more acres of taxable land than did the Garden City area. The Garden City precinct did not include more than 2,500 acres of farm ground. By the 1940s there were individual ranchers within the Laketown area who owned in excess of that figure. If Laketown precinct was paying the lion's share of the school taxes for North Rich High School, the reasoning went, the school should naturally be located at Laketown.

The prospect of building both a high school and elementary school at Garden City or a building large enough to house all grades was complicated by World War II. The United States had entered World War II in December 1941, and by February 1944 the military was preparing for the invasion of Europe which would follow in June. War preparations and demands required that citizens throughout the United States exercise restraint. Rationing of building supplies, gasoline, rubber products, and staple foods such as sugar and flour, was initiated. These restrictions placed a moratorium on building the new, larger school at Garden City and retarded the construction of even the smaller elementary school.

In hopes of expediting the situation, board member Cook proposed in March 1945 that a smaller elementary school be constructed at Garden City. In order to obtain community support for the smaller school, Cook also proposed that a large gymnasium be erected in conjunction with the school. Consensus was reached between Garden

City and Laketown on the issue, and a bond issue was voted on in March 1945. The bond called for thirty thousand dollars to be used for "purchasing school sites, for building or purchasing one or more school houses and supplying the same with furniture. . . ."[43] County voters turned the bond down by a two-to-one margin.

The schoolhouse that was eventually constructed in Garden City did not meet with the approval of the Garden City community. The building cost an estimated ten thousand dollars less than was originally planned, and although the school provided sufficient space for the students, the large gymnasium was scratched from the plans. This was done without bringing the issue again before the voters. The school board opted instead to work through Zions Bank of Salt Lake City which "offered to buy tax anticipation notes to be issued by the Rich district, to defray the construction costs of a school . . . at Garden City."[44]

The school board anticipated that the new Garden City school would be used for grades one through six. Since 1943 the district had adopted a policy of placing seventh and eighth grade students at one of the two high schools. The population throughout Rich County had declined during the difficult times of the depression and war years. In order to compensate, the school board voted to consolidate the seventh and eighth grades at Woodruff and Garden City with students at South and North Rich high schools. The move was first attempted at Woodruff where the board's decision was met with a "sit-down strike" in the Woodruff community. Seventh and eighth grade students simply stayed at home for two weeks. Gradually a reconciliation took place between the two communities and the Woodruff students returned to school at Randolph.[45]

The transporting of Garden City seventh and eighth grade students to Laketown was not settled within three weeks, however. Following the board's decision, many of the seventh and eighth grade Garden City students began attending school at Paris, Idaho. This placed the school board in an awkward position: with half of the area's seventh and eighth grade students attending school at Paris, the number of students in North Rich High School was insufficient to warrant the current teaching staff.

The Garden City community was still smarting from past school

board decisions which they perceived to be unjust. With the move to
Paris, Idaho, Garden City residents had finally found a way to reverse
the impotency of their position with the school board. Garden City
board member Parley N. Hodges offered an ultimatum in March
1943: Hodges reported that the Garden City community had met in
mass meeting and decided that they "would send all of their children
to Paris the next school year unless the high school [was] made in
Garden City."[46]

A year after Hodge's ultimatum, an interesting yet unrelated set
of events transpired: the Garden City school burned down in 1944;
the proposal to construct a larger school at Garden City with a gymnasium was turned down by the voters of the county; Parley Hodges
was voted off the school board in 1944 and replaced by Albert
Hodges, who resigned after a year; Clarence Cook, who was
appointed to fill the position in January 1945, died in office the following May. Everett Sims then assumed the vacant seat on the school
board in June 1945.

It would fall to Sims to try to unravel the tangle of ill will which
had developed between the two communities over the school issue.
The board proposed in 1946 to consolidate all the elementary grades
in northern Rich County at Garden City and the upper grades at
Laketown. Sims noted that regardless of the concessions some members of the community would still send their children to the Idaho
school unless the board rescinded its decision to remove the seventh
and eighth grade students from Garden City.[47]

Board member Sims was reminded by the board that a similar
controversy had developed at Woodruff and that if they allowed the
Garden City school to regroup with all eight grades they would be
obliged to allow Woodruff the same concession. The Garden City residents were serious about their boycott, however. During the first
week of school in September 1946, only one Garden City student registered for classes at North Rich High School. Furthermore, Laketown
school board member Vernon Robinson reported

> that the superintendent had informed him that two officials from
> the State Department of Health had appeared at the Laketown
> school . . . at the request of Board member Everett Sims, they had

made the trip to Rich County for the purpose of finding some cause for condemning and closing the Laketown school.[48]

The Paris, Idaho, schools appeared to have little problem accommodating the Garden City students. After meeting with the Rich County School Board in August 1946, the Idaho representatives advised Rich County that under the laws of the state of Utah the county could count the Garden City students as part of their "classroom unit" and could request reimbursement for those students from the Utah State Department of Public Instruction. According to the Paris officials, "Part of the money could be used to pay the tuitions at Paris and part could remain to increase the finances of Rich District."[49]

This, however, did not rectify the problem of diminishing enrollment at North Rich High School. Without the Garden City students, the studentbody at Laketown was too small to constitute a separate high school. At a meeting of the board in October 1946, the issue of the future of the Laketown school and the possibility of merging it with Randolph was discussed.

Mr. Robinson (board member from Laketown) stated that about three families in Laketown would permit their children to be transported to Randolph, but that the remaining families would strongly resist any present attempt at high school consolidation. Mr. Sims expressed the belief that if the Board would allow out-of-state tuition payments for the Garden City people until the road was completed over the hill and a new high school constructed in Randolph, many of the Garden City people would not object to supporting the high school at Randolph.[50]

Through the year 1951 the Garden City community continued to agitate for out-of-state tuition. In the interests of insulating the school at Laketown and of perpetuating the schools of Rich County in general, the school board voted in May 1951 "never to give time and consideration to the problem again, that the matter of out-of-state tuition payment was closed, and no further requests would be entertained."[51]

The students from Garden City eventually returned to Laketown and North Rich High School. The issue of consolidation was far from over, however. As the debate was taking place between Laketown and Garden City and between Garden City and the school board over out-of-state tuition, fire engulfed the South Rich High School on the evening of 21 January 1948. The destruction of the high school set immediately into motion a plan to erect a new building at Randolph. Bond elections for the purpose of constructing the new high school were held in the district as early as 1947, but the school board post-poned the construction of the building in order to await a more favorable market for building materials. The district was also in the middle of a debate over the future of North Rich High School and the probable secession of Garden City students. Nonetheless, the destruction by fire of South Rich High School made all other issues secondary. Financial difficulties continued to hamper the project, but by 1951 the new South Rich High School opened for business.[52]

As discussed by the county board of education in 1946, the most sensible course for the county to have taken would have been high-school consolidation at the new building in Randolph. The North Rich High School was old and in need of extensive repairs. Although this fact was certainly known prior to March 1953, the school board sought and received a state appropriation to remodel and improve the Laketown building. Board member Thelma McKinnon urged her fellow board members to entertain the idea of consolidation and to reconsider expending any more money at North Rich when the money could more profitably be used to improve the Randolph school. But with the district just beginning to recover from the Garden City incident, the other school board members were reluc-tant to engage in another consolidation fight. McKinnon's motion was voted down, and the board retained architect Karl C. Schaub to draw plans for the new North Rich addition.[53] The new high school opened in February 1955.[54]

With declining school enrollments, Rich County was soon forced to make some decisions concerning consolidation. In September 1960 school board members discussed the likelihood of Laketown Elementary School having insufficient enrollment to justify the employment of three teachers. On the other hand, the new Woodruff elementary school constructed in 1957 and opened in the fall of 1958, had an enrollment in excess of the normal workload of the two teachers currently employed there.[55] Faced with a difficult decision, the school board considered several options, including taking three grades from Woodruff and placing them at Randolph and consolidating the Garden City elementary classes with those of Laketown. The latter proposition met with some opposition in Garden City. A majority of eligible voters in the precinct signed a petition asking the school board to allow at least three grades to remain at Garden City. After considerable debate the school board decided to stay with their original plan, and the Garden City school was closed. The school district sold the building to the LDS church for two thousand dollars. Some board members felt that the price was too low; nonetheless the majority of the board felt that the building would best serve the needs of the community if placed in the hands of the local bishop.[56]

With the two Bear Lake communities consolidated at Laketown, it once again became evident that facilities countywide were not equal. A review team from the Utah State Board of Education visited the county in March 1966. They reported that while "the elementary school program tends to met basic requirements, the secondary school program appears to be woefully inadequate."[57] The review team made three main recommendations: consolidating the Woodruff school with the Randolph elementary, renovating North Rich High School for elementary purposes, and consolidating the county's two high schools at Randolph.

The consolidation of elementary schools was one thing, but high school consolidation was quite another. Few things typify the geographic peculiarities of Rich County more than its educational development. Garden City residents opposed high school consolidation for more than twenty years, even going so far as to send their children to the high school at Paris, Idaho. In many respects, Garden City retained closer ties with the communities of Fish Haven, Paris, and St. Charles, Idaho, than they did with Laketown. Laketown, on the other hand, maintained little affiliation with Randolph and Woodruff. Few things had changed over the years. In 1946 Laketown school board member Vernon Robinson stated that only about three families would be willing to send their children to Randolph for high school. The feeling remained about the same in 1966.

It appeared that these issues had to be approached with great sensitivity. South and North Rich high schools constituted a large part of the community identity in Laketown and Randolph; their geographic separation made them natural rivals. Rather than moving immediately to implement the recommendations of the state board of education, the Rich County School Board opted to try to improve the separate schools over a five-year period and then seek accreditation with the state board.[58] Major improvements were made, but accreditation was not achieved within the five-year period. Further renovations made in the late 1970s still did not meet state requirements. Finally, in 1984 the district moved to consolidate the two high schools at Randolph, and North and South Rich became Rich High School. This did not happen without significant public unrest. Superintendent Giles E. Parker largely bore the brunt of public dissatisfaction with the consolidation which contributed to his later resignation. School consolidation remained unpopular with adult residents within the county; students, however, generally had a positive experience. Overall, school consolidation was beneficial for the county. As former Rich County teacher Annie S. Wamsley has mentioned: "Although it has been painful to many, it has been for the good of the students."[59]

Rich County consistently expends more funds per student than the state average. In 1982 the county ranked fifth in overall expenditures, spending $3,035 per student. By 1987, although expenditures remained about the same, the county's ranking had dropped to number eight. In 1993 Rich County schools consisted of two elementary schools—one in Laketown and one in Randolph; one junior high school in Laketown; and one high school in Randolph. There were 283 elementary age students in Rich County in 1993; 99 students attended the junior high school in Laketown, and 167 students attended Rich High School in Randolph. The district employed thirty-two full-time teachers.[60] Maintaining educational opportunities is just one responsibility of administrators and officials within Rich County. As the school board oversaw educational matters, the Rich County Commission oversaw other aspects of county government. Among other matters, the county commission managed the maintenance of roads, the collection and disbursement of taxes, health and sanitation issues, and business regulations, as we shall see in the following pages.

ENDNOTES

1. John Clifton Moffitt, *The History of Public Education in Utah* (Salt Lake City: Deseret News Press, 1946), 2–8.

2. Ibid., 9.

3. *The Latter-day Saints' Millennial Star 10* (Liverpool, 1848): 85.

4. Ray L. DeBoer, *"A Historical Study of Mormon Education and the Influence of Its Philosophy on Public Education in Utah,"* (Ph.D. diss., University of Denver, 1951), 67. Furthermore, by 1854 the territorial assembly, "whether acting in civil or religious capacity, determined to use the schools as the agency in establishing the Deseret Alphabet." See Moffitt, *The History of Public Education in Utah,* 55.

Samuel C. Monson explained the circumstances surrounding the origin and adoption of the Deseret Alphabet before the Utah Academy of Sciences, Arts, and Letters in 1953. Explaining how most alphabets use Roman letters, Monson noted that a "notable exception is the Deseret Alphabet, proposed for use in Utah by Brigham Young." According to Monson, Brigham Young considered written English absurd and requested the Board of Regents of the newly created University of Deseret "to devise a better system." The system would be based upon phonetics. "Literacy was an ideal among the Mormons, and, if spelling were directly related to pronunciation, it would be much easier to teach English to foreigners, as well as to illiterate Americans." Monson also pointed out that the adoption of the Deseret Alphabet held the possibility of further isolating the Mormons—something which Brigham Young desired. "Although many writers disclaim the notion," he states, "isolationism . . . seems to have been a factor. When books in the alphabet finally appeared, an editorial in the *Deseret News* . . . suggested that if children were taught only the Deseret Alphabet they would be saved from contamination by a prurient and dangerous literature, which corrupts and distorts the minds and judgements of men"

The major force behind the creation of the new alphabet was George Watt, an English convert to Mormonism who, prior to emigration in 1842, had had considerable experience with "phonography" and shorthand. Monson describes the alphabet created by Watt as consisting of "thirty-eight characters . . . correspond[ing] in value to symbols of the International Phonetic Alphabet, with minor variations." Furthermore, "There was no distinction, other than in size, between capitals and lowercase letters. No cursive script was provided for handwriting. When the characters were used, they were disjunct." See Samuel C. Monson, "The Deseret Alphabet," *Utah Academy of Sciences, Arts, and Letters Proceedings* 10 (Salt Lake City: Utah Academy of Sciences, Arts and Letters, 1953): 23–29.

5. DeBoer, *A Historical Study of Mormon Education,* 61–2.

6. Ibid., 62–63.

7. Kate B. Carter, "Latter Day Saint Schools," in Lessons for December 1949 (Salt Lake City: Daughters of Utah Pioneers, 1949), 127.

8. *Journal History of the Church of Jesus Christ of Latter-day Saints,* manuscript, Department of Special Collections and Archives, Merrill Library, Utah State University, Logan, Utah (hereafter referred to as JH), 17 September 1883, 9.

9. JH, 29 May 1883, 6.

10. Earl F. Passey, "An Historical Study of Public Education in Rich County, Utah," (MS thesis, University of Utah, 1951), 33.

11. JH, 17 March 1883, 5.

12. JH, 5 April 1883, 5.

13. *Bear Lake Democrat,* Montpelier, Idaho, 21 November 1884. Quoted in JH, 19 November 1884, 10.

14. JH, 17 September 9.

15. JH, 22 February 1884, 3.

16. Passey, "An Historical Study of Public Education," 102. The school trustees in Laketown were John H. Weston, Manassah Kearl, and Joseph Moffatt.

17. See *Laws of the State of Utah: Passed at the Eleventh Regular Session of the Legislature of the State of Utah* (Salt Lake City: Century Printing Co., 1915), 98–101.

18. Passey, "An Historical Study of Public Education," 102–03.

19. Ibid., 59–63.

20. Mildred N. Thomson, comp., *Rich Memories: Some of the Happenings in Rich Country from 1863 to 1960* (Salt Lake City: Daughters of Utah Pioneers, 1962), 125.

21. Passey, "An Historical Study of Public Education," 22–26.

22. Sociologist Lowry Nelson devoted a lifetime of study to the characteristics of the Mormon village, and he more than anyone, popularized the idea. Nelson defined the Mormon village's structure as containing "first, wide streets intersecting each other at right angles, running in north-south and east-west directions; second, the square blocks thus formed are the location of the residence establishments of the farmers who cultivate the farm lands adjacent to the village proper." See Lowry Nelson, "The Mormon Village: A Study in Social Origins," reprint of article (n.p, n.d) 11, Special

Collections and Archives, Utah State University, Logan. See also the larger work, Lowry Nelson, *The Mormon Village: A Pattern and Technique of Land Settlement* (Salt Lake City: University of Utah Press, 1952).

23. Passey, "An Historical Study of Public Education," 56.

24. Passey, "An Historical Study of Public Education," 54. See also Manuscript History of Woodruff Ward, Bear Lake Stake, Rich County, Utah, 1900 Church Historian's Office, Church of Jesus Christ of Latter-day Saints, Salt Lake City (hereafter cited as WMH).

25. Passey, "An Historical Study of Public Education," 55.

26. Ibid., 54–58.

27. Ibid., 37.

28. See John D. Monnett, Jr., "The Mormon Church and Its Private School System in Utah: The Emergence of the Academies, 1880–1892," (Ph.D, diss., University of Utah, 1984), 222–23. The letter from Woodruff, sent to all area stake presidents and dated 8 June 1888, read as follows:

Dear Brethren:

A meeting of the General Board of Education was held to-day, and the subject of the educational interests of the Latter-day Saints was taken into consideration and discussed at some length. It was decided that a Board of Education, consisting of not less than five and not to exceed eight in number, should be selected in each Stake to take charge of and promote the interests of education in the Stake. This communication is addressed to you to inform you of this action, and to have you select energetic men who are friends of education, who understand the needs of the people, and who have influence with the Saints, to carry out any suggestions in this direction that may be deemed proper. In the decision which was made by our Board it was made the duty of these Boards to take into consideration the formation of Church schools and the best method of accomplishing this, and after arriving at proper conclusions, to report them to the General Board. Communications of this character may be addressed to Elder George Reynolds, who is Secretary of the Board. It was felt by the Board that, to begin with, there should be one State Academy established in each State as soon as practicable.

We feel that the time has arrived when the proper education of our children should be taken in hand by us as a people. Religious training is practically excluded from the District Schools. The perusal of books that we value as divine records is forbidden. Our children, if left to the training they receive in these schools, will grow up entirely ignorant of those principles of salvation for which the Latter-day Saints have made so many sacrifices. To permit this condition of things to exist among us would be criminal. The desire is universally expressed by all thinking people in the Church that we should have schools where the Bible, the Book of Mormon and the Book of

Doctrine and Covenants can be used as text books, and where the principles of our religion may form a part of the teaching of the schools. To effect this it will be necessary that funds be collected. The Church will doubtless do its share; but it cannot carry the entire burden. The Saints must be appealed to. There are hundreds of liberal-minded people among us who will be willing to contribute to this worthy object when they find the subject is receiving proper attention, and that definite and permanent arrangements are being made to establish academies of this character.

The brethren whom you select to form this Board should be men of character and integrity among the people, who will be able to use an influence in the collection of funds, so that academies may be established, good Faculties employed, and education be made so cheap that it will be within the reach of the humblest in the land. After you have made a proper selection for this Board, the names of the brethren composing it should be presented regularly at your Stake Conference as other authorities are, so that the people can vote for them.

> Very respectfully yours,
> Wilford Woodruff
> Chairman of the Church Board of Education
> George Reynolds
> Secretary

29. Monnett, "The Mormon Church and Its Private School System," 222.

30. Thomson, *Rich Memories,* 178.

31. Carter, "Latter Day Saint Schools," 127–29.

32. Monnett, "The Mormon Church and Its Private School System," 175–76.

33. Ibid., 176.

34. Ibid., 177.

35. Joseph F. Neville was born in England in 1876 and immigrated to Utah in 1880. He is credited with the construction of numerous buildings in Woodruff and elsewhere in Rich County. He was a talented carpenter, brick mason, and iron worker. See Woodruff Centennial Committee, *The First Hundred Years in Woodruff* (Springville, UT: Art City Publishing Co., 1970), 351.

36. Passey, "An Historical Study of Public Education," 70. Compared to the other six school districts which had operated in Rich County before 1915—Garden City, Round Valley, Sage, Laketown, Argyle, and Meadowville—the Woodruff District appeared well managed. For instance, while Woodruff held a surplus of one thousand dollars, the combined debt of the other districts amounted to over eighteen thousand dollars. Most of this

debt had been incurred in the North Randolph District (Sage), where a six-teen thousand dollar building bond had been issued. The Randolph District also required the highest mill levy of 13.5 to pay for district expenses. Furthermore, none of the other districts provided training beyond the eighth grade. See Passey, 64–73.

37. Passey, "An Historical Study of Public Education," 118.

38. Ibid., 79.

39. Ibid., 102.

40. Ibid., 103.

41. *Rich County Reaper* (Randolph, Utah), 24 February 1944, 1.

42. Passey, "An Historical Study of Public Education," 83.

43. Ibid., 85.

44. Ibid., 86.

45. Ibid., 123.

46. Ibid., 93.

47. Ibid., 95.

48. Ibid., 96.

49. Ibid., 97.

50. Ibid., 98.

51. The meeting held on 5 May 1951 included the following points of view as expressed by Everett Sims, the Garden City member, and Vern Hopkin, the member from Woodruff:

"At this time, Mr. Everett Sims and Mr. LaVon Sprouse of Garden City appeared before the Board with the request that the Rich County Board of Education pay the 1950–51 tuition bill for the Garden City students attending Paris, Idaho, schools. The entire arguments were again presented by this committee.

1. Rich County schools would profit financially by applying for state aid and using only part of such aid to pay the Idaho tuition.

2. Rich County schools were too small to be as good as the Paris schools.

3. The Garden City people desired better schools for their children than Rich County offered.

4. It would constitute an act of discrimination against the Garden City community if this tuition were not allowed.

A written petition was then presented to the Board, bearing the names of a large segment of the entire Garden City community.

Board member Hopkin led the other members of the Board in reply-ing to this request. He pointed out that to receive additional classroom units for the payment of the tuition cost would increase the total tax burden in the state of Utah. Since part of this additional money would be raised in Rich County, it could not benefit this district to tax itself a larger amount in order to have a smaller amount remaining for the particular use of Rich County Schools. Second, if Rich County's schools were too small to be efficient, they would be made still smaller as the result of the withdrawal of the Garden City students. Therefore, to allow the payment would be, in effect, working to the detriment of the very schools the Board were elected to manage, support, and upgrade. Third, evidence was amply available that Rich County school graduates were not handicapped above other students in later college study. In the matter of discrimination, it was pointed out that it was the first duty of Rich County citizens to support and build their own communities and by failing in this duty they were failing in their public trust as school board members. Further, that those citizens who were constantly working against our own school system were wholly to blame for the unhealthy condition existing in the north end of the county. See Passey, "An Historical Study of Public Education," 100–101.

52. Steven L. Thomson, Jane D. Digerness, and Mar Jean S. Thomson, *Randolph—A Look Back* (n.p., 1981), 176.

53. Rich County Board of Education minutes, 2 March 1953, Rich County School District, Randolph, Utah (hereafter referred to as Board of Education minutes).

54. Board of Education Minutes, 7 February 1955.

55. Board of Education Minutes, 12 September 1960.

56. Board of Education Minutes, 20 November 1962.

57. Utah State Board of Education, "Evaluation of the Rich County School District," 29 March 1966, 29.

58. Board of Education Minutes, 15 May 1968.

59. Annie S. Wamsley, "School Through the Years by a devoted Rich County, Utah, Teacher." Typescript. See appendix C.

60. *1993–94 Utah School Directory* (Salt Lake City: Utah State Office of Education, 1993), 118.

9

"In an Ever Broadening Role"

LOCAL GOVERNMENT IN RICH COUNTY

The boundaries of Richland County, Utah, were created by the Utah Territorial Assembly in January 1866 and included the area east of Cache County, north of Morgan and Summit counties, and west of the divide separating the Bear River and Green River drainages. The county was bounded on the north by the forty-second parallel.[1] Uncertain as to the exact location of the forty-second parallel dividing the territories of Utah and Idaho, the legislative assembly established the county seat of Richland County at St. Charles in what was actually Idaho.

Mormon settlers also were unaware of Bear Lake's unique location which placed half the valley in Utah Territory and half in Idaho Territory. But soon the settlers as well as both territorial legislative bodies suspected that at least a portion of Bear Lake was north of the forty-second parallel. Still, settlers in both the northern and southern Bear Lake settlements preferred affiliation with Utah and continued in their opinion even after the completion of the federal survey in 1872. As virtually the entire population of Bear Lake Valley was Mormon, their preference made sense. Given the interrelationship between ecclesiastical leadership and civil government in Bear Lake Valley, their affiliation with the territorial government of Utah seemed to best serve the needs of Bear Lake Valley settlers. Furthermore, it would have been impossible for local government in Bear Lake Valley to operate efficiently with the valley divided in half. One of the main purposes of early county governments was to provide the leadership necessary to begin to build the infrastructure— roads, bridges, and communication links—to join the communities together. Separate county governments in Bear Lake Valley would have made this much more difficult.

Mormon apostle Charles C. Rich was placed in charge of the Bear Lake settlements after their establishment in 1863. His duties included responsibility for both spiritual and temporal leadership. A semblance of county government began operation as early as May 1864.[2] In January 1866 the territorial assembly authorized the creation of an official county court to oversee county government. The act authorized by the territorial assembly provided for the election of three selectmen from each county who, along with the probate judge, constituted the county court.[3] The first county court to convene under the new legislation did so in 1866 at St. Charles and included as selectmen David B. Dille, John A. Hunt, and James H. Hart. The session was under the supervision of Probate Judge Preston Thomas.[4]

After the 1872 federal survey clearly established the location of the Idaho-Utah border, a new county court was appointed for Rich County, and the county seat was moved to Randolph. In February 1872 the territorial assembly amended the act establishing county boundaries to reflect the findings of the survey.[5]

Rich County's exact boundaries were still uncertain, however. The dividing line between Rich and Summit counties would remain in limbo for nearly eighty years. In 1895 the county court endeavored to determine the exact location of the border.[6] Two years later county surveyor J. H. Neville was authorized to fix the county line and set cedar posts to mark the boundary, but the border remained in dispute.[7] Of primary concern to both counties was the collection of taxes on livestock. As discussed in chapter six, Rich County was often deprived of its fair share of taxes because of the movement of sheep herds from summer to winter range. The Deseret Livestock

Company, in fact, was ultimately responsible for settling the controversy. The company had land holdings in Rich and Summit counties and was determined to find out just what share of its taxes each county was entitled to. In May 1936 the company sued the two counties in district court, and county commissions from both counties were forced to come to an understanding as to the location of the county line.[8] At the time of the court's decision, a survey map was prepared between November 1935 and March 1936 by J. W. Jones.[9] An additional twenty years elapsed before the final surveying was completed. J. F. Neville, Rich County Surveyor in 1952, wrote his counterpart in Summit County, J. Emerson Staples, that the surveying had finally been completed and that he hoped this would end the conflict "once and for all."[10]

The first county court for Rich County, Utah, convened on 5 May 1872. The court included selectmen William H. Lee, Randolph H. Stewart, and Ira Nebeker. James H. Hart was retained as probate judge from the previous county court at St. Charles.[11] The county was divided into districts which initially included Randolph, Woodruff, Meadowville, Round Valley, and Laketown, then later Argyle, Sage Creek, and Garden City. In addition to dividing the county into districts, the county court also organized the county into water districts which roughly paralleled the county districts. Another important consideration for the county court was the organization of estray pounds, including the appointment of pound keepers, in the various districts. Pound keepers were required to detain any stray stock found within their district. The animals generally were kept on the pound keeper's premises. At the conclusion of each term of the county court, each pound keeper reported to the court the number and kinds of strays within his district and received compensation from the court for the animals' upkeep. If strays were not claimed within the term of the court, they became the property of the county and were sold on bid at the conclusion of each term.

Road commissioners were also appointed for the various districts within the county, and the county court expended considerable time, effort, and finances in the maintenance of roads. As early as 1867 the county court took a major step in connecting the northern and southern portion of Bear Lake Valley when they authorized the construction of a road south from Fish Haven and a bridge over Swan Creek.[12] James H. Hart and John A. Hunt reported in September that $450 had been expended and that the project was satisfactory. Two years later, Joseph C. Rich was ordered to complete the county road south from the Swan Creek Bridge along the west shore of Bear Lake to Laketown.[13]

With the settlement of Randolph and Woodruff and the reorganization of Rich County in 1872, the foremost concern of county selectmen was the route from Laketown to Randolph. Laketown Canyon was the focal point for intercourse between the Bear Lake and Bear River portions of the county. Notwithstanding early comments on the accessibility of the Bear River Valley via the Laketown route, the road remained little more than a trail. Although David P. Kimball commented that his journey from Laketown to Evanston, Wyoming, in 1870 was by "a good road," and the manuscript history of Bear Lake Stake noted that the "pass or summit between Bear River and Bear Lake valleys is low and easily crossed,"[14] early Randolph resident John M. Baxter recalled that there was "no wagon road down Laketown Canyon, only an Indian trail."[15] The trip from Laketown to Randolph was possible only on foot or horseback. And that explains, as discussed in chapter three, why the original settlers into Randolph made the trip in the early spring with sleds.[16] In June 1871 the county court received a petition from the citizens of Laketown, Meadowville, and Randolph asking that a county road "be located from the southern terminus [Laketown] . . . through Laketown Canon by way of the Indian trail to Randolph."[17] In March 1873 a committee including William West and H. J. Harper of Randolph and John Nebeker and James Kearl of Laketown was appointed to locate the best possible route for the road.[18] During early summer of the following year, the county court authorized the employment of ten men from Randolph, five men from Woodruff, and five men from Laketown to begin work on the road at $2.50 per man per day plus $2.50 daily per team of horses. Selectman Ira Nebeker was authorized to purchase blasting powder, drills, hammers, and shovels.[19]

The original route of the road from Laketown to Randolph appears to have been different from either the present road or the

Bridge Out. Car being pulled from Bear River. The maintenance of bridges and roads was a constant problem and expense for county government. (Courtesy Nathell Hoffman.)

road used by the original settlers. The original settlers, after negotiating the canyon, apparently followed roughly the present-day road to Sage Creek. The report of the county court in 1875 noted that the old route by Sage Creek was "unavailable." A committee of Ira Nebeker, Randolph H. Stewart, and Wright A. Moore reported the old Indian trail to be the most "practical," and proposed a route from "Randolph to Otter Creek, thence up Otter Creek about 1/2 mile to Randolph Herd House[,] turn right and go in most direct route to head of Laketown Canyon."[20] Construction proceeded slowly. In 1877 the county court authorized additional expenditures on the road, noting that all taxes which could be spared from both Laketown and Randolph should be used in the construction of the road. Significant progress must have been made on the route, for by fall 1877 several families from Randolph had moved to Garden City using the Laketown route. Wright A. Moore even moved his cabin from Randolph to Garden City.[21] The road required continual upkeep, however, and travel plans were often at the mercy of the weather. Some communication between the two parts of the county could not wait for cooperative weather patterns; mail service, for instance, continued whether or not the Laketown Canyon road was open.

Although no official mail service existed in Bear Lake Valley upon the arrival of settlers in 1863, couriers were used to deliver letters from the valley to Franklin, Idaho. Often Bear Lake settlers would meet their counterparts from Franklin at the summit between Cache and Bear Lake valleys and exchange letters. The service was at best sporadic. Charles C. Rich decided to bid on an official contract for mail service from Huntsville to Bennington in Bear Lake Valley. However, Rich was undercut by a competitor. He complained about the competition to Brigham Young, stating that "Hershfield knew nothing of the country, and difficulties to be encountered in carrying a good sized weekly mail."[22] Rich must have been correct in his assessment of the difficulty of the Huntsville route, for a year later it was abandoned. Rich was later awarded a contract to carry mail from Bennington to Franklin. This route was used until the Oregon Shortline Railroad arrived at Montpelier in 1882.[23]

Railroad transportation brought increased efficiency to mail service in Rich County. After settlement of the Bear River Valley, mail service commenced from Evanston, Wyoming, to Randolph, and on to Laketown. Mail was brought from Evanston to Laketown by Joshua Eldredge. From Laketown, the mail traveled to St. Charles, Idaho, and was then taken over the divide to Franklin. James Kearl succeeded Eldredge as mail carrier during the 1880s. Until the advent of the automobile, mail service within Rich County required as much as six days. William J. Conger, grandson of James M. Conger who delivered mail in the early twentieth century, commented that it "took eight teams of horses for the trip." Two of the teams were extras and the remaining teams were "changed at Anson Call's at Woodruff, Luke Lynn's at Almy, Wyoming . . . Willis Johnson's in Laketown, and at Gardner's in Fish Haven."[24]

The most reliable and fastest form of early communication was the telegraph. The transcontinental telegraph completed at Salt Lake City in 1861 was the springboard which made possible the construction of the LDS church-owned Deseret Telegraph Company. According to historian Leonard J. Arrington, "the lack of timber for poles along this route, and the necessity of securing transportation for materials and sustenance for workmen, [made] it essential that the builders of the transcontinental line secure the approval and assistance of the Latter-day Saints Church."[25]

The Mormon church received a modest payment for assisting in the line's construction, but perhaps more important was the experience acquired by Mormons who worked in stringing the lines. Immediately after connections were made between Salt Lake City and Omaha, Nebraska, plans were made by church leaders to construct a similar but separate telegraph line within the territory. For the next four years the project was put on hold because of the Civil War. After the war's end the First Presidency issued a circular letter addressed to the "Bishops and Presiding Elders of the various wards and settlements of Utah Territory, from St. Charles, Richland County, in the north, to St. George, Washington County, in the south . . ." The letter read in part:

> Brethren - The proper time has arrived for us to take the necessary steps to build the telegraph line to run north and south through the Territory. . . . The necessity for the speedy construction of this work is pressing itself upon our attention, and scarcely a week passes that we do not feel the want of such a line.[26]

The "want" was particularly hard-felt in Rich County where mail service had proved inconsistent, and communication of any kind, both within and outside the area, was difficult. The original plan was to build the telegraph line through Logan Canyon. In 1869, however, Charles C. Rich contacted Brigham Young and remarked that if Logan Canyon was the intended route, "we will not be able to put it through the whole distance in and of ourselves." Rich suggested that a route from St. Charles to Franklin would be more practical and added: "We could put up the poles over the mountain to Franklin ourselves this fall, as it is but little over half the distance and better ground to set them in."[27]

Young liked the idea, and by fall 1871 the line to Franklin was complete. In the meantime, Joseph C. Rich had been pegged by his father to learn the rudiments of telegraphy. On 6 November 1871 Joseph sent the first of many messages to Salt Lake City:

> The wires of the Deseret Telegraph Company reached this place today at 4 P.M., bringing the people of Bear Lake Valley into instant communication with the world of mankind. In view of our isolated situation, no people in the mountains can better appreciate telegraphic communication. We heartily congratulate you on the extension of the line, and thank you for your labors in our behalf.[28]

Even after the arrival of the telegraph in St. Charles, the other communities of Bear Lake Valley as well as Woodruff and Randolph were still geographically isolated. The telegraph never extended to Laketown, nor did it connect with Randolph, the county seat after 1872. Communication outside the communities of Woodruff and Randolph was limited to the sporadic mail service or travel to Evanston, Wyoming, to send a message over the Western Union lines. In the 1890s telephone service was initiated from Evanston to Randolph. The Uinta-Rich Telephone Company began operation in 1898 and was under the direction of John M. Baxter, president; Charles Stone, secretary/treasurer; and Ed Chapman and Charles Kingston, trustees.[29] Within Bear Lake Valley, a small, Mormon church-owned telephone system began operation as early as 1882.[30]

Still, communication between the two parts of Rich County was difficult. During the early history of the county, this difficulty led to stronger individual communities within the county, but it also resulted in a weaker county government. Individualism characterized Rich County residents, as many families lived on their ranches rather than within town. Geographic barriers, sparse population, and the size of the county made it difficult for officials to collect taxes and oversee the operation of county government. A correspondent to the *Deseret News* wryly noted the condition of county buildings in Randolph. "This being the county seat of Rich County they of course have a county court house, which is very conspicuous for its smallness and looks more like an abandoned stable."[31]

The first courthouse in Randolph was a converted cabin which

Old Rich County Jail at Randolph. (Courtesy Nathell Hoffman.)

the county purchased from Harvey Harper.[32] In March 1888 the county court voted to consider building a new courthouse if the county's total indebtedness was less than $250.[33] The county had incurred some debt in 1881 when it undertook the construction of a jail. The county court voted to build a log structure, basing it upon a similar structure which had been built in Logan. Charles South was given until January 1882 to complete the project.[34] The county borrowed $260 at Evanston and deposited $300 worth of county funds as collateral.[35] By 1883 with the note on the jail coming due and other county obligations outstanding, the county court approached Cache Valley citizens C. C. Goodwin, John Wilkinson, and Charles Frank for an $850 loan.[36]

Indebtedness plagued the county court for many years, but by April 1888 the county was in good enough financial condition to begin plans for the new courthouse.[37] Bids were let in May. Joseph F. Neville underbid Smith and Cameron Company by several hundred dollars. Neville also agreed to build the foundation one foot higher than the plans called for and to provide the shutters at cost.[38]

Meanwhile, Selectman Joseph Kimball traveled to Cache County to explore the possibilities of securing a loan. In June Kimball reported that both First National Bank and Thatcher Brother's Bank were agreeable to loaning money to the county.[39] The county court decided to arrange the loan through Thatcher Brothers at one percent per month.[40] Joseph Neville was awarded $2,479 for the courthouse's construction, and a completion date was set for November 1888.[41]

The burden of debt continued to hamper the county, however. After construction of the courthouse, the territorial assembly changed the revenue laws affecting county government by limiting taxation to three mills on the dollar instead of six. In February 1894 the Rich County Court petitioned the territorial assembly to change the law back to the original mill levy, noting:

> That in the year 1888 said County built a County Court House at a cost of $4200, that said court house was built with the expectation of paying for the same under the operation of the old Revenue Law of a Tax of 6 mills on the Dollar . . . under the new Revenue Law said county has only been able to meet their Annual Current expenses and obliged at times to borrow money to pay interest on said indebtedness . . . they are confronted with the condition of being in debt with no possible way or prospect of liquidating said indebtedness. They therefore respectfully ask that the present Revenue Law be so amended that said County . . . be enabled to raise money for the purpose of paying their debts.[42]

In May 1894 a special election was held to bond the county for five thousand dollars to help meet expenses and to pay off the county's loans.[43] In 1896 Selectman Joshua Eldredge asked the court to entertain the idea of selling all the county's real estate to meet obligations owed to D. H. Perry of Ogden.[44]

Infusions of state monies for roads and schools following statehood in January 1896 gradually improved the county's financial condition. The change from territorial to state status also changed the manner in which county governments operated. Following statehood, county courts were supplanted by county commissions.[45] County courts, being under the direction of a probate judge, had

Old Rich County Courthouse. (Courtesy Nathell Hoffman.)

been a source of considerable strife within territorial Utah after passage of the Edmunds-Tucker Act in 1887. That act took the probate court out of the hands of the territorial assembly and made it a position appointed by the federal government. Consequently, virtually all probate judges within Utah from 1888 to statehood were non-Mormon. In Rich County, two non-Mormon probate judges served during this time period—Stephen V. Frazier and J. M. Grant. Both, however, fulfilled the duties of their office with little conflict. Only the conflict which developed over ownership of the public school/church in Woodruff as discussed in chapter seven dampened the relationship between Judge Frazier and the Mormon population of the county.

The first county commission to convene in Rich County included as members William H. Lee, Joseph Weston, and John

Kennedy. Among other things undertaken by the new commission
was the issue of contagious disease. The first state legislature passed
an act in 1896 requiring each county to form a board of health and
to appoint a county health officer.[46] Health committees were
appointed in the various precincts of Rich County in June 1898.[47]
Contagious diseases, particularly smallpox and diphtheria, had been
a problem throughout Utah since settlement. Because of the high
altitude and extreme cold, diphtheria was an acute problem in Rich
County. William H. Longhurst, an early Garden City settler, commented in 1884: "We have also some symptoms of this periodical disease which invariably makes its appearance at this season of the year,
and continues until the opening of the leaf."[48] The disease reached
near epidemic proportions at Laketown in 1887,[49] and in December
1892 both school and church were cancelled as virtually all of the
Bear Lake communities were placed under quarantine.[50] Because
diphtheria, or canker as it was referred to by early settlers, often took
the lives of the very young, it was viewed with special dread.
Consequently, the epidemics which periodically visited Rich County
communities became a part of the folk tradition, and a substantial
amount of folklore grew around them. As Niel Wilhelmsen, the son
of an early Bear Lake Valley family, related to folklorist Bonnie
Thompson, folk cures for diphtheria ranged from the sublime to the
ridiculous.

> When the early pioneers came to Bear Lake they had an epidemic
> of canker . . . Sometimes it would go down the throat and a black
> coat of canker would coat the throat and eventually choke the vic-
> tim to death . . .
>
> The Lord gave the prophet Joseph Smith the remedy for this
> dreaded disease and it was called canker medicine. I had an aunt
> who came down with this black canker. They gave her some of this
> medicine when she was near death. When it began to loosen the
> mucus in her throat, they took an old-style button hook and put
> that down her throat, and pulled up chunks of matter as big as a
> finger.[51]

Folk remedies were the only form of treatment available to early
pioneer settlers. Trained physicians did not begin arriving in Bear

Lake Valley until the 1880s. Dr. C. A. Hoover's arrival coincides with that of the Oregon Shortline Railroad in 1882.

Dr. Hoover saw to the needs of patients in Montpelier as well as other communities within Bear Lake Valley. Furthermore, he used the railroad to treat patients as far away as Pocatello, Idaho, and Evanston, Wyoming.[52]

Residents of Woodruff and Randolph may have benefitted from Dr. Hoover's rounds on the railroad, as well; but by the early 1890s resident physicians were practicing in Evanston.[53] In 1883 Caroline A. Mills and her husband Charles Frank Mills moved to Evanston. Caroline later traveled to Iowa where she attended four years of medical school. For a short period following her return, she practiced medicine in Evanston. Later Caroline, Charles, and their three daughters moved to Randolph where she set up practice and became the county's first doctor. While maintaining her office in Randolph, Dr. Mills also treated patients from Woodruff in the south of the county to Garden City in the north. Dr. Mills later relocated to Evanston and eventually to Lyman, Wyoming.[54]

Although she continued to care for the sick throughout Rich County, Doctor Mills's departure from Randolph left the county without a resident physician. The void was later filled by Doctor M. S. Reay. Reay was born in Randolph in 1877, but his family moved to Illinois when he was three years old. The move made it unlikely that he would ever return. Reay attended college in Illinois, graduating from Rush Medical College in 1902 and from the surgery unit of the University of Illinois in 1903. The young doctor then set up practice in Varden, Illinois. His excellent training made the prospects for a successful career likely which made even less likely his return to Rich County. Nevertheless, at his mother's request he returned to Randolph to visit his sick uncle, William Simpson. Finding no doctor within the county and the need for one great, he decided to stay. Doctor Reay served the citizens of Rich County for nearly forty years. He was county physician and county health examiner, serving through World War I and the influenza epidemic that followed. During World War II he was examining physician for Rich and Daggett counties. He was serving in this capacity when he passed away on 6 August 1943.[55]

Doctor Reay was the last physician to practice in Rich County. Since that time, the county has relied on the medical training of county residents. The Emergency Medical Technician Program did not officially begin until 1977; but, in conjunction with the county nurse, an emergency program was initiated during the 1950s. County Nurse Helen Cornia has recalled the many trips to one of the area's hospitals that she and Claude Reay took in a converted panel truck dubbed the "Black Wagon" during that time.[56] The son of Doctor M. S. Reay, Claude received advanced first-aid training and set up a first-aid station in his home with the help of doctors in Salt Lake City and Evanston. He was the first certified Emergency Medical Technician in Rich County and directed operations for over thirty years. Today, the legacy of Claude Reay is carried on by well-trained technicians and well-equipped ambulances. Two ambulances are maintained by the county—one in Laketown and the other at Randolph. Countless volunteer hours also have contributed to the success of the program. Given the remoteness of Rich County, emergency medical personnel are an absolute necessity.

Doctors and county nurses worked closely with county government. Medical issues were just one of many concerns with which the county commission dealt. Until 1905 all of the communities within Rich County were unincorporated; therefore, ordinances passed by the county court and county commission were applied throughout all areas of the county. Randolph was incorporated in 1905 and by 1909 had adopted its own set of ordinances to deal with health, disease, and other issues.[57] The first Randolph town council included Edward Benzley, president, with Robert McKinnon, A. W. Nebeker, Isaac Smith, and Joshua Eldredge as trustees.[58]

The other four major communities within the county remained unincorporated until the 1930s and 1940s. Woodruff petitioned the county commission for incorporation in December 1933. The first municipal board in Woodruff included B. D. Brown, president, with James Stuart, Rowena Stuart, Cloyd Eastman, and Sarah Cornia as trustees. A month later, Garden City proposed a similar petition with Charles W. Pope to act as president, and Alex Johnson, Thomas G. Hodges, Lavoy Hildt, and J. W. Gibbons, trustees.

The incorporation of Woodruff and Garden City appears to have been in response to an act passed by the state legislature in 1933 which more clearly defined the responsibilities and benefits of incorporation.[59] Furthermore, incorporated cities and towns were in a better position to take advantage of federal and state relief programs which came as a response to the Great Depression of the 1930s. In June 1935 residents near the southern boundaries of Garden City petitioned the county commission for incorporation.[60] The community had acquired rights to water in the canyon to the west from William Payne Spring with the thought of constructing a culinary water system. To accomplish this, the community sought a grant from the federal government's Public Works Administration. Technically the town did not have the necessary population to qualify for the funding, but through persistence and the help of Charles C. Pickel, a federal official, the town eventually secured the grant and completed its water system.[61] In gratitude for the help he had given them in working through the government "red tape," area residents (though they changed the spelling of his name) named the community Pickleville after him.[62] In 1979 a majority of residents from Garden City and Pickleville voted in favor of consolidation, thereby merging Pickleville with Garden City. Some local businesses continued using the name of Pickleville, however; one such was the Pickleville Playhouse which was opened in 1977 by the family of LaGrande C. Larsen of Logan and has operated continuously each summer since.[63]

Pickleville came into being because of the availability of federal funding for its first water system. Ironically, its consolidation with Garden City also came about in order to expedite federal grants for water development. Laketown, Garden City, and Woodruff also secured grants from the federal government to complete their culinary water systems. In 1935 water from springs west of Woodruff was piped into that town, marking the first time in history that water was "brought into the homes of the people."[64] Similarly, during early summer 1936 work commenced to pipe water northward four miles from Swan Creek Spring to Garden City. The project was completed in August, and the residents of Garden City also regarded the project as "one of the best accomplishments" in that community's history.

Although Laketown remained unincorporated throughout the

Great Depression, its residents also were able to use federal funds to improve their culinary system, initially installed in 1930.[65] A Public Works Administration project commenced in the fall of 1935 to build a rock-lined channel for the canyon stream and to construct a "cross channel" to "head off the underground water."[66] Laketown remained unincorporated until 1945 when its residents also petitioned for town status. The first town board consisted of Norman Weston, president, and Vernon Robinson, Arlo B. Weston, Grant Lamborn, and Parnell Johnson, trustees.[67]

Of all Rich County communities, only Randolph did not receive any federal support for its culinary water system. Randolph, however, was already incorporated and had the means to levy taxes in 1929 in order to complete its water system. Randolph City also received five hundred dollars from the county to construct the water system and to connect the water to the county courthouse.[68]

Municipal governments and county government took advantage of the fact that New Deal dollars were more plentiful during the depression than county revenue. In 1940 the county commission met with representatives from the Public Works Administration and the architectural firm of Ashton and Evans to discuss the possibility of constructing a new courthouse in Randolph. The commission was informed that the total cost of the new structure would be $42,297 and that the building could be constructed on the site of the present courthouse. Officials from the PWA informed the commission that the government would pay $22,297 of the construction costs, leaving the county with the obligation of coming up with the remaining twenty thousand dollars.[69] Under the supervision of Arthur Peck, the new courthouse was completed and occupied in 1942.[70]

Although the depression had an overall negative impact on Rich County, many community improvements such as the culinary water systems, the new courthouse, and some road improvements were made which would not have been possible under normal circumstances. Prices on farm commodities remained low throughout the depression, with beef cows selling for thirty dollars, steers for forty-five dollars, lambs for two dollars, and wheat selling for forty cents a bushel. There was considerable unemployment in the county as well.[71] In 1933 the state road commission agreed to match the county

Rich County Courthouse, ca. 1960. (Utah State Historical Society, Salt Lake City.)

up to six thousand dollars for unemployed workers to work on county and state roads. [72] As a result of this agreement and other funding, the highway between Woodruff and Evanston, Wyoming, received an oiled surface.[73]

Federal dollars also were used for the construction and improvement of canyon access roads. In 1933 a Civilian Conservation Corps (CCC) camp was established across the Idaho border in St. Charles Canyon.[74] The CCC was a program which brought unemployed youth throughout the United States to build roads, snow fences, and construct other conservation and reclamation measures. Ostensibly, the program was also planned to promote health and vitality by taking youth out of cities and transplanting them into nature.

Though unrelated to federal relief projects, historical markers began appearing along the highways in Rich County during the 1930s. A meeting in August 1937 attended by dignitaries from Oregon, California, and Utah preceded the unveiling of a marker commemorating the 1827 Bear Lake rendezvous.[75] Other historical markers placed within the county include the Daughters of Utah

Pioneers markers at Randolph and Woodruff commemorating the
first Mormon settlers in Bear River Valley, a marker located at the
Bear Lake scenic overlook above Garden City, and an Oregon Trail
marker located two miles south of the Idaho border.[76] The Daughters
of Utah Pioneers (DUP) also have erected two other markers in
Randolph, one at the park adjacent to the county courthouse and the
other commemorating the Wilford Woodruff home. Completed and
dedicated in May 1993, restoration of the Woodruff home commenced under Mayor Douglas Bingham and the Randolph City
Council with Councilwoman Flora Lamborn in charge. Blake
Thomson accomplished most of the restorative work on the wood.

At present there are two active DUP camps in Rich County:
Camp Ithaca at Laketown and Camp Randolph. The Daughters at
Camp Ithaca maintain a relic hall and museum which was established
through the efforts of many local women, especially Malita Robinson.
In Randolph, Thelma McKinnon and others collected and cared for
local artifacts for years before finally remodeling the old LDS church
welfare office for use as a relic hall.

The veteran's war memorial dedicated on 20 August 1988 is
another recent addition. The county had erected a monument to vet-
erans of World War I which had stood in its present location since
1922, but soldiers serving during the Second World War and the
Korean and Viet Nam conflicts had not been honored. Hoping to rectify the situation, supporters met with county commissioners in
September 1987 to solicit their support for a monument. Two
months later, a committee was formed including Willa Kennedy,
Elaine K. Cox, LaRue Lamborn, Dorothy Stringham, and County
Commissioner Kenneth Brown who was appointed chairman of the
committee. The committee set a goal of raising twenty thousand dollars for the monument's erection. Although the goal was set high, and
ultimately was not reached until only days prior to the dedication,
the committee managed to raise the entire cost of the monument
through donations. In its tribute, the monument lists fifty-eight vet-
erans who served in Korea and fifty who served in Viet Nam as well as
others serving during World War II.

During the two world wars of the twentieth century, citizens in
Rich County coped in much the same way as did citizens in other

rural parts of the country. As young men and women left home for training and active duty, the community turned out to support them. Dances were held, and donations were often taken up to help send the soldiers and nurses on their way. On the homefront, citizens supported the war effort in a number of ways—from planting victory gardens during World War I to buying war bonds during World War II. Though important to its outcome, United States involvement in World War I was brief and not nearly as all-consuming as was the country's involvement in World War II. Lucille Moffat Thornock recalled that the earlier war did not change life all that much. Without the benefit of nightly newscasts and with only infrequent access to newspapers, Lucille reported that "we just went on living."[77] But the war did impact the small communities of Rich County: eighty-one men from Rich County served during World War I and five died during the conflict.[78]

Lucille Thornock remembered the Second World War differently. She recalled that many young men were called to duty, leaving broken hearted sweethearts and a short supply of farm hands. A total of 244 Rich County citizens served during the Second World War, including two army nurses, Helen Kennedy Cornia and Lotamae Kennedy. Thornock recalled how some of them never returned. "It affected everybody's family," she said.[79] Soldiers who gave their lives in defense of their country during World War II include: Marine Corporal Kib A. Jacobson who died in 1945 on Okinawa; Ralph Eugene Hanney who, as a member of the Merchant Marine, died on a torpedoed oil tanker near France in 1944; Army Corporal Rex E. Schenck who fell victim to a land mine in France in 1944; Army Air Corps Master Sergeant John Morgan Rex who, as a crew chief on a fighter plane, died in 1942 as a result of enemy fire shortly after takeoff from Broome Field, Australia; Army Private First Class Dan M. Wilson who died in action in northern Italy two days prior to VE-Day in March 1945; and Army Sergeant Dale Brough Rex who died following the Battle of the Bulge in December 1944.[80] A total of eleven men from Rich County lost their lives during World War II.

The war not only took its toll on the families of those who did not return from battle, it also affected those who returned. Lotamae Kennedy of Randolph was trained as a nurse at Dee Hospital in

Ogden shortly before the United States entry into World War II. Lotamae found herself serving her country aboard the hospital ship the USS *Mercy* in the Pacific theater of the war. She administered to the sick and wounded at Guam, Eniwetok, New Caledonia, and the Philippines.

Her brother Floyd described the circumstances under which she served:

> [they included] the night-long vigils beside the dying, [and] the steeling of the senses in order to be able to endure the agonizing cries of the suffering. Under such stress, nurses, doctors and the entire medical staff ignored their own personal needs. They worked as a team, with only one thought in mind: to save lives, to serve. Yet when the bombing stopped and the tension dissolved, there were tears to be shed, their own fears to be recognized and something of their own lives to be resumed.[81]

According to Floyd, Lotamae never recovered from the reality of the war. Although she lived a full and fruitful life, she never forgot her war experiences, being reminded of them whenever tragedy occurred.

World War II permeated all aspects of American society. It was a war which the American people entered into without reservation, a war which most of them supported wholeheartedly. Government war-bond drives raised millions of dollars. Utah topped fourteen million dollars worth of bonds in 1944 with Rich County contributing 209 percent of its quota.[82]

Citizens throughout the United States were expected to contribute towards the war effort and to conserve materials essential to the war's successful prosecution. Paper, metal, and rubber were all rationed during the war. In each county of every state, quotas were established to limit the purchase of rationed materials. A branch of the Civil Defense Council was organized in Rich County in 1941. The committee included Lewis Longhurst, Ben Weston, Vern Hopkin, Leo McKinnon, and George Barker. Among other things, the council oversaw the allocation of rubber tires. The committee also existed to "take care of any emergency in Rich County and extend aid in adjacent areas if needed."[83]

The heartaches, fears, and privations of World War II gave way to jubilation once the war ended. Life gradually resumed in much the same manner as before. As the war ended, residents in Rich County took time to renew family ties and take comfort in their freedom. But new challenges awaited as the county moved from the post-war years into the 1950s.

Throughout the war years and immediately after, the population of Rich County declined from a high of 2,028 in 1940 to 1,673 in 1950.[84] Employment opportunities in the war industries and military duty account for most of the out-migration. Following the close of World War II, economic opportunity was greater in the more urbanized parts of the state and nation than it was in rural agricultural areas like Rich County. Only those with secure economic opportunities remained in or returned to Rich County following the war. Providing economic opportunity for citizens of the county would be an ongoing concern for elected county officials throughout the 1950s and 1960s. Agriculture still formed the basis for the county's economy, but it remained limited by available land, climate, and irrigation water. Most available agricultural land had been taken up by the 1920s, and ranchers and farmers had no control over the rigorous climate of the region. Therefore, agriculture was a somewhat static industry. It could supply a livelihood for a small entrenched population, but it did not hold out the possibility of creating many new jobs. In fact, the increased reliance on farm machinery following World War II actually decreased the number of farm laborers needed. As a result, the population of Rich County, like its agriculture, remained fairly static.

Until 1970 the population of Rich County remained at or below the 1950 level. Not until recreational development and natural gas and oil exploration began did the county's population increase—from 1,615 in 1970 to a high of 2,300 in 1984.[85] Increasing population strained the county's utilities and brought to the forefront new and demanding problems. As discussed in chapters four and five, the county commission working in conjunction with the Bear Lake Regional Commission met the demands and worked through the problems confronting the county. In addition to population pressures, government regulations made the administration of the county more complex. In 1972 Rich County became a member of the Bear River Association of Governments in order to better utilize funds available through the United States Office of Economic Opportunity.[86] The county commission also adopted new regulations for the disposal of sewage and waste in 1973 in order to comply with federal clean air and clean water mandates.[87] As recreational development increased in the Bear Lake area, sewage disposal became a major issue. Plans for sewage treatment around Bear Lake began taking shape in 1977 under a mandate from the Environmental Protection Agency. The sewer was to run from St. Charles, Idaho, to Pickleville, and was estimated to cost 2.5 million dollars. Under the terms of the agreement, the EPA would pick up 75 percent of the cost. The remaining expenses were to be met through a bond election. Ostensibly, the bonds would be purchased by the Farmers' Home Administration (FHA).[88]

A problem developed in the bureaucracy of the FHA, however, which made it difficult for two states to share one sewer line. It seems that the Idaho portion of the project was to be administered from the Seattle, Washington, office while the Utah portion was to be administered from Denver, Colorado. This required two sets of negotiations instead of one and led to delays and problems.[89] This problem eventually created an impasse which required that Utah and Idaho pursue separate plans for the sewer system. By 1984 construction of the Utah portion of the sewer system was underway, and a special district had been created at Fish Haven to complete the project in Idaho.[90]

The creation of special districts in both Idaho and Utah provided part of the financing for the west-side sewer. County improvement districts were authorized by the Utah State Legislature in 1979.[91] Under the act, counties in the state could create special service districts with the right to impose assessments on property owners for the construction of sewage-treatment facilities, waterworks, or other utilities. Citizens in Laketown and developers on Bear Lake's east shore opted not to participate in the west-side sewer project; instead, they announced their plans to create the South Shore Development Service District in 1979. The south shore project sought no federal funding, and without the bureaucratic red-tape which plagued the project on the west side was able to begin operation only six months after the creation of the special district[92] which was approved by the county commission in January 1979.[93] The south shore system proved to be inadequate, however, and as the Bear Lake Regional Commission noted in 1993 the area was targeted for future improvements.[94]

In March 1983 the Rich County Commission formulated a policy which in part read: "It shall be the policy of Rich County to encourage permanent growth and development in or adjacent to existing incorporated communities by following existing county zoning."[95] The county commission along with the Bear Lake Regional Commission as discussed in chapter four, assumed "an ever broadening role" in its attempt to deal effectively with growth.[96] But growth was something which Rich County had not had to deal with on any large scale. Little comprehensive planning had taken place there before recreational development and oil-and-gas exploration mandated it. In Woodruff, for instance, the city council was faced with an immediate request from local land owner Ray Cox to construct a 140-home development to accommodate oil-field workers in the area. Mayor Max Buck and the Woodruff town council placed a six-month moratorium on building until a city plan could be formulated.

That plan, along with similar plans formulated in other communities, provided Rich County with a direction for the future. At the time the county appeared poised for dramatic growth. Therefore, improvements in culinary water systems and sewage-disposal systems were designed to accommodate greater population growth than has thus far materialized. Viewed from that perspective, Rich County's flirtation with growth had a positive outcome. The area remained, and remains today, one with the potential for growth. The early 1980s gave county officials a crash course in community planning. The result was the putting in place of an infrastructure which would support future population growth, when it occurs. Rich County now has the luxury of feeling prepared for whatever the future might bring.

ENDNOTES

1. *Journal History of the Church of Jesus Christ of Latter-day Saints,* manuscript, Department of Special Collections and Archives, Merrill Library,

Utah State University, Logan, Utah (hereafter referred to as JH), 10 January 1866, 2.

2. County Book A, 5 May 1864.

3. *The Compiled Laws of Utah* (Salt Lake City: Deseret News, 1876), 123.

4. County Book A, 5 March 1866 through 3 September 1866. James H. Hart is a distinguished figure in Mormon history. He converted to Mormonism while still in London, England. He served with First Presidency member Erastus Snow during the Mormon migration west. Eventually, Hart was appointed Emigration Agent for the church. After settling in Bear Lake County, Idaho, he served several terms as a legislative assemblyman. In addition to his civic duties, he was also first counselor in the Bear Lake Stake. See Edward W. Tullidge, *Tullidge's Histories* (Salt Lake City: Juvenile Instructor Press, 1889) vol 2: 343.

John A. Hunt converted to Mormonism in 1840 at Nauvoo, Illinois. He served several missions for the church before settling in Salt Lake City and later at Grantsville, Tooele County, in 1856. He married Elizabeth Tilt in Grantsville, and the two immigrated to St. Charles in 1866. See Kate B. Carter, "They Came in 1856," Lessons for September 1856, Daughters of Utah Pioneers.

Little is known of David B. Dille except that he settled in Cache Valley before immigrating to Bear Lake Valley.

5. *Compiled Laws of the Territory of Utah (1876)*, 118. The amended portion of the act described Rich County as follows: "Commencing on the ridge west of Swan Creek on the Utah and Idaho territorial line, at the point dividing Cache and Rich Counties, thence southward on said ridge to a point near Wasatch and strike the railroad one mile east of Wasatch Station, thence along the north side of the railroad to where it enters Bear River Valley, thence directly east to the Wyoming line, thence north along said line to where it strikes Idaho, thence north along said line to where it strikes Idaho, thence west to the place of beginning, shall be known and designated under the name of Rich County and the town of Randolph is hereby constituted the County Seat." For a short period of time northern Bear Lake Valley became a part of Oneida County, Idaho, until the creation of Bear Lake County, Idaho, in 1875.

6. County Book A, 15 July 1895.

7. Ibid., 7 May 1897.

8. Deseret Livestock Company vs. Summit/Rich Counties, 27 May 1936. Copy in Rich County Recorder's Office, Rich County Courthouse, Randolph, Utah.

9. "Map of Divide Between Weber River and Bear River Valleys Which

is the Summit-Rich County Boundary Line, surveyed and mapped by J. W. Jones, November 1935–March 1936." File 4–6–36, entry 56711, Summit County Recorder's Office. Copy on file, Rich County Recorder's Office, Rich County Courthouse, Randolph, Utah.

10. J. F. Neville to J. Emerson Staples, 17 July 1952. Copy in Rich County Recorder's Office, Rich County Courthouse, Randolph, Utah.

11. County Book A, 5 May 1872.

12. Ibid., 3 June 1867.

13. Ibid., 1 March 1869.

14. JH, 18 December 1870, 5; and BLSMH, 23 January 1871.

15. John M. Baxter, *Life of John M. Baxter: Being a Brief Account of His Experiences as a Pioneer, Missionary, Bishop and Stake President* (Salt Lake City: Deseret News Press, 1932), 11–12.

16. See chapter three.

17. County Book A, 5 June 1871.

18. Ibid., 3 March 1873.

19. Ibid., 1 June 1874.

20. Ibid., 7 June 1875.

21. Manuscript History of Garden City Ward, Rich County, Utah, 1864, Historical Department of the LDS Church, Salt Lake City, Utah (hereafter referred to as GCMH), 1877.

22. Leonard J. Arrington, *Charles C. Rich* (Provo: Brigham Young University Press, 1974), 277.

23. Ibid.

24. Mildred H. Thomson, comp., *Rich Memories: Some of the Happenings in Rich County from 1863 to 1960* (Salt Lake City: Daughters of Utah Pioneers, 1962), 161.

25. Leonard J. Arrington, "The Deseret Telegraph—A Church-owned Public Utility"; reprint taken from *Journal of Economic History* (Spring 1951): 117.

26. *Deseret News,* 9 November, 1865. Quoted in Arrington, "The Deseret Telegraph," 121.

27. Arrington, *Charles C. Rich,* 275.

28. Ezra J. Poulsen, *Joseph C. Rich: Versatile Pioneer on the Mormon Frontier* (Salt Lake City: Granite Publishing Co., 1958), 232.

29. Steven L. Thomson, Jane D. Digerness, and Mar Jean S. Thomson, *Randolph—A Look Back* (n.p., 1981), 109.

30. Ibid., 277.

31. *Deseret News,* 10 November 1985; quoted in Thomson, *Randolph—A Look Back,* 22.

32. Thomson, *Rich Memories,* 7.

33. County Book A, 6 March 1888.

34. Ibid., 5 December 1881.

35. Ibid., 5 June 1882.

36. Ibid., 20 November 1883.

37. Ibid., 10 April 1888.

38. Ibid., 7 May 1888.

39. Ibid., 4 June 1888.

40. County Book A, 3 September 1888.

41. Ibid., 3 September 1888.

42. Ibid., 5 March 1894.

43. Ibid., 4 June 1894.

44. Ibid., 2 March 1896.

45. *The Revised Statutes of the State of Utah in Force January 1, 1898* (Lincoln, Nebraska: State Journal Co. Printers, 1897), 196.

46. Ibid., 317.

47. County Book A, 8 June 1898.

48. JH, 9 September 1884, 8.

49. Ibid., 27 May 1887, 4.

50. Ibid., 14 December 1892, 7.

51. Bonnie Thompson, *Folklore in the Bear Lake Valley* (master's thesis: Utah State University, 1972), 103–4. According to Wilhelmsen the concoction consisted of the following:

> 1 cup sugar
> 1 teaspoon burned green copper
> 1 teaspoon burned alum
> 1 teaspoon sulphur

Burn these ingredients on iron grate, mixing with a handle of a spoon. Add one cup boiling water.

52. J. Patrick Wilde, *Treasured Tidbits of Time: An Informal History of Mormon Conquest and Settlement of the Bear Lake Valley* (Montpelier, ID: author), 312.

53. Elizabeth Arnold Stone, *Uinta County: Its Place in History* (Glendale, CA: Arthur H. Clark Co., 1924), 163.

54. Thomson, *Rich Memories,* 171–72.

55. Thomson, *Rich Memories,* 173–75.

56. Helen Kennedy Cornia, "Rich County Public Health Nursing," typescript in possession of author. See appendix B.

57. Thomson, *Randolph—A Look Back,* 33–36.

58. Thomson, *Rich Memories,* 143.

59. *Revised Statutes of Utah, 1933,* 233–86.

60. County Book B, 17 June 1935.

61. There seems to be some controversy regarding the role played by Charles C. Pickel, as well as the spelling of his name. Most sources refer to him simply as Mr. Pickle. See, for example, Thomson, *Rich Memories,* 73. In his book on Utah place names, John W. Van Cott writes: "Charles C. Pickel was an engineer who supervised improvement of the town's water supply." See John W. Van Cott, *Utah Place Names: A Comprehensive Guide to the Origins of Geographic Names* (Salt Lake City: University of Utah Press, 1990), 294. In some agreement with Van Cott is Mark P. Hodges, whose family originally settled the area south of Garden City and founded the Hodges's Ranch. For some time the area was known as Hodgesville. Hodges uses the same spelling as Van Cott but claims that Mr. Pickel never even visited the town but was simply a bureaucrat working with the PWA who agreed to guide the town's application through the "red tape." See *Bear Lake Magazine* 1 (15 March 1978): 18. Regardless of spelling, Pickleville became the official name for the community.

62. Thomson, *Rich Memories,* 73.

63. *Bear Lake Magazine,* 1 (1 September 1977): 10.

64. Manuscript History of Woodruff Ward, Bear Lake Stake, Rich County, Utah, 1935. (Historian's Office, Church of Jesus Christ of Latter-day Saints, Salt Lake City, hereafter cited as WMH).

65. Laketown Ward Transcript History [1930], Historians Office, Church of Jesus Christ of Latter-day Saints, Salt Lake City (hereafter cited as LTMH).

66. LTMH, 31 December 1935.

67. County Book B, 3 July 1945.

68. County Book A, 1 July 1929.

69. Ibid., 13 July and 10 August 1940.

70. Thomson, *Rich Memories,* 7.

71. Randolph Ward Manuscript History, 1931, Historian's Office, Church of Jesus Christ of Latter-day Saints, Salt Lake City (hereafter cited as RMH).

72. County Book B, 2 October 1933.

73. WMH, 1935.

74. Manuscript History of Bear Lake Stake, 31 December 1933.

Historian's Office, Church of Jesus Christ of Latter-day Saints, Salt Lake City (hereafter cited as BLSMH).

75. LTMH, 30 September 1937. Those attending the meeting included George A. Smith, Howard R. Driggs, John D. Giles, F. N. Killman, Walter Mecham, Harry Claude Peterson, Walter M. Stockey, and Mr. and Mrs. Samuel O. Bennion.

76. *Rich County Land-Use Guide,* 57.

77. Willa Kennedy, interview with Lucille Moffat Thornock, 30 March 1977.

78. Paul M. VanSlyke, "Country Pride," *The Utah Veteran* (March-April 1992): 12.

79. Kennedy, interview with Lucille Moffat Thornock, 18.

80. Thomson, *Randolph—A Look Back,* 49–52.

81. Ibid., 57.

82. *Rich County Reaper,* 3 March 1944; quoted in Thomson, *Randolph—A Look Back,* 46.

83. *Rich County Reaper,* 2 January 1941. Quoted in Thomson, *Randolph—A Look Back,* 47.

84. *Statistical Abstract of Utah, 1954,* 16.

85. Ibid., 16–17.

86. County Book C, 7 June 1972.

87. Ibid., 7 March 1973 and 4 April 1973.

88. *Bear Lake Magazine* 1 (1 May 1977).

89. *Bear Lake Magazine* 2 (15 May 1978): 5.

90. *The News Examiner* (Montpelier, Idaho), 27 December 1984, B-1.

91. *Utah Code Annotated* (Charlottesville, VA: The Miche Company, 1991), 472.

92. *Bear Lake Magazine* 3 (15 June 1979): 7.

93. County Book C, 3 January 1979.

94. Bear Lake Regional Commission Historical Summary and Base Operations Report, February 1993.

95. County Book C, 3 March 1982.

96. Bear Lake Regional Commission Historical Summary and Base Operations Report, February 1993.

Appendix A

County Statistics, Prominent Educators, Religious Leaders, Civic Leaders, and Early Rich County Settlers

Population, Rich County, 1900–1990

1900 - 1,946	1970 - 1,615	1986 - 2,000
1910 - 1,883	1980 - 2,100	1987 - 1,900
1920 - 1,890	1981 - 2,200	1988 - 1,800
1930 - 1,873	1982 - 2,400	1989 - 1,700
1940 - 2,028	1983 - 2,400	1990 - 1,725
1950 - 1,673	1984 - 2,300	
1960 - 1,685	1985 - 2,100	

Population, Garden City, 1950–1990

1950 - 164	1970 - 134	1990 - 193
1960 - 168	1980 - 259	

Population, Pickleville, 1950–1960

1950 - 96
1960 - 94

Population, Laketown, 1950–1990

1950 - 217	1970 - 208	1990 - 261
1960 - 211	1980 - 271	

Population, Randolph, 1950–1990

1950 - 562   1970 - 500   1990 - 488
1960 - 537   1980 - 659

Population, Woodruff, 1950–1990

1950 - 175   1970 - 173   1990 - 135
1960 - 169   1980 - 222

Employment and Labor Force, Rich County, 1989–1991

Total Labor Force 829
Agriculture 464
Manufacturing 1
Mining 1
Transportation, Communication, and Utilities 13
Trade 67
Finance, Insurance, and Real Estate 33
Services and Misc. 52
Government 198

Farms and Acreages, Average Size of Farms in Acres, Rich County, 1930–1987

1930 - 1,396   1964 - 2,915
1935 - 1,551   1969 - 3,656
1940 - 2,172   1974 - 3,245
1945 - 2,307   1978 - 3,071
1950 - 2,335   1982 - 3,176
1954 - 2,055   1987 - 3,101
1959 - 2,635

Religious Leaders

Randolph Ward Bishops

Randolph H. Stewart
1870–1880

Archibald McKinnon, Sr.
1880 -1901

John C. Gray
1901 -1918

George A. Peart
1918 -1922

Oluf Larson
1922 -1929

Lawrence B. Johnson
1929–1940

George W. Peart
1940–1946

Earl F. Passey
1946–1953

Lynn McKinnon
1953–1962

Ross D. Jackson
1962 -1968

Roger W. Peart
1968–1975

Kenneth R. Brown
1975–1979

Randolph First Ward Bishops

Kenneth R. Brown
1979–1981

Glade B. Hatch
1981–1986

Douglas Balch
1986–1990

Perry Norris
1990–1993

Dean Davis
1993–

Randolph Second Ward Bishops

Fred A. Feller
1979–1986

Bart Argyle
1986–1992

Larry D. Johnson
1992–

Woodruff Ward Bishops

William Henry Lee
1871–1890

John M. Baxter
1898–1905

Peter McKinnon
1905–1912

Peter C. Cornia
Temporary

Carl G. Youngsburg
1913–1934

Thomas J. Tingey Jr.
1934–1942

LeRoy D. Tingey
1942–1956
W. Emerson Cox
1956–1962
Martin E. Frodsham
1962–1968
Keith L. Putnam
1968–
Ralph H. Eastman
1968–1971
Vernon S. Hopkins
1971–1975
Reed Cornia
1975–1979

Mark J. Frodsham
1979–1984
Steven G. Hutchinson
1984–1987
Dean Stuart
1987–1989
Wesley Tingey
1989–1990
Cleve Erickson
1990–1994
Kerry Stacey
1994–

Laketown Ward Bishops

John Oldfield
Presiding Elder in 1868
Ira Nebeker
Presiding Elder 1869–1877,
    Bishop 1877–1905
George H. Robinson
1905–1934
Vernon G. Robinson
1934–1936
John H. Weston
1936–1943
Norman E. Weston
1953–1961
Harold F. Johnson
1961–1967

Boyd H. Smart
1967–1972
Howard J. Lamborn
1972–1981
Lynn Jay Schow
1981–1985
Steven Rex
1985–1986
Stuart Wamsley
1986–1991
Craig Floyd
1991–

Garden City Ward Bishops

Wright A. Moore
Presiding Elder 1877–1879
Robert Calder
1879–1897
Samuel Weston
1897–1910
Charles Pope
1910–1923
Joseph W. Gibson
1923–1926
Clarence Cook
1926–1932
Paul A. Spence
1932–1941

Milford Loveland
1941–1947
Bryan L. Booth
1947–1954
Mitchell Sims
1954–1962
Clinton L. Tremelling
1962–1968
Mark P. Hodges
1968–1969
Oris Kaa Cook
1969–1974
Dale B. Weston
1974–

Bear Lake Ward Bishops

Dale B. Weston
1974–1976
Arlo B. Price
1976–1983
Michael J. Madsen
1983–1987

Don C. Huefner
1987–1992
Edward A. Price
1992–

Relief Society Presidents

Woodruff Ward

Harriet A. Lee
1874–1894
Esther Sessions
1894–1907
Charlotte Call
1907–1909
Eve C. Cornia
1909–1917
Sarah Lorinda (Rindy) Eastman
1917–1918

Rose Hunsaker
1918–1920
Betsy Maybell (Mae) D. Brown
1920–1930
Helen A. Cornia
1930–1932
Sophia Ashton
1932–1937
Ellen M. Kiddy
1937–1940

Helen A. Cornia
1940–1942
Cynthia M. Tingey
1942–1943
Christina Mae Stacey
1943–1945
Mary M. Tingey
1945–1948
Clara O. Dean
1948–1949
Emily G. Putnam
1949–1951
Nettie G. Staley
1951–1953
Alma J. Dean
1953–1954
Eddis L. Huffaker
1954–1956
Christina Mae Stacey
1956–1958
May S. Hopkin
1958–1961
Julia S. Mower
1961–1968

Grace M. Vernon
1968–1970
Lola A. Eastman
1970–1973
Mary M. Tingey
1973–1975
Vera T. Hopkin
1975–1980
Donnella Dean
1980–1982
Joan P. Stuart
1982–1986
Michelle C. McKinnon
1986–1988
Ruby G. Wilson
1988–1990
Cathy Cay S. Cox
1990–1992
Donnella B. Dean
1992–1994
Annie K. Erickson
1994–

Randolph Ward

Sarah Caldwell Tyson
1974–1903
Celia Ann C. Spencer
1903–1910
Annie E. Kearl Findley
1910–1920
Elsie W. Norris
1920–1923
Margaret B. Hatch
1923–1925
Adria B. Muir
1925–1935

Delora Brough Hatch
1935–1938
Myrtle Rex Jones
1938–1941
Ruby P. Rex
1941–1942
Julia Wahlstrom McKinnon
1942–1943
Counselors Phebe N. Smith,
Elaine Passey, and secretary
Lucille C. Hatch assumed lead-
ership between 1943 and 1944.

Delora Brough Hatch
1944–1946
Vera Hatch Peart
1946–1950
Ruby P. Rex
1950–
Mildred Hatch Thomson
1950–1951
Elizabeth Smith Rex
1952–1953
Ruth Smith Jackson
1953–1956
Vanice Moss Stuart
1956–1962

Donna McKinnon Groll
1962–1963
Sarah Schenck Hatch
1963–1966
Kathleen Rex Thornock
1966–1970
Billie Lou Cornia
1970–1976
Jane Ward Hatch
1979–1978
Judy Parker
1978–1979

Randolph First Ward

Judy Parker
1979–1980
JoAnn Vernon Bell
1980–1981
Helen Jackson Wamsley
1981–1986

Mary Putnam Argyle
1986–1990
Colleen Gray Rex
1990–1993
Vicky Humphreys Argyle
1993–

Randolph Second Ward

Debbie McKinnon
1979–1982
Margaret H. Wamsley
1982–1986
Dianna Jacobson
1986–

Irene Feller
1986–1988
Jeralene J. Groll
1988–1993
Cheri W. Nielson
1993–

Laketown Ward

Mary Woodcock Nebeker
1877–1883
Louisa Weston Hodges
1883–1901
Eliza Rachel Kearl Lamborn
1901–1911

Bessie Barker Weston
1911–1918
Melinda Weston Lamborn
1918–1925
Emma Weston Cheney
1925–1939

Lydia Weston Johnson
1939–1951

Larue Hatch Lamborn
1951–1952

Aileen Earley Weston
1952–1954

Loa Cook Lamborn
1954–1956

Elda Dixon Weston
1956–(died in office)

Lucy Earley Will
1957–1961

Mona Pugmire Kearl
1961–1965

Elgie Moss Robinson
1965–1969

Noma Lee Lamborn Pugmire
1969–1974

Jean Wright Jaussi
1974–1979

Larue Hatch Lamborn
1979–1983

Jean Johnson Willis
1983–1985

Gaye Calder Johnson
1985–1987

Doris Hunter Jex
1987–1989

Betty Burton Mills
1989–1992

Kathryn Wilson Lillywhite
1992–1995

Diane Kearl Wamsley
1995–

Garden City Ward

Ann Eliza Cook
1879–1896

Maranda Savage Linford
1897–1908

Amanda L. Pope
1908–1930

Celia Langford
1930–1939

Millie Sprouse
1939–1948

Leone Loveland
1948–1950

Theora Hodges
1950–1952

Virginia Whittington
1952–1956

Beatrice A. Hansen
1956–1958

Maxine Calder
1958–1961

Elva Satterthwaite
1961–1964

Merle Spence
1964–1965

Merinda Gibbons
1965–1967

Dorothea Garrett
1967–1969

Virginia Whittington
1969–1971

Darlene Booth
1971–1973

Noreen Hansen
1973–1975

Bear Lake Ward

Carol Howell
1975–1980

Dorothy Stringham
1980–1981

Wanda Stock
1981–

Pauline Bailey
1981–1982

Barbara Stringham
1982–

Gaylene Wamsley
1983–1984

Fern Nelson
1984–1986

Meryl Smith
1986–1988

Evelyn Wahlstrom
1988–1989

Carol Erickson
1989–1991

Bess McCellam
1991–1994

Elvira Luczak
1994–

Educational Administrators

County Superintendents from Statehood to Present

Oluf Larson
1896–1900

Josephine Reed
1900–1903

George H. Robinson
1903–1905

Fred R. Morgan
1905–1907

W. DeWitt Johnson
1907–1909

John Benson
1909–1915

Malcolm McKinnon
1915–1917

George N. Weston
1917–1929

Reuben D. Law
1929–1935

Verland L. Christensen
1935–1940

Earl F. Passey
1940–1959

Richard L. Harmon
1960–1968

Calvin Whatcott
1968–1975

Kenneth Lindsay
1975–1977

Giles Parker
1977–1984

Roger B. Brown
1984–1987

Martell Menlove
1987–1989

Daryl F. Nelson
1989–

School Board Members
Garden City

N. John Hodges
1915–1919

John C. Farner
1919–1923

Joseph W. Gibbons
1923–1927

Joseph N. Cook
1927–1931

Clarence Cook
1931–1935

Paul A. Spence
1935–1939

Parley N. Hodges
1939–1944

Albert Hodges
1944–1945

Clarence Cook
1945–died in office

Everett Sims
1945–1949

Clinton Tremelling
1949–1959

Lew Cook
1959–1961

Drew Cook
1961–1964

Arlo B. Price
1964–1970

Otto Mattsen
1970–1975

Gerry T. Brown
1975–1981

Mike Madsen
1981–1983

Stuart Wamsley
1983–1987

Arlo B. Price
1987–1990

Burdette Weston
1990–

School Board Members
Laketown

Alfred Kearl
1915–1917

George H. Robinson
1917–1935

William Lamborn
1937–1945

Vernon Robinson
1945–1950

DeWitt Johnson
1950–died in office

Stanley Mattson
1951–1953

Grant Lamborn
1953–1964

Keith Johnson
1964–1968

Norman Weston
1968–1979

Joseph S. Weston
1979–1987

Howard J. Lamborn
1987–

School Board Members
North Randolph

Fred R. Morgan
1915–1920

Jane Morgan
1920–1923

Margaret Hatch
1923–1927

J. G. Muir
1927–1931

Reay Kennedy
1931–1939

Norman L. Gray
1939–1946

G. Willard Peart
1946–1951

Lynn McKinnon
1951–1964

Roger Peart
1964–1970

William D. Cornia
1970–1977

Glade B. Hatch
1977–1985

Darlene Telford
1985–1993

Peter C. Cornia
1993–

School Board Members
South Randolph

James Kennedy
1915–1921

William Hoffman
1921–1933

William Johnson
1933–1937

Edna Smith
1937–1939

David Hoffman
1939–1942

Vloe B. Jackson
1942–1953

Thelma McKinnon
1953–1961

William Groll
1961–1965

Bryce F. Bell
1965–1970

Ross D. Jackson
1970–1975

Larry D. Johnson
1975–1981

Steve Rex
1981–1983

Merrill Muir
1983–

School Board Members
Woodruff

Lew Cook
1915–1919

Sarah R. Cornia
1919–1927

Frank Frazier
1927–1929

James Stuart
1929–1939

Marsh V. Eastman
1939–1948

Vern Hopkin
1948–1961

W. Emerson Cox
1961–1966

Keith Putnam
1966–1970

W. Emerson Cox
1970–1977

Kenneth Vernon
1977–1979

Charles M. Rex
1979–1981

Bill Hopkin
1981–1985

Charles M. Rex
1985–1993

Linda Kennedy
1993–

Total Enrollment of School-Age Children

1915–507	1945–395	1975 - 398
1920–517	1950–398	1980 - 459
1925–566	1955 - 410	1985 - 525
1930–610	1960 - 465	1990 - 488
1935–590	1965 - 446	
1940–503	1970 - 443	

Government

Members of the Rich County Court, 1872–1896

1872
James H. Hart - Probate Judge
William H. Lee - Selectman
Randolph H. Stewart - Selectman
Ira Nebeker - Selectman

1876
William H. Lee - Probate Judge
John Cox - Selectman
Ira Nebeker - Selectman
Randolph H. Stewart - Selectman

1878
William H. Lee - Probate Judge
Randolph H. Stewart - Selectman
Ira Nebeker - Selectman
Joseph Kimball - Selectman

1880
William H. Lee - Probate Judge
Archibald McKinnon - Selectman
Joseph Kimball - Selectman
Ira Nebeker - Selectman

1882
William H. Lee - Probate Judge
D. E. Fackrell - Selectman
Joseph Kimball - Selectman
Ira Nebeker - Selectman

1883
W. K. Walton - Probate Judge
Robert Calder - Selectman
Joseph Kimball - Selectman
Ira Nebeker - Selectman

1885
W. K. Walton - Probate Judge
Robert Calder - Selectman
John Cox - Selectman
Ira Nebeker - Selectman

1886

George A. Peart - Probate Judge
Robert Calder - Selectman
W. K. Walton - Selectman
Ira Nebeker - Selectman

1888

Stephen V. Frazier - Probate Judge
Robert Calder - Selectman
W. K. Walton - Selectman
Ira Nebeker - Selectman

1892

Stephen V. Frazier - Probate Judge
Ira Nebeker - Selectman
Anson C. Call - Selectman
David S. Cook - Selectman

1893

Stephen V. Frazier - Probate Judge
Anson C. Call - Selectman
David S. Cook - Selectman
Alma Findley - Selectman

1894

J. M. Grant - Probate Judge
Anson C. Call - Selectman
David S. Cook - Selectman
Alma Findley - Selectman

1895

J. M. Grant - Probate Judge
Anson C. Call - Selectman
David S. Cook - Selectman
Joshua Eldredge - Selectman

Members of the Rich County Commission, 1898–1994

1896
William H. Lee
John Kennedy
Joseph Weston

1899
Hyrum Nebeker
Nathanial M. Hodges
John Kennedy

1901
Peter McKinnon
Peter Johnson
Joseph E. Hatch

1903
Joshua Eldredge
Anson C. Call
Peter Johnson

1905
Isaac F. Price
Peter Johnson
D. W. Eastman

1907
Isaac F. Price
D. W. Eastman
George Kennedy

1909
George Kennedy
Thomas J. Tingey
Charles W. Pope

1911
Charles W. Pope
Joshua Eldredge
James Stuart

1913
James Stewart
William T. Rex
Edward S. Calder

1915
William T. Rex
Edward S. Calder
George A. Neville

1917
William T. Rex
Alfred Kearl
Shelby Huffaker

1919
Shelby Huffaker
George A. Peart Jr.
C. E. Booth

1921
George A. Peart Jr.
William Rees
DeWitt Johnson

1923
William Rees
DeWitt Johnson
Joseph Kennedy

1927
William Rees
Joseph Kennedy
Royal Pope

1929
L. B. Johnson
Marshall V. Eastman
Royal Pope

1931
L. B. Johnson
Marshall V. Eastman
William J. Lamborn

1933
L. B. Johnson
Marshall V. Eastman
Sidney Nebeker

1935
Alfred G. Rex
Sidney Nebeker
Orso Cornia

1937
Alfred G. Rex
Sidney Nebeker
William Rees

1939
William Rees
G. Willard Peart
Morton Kearl

1943
Nathanial J. Hodges
G. Willard Peart
J. Earl Stuart

1945
Nathanial J. Hodges
Wesley J. Kearl
J. Earl Stuart

1947
Wesley J. Kearl
Raymond Rees
Benjamin E. Weston

1949
Wesley J. Kearl
Lynn Huffaker
Harold Johnson

1951
Lynn Huffaker
Orval Johnson
Norman E. Weston

1953
Lynn Huffaker
Orval Johnson
Francis Frazier

1955
Orval Johnson
Francis Frazier
Norman E. Weston

1957
Francis Frazier
Kay Thornock
Russell Satterthwaite

1959
Russell Satterthwaite
Francis Frazier
Gale McKinnon

1961
Russell Satterthwaite
Gale McKinnon
Wayne Rees

1963
Wayne Rees
Del C. Cook
Wesley J. Kearl

1965
Del C. Cook
Sim Weston
Stuart Hopkin

1967
Sim Weston
Russell Satterthwaite
Stuart Hopkin

1971
Stuart Hopkin
Kay Thornock
Oris K. Cook

1973
Kay Thornock
Grant Lamborn
Keith Putnam

1977
Grant Lamborn
Delmore W. Eastman
Morrell Weston

1979
Morrell Weston
Norman H. Johnson
Louis M. Stuart

1981
Louis M. Stuart
LaVon Sprouse
Douglas Balch

1985
Kenneth Brown
Thad Mattson
Blair Francis

1987
Blair Francis
Kenneth Brown
Dee Johnson

1989
Dee Johnson
Kenneth Brown
Bill Cox

1991
Dee Johnson
Kenneth Brown
Blair Francis

1993
Louis Stuart
Kenneth Brown
Drew Cook

Appendix B

Rich County Public Health Nursing

by Helen Kennedy Cornia

I began working as a public health nurse in January 1941, and except for the year I spent in World War II as an army nurse in the European theatre, continued to work in public health nursing in Rich County until my retirement in 1982. These were rewarding and happy years, and I remember them with satisfaction.

Rural Utah has had great difficulty in attracting medical doctors. This has been true in Rich County, Utah, where but two physicians have practiced since the death of Doctor M. S. Reay in 1943. The nurses who worked in public health nursing programs came about in an effort to alleviate this pressing medical need.

The Utah State Department of Health is responsible for the organization of the counties into nine health districts. Each district has a medical director, and a director of nursing, who supervise the activities of the county nurse. In some counties several nurses are hired to perform the work. But while all the programs are alike in a broad

319

sense, their activities are tailored to meet the specific needs of each
county.

When first organized in with the Weber District, Rich County
was without a doctor. Physicians came from Ogden to assist the public health nurse in conducting clinics, such as well-baby conferences,
immunization, dental, orthopedic clinics, and others where a doctor's
services were essential. At a later date, Rich County was combined
with Box Elder, and Cache counties, and became known as Bear River
Health District number five. At this time doctors from Logan, along
with the full time district health officer, alternated in traveling to Rich
County to conduct clinics. Public health nurses and doctors were
often able to determine many abnormal conditions at these clinics
which were treated in early stages when complete cure was possible.
These clinics were also teaching and learning experiences that carried
down through families—from one generation to another.

Another aspect of public health nursing has been the school
nursing service. This is a delightful part of any program as one
worked with children from five years old through seniors in high
school. The school program is actually a continuation of the same
services provided to infants and pre-schoolers in well-baby and child
health conferences. Public health nurses also conducted yearly school
vision tests to help locate those students who needed glasses to see
both the world, and class blackboard. In times past, these tests were
often the only ones which students received. Today, owing strongly
to the past efforts of public health nurses, many parents have yearly
vision checks for their children on their own. But we still locate an
occasional child who has not seen an occulist, and badly needs visual
correction. Immunizations are another part of the school program,
though they are also given at public nursing clinics, and privately.
Immunizations have greatly reduced our cases of communicable diseases, and taken a great worry off the shoulders of parents, who used
to experience fear that their child would become infected. I gave so
many of these when I was working that I still meet young adults who
greet me by saying, " I know you. You're the shot lady!"

Home health nursing is another vital part of public health nursing in Rich County. People often became ill at the most inconvenient
hour. Often a frantic mother called at midnight, or early morning,

with a seriously ill child. Symtoms varied from high temperatures of 104 degrees, to labored breathing, or severe pain. Sometimes an immediate home visit was necessary so the nurse could safely determine if measures could be initiated to handle the problem until morning, or if the illness was of such severity to require the two and a half hour trip to the nearest hospital. Many have been able to return home days earlier from treatment at the hospital because the public health nurse was supplied with doctor's orders, and could give or supervise essential care.

In addition to unexpected illnesses were the unexpected farm accidents which happened all too frequently. During the 1950s, Claude Reay, a well trained and highly qualified first aid instructor, and I made countless trips in the county ambulance to one of the hospitals. These trips averaged four to six hours in travel time, and required considerable nursing skill. From the converted panel truck which Claude and I travelled in, today the county enjoys two well-equipped ambulances staffed by competent emergency medical technicians. Their services have saved many lives, and we all have a greater sense of security in knowing medical help is only a phone call away.

As medicine advances and additional needs become necessary, new clinics have been initiated. These include mammography clinics, cholestrol and glaucoma screenings, the WIC dietary program, and physicals for high school athletes. As other needs arise, I am confident that new programs will be created to make them available to the public. Public health nursing has been an ongoing ever changing and growing program. There have been many changes since its founding, and of necessity it will continue to change and grow as the need of our state and county, and their people continue to change.

Appendix C
School Through the Years

by Annie S. Wamsley

I was bubbling with enthusiasm in September 1925 when I came to Woodruff, Utah, to teach school. It was the beginning of some very thrilling and exciting years for me. I was twenty years old, and had a lot of energy for the challenges that I had to face. The first year in Woodruff I had forty students in my room, which was quite evenly divided between fifth and sixth grade. The classrooms were very large, and I especially liked that because it provided opportunities for many activities that we all enjoyed.

The school house had been built by the pioneers in 1886, of bricks made in the local brick yard. It consisted of two large spacious classrooms on the first level, and one large room upstairs that was used for both a classroom and an assembly room. There was also a smaller classroom, and a principal's office. The basement consisted of one large room where the children could play on stormy days. There was a long wooden sidewalk extending from the front gate to the double doors at the entrance, and a large bell hung from the belfry, waiting to announce the beginning of the school day. The bell rang at 8:30 A.M. At nine o'clock, students were expected to be lined up on the walk to march to the beat of the triangle, and off to their respective rooms.

There was no bus service at this time. The children from ranch homes were brought to school by their parents, or some rode horses, which they kept in a neighboring barn. The children would water and feed their horses during the noon hour. After these chores, and at recess, the children played such games as run-sheep-run, wolf-over-the-river, kick-the-can, and softball.

There was no water in the building. A large "tank like" water fountain was in the entrance hall. This was kept full of water by the custodian. He carried water by bucket from a nearby well. A small table in the hall with a bucket of water, a wash basin, a bar of soap, and a towel was the only facility we had for washing our hands. Two toilets about three hundred feet west of the building with a tall board fence between them were the only toilet facilities available. As the years passed on, the water system was installed in Woodruff City, and was piped into the school building. Toilet and hand-basin connections now made it possible for us to raise our standard of hygiene.

At this time there was no school lunch. The smaller children would bring a small jar of milk to school, where it was placed in the west window to keep it cool until it was drunk at the mid-morning lunch time. Most of the children went home for lunch. Those children from ranches brought their lunch in their lunch buckets. When the lunch program was first installed it was rather meager, and cost about three cents per meal. The school lunch program grew and progressed over the years, until eventually it was available in all of the schools. Excellent cooks prepared well balanced meals making it possible to serve not only those children who were not getting the proper nourishment, but all children had the opportunity to participate.

As the years went by, the old school house came in need of renovation. Either much repair needed to be done, or a new building needed to be provided. The school board began considering consolidation as an option. This was very unpopular in the town. The school was the nucleus of activity in the community. Consolidation had been a hated work in our school history, and this was the second time in my teaching career where consolidation had been used. The residents of the community were very upset when the ninth and tenth grades were taken to Randolph. This occurred in the first year of my teaching.

Finally, it was decided that the best solution to the problem was to take the seventh and eighth grades to Randolph, and build a two room school house. This was completed in 1958, and the first six grades remained in Woodruff. In 1967 grades three, four, five, and six were also bussed to Randolph, and the first and second grades were brought from Randolph to Woodruff. The same problem arose again. This time it was the Randolph parents who objected to their children coming to Woodruff to school. This plan lasted about four or five years before all of the children from Woodruff were taken to Randolph by bus to school.

As I meditate over the past years of the school, I am very grateful for the progress, although it has been painful to many, it has been for the good of the students. Many opportunities are now provided that were not available in the "good old days." The hope is that we will keep our eyes on the future and continue to progress.

Appendix D

The Bear Lake Monster

The following accounts were provided to the *Deseret News* by Joseph C. Rich, who actively promoted Bear Lake. Though he never claimed to have seen the Bear Lake Monster himself, he implied that many of the most respected members of Bear Lake Valley had.

All lakes, caves and dens have their legendary histories. Tradition loves to throw her magic wand over beautiful dells and lakes and people them with fairies, giants and monsters of various kinds. Bear Lake has also its monster take to tell, and when I have told it, I will leave you to judge whether or not its merits are merely traditionary.

The Indians say there is a monster animal which lives in the Lake that has captured and carried away Indians while in the Lake swimming; but they say it has not been seen by them for many years, not since the buffalo inhabited the valley. They represent it as being of the serpent kind, but having legs about eighteen inches long on which they sometimes crawl out of the water a short distance on the shore. They also say it spurts water upwards out of its mouth.

Since the settlement of this valley several persons have reported seeing a huge animal of some kind that they could not describe; but such persons have generally been alone when they saw it, and but little credence have been attached to the matter, and until this summer the "monster question" had about died out.

About three weeks ago Mr. S. M. Johnson, who lives on the east side of the lake at a place called South Eden was going to the Round Valley settlement, six miles to the South of this place and when about half way he saw something in the lake which at the time, he thought to be a drowned person. The road being some distance from the water's edge he rode to the beach and the waves were running pretty high. He thought it would soon wash to shore. In a few minutes two or three feet of some kind of animal that he had never seen before were raised out of the water. He did not see the body, only the head and what he supposed to be part of the neck. It had ears or bunches on the side of its head nearly as large as a pint cup. The waves at the times would dash over its head, when it would throw water from its mouth or nose. It did not drift landward, but appeared stationary, with the exception of turning its head. Mr. Johnson thought a portion of the body must lie on the bottom of the lake or it would have drifted with the action of the water. This is Mr. Johnson's version as he told me.

The next day an animal of a monster kind was seen near the same place by a man and three women, who said it was swimming when they first saw it. They represented [it] as being very large, and say it swam much faster than a horse could run on land. These recent discoveries again revive the `monster question'. Those who had seen it before brought in their claims anew, and many people began to think the story was not altogether moonshine.

On Sunday last as N. C. Davis and Allen Davis, of St. Charles, and Thomas Slight [Sleight?] and J. Collings of Paris, with six women, were returning from Fish Haven, when about midway from the latter named place to St. Charles their attention was suddenly attracted to a peculiar motion or wave in the water, about three miles distant. The lake was not rough, only a little disturbed by a light wind. Mr.

Slight says he distinctly saw the sides of a very large animal that he would suppose to be not less than ninety feet in length. Mr. Davis don't think he (Davis) saw any part of the body, but is positive it must have been not less than 40 feet in length, judging by the wave it rolled upon both sides of it as it swam, and the wake it left in the rear. It was going South, and all agreed that it swam with a speed almost incredible to their senses. Mr. Davis says he never saw a locomotive travel faster, and thinks it made a mile a minute, easy. In a few minutes after the discovery of the first, a second one followed in its wake; but it seemed to be much smaller, appearing to Mr. Slight about the size of a horse. A large one, in all, and six small ones had [headed] southward out of sight.

One of the large ones before disappearing made a sudden turn to the west, a short distance; then back to its former track. At this turn Mr. Slight says he could distinctly see it was of a brownish color. They could judge somewhat of their speed by observing known distances on the side of the lake, and all agree that the velocity with which they propelled themselves through the water was astonishing. They represent the waves that rolled up in front and on each side of them as being three feet high from where they stood. This is substantially their statement as they told me. Messrs. Davis and Slight are prominent men, well known in this country, and all of them are reliable persons whose veracity is undoubted. I have no doubt they would be willing to make affidavits to their statement.

There you have the monster story so far as completed, but I hope it will be concluded by the capture of one sometime. If so large an animal exists in this altitude and in so small a lake, what could it be? It must be something new under the sun, the scriptural text to the contrary, not withstanding. Is it fish, flesh or serpent, amphibious and fabulous or a great big fish, or what is it? Give it up but have hopes of someday seeing it, if it really exists, and I have no reason to doubt the above statements. Here is an excellent opportunity for some company to bust Barnum on a dicker for the monster, if they can only catch one; already some settlers talk of forming a joint stock arrangement and what they can do to the business."

When disbelievers began surfacing, Rich fired off another tongue-in-cheek letter: "I am sorry they don't believe the story

because they might come up here some day and through their unbe-
lief be thrown off their guard and be gobbled up by the water devil.
There are a few people even here who disbelieve the monster story,
but as a general rule they have not prospered in what they undertake
and their intellects are tottering; they are not considered competent
to act as fence viewers; and no doubt the government will in time
withhold from them the blessing of paying internal revenue."

Ever the joker, Rich even had a plan for catching the monster:
"Phineas Cook expects to use a barbed hook, attached to twenty feet
of cable, which in turn would be fastened to three hundred feet of
one inch rope; at the end of the rope would be a large buoy with a
flag-staff in a perpendicular position. The stars and stripes were to
float from the top of the staff. To this buoy would be attached
another one hundred yards of 3/4 inch rope fastened to the switch
end of a tree on shore. The hook would be baited by a leg of mutton
. . . and allowed to sink twenty feet in the water, being held at that
depth by a smaller buoy. Naturally, when the monster swallowed the
hook there would be a great commotion in the water; but the flag
would always indicate the position of the monster, regardless of
where he went in the lake."

(The original Joseph C. Rich account was published in the
Deseret News, 27 July 1868, and was quoted in Austin E. Fife, "The
Bear Lake Monsters," *Utah Humanities Review,* 2, no. 2 [April, 1948]:
99-101. See also *Bear Lake Magazine* 3 [1 December 1979].)

Selected Bibliography

Adams, Luella Nebeker. *Phebe Almira Hulme Nebeker*. Salt Lake City: n.p., 1955.

Alexander, Thomas G. *Things in Heaven and Earth : The Life and Times of Wilford Woodruff, A Mormon Prophet*. Salt Lake City: Signature Books, 1991.

Alter, J. Cecil. *Jim Bridger*, rev. ed. Norman: University of Oklahoma Press, 1962.

Arrington, Leonard J. *Brigham Young: American Moses*. New York: Alfred A. Knopf, 1985.

———. *Charles C. Rich*. Provo: Brigham Young University Press, 1974.

———. *Great Basin Kingdom: An Economic History of the Latter-day Saints 1830–1900*. Cambridge: Harvard University Press, 1958.

Baxter, John M., *Life of John M. Baxter: Being a Brief Account of His Experiences as a Pioneer, Missionary, Bishop and Stake President*. Salt Lake City: The Deseret News Press, 1932,

Budge, Jesse R. S. *The Life of William Budge*. Salt Lake City: Deseret News, 1915.

Fredrickson, Lars. *History of Weston, Idaho.* Logan: Utah State University, 1972.

Haddock, Edith Parker, and Dorothy Hardy Matthews, comp., *Bear Lake Pioneers* Salt Lake City: DUP, Bear Lake County, Idaho, 1968.

Hatch, Charles M. "Creating Ethnicity in the Hydraulic Village of the Mormon West." Master's thesis, Utah State University, 1991.

Kenney, Scott G. ed. *Wilford Woodruff's Journal, 1833–1898,* Typescript, 9 vols. Midvale, UT: Signature Books, 1983–1991.

Kimball, Solomon F. *Life of David P. Kimball and other Sketches* Salt Lake City: Deseret News, 1918.

Larson, Gustive O. *The "Americanization" of Utah for Statehood.* San Marino, CA: Huntington Library, 1971.

————. *Prelude to the Kingdom, Mormon Desert Conquest: A Chapter in American Cooperative Experience.* Francestown, NH: M. Jones Co., 1947.

McCarthy, Max R. *The Last Chance Canal Company.* Provo: Brigham Young University, 1987.

McConnell, William J., Clark and William F. Sigler, *Bear Lake: Its Fish and Fishing.* Salt Lake City: Utah State Department of Fish and Game, 1957.

McMurrin, Jean Ann. "The Deseret Live Stock Company: The First Fifty Years, 1890–1940." Master's thesis, University of Utah, 1989.

Madsen, Brigham D. Madsen. *The Shoshoni Frontier and the Bear River Massacre.* Salt Lake City: University of Utah Press, 1985.

May, Dean L. "Mormon Cooperatives in Paris, Idaho, 1869–1896," *Idaho Yesterdays,* 21 (Summer 1975).

Moffitt, John Clifton. *The History of Public Education in Utah.* Salt Lake City: The Deseret News Press, 1946.

Nelson, Lowry. *The Mormon Village: A Pattern and Technique of Land Settlement.* Salt Lake City: University of Utah Press, 1952.

Nunis, Doyce B. *The Bidwell-Bartleson Party, 1841: California Emigrant Adventure.* Santa Cruz, CA: Western Tanager Press, 1991.

Parson, Robert "Prelude to the Taylor Grazing Act: Don B. Colton and the Utah Public Domain Committee, 1927–1932," *Encyclia: The Journal of the Utah Academy of Sciences, Arts, and Letters,* 68 (1991).

Passey, Earl F. "An Historical Study of Public Education in Rich County, Utah," Master's thesis, University of Utah, 1951

Poll, Richard, et al., ed. *Utah's History.* Logan: Utah State University Press, 1989.

Poulsen, Ezra J. *Joseph C. Rich: Versatile Pioneer on the Mormon Frontier.* Salt Lake City: Granite Publishing Co., 1958.

Quinn, D. Michael. *J. Reuben Clark: The Church Years.* Provo: Brigham Young University Press, 1983.

Rich, A. McKay Rich, "The History of Montpelier From 1864 to 1925." Master's thesis, Utah State Agricultural College, 1957.

Rich, Russell R. *Land of the Sky-Blue Water: A History of the L.D.S. Settlement of the Bear Lake Valley.* Provo: Brigham Young University, 1963.

Sigler, William F. *Bear Lake and Its Future.* Logan: Utah State University Faculty Association, 1962.

Simmonds, A. J. *The Gentile Comes to Cache Valley: A Study of the Logan Apostasies of 1874 and the Establishment of Non-Mormon Churches in Cache Valley, 1873–1913.* Logan: Utah State University Press, 1976.

Smith, George D. ed. *An Intimate Chronicle: The Journals of William Clayton.* Salt Lake City: Signature Books, 1991.

Thompson, Bonnie. "Folklore in the Bear Lake Valley." Master's thesis: Utah State University, 1972.

Thomson, Mildred H. comp. *Rich Memories: Some of the Happenings in Rich County from 1863 to 1960.* Salt Lake City: Daughters of Utah Pioneers, 1962.

Thomson, Steven L., Jane D. Digerness, and Mar Jean S. Thomson, *Randolph—A Look Back.* n.p., 1981.

Wells, Merle W. *Anti-Mormonism in Idaho, 1872–92.* Provo: Brigham Young University Press, 1978.

Wilde, J. Patrick. *Treasured Tidbits of Time: An Informal History of Mormon Conquest and Settlement of the Bear Lake Valley.* Montpelier, ID: the author.

Willard, Allen D. "Surficial Geology of Bear Lake Valley, Utah." Master's thesis, Utah State University, 1959.

Winsor, Luther M. *Life History of Luther M. Winsor.* Murray, UT: R. Fenton Murray, 1962.

Woodruff Centennial Committee, *The First Hundred Years In Woodruff.* Springville, UT: Art City Publishing Co., 1972.

Wright, Charlotte M. "Bear Lake Blizzard: A History of Family and Community Conflict in Bennington, Idaho, 1864–1915." Master's thesis, Utah State University, 1986.

Index